JUSTICE

Key Concepts in Critical Theory

Series Editor
Roger S. Gottlieb

Published

JUSTICE
Edited by Milton Fisk

DEMOCRACY
Edited by Philip Green

ALIENATION AND SOCIAL CRITICISM
Edited by Richard Schmitt and Thomas E. Moody

Forthcoming

GENDER
Edited by Carol Gould

RACISM
Edited by Leonard Harris

DECONSTRUCTION AND SOCIAL THEORY
Edited by Bill Martin

ECOLOGY
Edited by Carolyn Merchant

EXPLOITATION
Edited by Kai Nielsen and Robert Ware

IMPERIALISM AND GLOBAL CAPITALISM
Edited by Robert Ross

Key Concepts in Critical Theory

JUSTICE

EDITED BY
Milton Fisk

HUMANITIES PRESS

NEW JERSEY

This collection first published in 1993 by Humanities Press International, Inc.,
Atlantic Highlands, NJ 07716–1289

© 1993 by Humanities Press

Library of Congress Cataloging-in-Publication Data
Justice / edited by Milton Fisk.
p.   cm.   — (Key concepts in critical theory)
Includes bibliographical references and index.
ISBN 0-391–03777-3 (pbk)
1. Justice.   I. Fisk, Milton.   II. Series.
JC578.J882   1993
320'.01'1—dc20   92–14915
CIP

A catalog record for this book is available from the British Library.

Printed in the United States of America

CONTENTS

PART IV: EXPLOITATION AND ENVIRONMENT

PART V: RACE AND GENDER

SERIES EDITOR'S PREFACE

THE VISION OF A rational, just, and fulfilling social life, present in Western thought from the time of the Judaic prophets and Plato's *Republic*, has since the French Revolution been embodied in systematic *critical theories* whose adherents seek a fundamental political, economic, and cultural transformation of society.

These critical theories—varieties of Marxism, socialism, anarchism, feminism, gay/lesbian liberation, ecological perspectives, discourses by antiracist, anti-imperialist, and national liberation movements, and utopian/critical strains of religious communities—have a common bond that separates them from liberal and conservative thought. They are joined by the goal of sweeping social change; the rejection of existing patterns of authority, power, and privilege; and a desire to include within the realms of recognition and respect the previously marginalized and oppressed.

Yet each tradition of critical theory also has its distinct features: specific concerns, programs, and locations within a geometry of difference and critique. Because of their intellectual specificity and the conflicts among the different social groups they represent, these theories have often been at odds with one another, differing over basic questions concerning the ultimate cause and best response to injustice, the dynamics of social change, the optimum structure of a liberated society, the identity of the social agent who will direct the revolutionary change, and in whose interests the revolutionary change will be made.

In struggling against what is to some extent a common enemy, in overlapping and (at times) allying in the pursuit of radical social change, critical theories to a great extent share a common conceptual vocabulary. It is the purpose of this series to explore that vocabulary, revealing what is common and what is distinct, in the broad spectrum of radical perspectives.

For instance, although both Marxists and feminists may use the word "exploitation," it is not clear that they really are describing the same phenomenon. In the Marxist paradigm the concept identifies the surplus labor appropriated by the capitalist as a result of the wage-labor relation. Feminists have used the same term to refer as well to the unequal amounts of housework, emotional nurturance, and child raising performed by women in the nuclear family. We see some similarity in the notion of group inequality (capitalists/workers, husbands/wives) and of unequal exchange. But we also see critical differences: a previously "public" concept extended to the private realm; one first centered in the economy of goods now moved into the life of emotional relations. Or, for another example, when deep ecologists speak of "alienation" they may be exposing the contradictory and destructive relations of humans *to* nature. For socialists and anarchists, by contrast, "alienation" basically refers only to relations among human beings. Here we find a profound contrast between what is and is not included in the basic arena of politically significant relationships.

What can we learn from exploring the various ways different radical perspectives utilize the same terminology?

Most important, we see that these key concepts have histories and that the theories of which they are a part and the social movements whose spirit they embody take shape through a process of political struggle as well as of intellectual reflection. As a corollary, we can note that the creative tension and dissonance among the different uses of these concepts stem not only from the endless play of textual interpretation (the different understandings of classic texts, attempts to refute counterexamples or remove inconsistencies, rereadings of history, reactions to new theories), but also from the continual movement of social groups. Oppression, domination, resistance, passion, and hope are crystallized here. The feminist expansion of the concept of exploitation could only grow out of the women's movement. The rejection of a purely anthropocentric (human-centered, solely humanistic) interpretation of alienation is a fruit of people's resistance to civilization's lethal treatment of the biosphere.

Finally, in my own view at least, surveys of the differing applications of these key concepts of critical theory provide compelling reasons to see how complementary, rather than exclusive, the many radical perspectives are. Shaped by history and embodying the spirit of the radical movements that created them, these varying applications each have in them some of the truth we need in order to face the darkness of the current social world and the ominous threats to the earth.

ROGER S. GOTTLIEB

PREFACE

IN SELECTING THE MATERIALS for this anthology I was guided by several things. First, I wanted to give the reader a view of contemporary debates on justice. It was not to be a book of classics, with something from each of the major periods and schools. This limited the field considerably, but there remained a lot to choose from since the recent past has seen an outpouring of work on justice. From that outpouring I neglected, among other things, the libertarian approach to justice, though a number of the authors I have included provide critical comment on it.

Second, I wanted to focus on debates in which the sides assume, at least implicitly, that justice pushes us in the direction of greater equality. Thus, not only views that treat as just any arrangements which perpetuate an elite with certain special qualities, but also views that treat as just any circumstances brought about by a free market are neglected except for scattered comments. Equality is, to be sure, a complex notion, having social, economic, and political dimensions. It is, then, relevant in considering such diverse matters as relations between the sexes, the control of production, and democratic governance. In view of this complexity, the egalitarian thrust of most of the authors is never expressed simply in terms of material equality.

Each of the five parts of the anthology serves a distinct aim. Nineteenth-century writers associated with reform or revolutionary movements are represented in Part I in order to provide a background for contemporary debates. One of the major current debates is that between liberals and communitarians, who appear in Part II not necessarily in pure form but in ways that indicate how they have affected one another. The state, as is clear in Part III, is a central factor not merely in administering justice but also in formulating standards of justice under pressures sparked by outrage at prevailing conditions.

The justice of an economic system depends in a significant way on the role its workers have within it. The first three chapters of Part IV take up this issue in the form of recent debates on the justice of exploitation. The remainder of Part IV looks at issues of poverty and future generations in an environmental context. Opposed positions on the justice of affirmative action for African Americans are represented in Part V along with opposed positions on whether liberal justice is an adequate basis for justice for women.

My introductory essay is an effort to detail some of the problems regarding justice which the various authors included here have had to face. The directions you will find them taking are responses to some of those problems. The suggestions in that essay about where thinking about justice should be going in order to avoid dead ends summarize my own work on the issue. In almost all of the selections footnotes have been dropped, but there is instead a bibliography at the end of this collection referring to major sources for recent views of justice.

MILTON FISK

INTRODUCTION

The Problem of Justice

MILTON FISK

FINDING A JUST SOLUTION to a problem involves finding a way out of a morass of conflicting claims. Without conflicts of claims, the morality of action would be more straightforward. One could then hope for unambiguous and uncontested statements of value to light the way to action. But justice is rarely a matter of clear and evident principles alone, which prove to be of little avail when it comes to finding the way out of such a morass. Instead, getting the just solution demands sensitivity to the genuine appeal that conflicting principles have to the different contending parties.

This link between justice and conflict is not accidental. In a society of an ideal homogeneity, the search for just solutions would be less pressing, not because justice was realized but because no appeal could be made to justice. Of course, there would be cases where rights are violated, and we might for that reason speak of unfairness or even injustice. But in fact views about rights provide adequate conceptual tools by themselves for handling such cases. Justice, though, is something that takes us beyond the conceptual tools of rights discourse. There has to be at least a conflict based on an actual lack of homogeneity for what is distinctive about justice to become relevant.

Plato himself was aware of the conflict in his society between workers, warriors, and rulers. His effort in *The Republic* to transcend that conflict led him to claim that the ideal function of each of those classes was totally different from that of any of the rest. By not straying from its ideal function, Plato thought each class would steer clear of conflict with the others. He sought, in effect, a just solution to conflict by positing a basic inequality between humans in the various classes.

The search for a just solution would seem then to lead toward the universal—a theory of human nature, of preeminent values, or of a pattern of relevant factors—and away from the particular. The just solution is often not found merely by taking one of the various sides to a dispute. For that would, if practiced in a consistent way, deny the other side the validity of its rights and

1

proclaim a solution by privileging the rights of a particular group. The just solution generally goes beyond all of the sides, and is in that sense universal.

There is a social reason for this. Except in extreme cases, the contending parties are going to continue to participate in the same society. Social cohesiveness is rarely lacking as a motive in seeking justice. The distributions of the modern welfare state are too great in the eyes of the "haves," who think they sacrifice too much for them, and too small in the eyes of the "have-nots," who depend on them for even a low standard of living. But in seeking just distributions the idea is not to please the contenders but to transcend their particular demands. This transcendence is generally fashioned in a way that preserves the basic features of the social order, perhaps in some reformed conception of it.

The transcendence involved in going beyond particular values can easily suggest that justice leads us toward an absolute. It does indeed lead toward the universal and away from the particular. But universality is, in the view of many, to be distinguished from absoluteness. One can start from a particular set of values to reach a solution that others, who do not accept those values, can live with. This process is, then, universalizing also in a second sense: that it moves one from a narrower to a broader consensus.

There remains the question as to whether the view for which there may be a broader consensus isn't itself a view that reflects, in a general way, the standpoint of some contending party. Perhaps it is a view expressing the way that a particular contending party, but not others, would devise a solution to a conflict without alienating all other contending parties, thereby breaking the social bond. If this is a feasible interpretation of the kind of universality involved in just solutions, then that universality is in no sense absolute but is quite clearly perspectival.

The question "Must justice be absolute in order to provide a universal that transcends the conflict of particular values?" comes up over and over again in contemporary debates on justice. The general form of the absolutist view, as suggested by the work of Jürgen Habermas, is that moral discourse in which there are sufficient resources to carry on discussion about competing values presupposes a moral stance that is not tied to the perspective of any particular social grouping. Thus, the content of such a moral stance is neutral between social perspectives, giving it a claim to absoluteness. The search for a just solution to any problem is necessarily entwined in moral discourse about competing values, and hence presupposes at least some absolute principles of justice.

Though this can serve as the general form of the absolutist view, there remain differences over exactly how to find the content of the principles of absolute justice. Various ways have been proposed for finding it. Mill had a utilitarian way: justice transcends disputes over different claims by deciding on the basis of utility to the society what it is right to do, where what is to count as utility is a neutral matter. Rawls, at least in his *A Theory of Justice* (1971), had a way of detachment: the just solution is one people would decide on if they could detach themselves from the circumstances, such as wealth, that might bias their judgment in their own favor. Great care is taken in all such methods to assure that the process of finding justice is not limited by adopting any particular perspective.

Those who counter the absolutist view tend to emphasize the society-specific nature of many of the arguments used by the absolutists. Such attacks on absolutism belong to a venerable tradition. David Hume, in *An Enquiry Concerning the Principles of Morals* (1751), contributed to that tradition when he insisted that justice owes the approval that humanity gives it solely to its tendency to preserve order in society. Hume saw that social order will be different where birth and the military are preeminent from what it is where industry and wealth are preeminent. Thus, a Humean would expect a difference between the justice of a monarchical society, which fits the former order, and that of a republican society, which fits the latter.

Today's communitarians—like Alasdair MacIntyre and Michael Sandel—are more recent members of the same venerable tradition of anti-absolutists. Their attachment to this tradition follows from their criticism of liberalism as a contributor to or at least as incapable of rescuing us from the contemporary moral wasteland with its rootless selves. The particular form of liberalism they attack is characterized by two theses. First, it bases tolerance for multiple conceptions of individual and social goods on there being no basis for deciding among them. Second, it requires that a fair regulation of conflicts within this pluralism of goods be independent of any overarching view of the good for individuals and society. The communitarians argue that the moral wasteland emerges from or persists due to just such a detachment in the liberal position from any commitment to particular values. How is this to be shown?

The first liberal thesis casts a shadow over organized efforts, by the state or private groups, to inculcate particular values. For moral education and political proselytization cannot then avoid the charge of manipulating the unsuspecting. There are, on this liberal view, no rational arguments for one concept of the good rather than another, leaving manipulation as the only tool. And those who get their moral outlook by being manipulated will defend themselves from alternative outlooks not by rational argument but by intolerance. Ending moral education would certainly avoid having objectionable creeds imposed on the new generation, but it is doubtful that moral education could be ended since social organization depends on it. As communitarians would observe, it is through moral education that a new generation will learn the difference between right and wrong in a way that is relevant to carrying on a given social order.

As regards the second liberal thesis, communitarians argue that the motivation for accepting any proposal for the fair regulation of conflicts is fatally lacking. For, as Hume said, people will accept a view of justice when they can see how it supports a social order to which they are attached. Yet liberal justice is not supposed to support any one such social order, since it is not tied to any one concept of the good. Liberals would counter that their justice would support instead a variety of social orders, merely as social orders and not in their distinctiveness. But there is room to doubt that there is a neutral concept of social order since communities conceive of social order itself in terms of their own distinctive goods. As a consequence people will ignore liberal justice. No wonder, then, that contemporary society, under the influence of liberalism, is a war of each against all unregulated by justice.

The turn to community in order to give a foundation to political morality— to normative concerns integral to politics—has been at best a qualified success. To what community do we turn? John Dewey, in *The Public and Its Problems* (1927), noted that the market and industrialism had effectively ruptured the social bond. Community had to be a project, rather than a place ready for occupancy. His Great Community was a project drawn to Dewey's own specifications, and thus it reflected his political morality rather than giving it a foundation.

To avoid this problem, one could instead look to an existing tradition for community, as MacIntyre did to the Aristotelian tradition in his *After Virtue* (1981). He felt the need for this particular intellectual community, with its emphasis on a virtue-based ethics, as a context from within which he could project local practical communities, where people of good will could survive this modern moral wasteland. The choice of such a tradition is a commitment that excludes others without a satisfactory account being given as to the relations between such traditions. The liberal demand that such a commitment not lead to intolerance goes unaddressed.

In view of all these problems, one must welcome the clear signs of efforts to go beyond the liberal/communitarian duality. Each of those positions made its contribution. Liberalism insisted on the need for a kind of justice that transcends particular values. It upheld the universalist aspect of justice. But it has often encouraged the confusion of universality with absolute justice. Communitarianism, in opposition, began from an insistence on the particular and historical nature of political morality. A just solution then transcends conflicting values but at the same time is itself rooted in particular social understandings, understandings that will not be universally shared. Any satisfactory future account of justice might well have to combine both the universal element required for transcending conflicts and the particular element required by shared understandings. In the 1980s Rawls himself has been in the lead in pushing toward a feasible combination of these elements.

Nonetheless, combining these elements calls for a more careful look than either liberalism or communitarianism ever gave at the social backdrop for justice. Liberalism supposes that groups with divergent goods can be made to tolerate one another; communitarianism, of the sort espoused by Michael Walzer and others who emphasize a republican form of community, supposes the bond in state-sized societies can be shared values. There is in fact a common assumption here, that homogeneity runs deeper than heterogeneity in the relevant state-sized units. Were we to make the opposite assumption, that heterogeneity runs deeper than homogeneity, both liberal and this kind of communitarian reasoning would be undermined.

The liberal, for example, is committed to tolerance in respect to diverse goods. If, though, the As see their good as getting what they can from the Bs by beating up on the Bs and the Bs see their good as subverting the whole system that makes them the As' victims, then tolerance is not a prime requisite in a political morality for a society with As and Bs. It would, rather, be plausible to judge both the slogan "A Better Future through B-Bashing!" and the slogan "Smash A-Rule to Feel Secure!" as "fighting words" and not as speech to be protected by rules of tolerance. If, instead, liberal tolerance were to be upheld, then goods such as those expressed by these slogans would have to be put off the agenda. But doing so would call for adopting a particular view of goods and rights, one that fits neatly only a more homogeneous society.

The communitarian is, in turn, committed to the view that for there to be a political morality for a state there must be shared understandings about what is good and that from these justice can be inferred. If, though, there is the sort of radical heterogeneity we have just imagined, such shared understandings can only be the result of thought control. (To achieve them without thought control would require the kind of social revolution that would eliminate heterogeneity based on the domination of some by others.) But surely no genuine political morality can be the product of thought control, for that would contradict the intuitive idea that a community freely develops its morality. Rather than reject this intuitive idea, the communitarian has to make the assumption that only quite homogeneous societies can have a political morality.

Since most societies are divided along one or more dimensions, it is important that heterogeneity be an integral part of the social backdrop of justice. The consequence of this that impacts forcefully against the liberal side is that there may be no unique or absolute content for justice. Justice may be as diverse as the areas defined by a divided society's fracture lines. The various contents given to justice will then be dependent on the views of the good behind such lines, a position rejected by liberals.

Since the areas defined by the fracture lines are not merely areas of conflicting beliefs but areas involved in social conflict with other areas, tolerance is no longer the main motif of justice. Justice will, to be sure, require tolerance but only a tolerance that does not drastically inhibit the pursuit of the good associated with a given group. Liberalism, as we just saw, avoids considering the importance of the social good as a background for tolerance only by ruling the pursuit of at least some of the goods of groups in conflict off the moral agenda.

There is also a consequence of making heterogeneity part of the backdrop for justice that impacts forcefully against the communitarianism side, at least in its contemporary forms. It is that the focus can no longer be on the shared beliefs and common meanings emphasized by communitarians but has to shift to social positions defined by the fracture lines in a society. This is a shift from a focus on ideas to a focus on interests and social relations. After all, shared beliefs can be imposed to get a uniformity that papers over fractures in society. Moreover, different systems of shared beliefs may coexist with any one social position as defined by a set of fracture lines. It is, as a Marxian view of morality would claim, not how people see themselves at a given time but what their real social relations are that provides the framework for structuring a morality consonant with who they are. We find, then, that current political morality has begun to stress the relevance of social position, of heterogeneity, and of the diversity of underlying perspectives. In doing so it goes beyond both liberalism and communitarianism.

However, in contemporary debates, communitarianism sides with poststructuralism by emphasizing beliefs and discourses. And this is a limitation of its current form. The historical and the particular element in our conception of justice cannot be adequately captured by the vagaries of discourse but must include social structures. Beliefs, meanings, and discourses fail here for the reasons indicated. On the one hand, they cannot, without being imposed, span social fracture lines in order to provide the basis for state-sized communities. On the other hand, even where there are no social fracture lines and hence the prospects for community are optimal, there will be multiple discourses and conflicting meanings. Despite multiple discourses in the penumbra of any group, a challenge from outside it will have a unifying effect as regards action, an effect that can be made sense of by the fact that there is one social position involved.

A great prod to this departure from both liberalism and communitarianism has been reflection on the reemergence of powerful social movements. The feminist movement, the movements of people of color, nationalist movements fracturing countries in the East, workers' movements in the 1980s from Poland to Brazil and on to South Korea, the gay and lesbian movements, and the ecological movement—all of these and others dispel the assumption of homogeneity common to liberalism and certain forms of communitarianism. These movements made clear that state-sized communities were still a long way from Dewey's Great Community. In fact, their struggles made the state-sized community a myth. Of course, some communitarians had, all along, emphasized units different from state-sized communities—either smaller communities or communities cutting across nation-states. But unlike them, participants in these new movements weren't so much trying to form communities, defined by coherent discourses, within the fragments of state-sized societies. Rather, they were trying, in the short run, to win concessions from others to alleviate oppression and, in the long run, to change whole social systems to end oppression.

The deep fractures in the social structure made evident by these movements helped define concepts of the social good that wouldn't easily fit onto the liberal agenda along with more standard ones. Such movements generated proclamations of difference and uncompromising refusals to be fit into pregiven views of social homogeneity. The idea of seeking justice apart from the movements' concepts of the good is condemned within them as little more than a capitulation to those who had been enjoying a privileged status.

Nonetheless, there is still no common discourse within these movements when it comes to the topic of justice. There are African-American and feminist writers who still insist that justice is to be measured by a common human yardstick. But there are others, like Bernard Boxill in *Blacks and Social Justice* (1984) and Iris Young in *Justice and the Politics of Difference* (1990), who insist that there can, at least now, not be a race- or a gender-blind justice. For them a neutral justice abstracted from the perspective of an oppressed group may, whether consciously or not, serve to maintain oppression.

It seems incredible that such a neutral and allegedly absolute justice could actually promote oppression. But consider the effect it has of undermining the distinctiveness of racial, gender, and other groups. It has this effect since it claims that the perspective of any such group is irrelevant as a basis for a view of political morality and of justice in particular. Social and cultural distinctiveness cannot be reduced to wearing traditional garb and having a unique diet; a group's own moral perspective is an integral part of its distinctiveness. An absolute view of justice would lessen the worth of the distinctiveness of a group by usurping its moral perspective. It promotes oppression, since in not allowing the group its full distinctiveness it subjects it to forces from without.

Care is needed in not drawing the wrong conclusion from the situated and particular character of justice. As already emphasized, justice is inherently universal. And this universality needs to be combined with the particularity due to justice's pertaining to a given social position. Recall that justice is universal insofar as it overarches a conflict that may be based in irreconcilable values, ones that come from conflicting social positions.

This, though, does not mean that justice itself is independent of some of these values. But being dependent doesn't necessarily imply that it one-sidedly favors the values of the position it is rooted in. In a world of antagonistic forces, no group can suppose its right will conquer all. In most circumstances groups must leave room for other groups to maneuver in. This introduces another sense of being dependent, one implying that just solutions are sought in a way that avoids deepening conflict while still moving in the direction of, without fully realizing, the values of a particular social position. Justice is then a way of considering the big picture, but from a point of view somewhere within it. The broad outlines for this perspectival universalism were sketched by Antonio Gramsci in the 1930s within the context of his theory of hegemony in his *Prison Notebooks*.

Nowhere is this perspectival universalism more evident than in the state itself. Those with power in the state want to retain their power. It seems a good bet that they can retain it better if they ally with those who are most powerful in the society. But there are limits to the advantages of such an alliance. Those with less power in the society could be provoked by a state that worked for the benefit of only a few powerful citizens. Those in the ruling group can avoid making such a provocation by adopting measures of justice.

They adopt measures of justice by seeking to limit the losses of the many and the benefits of the few through a variety of devices, such as welfare and civil rights. These devices then define the pattern of official justice of the state. If such a pattern of justice is not made into a hoax by corrupt administration, then it can truthfully be said that the state rules for all, since the losses of all are limited.

Nonetheless, the state's justice, even though it is universal in this way, is fashioned from the perspective of the need to avoid provocations that would destabilize rule, and hence threaten those with power. Thus, we find that studies of the legitimacy of state institutions, such as the courts, raise the problem of justice, the problem of how it can be universal and at the same time dependent on a particular context.

PART I

Utility, Production, and Society

On the Connection between Justice and Utility*

JOHN STUART MILL

IN ALL AGES OF speculation one of the strongest obstacles to the reception of the doctrine that utility or happiness is the criterion of right and wrong has been drawn from the idea of justice. The powerful sentiment and apparently clear perception which that word recalls with a rapidity and certainty resembling an instinct have seemed to the majority of thinkers to point to an inherent quality in things; to show that the just must have an existence in nature as something absolute, generically distinct from every variety of the expedient and, in idea, opposed to it, though (as is commonly acknowledged) never, in the long run, disjoined from it in fact.

In the case of this, as of our other moral sentiments, there is no necessary connection between the question of its origin and that of its binding force. That a feeling is bestowed on us by nature does not necessarily legitimate all its promptings. The feeling of justice might be a peculiar instinct, and might yet require, like our other instincts, to be controlled and enlightened by a higher reason. If we have intellectual instincts leading us to judge in a particular way, as well as animal instincts that prompt us to act in a particular way, there is no necessity that the former should be more infallible in their sphere than the latter in theirs; it may as well happen that wrong judgments are occasionally suggested by those, as wrong actions by these. But though it is one thing to believe that we have natural feelings of justice, and another to acknowledge them as an ultimate criterion of conduct, these two opinions are very closely connected in point of fact. Mankind are always predisposed to believe that any subjective feeling, not otherwise accounted for, is a revelation of some objective reality. Our present

*This selection is from chapter 5 of Mill's *Utilitarianism* (1861).

object is to determine whether the reality to which the feeling of justice corresponds is one which needs any such special revelation, whether the justice or injustice of an action is a thing intrinsically peculiar and distinct from all its other qualities or only a combination of certain of those qualities presented under a peculiar aspect. For the purpose of this inquiry it is practically important to consider whether the feeling itself, of justice and injustice, is sui generis, like our sensations of color and taste, or a derivative feeling formed by a combination of others. And this it is the more essential to examine, as people are in general willing enough to allow that objectively the dictates of justice coincide with a part of the field of general expediency; but inasmuch as the subjective mental feeling of justice is different from that which commonly attaches to simple expediency, and, except in the extreme cases of the latter, is far more imperative in its demands, people find it difficult to see in justice only a particular kind or branch of general utility, and think that its superior binding force requires a totally different origin.

To throw light upon this question, it is necessary to attempt to ascertain what is the distinguishing character of justice, or of injustice; what is the quality, or whether there is any quality, attributed in common to all modes of conduct designated as unjust (for justice, like many other moral attributes, is best defined by its opposite), and distinguishing them from such modes of conduct as are disapproved, but without having that particular epithet of disapprobation applied to them. If in everything which men are accustomed to characterize as just or unjust some one common attribute or collection of attributes is always present, we may judge whether this particular attribute or combination of attributes would be capable of gathering round it a sentiment of that peculiar character and intensity by virtue of the general laws of our emotional constitution, or whether the sentiment is inexplicable and requires to be regarded as a special provision of nature. If we find the former to be the case, we shall, in resolving this question, have resolved also the main problem; if the latter, we shall have to seek for some other mode of investigating it.

To find the common attributes of a variety of objects, it is necessary to begin by surveying the objects themselves in the concrete. Let us therefore advert successively to the various modes of action and arrangements of human affairs which are classed, by universal or widely spread opinion, as just or as unjust. The things well known to excite the sentiments associated with those names are of a very multifarious character. I shall pass them rapidly in review, without studying any particular arrangement.

In the first place, it is mostly considered unjust to deprive anyone of his personal liberty, his property, or any other thing which belongs to him by law. Here, therefore, is one instance of the application of the terms "just" and "unjust" in a perfectly definite sense, namely, that it is just to respect, unjust to violate, the *legal rights* of anyone. But this judgment admits of several exceptions, arising from the other forms in which the notions of justice and injustice present themselves. For example, the person who suffers the deprivation may (as the phrase is) *have forfeited* the *rights* which he is so deprived of—a case to which we shall return presently. But also—

Secondly, the legal rights of which he is deprived may be rights which *ought* not to have belonged to him; in other words, the law which confers on him these rights may be a bad law. When it is so or when (which is the same thing for our purpose) it is supposed to be so, opinions will differ as to the justice or injustice of infringing it. Some maintain that no law, however bad, ought to be disobeyed by an individual citizen; that his opposition to it, if shown at all, should only be shown in endeavoring to get it altered by competent authority. This opinion (which condemns many of the most illustrious benefactors of mankind, and would often protect pernicious institutions against the only weapons which, in the state of things existing at the time, have any chance of succeeding against them) is defended by those who hold it on grounds of expediency, principally on that of the importance to the common interest of mankind, of maintaining inviolate the sentiment of submission to law. Other persons, again, hold the directly contrary opinion that any law, judged to be bad, may blamelessly be disobeyed, even though it be not judged to be unjust but only inexpedient, while others would confine the license of disobedience to the case of unjust laws; but, again, some say that all laws which are inexpedient are unjust, since every law imposes some restriction on the natural liberty of mankind, which restriction is an injustice unless legitimated by tending to their good. Among these diversities of opinion it seems to be universally admitted that there may be unjust laws, and that law, consequently, is not the ultimate criterion of justice, but may give to one person a benefit, or impose on another an evil, which justice condemns. When, however, a law is thought to be unjust, it seems always to be regarded as being so in the same way in which a breach of law is unjust, namely, by infringing somebody's right, which, as it cannot in this case be a legal right, receives a different appellation and is called a moral right. We may say, therefore, that a second case of injustice consists in taking or withholding from any person that to which he has a moral right.

Thirdly, it is universally considered just that each person should obtain that (whether good or evil) which he *deserves*, and unjust that he should obtain a good or be made to undergo an evil which he does not deserve. This is, perhaps, the clearest and most emphatic form in which the idea of justice is conceived by the general mind. As it involves the notion of desert, the question arises what constitutes desert? Speaking in a general way, a person is understood to deserve good if he does right, evil if he does wrong; and in a more particular sense, to deserve good from those to whom he does or has done good, and evil from those to whom he does or has done evil. The precept of returning good for evil has never been regarded as a case of the fulfillment of justice, but as one in which the claims of justice are waived, in obedience to other considerations.

Fourthly, it is confessedly unjust to *break faith* with anyone: to violate an engagement, either express or implied, or disappoint expectations raised by our own conduct, at least if we have raised those expectations knowingly and voluntarily. Like the other obligations of justice already spoken of, this one is not regarded as absolute, but as capable of being overruled by a stronger obligation of justice on the other side, or by such conduct on the part of the person concerned as is deemed to absolve us from our obligation to him and to constitute a *forfeiture* of the benefit which he has been led to expect.

Fifthly, it is, by universal admission, inconsistent with justice to be partial— to show favor or preference to one person over another in matters to which favor and preference do not properly apply. Impartiality, however, does not seem to be regarded as a duty in itself, but rather as instrumental to some other duty; for it is admitted that favor and preference are not always censurable, and, indeed, the cases in which they are condemned are rather the exception than the rule. A person would be more likely to be blamed than applauded for giving his family or friends no superiority in good offices over strangers when he could do so without violating any other duty; and no one thinks it unjust to seek one person in preference to another as a friend, connection, or companion. Impartiality where rights are concerned is of course obligatory, but this is involved in the more general obligation of giving to everyone his right. A tribunal, for example, must be impartial because it is bound to award, without regard to any other consideration, a disputed object to the one of two parties who has the right to it. There are other cases in which impartiality means being solely influenced by desert, as with those who, in the capacity of judges, preceptors, or parents, administer reward and punishment as such. There are cases, again, in which it means being solely influenced by consideration for the public interest, as in making a selection among candidates for a government employment. Impartiality, in short, as an obligation of justice, may be said to mean being exclusively influenced by the considerations which it is supposed ought to influence the particular case in hand, and resisting solicitation of any motives which prompt to conduct different from what those considerations would dictate.

Nearly allied to the idea of impartiality is that of *equality*, which often enters as a component part both into the conception of justice and into the practice of it, and, in the eyes of many persons, constitutes its essence. But in this, still more than in any other case, the notion of justice varies in different persons, and always conforms in its variations to their notion of utility. Each person maintains that equality is the dictate of justice, except where he thinks that expediency requires inequality. The justice of giving equal protection to the rights of all is maintained by those who support the most outrageous inequality in the rights themselves. Even in slave countries it is theoretically admitted that the rights of the slave, such as they are, ought to be as sacred as those of the master, and that a tribunal which fails to enforce them with equal strictness is wanting in justice; while, at the same time, institutions which leave to the slave scarcely any rights to enforce are not deemed unjust because they are not deemed inexpedient. Those who think that utility requires distinctions of rank do not consider it unjust that riches and social privileges should be unequally dispensed; but those who think this inequality inexpedient think it unjust also. Whoever thinks that government is necessary sees no injustice in as much inequality as is constituted by giving to the magistrate powers not granted to other people. Even among those who hold leveling doctrines, there are differences of opinion about expediency. Some communists consider it unjust that the produce of the labor of the community should be shared on any other principle than that of exact equality; others think it just that those should receive most whose wants are greatest; while others hold that those who work harder, or who produce more, or whose services are more valuable to the community, may justly claim a larger quota in the division of the produce. And the sense of natural justice may be plausibly appealed to in behalf of every one of these opinions.

Among so many diverse applications of the term "justice," which yet is not regarded as ambiguous, it is a matter of some difficulty to seize the mental link which holds them together, and on which the moral sentiment adhering to the term essentially depends. Perhaps, in this embarrassment, some help may be derived from the history of the word, as indicated by its etymology.

In most if not in all languages, the etymology of the word which corresponds to "just" points distinctly to an origin connected with the ordinances of law. *Justum* is a form of *jussum*, that which has been ordered. *Dikaion* comes directly from *dike*, a suit at law. *Recht*, from which came *right* and *righteous*, is synonymous with law. The courts of justice, the administration of justice, are the courts and the administration of law. *La justice*, in French, is the established term for judicature. I am not committing the fallacy, imputed with some show of truth to Horne Tooke, of assuming that etymology is slight evidence of what the idea now signified is, but the very best evidence of how it sprang up. There can, I think, be no doubt that the *idée mère*, the primitive element, in the formation of the notion of justice was conformity to law. It constituted the entire idea among the Hebrews, up to the birth of Christianity; as might be expected in the case of a people whose laws attempted to embrace all subjects on which precepts were required, and who believed those laws to be a direct emanation from the Supreme Being. But other nations, and in particular the Greeks and Romans, who knew that their laws had been made originally, and still continued to be made, by men, were not afraid to admit that those men might make bad laws; might do, by law, the same things, and from the same motives, which if done by individuals without the sanction of law would be called unjust. And hence the sentiment of injustice came to be attached, not to all violations of law, but only to violations of such laws as *ought* to exist, including such as ought to exist but do not, and to laws themselves if supposed to be contrary to what ought to be law. In this manner the idea of law and of its injunctions was still predominant in the notion of justice, even when the laws actually in force ceased to be accepted as the standard of it.

It is true that mankind considers the idea of justice and its obligations as applicable to many things which neither are, nor is it desired that they should be, regulated by law. Nobody desires that laws should interfere with the whole detail of private life; yet everyone allows that in all daily conduct a person may and does show himself to be either just or unjust. But even here, the idea of the breach of what ought to be law still lingers in a modified shape. It would always give us pleasure, and chime in with our feelings of fitness, that acts which we deem unjust should be punished, though we do not always think it expedient that this should be done by the tribunals. We forego that gratification on account of incidental inconveniences. We should be glad to see just conduct enforced and injustice repressed, even in the minutest details, if we were not, with reason, afraid of trusting the magistrate with so unlimited an amount of power over individuals. When we think that a person is bound in justice to do a thing, it is an ordinary form of language to say that he ought to be compelled to do it. We should be gratified to see the obligation enforced by anybody who had the power. If we see that its enforcement by law would be inexpedient, we lament the impossibility, we consider the impunity given to injustice as an evil, and strive to make amends for it by bringing a strong expression of our own and the public disapprobation to bear upon the offender. Thus the idea of legal constraint is still the generating idea of the notion of justice, though undergoing several transformations before that notion as it exists in an advanced state of society becomes complete.

The above is, I think, a true account, as far as it goes, of the origin and progressive growth of the idea of justice. But we must observe that it contains as yet nothing to distinguish that obligation from moral obligation in general. For the truth is that the idea of penal sanction, which is the essence of law, enters not only into the conception of injustice, but into that of any kind of wrong. We do not call anything wrong unless we mean to imply that a person ought to be punished in some way or other for doing it—if not by law, by the opinion of his fellow creatures; if not by opinion, by the reproaches of his own conscience. This seems the real turning point of the distinction between morality and simple expediency. It is a part of the notion of duty in every one of its forms that a person may rightfully be compelled to fulfill it. Duty is a thing which may be *exacted* from a person, as one exacts a debt. Unless we think that it may be exacted from him, we do not call it his duty. Reasons of prudence, or the interest of other people, may militate against actually exacting it, but the person himself, it is clearly understood, would not be entitled to complain. There are other things, on the contrary, which we wish that people should do, which we like or admire them for doing, perhaps dislike or despise them for not doing, but yet admit that they are not bound to do; it is not a case of moral obligation; we do not blame them, that is, we do not think that they are proper objects of punishment. How we come by these ideas of deserving and not deserving punishment will appear, perhaps, in the sequel; but I think there is no doubt that this distinction lies at the bottom of the notions of right and wrong; that we call any conduct wrong, or employ, instead, some other term of dislike or disparagement, according as we think that the person ought, or ought not, to be punished for it; and we say it would be right to do so and so, or merely that it would be desirable or laudable, according as we would wish to see the person whom it concerns compelled, or only persuaded and exhorted, to act in that manner.

This, therefore, being the characteristic difference which marks off, not justice, but morality in general from the remaining provinces of expediency and worthiness, the character is still to be sought which distinguishes justice from other branches of morality. Now it is known that ethical writers divide moral duties into two classes, denoted by the ill-chosen expressions, duties of perfect and of imperfect obligation; the latter being those in which, though the act is obligatory, the particular occasions of performing it are left to our choice, as in the case of charity or beneficence, which we are indeed bound to practice but not toward any definite person, nor at any prescribed time. In the more precise language of philosophic jurists, duties of perfect obligation are those duties in virtue of which a correlative *right* resides in some person or persons; duties of imperfect obligation are those moral obligations which do not give birth to any right. I think it will be found that this distinction exactly coincides with that which exists between justice and the other obligations of morality. In our survey of the various popular acceptations of justice, the term appeared generally to involve the idea of a personal right—a claim on the part of one or more individuals, like that which the law gives when it confers a proprietary or other legal right. Whether the injustice consists in depriving a person of a possession, or in breaking faith with him, or in treating him worse than he deserves, or worse than other people who have no greater claims—in each case the supposition implies two things: a wrong done, and some assignable person who is wronged. Injustice may also be done by treating a person better than others; but the wrong in this case is to his competitors, who are also assignable persons. It seems to me that this feature in the case—a right in some person, correlative to the moral obligation—constitutes the specific difference between justice and generosity or beneficence. Justice implies something which it is not only right to do, and wrong not to do, but which some individual person can claim from us as his moral right. No one has a moral right to our generosity or beneficence because we are not morally bound to practice those virtues toward any given individual. And it will be found with respect to this as to every correct definition that the instances which seem to connect with it are those which most confirm it. For if a moralist attempts, as some have done, to make out that mankind generally, though not any given individual, have a right to all the good we can do them, he at once, by that thesis, includes generosity and beneficence within the category of justice. He is obliged to say that our utmost exertions are *due* to our fellow creatures, thus assimilating them to a debt; or that nothing less can be a sufficient *return* for what society does for us, thus classing the case as one of gratitude; both of which are acknowledged cases of justice, and not of the virtue of beneficence; and whoever does not place the distinction between justice and morality in general, where we have now placed it, will be found to make no distinction between them at all, but to merge all morality in justice.

Having thus endeavored to determine the distinctive elements which enter into the composition of the idea of justice, we are ready to enter on the inquiry whether the feeling which accompanies the idea is attached to it by a special dispensation of nature, or whether it could have grown up, by any known laws, out of the idea itself; and, in particular, whether it can have originated in considerations of general expediency.

I conceive that the sentiment itself does not arise from anything which would commonly or correctly be termed an idea of expediency, but that, though the sentiment does not, whatever is moral in it does.

We have seen that the two essential ingredients in the sentiment of justice are the desire to punish a person who has done harm and the knowledge or belief that there is some definite individual or individuals to whom harm has been done.

Now it appears to me that the desire to punish a person who has done harm to some individual is a spontaneous outgrowth from two sentiments, both in the highest degree natural and which either are or resemble instincts: the impulse of self-defense and the feeling of sympathy.

It is natural to resent and to repel or retaliate any harm done or attempted against ourselves or against those with whom we sympathize. The origin of this sentiment it is not necessary here to discuss. Whether it be an instinct or a result of intelligence, it is, we know, common to all animal nature; for every animal tries to hurt those who have hurt, or who it thinks are about to hurt, itself or its young. Human beings, on this point, only differ from other animals in two particulars. First, in being capable of sympathizing, not solely with their offspring, or, like some of the more noble animals, with some superior animal who is kind to them, but with all human, and even with all sentient, beings; secondly, in having a more developed intelligence, which gives a wider range to the whole of their sentiments, whether self-regarding or sympathetic. By virtue of his superior intelligence, even apart from his superior range of sympathy, a human being is capable of apprehending a community of interest between himself and the human society of which he forms a part, such that any conduct which threatens the security of the society generally is threatening to his own, and calls forth his instinct (if instinct it be) of self-defense. The same superiority of intelligence, joined to the power of sympathizing with human beings generally, enables him to attach himself to the collective idea of his tribe, his country, or mankind in such a manner that any act hurtful to them raises his instinct of sympathy and urges him to resistance.

The sentiment of justice, in that one of its elements which consists of the desire to punish, is thus, I conceive, the natural feeling of retaliation or vengeance, rendered by intellect and sympathy applicable to those injuries, that is, to those hurts, which wound us through, or in common with, society at large. This sentiment, in itself, has nothing moral in it; what is moral is the exclusive subordination of it to the social sympathies, so as to wait on and obey their call. For the natural feeling would make us resent indiscriminately whatever anyone does that is disagreeable to us; but, when moralized by the social feeling, it only acts in the directions conformable to the general good: just persons resenting a hurt to society, though not otherwise a hurt to themselves, and not resenting a hurt to themselves, however painful, unless it be of the kind which society has a common interest with them in the repression of.

It is no objection against this doctrine to say that, when we feel our sentiment of justice outraged, we are not thinking of society at large or of any collective interest, but only of the individual case. It is common enough, certainly, though the reverse of commendable, to feel resentment merely because we have suffered pain; but a person whose resentment is really a moral feeling, that is, who considers whether an act is blamable before he allows himself to resent it—such a person, though he may not say expressly to himself that he is standing up for the interest of society, certainly does feel that he is asserting a rule which is for the benefit of others as well as for his own. If he is not feeling this, if he is regarding the act solely as it affects him individually, he is not consciously just; he is not concerning himself about the justice of his actions. This is admitted even by anti-utilitarian moralists. When Kant (as before remarked) propounds as the fundamental principle of morals, "So act that thy rule of conduct might be adopted as a law by all rational beings," he virtually acknowledges that the interest of mankind collectively, or at least of mankind indiscriminately, must be in the mind of the agent when conscientiously deciding on the morality of the act. Otherwise he uses words without a meaning; for that a rule even of utter selfishness could not *possibly* be adopted by all rational beings—that there is any insuperable obstacle in the nature of things to its adoption—cannot be even plausibly maintained. To give any meaning to Kant's principle, the sense put upon it must be that we ought to shape our conduct by a rule which all rational beings might adopt *with benefit to their collective interest*.

To recapitulate: the idea of justice supposes two things—a rule of conduct and a sentiment which sanctions the rule. The first must be supposed common to all mankind and intended for their good. The other (the sentiment) is a desire that punishment may be suffered by those who infringe the rule. There is involved, in addition, the conception of some definite person who suffers by the infringement, whose rights (to use the expression appropriated to the case) are violated by it. And the sentiment of justice appears to me to be the animal desire to repel or retaliate a hurt or damage to oneself or to those with whom one sympathizes, widened so as to include all persons, by the human capacity of enlarged sympathy and the human conception of intelligent self-interest. From the latter elements the feeling derives its morality; from the former, its peculiar impressiveness and energy of self-assertion.

I have, throughout, treated the idea of a *right* residing in the injured person and violated by the injury, not as a separate element in the composition of the idea and sentiment, but as one of the forms in which the other two elements clothe themselves. These elements are a hurt to some assignable person or persons, on the one hand, and a demand for punishment, on the other. An examination of our own minds, I think, will show that these two things include all that we mean when we speak of violation of a right. When we call anything a person's right, we mean that he has a valid claim on society to protect him in the possession of it, either by the force of law or by that of education and opinion. If he has what we consider a sufficient claim, on whatever account, to have something guaranteed to him by society, we say that he has a right to it. If we desire to prove that anything does not belong to him by right, we think this done as soon as it is admitted that society ought not to take measures for securing it to him, but should leave him to chance or to his own exertions. Thus a person is said to have a right to what he can earn in fair professional competition, because society ought not to allow any other person to hinder him from endeavoring to earn in that manner as much as he can. But he has not a right to three hundred a year, though he may happen to be earning it; because society is not called on to provide that he shall earn that sum. On the contrary, if he owns ten thousand pounds 3 percent stock, he *has* a right to three hundred a year because society has come under an obligation to provide him with an income of that amount.

To have a right, then, is, I conceive, to have something which society ought to defend me in the possession of. If the objector goes on to ask why it ought, I can give him no other reason than general utility. If that expression does not seem to convey a sufficient feeling of the strength of the obligation, nor to account for the peculiar energy of the feeling, it is because there goes to the composition of the sentiment, not a rational only but also an animal element— the thirst for retaliation; and this thirst derives its intensity, as well as its moral justification, from the extraordinarily important and impressive kind of utility which is concerned. The interest involved is that of security, to everyone's feelings the most vital of all interests. All other earthly benefits are needed by one person, not needed by another; and many of them can, if necessary, be cheerfully foregone or replaced by something else; but security no human being can possibly do without; on it we depend for all our immunity from evil and for the whole value of all and every good, beyond the passing moment, since nothing but the gratification of the instant could be of any worth to us if we could be deprived of everything the next instant by whoever was momentarily stronger than ourselves. Now this most indispensable of all necessaries, after physical nutriment, cannot be had unless the machinery for providing it is kept unintermittedly in active play. Our notion, therefore, of the claim we have on our fellow creatures to join in making safe for us the very groundwork of our existence gathers feelings around it so much more intense than those concerned in any of the more common cases of utility that the difference in degree (as is often the case in psychology) becomes a real difference in kind. The claim assumes that character of absoluteness, that apparent infinity and incommensurability with all other considerations which constitute the distinction between the feeling of right and wrong and that of ordinary expediency and inexpediency. The feelings concerned are so powerful, and we count so positively on finding a responsive feeling in others (all being alike interested) that *ought* and *should* grow into *must*, and recognized indispensability becomes a moral necessity, analogous to physical, and often not inferior to it in binding force.

If the preceding analysis, or something resembling it, be not the correct account of the notion of justice—if justice be totally independent of utility, and be a standard per se, which the mind can recognize by simple introspection of itself—it is hard to understand why that internal oracle is so ambiguous, and why so many things appear either just or unjust, according to the light in which they are regarded.

We are continually informed that utility is an uncertain standard, which every different person interprets differently, and that there is no safety but in the immutable, ineffaceable, and unmistakable dictates of justice, which carry their evidence in themselves and are independent of the fluctuations of opinion. One would suppose from this that on questions of justice there could be no controversy; that, if we take that for our rule, its application to any given case could leave us in as little doubt as a mathematical demonstration. So far is this from being the fact that there is as much difference of opinion, and as much discussion, about what is just as about what is useful to society. Not only have different nations and individuals different notions of justice, but in the mind of one and the same individual, justice is not some one rule, principle, or maxim, but many which do not always coincide in their dictates, and, in choosing between which, he is guided either by some extraneous standard or by his own personal predilections.

For instance, there are some who say that it is unjust to punish anyone for the sake of example to others, that punishment is just only when intended for the good of the sufferer himself. Others maintain the extreme reverse, contending that to punish persons who have attained years of discretion, for their own benefit, is despotism and injustice, since, if the matter at issue is solely their own good, no one has a right to control their own judgment of it; but that they may justly be punished to prevent evil to others, this being the exercise of the legitimate right of self-defense. Mr. Owen, again, affirms that it is unjust to punish at all, for the criminal did not make his own character; his education and the circumstances which surrounded him have made him a criminal, and for these he is not responsible. All these opinions are extremely plausible; and so long as the question is argued as one of justice simply, without going down to the principles which lie under justice and are the source of its authority, I am unable to see how any of these reasoners can be refuted. For in truth every one of the three builds upon rules of justice confessedly true. The first appeals to the acknowledged injustice of singling out an individual and making him a sacrifice, without his consent, for other people's benefit. The second relies on the acknowledged justice of self-defense and the admitted injustice of forcing one person to conform to another's notions of what constitutes his good. The Owenite invokes the admitted principle that it is unjust to punish anyone for what he cannot help. Each is triumphant so long as he is not compelled to take into consideration any other maxims of justice than the one he has selected; but as soon as their several maxims are brought face to face, each disputant seems to have exactly as much to say for himself as the others. No one of them can carry out his own notion of justice without trampling upon another equally binding. These are difficulties; they have always been felt to be such; and many devices have been invented to turn rather than to overcome them. As a refuge from the last of the three, men imagined what they called the freedom of the will— fancying that they could not justify punishing a man whose will is in a thoroughly hateful state unless it be supposed to have come into that state through no influence of anterior circumstances. To escape from the other difficulties, a favorite contrivance has been the fiction of a contract whereby at some un- known period all the members of society engaged to obey the laws and consented to be punished for any disobedience to them, thereby giving to their legislators the right, which it is assumed they would not otherwise have had, of punishing them, either for their own good or for that of society. This happy thought was considered to get rid of the whole difficulty and to legitimate the infliction of punishment, in virtue of another received maxim of justice, *volenti non fit injuria*—that is not unjust which is done with the consent of the person who is supposed to be hurt by it. I need hardly remark that, even if the consent were not a mere fiction, this maxim is not superior in authority to the others which it is brought in to supersede. It is, on the contrary, an instructive specimen of the loose and irregular manner in which supposed principles of justice grow up. This particular one evidently came into use as a help to the coarse exigencies of courts of law, which are sometimes obliged to be content with very uncertain presumptions, on account of the greater evils which would often arise from any attempt on their part to cut finer. But even courts of law are not able to adhere consistently to the maxim, for they allow voluntary engagements to be set aside on the ground of fraud, and sometimes on that of mere mistake or misinformation.

Again, when the legitimacy of inflicting punishment is admitted, how many conflicting conceptions of justice come to light in discussing the proper apportionment of punishments to offenses. No rule on the subject recommends itself so strongly to the primitive and spontaneous sentiment of justice as the *lex talionis*, an eye for an eye and a tooth for a tooth. Though this principle of the Jewish and of the Mohammedan law has been generally abandoned in Europe as a practical maxim, there is, I suspect, in most minds, a secret hankering after it; and when retribution accidentally falls on an offender in that precise shape, the general feeling of satisfaction evinced bears witness how natural is the sentiment to which this repayment in kind is acceptable. With many, the test of justice in penal infliction is that the punishment should be proportioned to the offense, meaning that it should be exactly measured by the moral guilt of the culprit (whatever be their standard for measuring moral guilt), the consideration what amount of punishment is necessary to deter from the offense having nothing to do with the question of justice, in their estimation; while there are others to whom that consideration is all in all, who maintain that it is not just, at least for man, to inflict on a fellow creature, whatever may be his offenses, any amount of suffering beyond the least that will suffice to prevent him from repeating, and others from imitating, his misconduct.

To take another example from a subject already once referred to. In cooperative industrial association, is it just or not that talent or skill should give a title to superior remuneration? On the negative side of the question it is argued that whoever does the best he can deserves equally well, and ought not in justice to be put in a position of inferiority for no fault of his own; that superior abilities have already advantages more than enough, in the admiration they excite, the personal influence they command, and the internal sources of satisfaction attending them, without adding to these a superior share of the world's goods; and that society is bound in justice rather to make compensation to the less favored for this unmerited inequality of advantages than to aggravate it. On the contrary side it is contended that society receives more from the more efficient laborer; that, his services being more useful, society owes him a larger return for them; that a greater share of the joint result is actually his work, and not to allow his claim to it is a kind of robbery; that, if he is only to receive as much as others, he can only be justly required to produce as much, and to give a smaller amount of time and exertion, proportioned to his superior efficiency. Who shall decide between these appeals to conflicting principles of justice? Justice has in this case two sides to it, which it is impossible to bring into harmony, and the two disputants have chosen opposite sides; the one looks to what it is just that the individual should receive, the other to what it is just that the community should give. Each, from his own point of view, is unanswerable; and any choice between them, on grounds of justice, must be perfectly arbitrary. Social utility alone can decide the preference.

How many, again, and how irreconcilable are the standards of justice to which reference is made in discussing the repartition of taxation. One opinion is that payment to the state should be in numerical proportion to pecuniary means. Others think that justice dictates what they term graduated taxation—taking a higher percentage from those who have more to spare. In point of natural justice a strong case might be made for disregarding means altogether, and taking the same absolute sum (whenever it could be got) from everyone; as the subscribers to a mess or to a club all pay the same sum for the same privileges, whether they can all equally afford it or not. Since the protection (it might be said) of law and government is afforded to and is equally required by all, there is no injustice in making all buy it at the same price. It is reckoned justice, not injustice, that a dealer should charge to all customers the same price for the same article, not a price varying according to their means of payment. This doctrine, as applied to taxation, finds no advocates because it conflicts so strongly with man's feelings of humanity and of social expediency; but the principle of justice which it invokes is as true and as binding as those which can be appealed to against it. Accordingly it exerts a tacit influence on the line of defense employed for other modes of assessing taxation. People feel obliged to argue that the state does more for the rich man than for the poor, as a justification for its taking more from them, though this is in reality not true, for the rich would be far better able to protect themselves, in the absence of law or government, than the poor, and indeed would probably be successful in converting the poor into their slaves. Others, again, so far defer to the same conception of justice as to maintain that all should pay an equal capitation tax for the protection of their persons (these being of equal value to all), and an unequal tax for the protection of their property, which is unequal. To this others reply that the all of one man is as valuable to him as the all of another. From these confusions there is no other mode of extrication than the utilitarian.

Is, then, the difference between the just and the expedient a merely imaginary distinction? Have mankind been under a delusion in thinking that justice is a more sacred thing than policy, and that the latter ought only to be listened to after the former has been satisfied? By no means. The exposition we have given of the nature and origin of the sentiment recognizes a real distinction; and no one of those who profess the most sublime contempt for the consequences of actions as an element in their morality attaches more importance to the distinc-tion than I do. While I dispute the pretensions of any theory which sets up an imaginary standard of justice not grounded on utility, I account the justice which is grounded on utility to be the chief part, and incomparably the most sacred and binding part, of all morality. Justice is a name for certain classes of moral rules which concern the essentials of human well-being more nearly, and are therefore of more absolute obligation, than any other rules for the guidance of life; and the notion which we have found to be of the essence of the idea of justice—that of a right residing in an individual—implies and testifies to this more binding obligation.

The moral rules which forbid mankind to hurt one another (in which we must never forget to include a wrongful interference with each other's freedom) are more vital to human well-being than any maxims, however important, which only point out the best mode of managing some department of human affairs. They have also the peculiarity that they are the main element in determining the whole of the social feelings of mankind. It is their observance which alone preserves peace among human beings; if obedience to them were not the rule, and disobedience the exception, everyone would see in everyone else an enemy against whom he must be perpetually guarding himself. What is hardly less important, these are the precepts which mankind have the strongest and the most direct inducements for impressing upon one another. By merely giving to each other prudential instruction or exhortation, they may gain, or think they gain, nothing; in inculcating on each other the duty of positive beneficence, they have an unmistakable interest, but far less in degree; a person may possibly not need the benefits of others, but he always needs that they should not do him hurt. Thus the moralities which protect every individual from being harmed by others, either directly or by being hindered in his freedom of pursuing his own good, are at once those which he himself has most at heart and those which he has the strongest interest in publishing and enforcing by word and deed. It is by a person's observance of these that his fitness to exist as one of the fellowship of human beings is tested and decided; for on that depends his being a nuisance or not to those with whom he is in contact. Now it is these moralities primarily which compose the obligations of justice. The most marked cases of injustice, and those which give the tone to the feeling of repugnance which characterizes the sentiment, are acts of wrongful aggression or wrongful exercise of power over someone; the next are those which consist in wrongfully withholding from him something which is his due—in both cases inflicting on him a positive hurt, either in the form of direct suffering or of the privation of some good which he had reasonable ground, either of a physical or of a social kind, for counting upon.

The same powerful motives which command the observance of these primary moralities enjoin the punishment of those who violate them; and as the impulses of self-defense, of defense of others, and of vengeance are all called forth against such persons, retribution, or evil for evil, becomes closely connected with the sentiment of justice, and is universally included in the idea. Good for good is also one of the dictates of justice; and this, though its social utility is evident, and though it carries with it a natural human feeling, has not at first sight that obvious connection with hurt or injury which, existing in the most elementary cases of just and unjust, is the source of the characteristic intensity of the sentiment. But the connection, though less obvious, is not less real. He who accepts benefits and denies a return of them when needed inflicts a real hurt by disappointing one of the most natural and reasonable of expectations, and one which he must at least tacitly have encouraged, otherwise the benefits would seldom have been conferred. The important rank, among human evils and wrongs, of the disappointment of expectation is shown in the fact that it constitutes the principal criminality of two such highly immoral acts as a breach of friendship and a breach of promise. Few hurts which human beings can sustain are greater, and none wound more, than when that on which they habitually and with full assurance relied fails them in the hour of need; and few wrongs are greater than this mere withholding of good; none excite more resentment, either in the person suffering or in a sympathizing spectator. The principle, therefore, of giving to each what they deserve, that is, good for good as well as evil for evil, is not only included within the idea of justice as we have defined it, but is a proper object of that intensity of sentiment which places the just human estimation above the simply expedient.

Most of the maxims of justice current in the world, and commonly appealed to in its transactions, are simply instrumental to carrying into effect the principles of justice which we have now spoken of. That a person is only responsible for what he has done voluntarily, or could voluntarily have avoided, that it is unjust to condemn any person unheard, that the punishment ought to be proportioned to the offense, and the like, are maxims intended to prevent the just principle of evil for evil from being perverted to the infliction of evil without that justification. The greater part of these common maxims have come into use from the practice of courts of justice, which have been naturally led to a more complete recognition and elaboration than was likely to suggest itself to others, of the rules necessary to enable them to fulfill their double function—of inflicting punishment when due, and of awarding to each person his right. . . .

Critique of the
Gotha Program *

KARL MARX

1. "LABOR IS THE SOURCE *of all wealth and all culture,* and since *useful labor is possible only in society and through society, the proceeds of labor belong undiminished with equal right to all members of society.*"

First Part of the Paragraph: "Labor is the source of all wealth and all culture."

Labor is *not the source* of all wealth. *Nature* is just as much the source of use values (and it is surely of such that material wealth consists!) as is labor, which itself is only the manifestation of a natural force, human labor power. That phrase is to be found in all children's primers and is correct insofar as it is *implied* that labor proceeds with the appropriate subjects and instruments. But a socialist program cannot allow such bourgeois phrases to cause the *conditions* to be ignored that alone give them meaning. And insofar as man from the beginning behaves toward nature, the primary source of all instruments and subjects of labor, as her owner, treats her as belonging to him, his labor becomes the source of use values, therefore also of wealth. The bourgeois have very good grounds for fancifully ascribing *supernatural creative power* to labor, since it follows precisely from the fact that labor depends on nature, that the man who possesses no other property than his labor power must, in all conditions of society and culture, be the slave of other men who have made themselves the owners of the material conditions of labor. He can work only with their permission, hence only live with their permission.

*Excerpt from *Critique of the Gotha Programme* (1875) by Karl Marx, translated by C. P. Dutt. Copyright ©1966 by International Publishers Co., Inc. Reprinted by permission.

Let us now leave the sentence as it stands, or rather limps. What would one have expected as conclusion? Obviously this:

"Since labor is the source of all wealth, no one in society can appropriate wealth except as the product of labor. Therefore, if he himself does not work, he lives by the labor of others and also acquires his culture at the expense of the labor of others."

Instead of this, by means of the words "*and since*" a second proposition is added in order to draw a conclusion from this and not from the first one.

Second Part of the Paragraph: "Useful labor is possible only in society and through society."

According to the first proposition, labor was the source of all wealth and all culture; therefore no society is possible without labor. Now we learn, conversely, that no "useful" labor is possible without society.

One could just as well have said that only in society can useless and even socially harmful labor become a gainful occupation, that only in society can one live by being idle, etc., etc.—in short, one could just as well have copied the whole of Rousseau.

And what is "useful" labor? Surely only labor which produces the intended useful result. A savage—and man was a savage after he had ceased to be an ape—who kills an animal with a stone, who collects fruits, etc., performs "useful" labor.

Thirdly: The Conclusion: "And since useful labor is possible only in society and through society, the proceeds of labor belong undiminished with equal right to all members of society."

A fine conclusion! If useful labor is possible only in society and through society, the proceeds of labor belong to society—and only so much therefrom accrues to the individual worker as is not required to maintain the "condition" of labor, society.

In fact, this proposition has at all times been made use of by *the champions of the state of society prevailing at any given time*. First come the claims of the government and everything that sticks to it, since it is the social organ for the maintenance of the social order; then come the claims of the various kinds of private owners for the various kinds of private property are the foundations of society, etc. One sees that such hollow phrases can be twisted and turned as desired.

The first and second parts of the paragraph have some intelligible connection only in the following wording:

"Labor becomes the source—of wealth and culture only as social labor," or, what is the same thing, "in and through society."

This proposition is incontestably correct, for although isolated labor (its material conditions presupposed) can create use values, it can create neither wealth nor culture.

But equally incontestable is the other proposition:

"In proportion as labor develops socially, and becomes thereby a source of wealth and culture, poverty and destitution develop among the workers, and wealth and culture among the nonworkers."

This is the law of all history hitherto. What, therefore, had to be done here, instead of setting down general phrases about "labor" and "*society*," was to prove concretely how in present capitalist society the material, etc., conditions have at last been created which enable and compel the workers to lift this historical curse.

In fact, however, the whole paragraph, bungled in style and content, is only there in order to inscribe the Lassallean catchword of the "undiminished proceeds of labor" as a slogan at the top of the party banner. I shall return later to the "proceeds of labor," "equal right," etc., since the same thing recurs in a somewhat different form further on.

2. *"In present-day society, the instruments of labor are the monopoly of the capitalist class; the resulting dependence of the working class is the cause of misery and servitude in all their forms."*

This sentence, borrowed from the Statutes of the International, is incorrect in this "improved" edition.

In present-day society the instruments of labor are the monopoly of the landowners (the monopoly of land ownership is even the basis of the monopoly of capital) *and* the capitalists. In the passage in question, the Statutes of the International mention neither the one nor the other class of monopolists. They speak of the *"monopoly of the means of labor, that is, the sources of life."* The addition, "source of life," makes it sufficiently clear that land is included in the instruments of labor.

The correction was introduced because Lassalle, for reasons now generally known, attacked *only* the capitalist class and not the landowners. In England, the capitalist is mostly not even the owner of the land on which his factory stands.

3. *"The emancipation of labor demands the promotion of the instruments of labor to the common property of society, and the cooperative regulation of the total labor with equitable distribution of the proceeds of labor."*

"The promotion of the instruments of labor to common property" ought obviously to read, their "conversion into common property," but this only in passing.

What are *"proceeds of labor"*? The product of labor or its value? And in the latter case, is it the total value of the product or only that part of the value which labor has newly added to the value of the means of production consumed?

"Proceeds of labor" is a loose notion which Lassalle has put in the place of definite economic concepts.

What is "equitable distribution"?

Do not the bourgeois assert that present-day distribution is "equitable"? And is it not, in fact, the only "equitable" distribution on the basis of the present-day mode of production? Are economic relations regulated by legal concepts or do not, on the contrary, legal relations arise from economic ones? Have not also the socialist sectarians the most varied notions about "equitable" distribution?

To understand what is implied in this connection by the phrase "equitable distribution," we must take the first paragraph and this one together. The latter presupposes a society wherein "the instruments of labor are common property and the total labor is cooperatively regulated," and from the first paragraph we learn that "the proceeds of labor belong undiminished with equal right to all members of society."

"To all members of society"? To those who do not work as well? What remains then of "the undiminished proceeds of labor"? Only to those members of society who work? What remains then of "the equal right" of all members of society?

But "all members of society" and "equal right" are obviously mere phrases. The crucial point is this, that in this communist society every worker must receive his "undiminished" Lassallean "proceeds of labor."

Let us take first of all the words "proceeds of labor" in the sense of the product of labor; then the collective proceeds of labor are the *total social product*.

From this must now be deducted:

First, cover for replacement of the means of production used up.

Secondly, additional portion for expansion of production.

Thirdly, reserve or insurance funds to provide against accidents, disturbances caused by natural factors, etc.

These deductions from the "undiminished proceeds of labor" are an economic necessity and their magnitude is to be determined according to available means and forces, and partly by computation of probabilities, but they are in no way calculable by equity.

There remains the other part of the total product, intended to serve as means of consumption.

Before this is divided among the individuals, there has to be again deducted from it:

First, the general costs of administration not directly appertaining to production.

This part will, from the outset, be very considerably restricted in comparison with present-day society and it diminishes in proportion as the new society develops.

Secondly, that which is intended for the common satisfaction of needs, such as schools, health services, etc.

From the outset this part grows considerably in comparison with present-day society and it grows in proportion as the new society develops.

Thirdly, funds for those unable to work, etc., in short, for what is included under so-called official poor relief today.

Only now do we come to the "distribution" which the program, under Lassallean influence, has alone in view in its narrow fashion, namely, to that part of the means of consumption which is divided among the individual producers of the collective.

The "undiminished proceeds of labor" have already unnoticeably become converted into the "diminished" proceeds, although what the producer is deprived of in his capacity as a private individual benefits him directly or indirectly in his capacity as a member of society.

Just as the phrase of the "undiminished proceeds of labor" has disappeared, so now does the phrase of the "proceeds of labor" disappear altogether.

Within the cooperative society based on common ownership of the means of production, the producers do not exchange their products; just as little does the labor employed on the products appear here *as the value* of these products, as a material quality possessed by them, since now, in contrast to capitalist society, individual labor no longer exists in an indirect fashion but directly as a component part of the total labor. The phrase "proceeds of labor," objectionable even today on account of its ambiguity, thus loses all meaning.

What we are dealing with here is a communist society, not as it has *developed* on its own foundations, but on the contrary, just as it *emerges* from capitalist society, which is thus in every respect, economically, morally and intellectually, still stamped with the birth-marks of the old society from whose womb it emerges. Accordingly, the individual producer receives back from society— after the deductions have been made—exactly what he gives to it. What he has given to it is his individual quantum of labor. For example, the social working day consists of the sum of the individual hours of work; the individual labor time of the individual producer is the part of the social working day contributed by him, his share in it. He receives a certificate from society that he has furnished such and such an amount of labor (after deducting his labor for the common funds), and with this certificate he draws from the social stock of means of consumption as much as the same amount of labor costs. The same amount of labor which he has given to society in one form he receives back in another.

Here obviously the same principle prevails as that which regulates the exchange of commodities, as far as this is the exchange of equal values. Content and form are changed, because under the altered circumstances no one can give anything except his labor, and because, on the other hand, nothing can pass to the ownership of individuals except individual means of consumption. But, as far as the distribution of the latter among the individual producers is concerned, the same principle prevails as in the exchange of commodity-equivalents, so much labor in one form is exchanged for an equal amount of labor in another form.

Hence, *equal right* here is still in principle—*bourgeois right*, although principle and practice are no longer in conflict, while the exchange of equivalents in commodity exchange only exists *on the average* and not in the individual case.

In spite of this advance, this *equal right* is still constantly encumbered by a bourgeois limitation. The right of the producers is *proportional* to the labor they supply; the equality consists in the fact that measurement is made with an *equal standard*, labor.

But one man is superior to another physically or mentally and so supplies more labor in the same time, or can work for a longer time: and labor, to serve as a measure, must be defined by its duration or intensity, otherwise it ceases to be a standard of measurement. This *equal* right is an unequal right for unequal labor. It recognizes no class distinctions, because everyone is only a worker like everyone else; but it tacitly recognizes the unequal individual endowment and thus productive capacity of the workers as natural privileges. *It is, therefore, a right of inequality in its content, like every right.* Right by its nature can exist only as the application of an equal standard; but unequal individuals (and they would not be different individuals if they were not unequal) are only measurable by an equal standard insofar as they are brought under an equal point of view, are taken from one *definite* side only, e.g., in the present case are regarded *only as workers*, and nothing more is seen in them, everything else being ignored. Besides, one worker is married, another not; one has more children than another, etc., etc. Thus, given an equal amount of work done, and hence an equal share in the social consumption fund, one will in fact receive more than another, one will be richer than another, etc. To avoid all these defects, right would have to be unequal rather than equal.

But these defects are inevitable in the first phase of communist society as it is when it has just emerged after prolonged birthpangs from capitalist society. Right can never be higher than the economic structure of society and the cultural development thereby determined.

In a higher phase of communist society, after the enslaving subordination of the individual to the division of labor, and thereby also the antithesis between mental and physical labor, has vanished; after labor has become not only a means of life but life's prime want; after the productive forces have also increased with the all-round development of the individual, and all the springs of cooperative wealth flow more abundantly—only then can the narrow horizon of bourgeois right be crossed in its entirety and society inscribe on its banners: From each according to his ability, to each according to his needs!

I have dealt at greater length with the "undiminished proceeds of labor," on the one hand, and with "equal right" and "equitable distribution," on the other, in order to show what a crime it is to attempt, on the one hand, to force on our Party again, as dogmas, ideas which in a certain period had some meaning but have now become obsolete verbal rubbish, while again perverting, on the other, the realistic outlook, which it cost so much effort to instil into the Party but which has now taken root in it, by means of ideological, legal, and other trash so common among the Democrats and French Socialists.

Quite apart from the analysis so far given, it was in general a mistake to make a fuss about so-called *distribution* and put the principal stress on it.

Any distribution whatever of the means of consumption is only a consequence of the distribution of the conditions of production themselves. The latter distribution, however, is a feature of the mode of production itself. The capitalist mode of production, for example, rests on the fact that the material conditions of production are in the hands of non-workers in the form of capital and land ownership, while the masses are only owners of the personal condition of production, of labor power. If the elements of production are so distributed, then the present-day distribution of the means of consumption results automatically. If the material conditions of production are the cooperative property of the workers themselves, then there likewise results a distribution of the means of consumption different from the present one. The vulgar socialists (and from them in turn a section of the Democrats) have taken over from the bourgeois economists the consideration and treatment of distribution as independent of the mode of production and hence the presentation of socialism as turning principally on distribution. After the real relation has long been made clear, why go back again?

4. *"The emancipation of labor must be the work of the working class, in relation to which all other classes are* only one reactionary mass."

The main clause is taken from the introductory words of the Statutes of the International, but "improved." There it is said: "The emancipation of the working classes must be the act of the workers themselves"; here, on the contrary, the "working class" has to emancipate—what? "Labor." Let him understand who can.

In compensation, the subordinate clause, on the other hand, is a Lassallean quotation of the first water: "in relation to which (the working class) all other classes are *only one reactionary mass.*"

In the *Communist Manifesto* it is said: "Of all the classes that stand face to face with the bourgeoisie today, the proletariat alone is a *really revolutionary class.* The other classes decay and finally disappear in the face of Modern Industry; the proletariat is its special and essential product."

The bourgeoisie is here conceived as a revolutionary class—as the bearer of large-scale industry—in relation to the feudal lords and the middle estates, who desire to maintain all social positions that are the creation of obsolete modes of production. Thus they do not form *together* with the *bourgeoisie* only one reactionary mass.

On the other hand, the proletariat is revolutionary in relation to the bourgeoisie because, having itself grown up on the basis of large-scale industry, it strives to strip off from production the capitalist character that the bourgeoisie seeks to perpetuate. But the *Manifesto* adds that the "middle estates" are becoming revolutionary "in view of their impending transfer into the proletariat."

From this point of view, therefore, it is again nonsense to say that they, "together with the bourgeoisie," and with the feudal lords into the bargain, "form only one reactionary mass" in relation to the working class.

Did anyone proclaim to the artisans, small manufacturers, etc., and *peasants* during the last elections: In relation to us you, together with the bourgeoisie and feudal lords, form only one reactionary mass?

Lassalle knew the *Communist Manifesto* by heart, as his faithful followers know the gospels written by him. If, therefore, he has falsified it so grossly, this has occurred only to put a good color on his alliance with absolutist and feudal opponents against the bourgeoisie.

In the above paragraph, moreover, his oracular saying is dragged in by the hair, without any connection with the botched quotation from the Rules of the International. Thus it is here simply an impertinence, and indeed not at all displeasing to Mr. Bismarck, one of those cheap pieces of insolence in which the Marat of Berlin deals.

5. *"The working class strives for its emancipation first of all* within the framework of the present-day national state, *conscious that the necessary result of its efforts, which are common to the workers of all civilized countries, will be the international brotherhood of peoples."*

Lassalle, in opposition to the *Communist Manifesto* and to all earlier socialism, conceived the workers' movement from the narrowest national standpoint. He is being followed in this—and that after the work of the International!

It is altogether self-evident that, to be able to fight at all, the working class must organize itself at home *as a class* and that its own country is the immediate arena of its struggle. To this extent its class struggle is national, not in substance, but, as the *Communist Manifesto* says, "in form." But the "framework of the present-day national state," for instance, the German Empire, is itself in its turn economically "within the framework of the world market," politically "within the framework of the system of states." Every businessman knows that German trade is at the same time foreign trade, and the greatness of Mr. Bismarck consists, to be sure, precisely in his pursuing his kind of *international* policy.

And to what does the German workers' party reduce its internationalism? To the consciousness that the result of its efforts "will be the *international brotherhood of peoples"*—a phrase borrowed from the bourgeois League of Peace and Freedom, which is intended to pass as equivalent to the international brotherhood of the working classes in the joint struggle against the ruling classes and their governments. So not a word *about the international functions* of the German working class! And it is thus that it is to defy its own bourgeoisie—which is already linked up in brotherhood against it with the bourgeois of all other countries—and Mr. Bismarck's international policy of conspiracy!

In fact, the internationalism of the program stands *even infinitely below* that of the Free Trade Party. The latter also asserts that the result of its efforts will be "the international brotherhood of peoples." But it also *does* something to make trade international and by no means contents itself with the consciousness— that all peoples are carrying on trade at home.

The international activity of the working classes does not in any way depend on the existence of the *"International Working Men's Association."* This was only the first attempt to create a central organ for that activity; an attempt which was a lasting success on account of the impulse which it gave, but which was no longer realizable in its *first historical form* after the fall of the Paris Commune.

Bismarck's *Norddeutsche* was absolutely right when it announced, to the satisfaction of its master, that the German workers' party had forsworn internationalism in the new program.

Rights and Justice*

THOMAS HILL GREEN

HAS THE CITIZEN RIGHTS AGAINST THE STATE?

138. IT IS EQUALLY IMPOSSIBLE, then, to hold that the right of the sovereign power in a state over its members is dependent on their consent, and, on the other hand, that these members have no rights except such as are constituted and conferred upon them by the sovereign. The sovereign, and the state itself as distinguished by the existence of a sovereign power, presupposes rights and is an institution for their maintenance. But these rights do not belong to individuals as they might be in a state of nature, or as they might be if each acted irrespectively of others. They belong to them as members of a society in which each recognizes the other as an originator of action in the same sense in which he is conscious of being so himself (as an "ego"—as himself the object which determines the action), and thus regards the free exercise of his own powers as dependent upon his allowing an equally free exercise of his powers to every other member of the society. There is no harm in saying that they belong to individuals as such, if we understand what we mean by "individual," and if we mean by "individual" a self-determining subject conscious of itself as one among other such subjects, and of its relation to them as making it what it is; for then there is no opposition between the attachment of rights to the individuals as such and their derivation from society. They attach to the individual, but only as a member of a society of free agents, as recognizing himself and recognized by others to be such a member, as doing and done by accordingly. A right, then, to act unsocially—to act otherwise than as belonging to a society of which each member keeps the exercise of his powers within the limits necessary to the like

*Selections from T. H. Green: *Lectures on the Principles of Political Obligation and Other Writings.* Copyright © Cambridge University Press, 1986. Reprinted with the Permission of Cambridge University Press.

exercise by all the other members—is a contradiction. No one can say that, unless he has consented to such a limitation of his powers, he has a right to resist it. The fact of his not consenting would be an extinction of all right on his part.

139. The state then presupposes rights, and *rights of individuals.* It is a form which society takes in order to maintain them. But rights have no being except in a society of men recognizing each other as *isoi kai homoioi* [equals]. They are constituted by that mutual recognition. In analyzing the nature of any right, we may conveniently look at it on two sides, and consider it as on the one hand a claim of the individual, arising out of his rational nature, to the free exercise of some faculty; on the other, as a concession of that claim by society, a power given to the individual of putting the claim in force by society. But we must be on our guard against supposing that these distinguishable sides have any really separate existence. It is only a man's consciousness of having an object in common with others, a well-being which is consciously his in being theirs and theirs in being his—only the fact that they are recognized by him and he by them as having this object—that gives him the claim described. There can be no reciprocal claim on the part of a man and an animal each to exercise his powers unimpeded by the other, because there is no consciousness common to them. But a claim founded on such a common consciousness is already a claim conceded; already a claim to which reality is given by social recognition and thus implicitly a right.

140. It is in this sense that a slave has "natural rights." They are "natural" in the sense of being independent of, and in conflict with, the laws of the state in which he lives, but they are not independent of social relations. They arise out of the fact that there is a consciousness of objects common to the slave with those among whom he lives—whether other slaves or the family of his owner—and that this consciousness constitutes at once a claim on the part of each of those who share it to exercise a free activity conditionally upon his allowing a like activity in the others, and a recognition of this claim by the others, through which it is realized. The slave thus derives from his social relations a real right which the law of the state refuses to admit. The law cannot prevent him from acting and being treated, within certain limits, as a member of a society of persons freely seeking a common good. And as that capability of living in a certain limited community with a certain limited number of human beings, which the slave cannot be prevented from exhibiting, is in principle a capability of living in a community with any other human beings, supposing the necessary training to be allowed; and as every such capability constitutes a right, we are entitled to say that the slave has a right to citizenship—to a recognized equality of freedom with any and every one with whom he has to do—and that in refusing him not only citizenship but the means of training his capability of citizenship, the state is violating a right, founded on that common human consciousness which is evinced both by language which the slave speaks and by

actual social relations subsisting between him and others. And on the same principle upon which a state is violating natural rights in maintaining slavery, it does the same in using force, except under necessity of self-defense, against members of another community. Membership of any community is so far in principle membership of all communities as to constitute a right to be treated as a freeman by all other men, to be exempt from subjection to force except for prevention of force.

PRIVATE RIGHTS: THE RIGHT TO LIFE AND LIBERTY

148. In order then to understand the nature of the state, we must understand the nature of those rights which do not come into being with it but arise out of social relations that may exist where a state is not; it being the first, though not the only, office of the state to maintain those rights. They depend for their existence, indeed, on society—a society of men who recognize each other as *isoi kai homoioi* [equals], as capable of a common well-being—but not on society's having assumed the form of a state. They may therefore be treated as claims of the individual without reference to the form of the society which concedes or recognizes them, and on whose recognition, as we have seen, their nature as rights depends. Only it must be borne in mind that the form in which these claims are admitted and acted on by men in their dealings with each other varies with the form of society—that the actual form, e.g., in which the individual's right of property is admitted under a patriarchal *régime* is very different from that in which it is admitted in a state—and that though the principle of each right is throughout the same, it is a principle which only comes to be fully recognized and acted on when the state has not only formed, but fully developed according to its idea.

149. The rights which may be treated as independent of the state in the sense explained are of course those which are commonly distinguished as *private*, in opposition to *public* rights.

> [I]f rights be analyzed, they will be found to consist of several kinds. For first they are such as regard a man's own person; secondly, such as regard his dominion over the external and sensible things by which he is surrounded; thirdly, such as regard his private relations, as a member of a family; fourthly, such as regard his social state or condition, as a member of the community; the first of which classes may be designated as *personal rights*, the second, as *rights of property*, the third, as *rights in private relations*, and the fourth, as *public rights*.

150. An objection might fairly be made to distinguishing one class of rights as *personal*, on the ground that all rights are so—not merely in the legal sense of "person," according to which the proposition is a truism, since every right

implies a person as its subject, but in the moral sense, since all rights depend on that capacity in the individual for being determined by a conception of well-being, as an object at once for himself and for others, which constitutes personality in the moral sense. By personal rights in the above classification are meant the rights of life and liberty—i.e., of preserving one's body from the violence of other men, and of using it as an instrument only of one's own will—if of another's, still only through one's own. The reason why these come to be spoken of as "personal" is probably the same with the reason why we talk of a man's "person" in the sense simply of his body. They may, however, be reckoned in a special sense personal even by those who consider all rights personal because the person's possession of a body and its exclusive determination by his own will is the condition of his exercising any other rights—indeed, of all manifestation of personality. Prevent a man from possessing property (in the ordinary sense), and his personality may still remain. Prevent him (if it were possible) from using his body to express a will, and the will itself could not become a reality; he would not be really a person.

151. If there are such things as rights at all, then, there must be a right to life and liberty, or, to put it more properly, to free life. No distinction can be made between the right to life and the right to liberty, for there can be no right to mere life—no right to life on the part of a being that has not also the right to direct the life according to the motions of its own will. What is the foundation of this right? The answer is, capacity on the part of the subject for membership of a society—for determination of the will, and through it of the bodily organization, by the conception of a well-being as common to self with others. This capacity is the *foundation* of the right, or the right *potentially*, which becomes *actual* through recognition of the capacity by a society, and through the power which the society in consequence secures to the individual of acting according to the capacity. In principle, or intrinsically, or in respect of that which it has it in itself to become, the right is one that belongs to every man in virtue of his human nature (of the qualities which render him capable of any fellowship with any other men), and is a right as between him and all men; because, as we have seen, the qualities which enable him to act as a member of any one society having the general well-being of its members for its object (as distinct from any special object requiring special talent for its accomplishment) form a capacity for membership of any other such society. But actually, or as recognized, it only gradually becomes a right of a man, as man, and against all men.

THE RIGHT OF THE STATE TO PUNISH

185. The idea of punishment implies on the side of the person punished at once a capacity for determination by conception of a common or public good, or in

other words a practical understanding of the nature of rights as founded on relations to such public good, and an actual violation of a right or omission to fulfil an obligation, the right or obligation being one of which the agent might have been aware and the violation or omission one which he might have prevented. On the side of the authority punishing, it implies equally a conception of right founded on relation to public good, and one which, unlike that on the part of the criminal, is realized in act; a conception of which the punitive act, as founded on a consideration of what is necessary for the maintenance of rights, is the logical expression. A punishment is unjust if either element is absent; if either the act punished is not a violation of known rights or omission to fulfil known obligations of a kind which the agent might have prevented, or punishment is one that is not required for the maintenance of rights, or (which comes to the same thing) if the ostensible rights for maintenance of which the punishment is required are not real rights—not liberties of action or acquisition which there is any real public interest in maintaining.

189. It is true that there can be no a priori criterion of just punishment, except of an abstract and negative kind. We may say that no punishment is just, unless the rights which it serves to protect are powers on the part of individuals or corporations of which the general maintenance is necessary to the well-being of society on the whole and unless the terror which the punishment is calculated to inspire is for their maintenance. For a positive and detailed criterion of just punishment we must wait till a system of rights has been established in which the claims of all men, as founded on their capacities for contributing to social well-being, are perfectly harmonized, and till experience has shown the degree and kind of terror with which men must be affected in order to the suppression of the antisocial tendencies which might lead to the violation of such a system of rights. And this is perhaps equivalent to saying that no complete criterion of just punishment can be arrived at till punishment is no longer necessary, for the state of things supposed could scarcely be realized without bringing with it an extinction of the tendencies which state-punishment is needed to suppress. Meanwhile there is no method of approximation to justice in punishment but that which consists in gradually making the system of established rights just, i.e., in harmonizing the true claims of all men, and in discovering by experience the really efficient means of restraining tendencies to violation of rights. An intentional violation of a right must be punished, whether the right violated is one that should be a right or no, on the principle that social well-being suffers more from violation of any established right, whatever the nature of the right, than from the establishment as a right of a power which should not be so established; and it can only be punished in the way which for the time is thought most efficient by the maintainers of law for protecting the right in question by associating terror with its violation. This, however, does not alter the moral duty, on the part of the society authorizing the punishment, to make its

punishments just by making the system of rights which it maintains just. The justice of the punishment depends on the justice of the general system of rights—not merely on the propriety with reference to social well-being of maintaining this or that particular right which the crime punished violates, but on the question whether the social organization in which a criminal has lived and acted is one that has given him a fair chance of not being a criminal.

200. The principle above stated, as that according to which punishment by the state should be inflicted and regulated, also justifies a distinction between crimes and civil injuries, i.e., between breaches of right for which the state inflicts punishment without redress to the person injured, and those for which it procures or seeks to procure redress to the person injured without punishment of the person causing the injury. We are not here concerned with the history of this distinction, nor with the question whether many breaches of right now among us treated as civil injuries ought not to be treated as crimes, but with the justification that exists for treating certain kinds of breach of right as cases in which the state should interfere to procure redress for the person injured, but not in the way of inflicting punishment on the injurer until he willfully resists the order to make redress. The principle of the distinction as ordinarily laid down, viz., that civil injuries "are violations of public or private rights, when considered in reference to the injury sustained by the individual," while crimes are "violations of public or private rights, when considered in reference to their evil tendency as regards the community at large" is misleading because if the well-being of the community did not suffer in the hurt done to the individual, that hurt would not be a violation of a right in the true sense at all, nor would the community have any ground for insisting that the hurt shall be redressed, and for determining the mode in which it shall be redressed. A violation of right cannot in truth be considered merely in relation to injury sustained by an individual, for thus considered it would not be a violation of right. It may be said that the state is only concerned in procuring redress for civil injuries because if it left an individual to procure redress in his own way, there would be no public peace. But there are other and easier ways of preventing fighting than by procuring redress of wrongs. We prevent our dogs from fighting, not by redressing wrongs which they sustain from each other (of wrongs as of rights they are in the proper sense incapable), but by beating them or tying them up. The community would not keep the peace by procuring redress for hurt or damage sustained by individuals unless it conceived itself as having interest in the security of individuals from hurt and damage, unless it considered the hurt done to individuals as done to itself. The true justification for treating some breaches of right as cases merely for redress, others as cases for punishment, is that, in order to the general protection of rights, with some it is necessary to associate a certain terror, with others it is not.

204. According to the view here taken, then, there is no *direct* reference in

punishment by the state, either retrospective or prospective, to moral good or evil. The state in its judicial action does not look to the moral guilt of the criminal whom it punishes, or to the promotion of moral good by means of his punishment in him or others. It looks not to virtue and vice but to rights and wrongs. It looks back to the wrong done in the crime which it punishes; not, however, in order to avenge it but in order to the consideration of the sort of terror which needs to be associated with such wrongdoing in order to the future maintenance of rights. If the character of the criminal comes into account at all, it can only be properly as an incident of this consideration. Thus punishment of crime is preventive in its object; not, however, preventive of any or every evil or by any and every means, but (according to its idea or as it should be) *justly* preventive of *injustice*; preventive of interference with those powers of action and acquisition which it is for the general well-being that individuals should possess, and according to laws which allow those powers equally to all men. But in order effectually to attain its preventive object and to attain it *justly*, it should be reformatory. When the reformatory office of punishment is insisted on, the reference may be, and from the judicial point of view must be, not to the moral good of the criminal as an ultimate end, but to his recovery from criminal habits as a means to that which is the proper and direct object of state-punishment, viz., the general protection of rights. The reformatory function of punishment is from this point of view an incident of its preventive function, as regulated by consideration of what is just to the criminal as well as to others. For the fulfillment of this latter function, the great thing, as we have seen, is by the punishment of an actual criminal to deter other possible criminals, but for the same purpose, unless the actual criminal is to be put out of the way or locked up for life, it must be desirable to reform him so that he may not be dangerous in the future. Now when it is asked why he should not be put out of the way it must not be forgotten that among the rights which the state has to maintain are included rights of the criminal himself. These indeed are for the time suspended by his action in violation of rights, but founded as they are on the capacity for contributing to social good, they could only be held to be finally forfeited on the ground that this capacity was absolutely extinct.

205. This consideration limits the kind of punishment which the state may justly inflict. It ought not in punishing unnecessarily to sacrifice to the maintenance of rights in general what may be called the reversionary rights of the criminal—rights which, if properly treated, he might ultimately become capable of exercising for the general good. Punishment therefore either by death or by perpetual imprisonment is justifiable only on one of two grounds; either that association of the extremest terror with certain actions is under certain conditions necessary to preserve the possibility of a social life based on observance of rights, or that the crime punished affords a presumption of a permanent incapacity for rights on the part of the criminal. The first justification may be pleaded for

the executions of men concerned in treasonable outbreaks, or guilty of certain breaches of discipline in war (on supposition that the war is necessary for the safety of the state and that such punishments are a necessary incident of war). Whether the capital punishment is really just in such cases must depend, not only on its necessity as an incident in defense of a certain state, but on the question whether that state itself is fulfilling its function as a sustainer of true rights. For the penalty of death for murder both justifications may be urged. It cannot be defended on any other ground, but it may be doubted whether the presumption of permanent incapacity for rights is one which in our ignorance we can ever be entitled to make. As to the other plea, the question is whether, with a proper police system and sufficient certainty of detection and conviction, the association of this extremest terror with the murderer is necessary to the security of life. Where the death penalty, however, is unjustifiable, so must be that of really permanent imprisonment; one as much as the other is an absolute deprivation of free social life, and of the possibilities of moral development which that life affords. The only justification for a sentence of permanent imprisonment in a case where there would be none for capital punishment would be that, though inflicted as permanent, the imprisonment might be brought to an end in the event of any sufficient proof appearing of the criminal's amendment. But such proof could only be afforded if the imprisonment were so modified as to allow the prisoner a certain amount of liberty.

206. If punishment then is to be just, in the sense that in its infliction due account is taken of all rights, including the suspended rights of the criminal himself, it must be, so far as public safety allows, reformatory. It must tend to qualify the criminal for the resumption of rights. As reformatory, however, punishment has for its direct object the qualification for the exercise of rights, and is only concerned with true moralization of the criminal indirectly so far as it may result from the exercise of rights. But even where it cannot be reformatory in this sense, and over and above its reformatory function in cases where it has one, punishment has a moral end. Just because punishment by the state has for its direct object the maintenance of rights, it has, like every other function of the state, indirectly a moral object, because true rights according to our definition, are powers which it is for the general well-being that the individual (or association) should possess, and that well-being is essentially a moral well-being. Ultimately, therefore, the just punishment of crime is for the moral good of the community. It is also for the moral good of the criminal himself, unless—and it is a supposition which we ought not to make—he is beyond the reach of moral influences. Though not inflicted for that purpose, and though it would not the less have to be inflicted if no moral effect on the criminal could be discerned, it is morally the best thing that can happen to him. It is so, even if a true social necessity requires that he be punished with death. The fact that society is obliged so to deal with him affords the best chance of bringing home to him the

antisocial nature of his act. It is true that the last utterances of murderers generally convey the impression that they consider themselves interesting persons, quite sure of going to heaven, but these are probably conventional. At any rate if the solemn infliction of punishment on behalf of human society, and without any sign of vindictiveness, will not breed the shame, which is the moral new birth, presumably nothing else within human reach will.

The Right of the State to Promote Morality

207. The right of the individual man, as such, to free life on its negative side is constantly gaining more general recognition. It is the basis of the growing scrupulosity in regard to punishments which are not reformatory, which put rights finally out of the reach of a criminal instead of qualifying him for their renewed exercise. But the only rational foundation for the ascription of this right is ascription of capacity for free contribution to social good. Is it then reasonable for us as a community to treat this capacity in the man whose crime has given proof of its having been overcome by antisocial tendencies, as yet giving him a title to a further chance of its development; on the other hand, to act as if it conferred no title on its possessors, before a crime has been committed, to be placed under conditions in which its realization would be possible? Are not all modern states so acting allowing their ostensible members to grow up under conditions which render the development of social capacity practically impossible? Was it no more reasonable, as in the ancient states, to deny the right to life in the human subject as such, than to admit it under conditions which prevent the realization of the capacity that forms the ground of its admission? This brings us to the fourth of the questions that arose out of the assertion of the individual's right to free life. What is the nature and extent of the individual's claim to be enabled positively to realize that capacity for freely contributing to social good which is the foundation of his right to free life?

208. In dealing with this question, it is important to bear in mind that the capacity we are considering is essentially a free or (what is the same) a moral capacity. It is a capacity, not for action determined by relation to a certain end, but for action determined by a conception of the end to which it is relative. Only thus is it a foundation of rights. The action of an animal or plant may be made contributory to social good, but it is not therefore a foundation of rights on the part of an animal or plant, because they are not affected by the conception of the good to which they contribute. A right is a power (of acting for his own ends—for what he conceives to be his good) secured to an individual by the community, on the supposition that its exercise contributes to the good of the community. But the exercise of such a power cannot be so contributory unless the individual, in acting for his own ends, is at least affected by the conception of a good as common to himself with others. The condition of making the

animal contributory to human good is that we do not leave him free to determine the exercise of his powers—that we determine them for him, that we use him merely as an instrument; and this means that we do not, because we cannot, endow him with rights. We cannot endow him with rights because there is no conception of a good common to him with us which we can treat as a motive to him to do to us as he would have us do to him. It is not indeed necessary to a capacity for rights, as it is to true moral goodness, that interest in a good conceived as common to himself with others should be a man's dominant motive. It is enough if that which he presents to himself from time to time as his good, and which accordingly determines his action, is so far affected by consideration of the position in which he stands to others—of the way in which this or that possible action of his would affect them, and of what he would have to expect from them in return—as to result habitually, without force or fear of force, in action not incompatible with conditions necessary to the pursuit of a common good on the part of others. In other words, it is the presumption that a man in his general course of conduct will of his own motion have respect to the common good, which entitles him to rights at the hands of the community. The question of the moral value of the motive which may induce this respect— whether an unselfish interest in common good or the wish for personal pleasure and fear of personal pain—does not come into the account at all. An agent, indeed, who could only be induced by fear of death or bodily harm to behave conformably to the requirements of the community, would not be a subject of rights, because this influence could never be brought to bear on him so constantly, if he were free to regulate his own life, as to secure the public safety. But a man's desire for pleasure to himself and aversion from pain to himself, though dissociated from any desire for a higher object—for any object that is desired because good for others—may constitute a capacity for rights, if his imagination of pleasure and pain is so far affected by sympathy with the feeling of others about him as to make him, independently of force or fear of punishment, observant of established rights. In such a case the fear of punishment may be needed to neutralize antisocial impulses under circumstances of special temptation, but by itself it could never be a sufficiently uniform motive to qualify a man, in the absence of more spontaneously social feelings, for the life of a free citizen. The qualification for such a life is a spontaneous habit of acting with reference to a common good, whether that habit be founded on an imagination of pleasures and pains or on a conception of what ought to be. In either case the habit implies at least an understanding that there is such a thing as a common good, and a regulation of egoistic hopes and fears, if not an inducing of more "disinterested" motives, in consequence of that understanding.

209. The capacity for rights, then, being a capacity for spontaneous action regulated by a conception of a common good—either so regulated through an interest which flows directly from that conception or through hopes and fears

which are affected by it through more complex channels of habit and association—is a capacity which cannot be generated—which on the contrary is neutralized—by any influences that interfere with the spontaneous action of social interests. Now any direct enforcement of the outward conduct, which ought to flow from social interests, by means of threatened penalties—and a law requiring such conduct necessarily implies penalties for disobedience to it—does interfere with the spontaneous action of those interests, and consequently checks the growth of the capacity which is the condition of the beneficial exercise of rights. For this reason the effectual action of the state, i.e., the community as acting through law, for the promotion of habits of true citizenship, seems necessarily to be confined to the removal of obstacles. Under this head, however, there may and should be included much that most states have hitherto neglected, and much that at first sight may have the appearance of an enforcement of moral duties, e.g., the requirement that parents have their children taught the elementary arts. To educate one's children is no doubt a moral duty, and it is not one of those duties, like that of paying debts, of which the neglect directly interferes with the rights of someone else. It might seem, therefore, to be a duty with which positive law should have nothing to do, any more than with the duty of striving after a noble life. On the other hand, the neglect of it does tend to prevent the growth of the capacity for beneficially exercising rights on the part of those whose education is neglected, and it is on this account—not as a purely moral duty on the part of a parent, but as the prevention of a hindrance to the capacity for rights on the part of children— that education should be enforced by the state. It may be objected, indeed, that in enforcing it we are departing in regard to the parents from the principle above laid down—that we are interfering with the spontaneous action of social interests, though we are doing so with a view to promoting this spontaneous action in another generation. But the answer to this objection is, that a law of compulsory education, if the preferences, ecclesiastical or other, of those parents who show any practical sense of their responsibility are duly respected, is from the beginning only felt as compulsion by those in whom, so far as this social function is concerned, there is no spontaneity to be interfered with, and that in the second generation, though the law with its penal sanctions still continues, it is not felt as a law, as an enforcement of action by penalties, at all.

210. On the same principle the freedom of contract ought probably to be more restricted in certain directions than is at present the case. The freedom to do as they like on the part of one set of men may involve the ultimate disqualification of many others, or of a succeeding generation, for the exercise of rights. This applies most obviously to such kinds of contract or traffic as affect the health and housing of the people, the growth of population relatively to the means of subsistence, and the accumulation or distribution of landed property. In the hurry of removing those restraints on free dealing between man and man,

which have arisen partly perhaps from some confused idea of maintaining morality, but much more from the power of class interests, we have been apt to take too narrow a view of the range of persons—not one generation merely but succeeding generations—whose freedom ought to be taken into account, and of the conditions necessary to their freedom ("freedom" here meaning their qualification for the exercise of rights). Hence the massing of population without regard to conditions of health; unrestrained traffic in deleterious commodities; unlimited upgrowth of the class of hired laborers in particular industries which circumstances have suddenly stimulated, without any provision against the dangers of an impoverished proletariate in following generations. Meanwhile, under pretense of allowing freedom of bequest and settlement, a system has grown up which prevents the landlords of each generation from being free either in the government of their families or in the disposal of their land, and aggravates the tendency to crowd into towns, as well as the difficulties of providing healthy house-room, by keeping land in a few hands. It would be out of place here to consider in detail the remedies for these evils, or to discuss the question how far it is well to trust to the initiative of the state or individuals in dealing with them. It is enough to point out the directions in which the state may remove obstacles to the realization of the capacity for beneficial exercise of rights without defeating its own object by vitiating the spontaneous character of that capacity.

PART II

Liberty and Community

Justice as Fairness:
Political Not Metaphysical*

JOHN RAWLS

IN THIS DISCUSSION I shall make some general remarks about how I now understand the conception of justice that I have called "justice as fairness" (presented in my book A *Theory of Justice*). I do this because it may seem that this conception depends on philosophical claims I should like to avoid, for example, claims to universal truth, or claims about the essential nature and identity of persons. My aim is to explain why it does not. I shall first discuss what I regard as the task of political philosophy at the present time and then briefly survey how the basic intuitive ideas drawn upon in justice as fairness are combined into a political conception of justice for a constitutional democracy. Doing this will bring out how and why this conception of justice avoids certain philosophical and metaphysical claims. Briefly, the idea is that in a constitutional democracy the public conception of justice should be, so far as possible, independent of controversial philosophical and religious doctrines. Thus, to formulate such a conception, we apply the principle of toleration to philosophy itself: the public conception of justice is to be political, not metaphysical. Hence the title.

I want to put aside the question whether the text of A *Theory of Justice* supports different readings than the one I sketch here. Certainly on a number of points I have changed my views, and there are no doubt others on which my views have changed in ways that I am unaware of. I recognize further that certain faults of exposition as well as obscure and ambiguous passages

*From Rawls, John, "Justice as Fairness: Political Not Metaphysical," *Philosophy and Public Affairs* 14, no. 3, 1985. Copyright © 1985 by Princeton University Press. Reprinted by permission of Princeton University Press.

in A *Theory of Justice* invite misunderstanding; but I think these matters need not concern us and I shan't pursue them. For our purposes here, it suffices first, to show how a conception of justice with the structure and content of justice as fairness can be understood as political and not metaphysical, and second, to explain why we should look for such a conception of justice in a democratic society.

I

One thing I failed to say in A *Theory of Justice* or failed to stress sufficiently, is that justice as fairness is intended as a political conception of justice while a political conception of justice is, of course, a moral conception, it is a moral conception worked out for a specific kind of subject, namely, for political, social, and economic institutions. In particular, justice as fairness is framed to apply to what I have called the "basic structure" of a modern constitutional democracy. (I shall use "constitutional democracy" and "democratic regime" and similar phrases interchangeably.) By this structure I mean such a society's main political, social, and economic institutions, and how they fit together into one unified system of social cooperation. Whether justice as fairness can be extended to a general political conception for different kinds of societies existing under different historical and social conditions or whether it can be extended to a general moral conception, or a significant part thereof, are altogether separate questions. I avoid prejudging these larger questions one way or the other.

It should also be stressed that justice as fairness is not intended as the application of a general moral conception to the basic structure of society as if this structure were simply another case to which that general moral conception is applied. In this respect justice as fairness differs from traditional moral doctrines for these are widely regarded as such general conceptions. Utilitarianism is a familiar example, since the principle of utility, however it is formulated, is usually said to hold for all kinds of subjects ranging from the actions of individuals to the law of nations. The essential point is this: as a practical political matter no general moral conception can provide a publicly recognized basis for a conception of justice in a modern democratic state. The social and historical conditions of such a state have their origins in the Wars of Religion following the Reformation and the subsequent development of the principle of toleration and in the growth of constitutional government and the institutions of large industrial market economies. These conditions profoundly affect the requirements of a workable conception of political justice: such a conception must allow for a diversity of doctrines and the plurality of conflicting, and indeed incommensurable conceptions of the good affirmed by the members of existing democratic societies.

Finally, to conclude these introductory remarks, since justice as fairness is intended as a political conception of justice for a democratic society, it tries to draw solely upon basic intuitive ideas that are embedded in the political institutions of a constitutional democratic regime and the public traditions of their interpretation. Justice as fairness is a political conception in part because it starts from within a certain political tradition. We hope that this political conception of justice may at least be supported by what we may call an "overlapping consensus" that includes all the opposing philosophical and religious doctrines likely to persist and to gain adherents in a more or less just constitutional democratic society.

II

There are, of course, many ways in which political philosophy may be understood, and writers at different times, faced with different political and social circumstances, understand their work differently. Justice as fairness I would now understand as a reasonable systematic and practicable conception of justice for a constitutional democracy, a conception that offers an alternative to the dominant utilitarianism of our tradition of political thought. Its first task is to provide a more secure and acceptable basis for constitutional principles and basic rights and liberties that utilitarianism seems to allow. The need for such a political conception arises in the following way.

There are periods, sometimes long periods, in the history of any society during which certain fundamental questions give rise to sharp and divisive political controversy, and it seems difficult, if not impossible, to find any shared basis of political agreement. Indeed certain questions may prove intractable and may never be fully settled. One task of political philosophy in a democratic society is to focus on such questions and to examine whether some underlying basis of agreement can be uncovered and a mutually acceptable way of resolving these questions publicly established. Or if these questions cannot be fully settled, as may well be the case, perhaps the divergence of opinion can be narrowed sufficiently so that political cooperation on a basis of mutual respect can still be maintained.

The course of democratic thought over the past two centuries or so makes plain that there is no agreement on the way basic institutions of a constitutional democracy should be arranged if they are to specify and secure that basic rights and liberties of citizens and answer to the claims of democratic equality when citizens are conceived as free and equal persons (as explained in the last three paragraphs of section III). A deep disagreement exists as to how the values of liberty and equality are best realized in the basic structure of society. To simplify we may think of this disagreement as a conflict within the tradition of democratic thought itself, between the tradition associated with Locke, which gives greater weight to what Constant called "the liberties of the moderns," freedom of thought and conscience, certain basic rights of the person and of property, and the rule of law, and the tradition associated with Rousseau, which gives greater weight to what Constant called "the liberties of the ancients," the equal political liberties, and the values of public life. This is a stylized contrast and historically inaccurate, but it serves to fix ideas.

Justice as fairness tries to adjudicate between these contending traditions first, by proposing two principles of justice to serve as guidelines for how basic institutions are to realize the values of liberty and equality and second, by specifying a point of view from which these principles can be seen as more appropriate than other familiar principles of justice to the nature of democratic citizens viewed as free and equal persons. What it means to view citizens as free and equal persons is, of course, a fundamental question and is discussed in the following sections. What must be shown is that a certain arrangement of the basic structure, certain institutional forms, are more appropriate for realizing the values of liberty and equality when citizens are conceived as such persons, that is (very briefly), as having the requisite powers of moral personality that enable them to participate in society viewed as a system of fair cooperation for mutual advantage. So to continue, the two principles of justice (mentioned above) read as follows:

1. Each person has an equal right to a fully adequate scheme of equal basic rights and liberties, which scheme is compatible with a similar scheme for all.
2. Social and economic inequalities are to satisfy two conditions: first, they must be attached to offices and positions open to all under conditions of fair equality of opportunity; and second they must be to the greatest benefit of the least advantaged members of society.

Each of these principles applies to a different part of the basic structure; and both are concerned not only with basic rights, liberties and opportunities, but also with the claims of equality; while the second part of the second principle underwrites the worth of these institutional guarantees. The two principles together, when the first is given priority over the second, regulate the basic institutions which realize these values. But these details, although important, are not our concern here.

We must now ask: how might political philosophy find a shared basis for settling such a fundamental question as that of the most appropriate institutional forms for liberty and equality? Of course, it is likely that the most that can be done is to narrow the range of public disagreement. Yet even firmly held convictions gradually change: religious toleration is now accepted, and arguments for persecutions are no longer openly professed; similarly, slavery is rejected as inherently unjust, and however much the aftermath of slavery may persist in social practices and unavowed attitudes, no one is willing to defend it.

We collect such settled convictions as the belief in religious toleration and the rejection of slavery and try to organize the basic ideas and principles implicit in these convictions into a coherent conception of justice. We can regard these convictions as provisional fixed points which any conception of justice must account for if it is to be reasonable for us. We look, then, to our public political culture itself, including its main institutions and the historical traditions of their interpretation, as the shared fund of implicitly recognized basic ideas and principles. The hope is that these ideas and principles can be formulated clearly enough to be combined into a conception of political justice congenial to our most firmly held convictions. We express this by saying that a political conception of justice, to be acceptable, must be in accordance with our considered convictions, at all levels of generality, on due reflection (or in what I have called "reflective equilibrium").

The public political culture may be of two minds even at a very deep level. Indeed, this must be so with such an enduring controversy as that concerning the most appropriate institutional forms to realize the values of liberty and equality. This suggests that if we are to succeed in finding a basis of public agreement, we must find a new way of organizing familiar ideas and principles into a conception of political justice so that the claims in conflict, as previously understood, are seen in another light. A political conception need not be an original creation but may only articulate familiar intuitive ideas and principles so that they can be recognized as fitting together in a somewhat different way than before. Such a conception may, however, go further than this: it may organize these familiar ideas and principles by means of a more fundamental intuitive idea within the complex structure of which the other familiar intuitive ideas are then systematically connected and related. In justice as fairness, as we shall see in the next section, this more fundamental idea is that of society as a system of fair social cooperation between free and equal persons. The concern of this section is how we might find a public basis of political agreement. The point is that a conception of justice will only be able to achieve this aim if it provides a reasonable way of shaping into one coherent view the deeper bases of agreement embedded in the public political culture of a constitutional regime and acceptable to its most firmly held considered convictions.

Now suppose justice as fairness were to achieve its aim and a publicly acceptable political conception of justice is found. Then this conception provides a publicly recognized point of view from which all citizens can examine before one another whether or not their political and social institutions are just. It enables them to do this by citing what are recognized among them as valid and sufficient reasons singled out by that conception itself. Society's main institutions and how they fit together into one scheme of social cooperation can be examined on the same basis by each citizen, whatever the citizen's social position or more particular interests. It should be observed that, on this view, justification is not regarded simply as valid argument from lists premises, even should these premises be true. Rather, justification is addressed to others who disagree with us, and therefore it must always proceed from some consensus, that is, from premises that we and others publicly recognize as true; or better, publicly recognize as acceptable to us for the purpose of establishing a working agreement on the fundamental questions of political justice. It goes without saying that this agreement must be informed and uncoerced, and reached by citizens in ways consistent with their being viewed as free and equal persons.

Thus, the aim of justice as fairness as a political conception is practical, and not metaphysical or epistemological. That is, it presents itself not as a conception of justice that is true, but one that can serve as a basis of informed and willing political agreement between citizens viewed as free and equal persons. This agreement, when securely founded in public political and social attitudes, sustains the goods of all persons and associations within a just democratic regime. To secure this agreement we try, so far as we can, to avoid disputed philosophical, as well as disputed moral and religious, questions. We do this not because these questions are unimportant or regarded with indifference, but because we think them too important and recognize that there is no way to resolve them politically. The only alternative to a principle of toleration is the autocratic use of state power. Thus, justice as fairness deliberately stays on the surface, philosophically speaking. Given the profound differences in belief and conceptions of the good at least since the Reformation, we must recognize that, just as on questions of religious and moral doctrine, public agreement on the basic questions of philosophy cannot be obtained without the state's infringement of basic liberties. Philosophy as the search for truth about an independent metaphysical and moral order cannot, I believe, provide a workable and shared basis for a political conception of justice in a democratic society.

We try, then, to leave aside philosophical controversies whenever possible, and look for ways to avoid philosophy's long-standing problems. Thus, in what I have called "Kantian constructivism," we try to avoid the problem of truth and the controversy between realism and subjectivism about the status of moral and political values. This form of constructivism neither asserts nor denies these doctrines. Rather, it recasts ideas from the tradition of the social contract to achieve a practicable conception of objectivity and justification founded on public agreement in judgment on due reflection. The aim is free agreement, reconciliation through public reason. And similarly, as we shall see (in section V), a conception of the person in a political view, for example, the conception of citizens as free and equal persons, need not involve, so I believe, questions of philosophical psychology or a metaphysical doctrine of the nature of the self. No political view that depends on these deep and unresolved matters can serve as a public conception of justice in a constitutional democratic state. As I have said, we must apply the principle of toleration to philosophy itself. The hope is that, by this method of avoidance, as we might call it, existing differences between contending political views can at least be moderated, even if not entirely removed, so that social cooperation on the basis of mutual respect can be maintained. Or if this is expecting too much, this method may enable us to conceive how, given a desire for free and uncoerced agreement, a public understanding could arise consistent with the historical conditions of constraints of our social world. Until we bring ourselves to conceive how this could happen, it can't happen.

III

Let's now survey briefly some of the basic ideas that make up justice as fairness in order to show that these ideas belong to a political conception of justice. As I have indicated, the overarching fundamental intuitive idea, within which other basic intuitive ideas are systematically connected, is that of society as a fair system of cooperation between free and equal persons. Justice as fairness starts from this idea as one of the basic intuitive ideas which we take to be implicit in the public culture of a democratic society. In their political thought, and in the context of public discussion of political questions, citizens do not view the social order as a fixed natural order, or as an institutional hierarchy justified by religious or aristocratic values. Here it is important to stress that from other points of view, for example, from the point of view of personal morality, or from the point of view of members of an association, or of one's religious or philosophical doctrine, various aspects of the world and one's relation to it, may be regarded in a different way. But these other points of view are not to be introduced into political discussion.

We can make the idea of social cooperation more specific by noting three of its elements:

1. Cooperation is distinct from merely socially coordinated activity, for example, from activity coordinated by orders issued by some central authority. Cooperation is guided by publicly recognized rules and procedures which those who are cooperating accept and regard as properly regulating their conduct.

2. Cooperation involves the idea of fair terms of cooperation: these are terms that each participant may reasonably accept, provided that everyone else likewise accepts them. Fair terms of cooperation specify an idea of reciprocity or mutuality: all who are engaged in cooperation and who do their part as the rules and procedures require, are to benefit in some appropriate way as assessed by a suitable benchmark of comparison. A conception of political justice characterizes the fair terms of social cooperation. Since the primary subject of justice is the basic structure of society, this is accomplished in justice as fairness by formulating principles that specify basic rights and duties within the main institutions of society, and by regulating the institutions of background justice

over time so that the benefits produced by everyone's efforts are fairly acquired and divided from one generation to the next.

3. The idea of social cooperation requires an idea of each participant's rational advantage, or good. This idea of good specifies what those who are engaged in cooperation, whether individuals, families, or associations, or even nation-states, are trying to achieve, when the scheme is viewed from their own standpoint.

Now consider the idea of the person. There are, of course, many aspects of human nature that can be singled out as especially significant depending on our point of view. This is witnessed by such expressions as *homo politicus, homo oeconomicus, homo faber,* and the like. Justice as fairness starts from the idea that society is to be conceived as a fair system of cooperation and so it adopts a conception of the person to go with this idea. Since Greek times, both in philosophy and law, the concept of the person has been understood as the concept of someone who can take part in, or who can play a role in, social life, and hence exercise and respect its various rights and duties. Thus, we say that a person is someone who can be a citizen, that is, a fully cooperating member of society over a complete life. We add the phrase "over a complete life" because a society is viewed as a more or less complete and self-sufficient scheme of cooperation, making room within itself for all the necessities and activities of life, from birth until death. A society is not an association for more limited purposes; citizens do not join society voluntarily but are born into it, where, for our aims here, we assume they are to lead their lives.

Since we start within the tradition of democratic thought, we also think of citizens as free and equal persons. The basic intuitive idea is that in virtue of what we may call their moral powers, and the powers of reason, thought, and judgment connected with those powers, we say that persons are free. And in virtue of their having these powers to the requisite degree to be fully cooperating members of society, we say that persons are equal. We can elaborate this conception of the person as follows. Since persons can be full participants in a fair system of social cooperation, we ascribe to them the two moral powers connected with the elements in the idea of social cooperation noted above: namely, a capacity for a sense of justice and a capacity for a conception of the good. A sense of justice is the capacity to understand, to apply, and to act from the public conception of justice which characterizes the fair terms of social cooperation. The capacity for a conception of the good is the capacity to form, to revise, and rationally to pursue a conception of one's rational advantage, or good. In the case of social cooperation, this good must not be understood narrowly but rather as a conception of what is valuable in human life. Thus, a conception of the good normally consists of a more or less determinate scheme of final ends, that is, ends we want to realize for their own sake, as well as of attachments to other persons and loyalties to various groups and associations.

These attachments and loyalties give rise to affections and devotions, and therefore the flourishing of the persons and associations who are the objects of these sentiments is also part of our conception of the good. Moreover, we must also include in such a conception a view of our relation to the world—religious, philosophical, or moral—by reference to which the value and significance of our ends and attachments are understood.

In addition to having the two moral powers, the capacities for a sense of justice and a conception of the good, persons also have at any given time a particular conception of the good that they try to achieve. Since we wish to start from the idea of society as a fair system of cooperation, we assume that persons as citizens have all the capacities that enable them to be normal and fully cooperating members of society. This does not imply that no one ever suffers from illness or accident; such misfortunes are to be expected in the ordinary course of human life; and provision for these contingencies must be made. But for our purposes here I leave aside permanent physical disabilities or mental disorders so severe as to prevent persons from being normal and fully cooperating members of society in the usual sense.

Now the conception of persons as having the two moral powers, and therefore as free and equal, is also a basic intuitive idea assumed to be implicit in the public culture of a democratic society. Note, however, that it is formed by idealizing and simplifying in various ways. This is done to achieve a clear and uncluttered view of what for us is the fundamental question of political justice: namely, what is the most appropriate conception of justice for specifying the terms of social cooperation between citizens regarded as free and equal persons, and as normal and fully cooperating members of society over a complete life. It is this question that has been the focus of the liberal critique of aristocracy, of the socialist critique of liberal constitutional democracy, and of the conflict between liberals and conservatives at the present time over the claims of private property and the legitimacy (in contrast to the effectiveness) of social policies associated with the so-called welfare state.

IV

I now take up the idea of the original position. This idea is introduced in order to work out which traditional conception of justice, or which variant of one of those conceptions, specifies the most appropriate principles for realizing liberty and equality once society is viewed as a system of cooperation between free and equal persons. Assuming we had this purpose in mind, let's see why we would introduce the idea of the original position and how it serves its purpose.

Consider again the idea of social cooperation. Let's ask: how are the fair terms of cooperation to be determined? Are they simply laid down by some outside agency distinct from the persons cooperating? Are they, for example, laid down by God's law? Or are these terms to be recognized by these persons as fair by reference to their knowledge of a prior and independent moral order? For example, are they regarded as required by natural law, or by a realm of values known by rational intuition? Or are these terms to be established by an undertaking among these persons themselves in the light of what they regard as their mutual advantage? Depending on which answer we give, we get a different conception of cooperation.

Since justice as fairness recasts the doctrine of the social contract, it adopts a form of the last answer: the fair terms of social cooperation are conceived as agreed to by those engaged in it, that is, by free and equal persons as citizens who are born into the society in which they lead their lives. But their agreement, like any other valid agreement, must be entered into under appropriate conditions. In particular, these conditions must situate free and equal persons fairly and must not allow some persons greater bargaining advantages than others. Further, threats of force and coercion, deception and fraud, and so on, must be excluded.

So far so good. The foregoing considerations are familiar from everyday life. But agreements in everyday life are made in some more or less clearly specified situation embedded within the background institutions of the basic structure. Our task, however, is to extend the idea of agreement to this background framework itself. Here we face a difficulty for any political conception of justice that uses the idea of a contract, whether social or otherwise. The difficulty is this: we must find some point of view, removed from and not distorted by the particular features and circumstances of the all-encompassing background framework, from which a fair agreement between free and equal persons can be reached. The original position, with the feature I have called "the veil of ignorance," is this point of view. And the reason why the original position must abstract from and not be affected by the contingencies of the social world is that the conditions for a fair agreement on the principles of political justice between free and equal persons must eliminate the bargaining advantages which inevitably arise within background institutions of any society as the result of cumulative social, historical, and natural tendencies. These contingent advantages and accidental influences from the past should not influence an agreement on the principles which are to regulate the institutions of the basic structure itself from the present into the future.

Here we seem to face a second difficulty, which is, however, only apparent. To explain: from what we have just said it is clear that the original position is to be seen as a device of representation and hence any agreement reached by the parties must be regarded as both hypothetical and nonhistorical. But if so since hypothetical agreements cannot bind, what is the significance of the original position? The answer is implicit in what has already been said: it is given by the role of the various features of the original position as a device of representation. Thus, that the parties are symmetrically situated is required if they are to be seen as representatives of free and equal citizens who are to reach an agreement under conditions that are fair. Moreover, one of our considered convictions, I assume, is this: the fact that we occupy a particular social position is not a good reason for us to accept, or to expect others to accept, a conception of justice that favors those in this position. To model this conviction in the original position the parties are not allowed to know their social position; and the same idea is extended to other cases. This is expressed figuratively by saying that the parties are behind a veil of ignorance. In sum, the original position is simply a device of representation: it describes the parties, each of whom are responsible for the essential interests of a free and equal person, as fairly situated and as reaching an agreement subject to appropriate restrictions on what are to count as good reasons.

Both of the above mentioned difficulties, then, are overcome by viewing the original position as a device of representation: that is, this position models what we regard as fair conditions under which the representatives of free and equal persons are to specify the terms of social cooperation in the case of the basic structure of society; and since it also models what, for this case, we regard as acceptable restrictions on reasons available to the parties for favoring one agreement rather than another, the conception of justice the parties would adopt identifies the conception we regard—*here and now*—as fair and supported by the best reasons. We try to model restrictions on reasons in such a way that it is perfectly evident which agreement would be made by the parties in the original position as citizens' representatives. Even if there should be, as surely there will be, reasons for and against each conception of justice available, there may be an overall balance of reasons plainly favoring one conception over the rest. As a device of representation the idea of the original position serves as a means of public reflection and self-clarification. We can use it to help us work out what we now think, once we are able to take a clear and uncluttered view of what justice requires when society is conceived as a scheme of cooperation between free and equal persons over time from one generation to the next. The original position serves as a unifying idea by which our considered convictions at all levels of generality are brought to bear on one another so as to achieve greater mutual agreement and self-understanding.

To conclude: we introduce an idea like that of the original position because there is no better way to elaborate a political conception of justice for the basic structure from the fundamental intuitive idea of society as a fair system of cooperation between citizens as free and equal persons. There are, however, certain hazards. As a device of representation the original position is likely to seem somewhat abstract and hence open to misunderstanding. The description of the parties may seem to presuppose some metaphysical conception of the person, for example, that the essential nature of persons is independent of and prior to their contingent attributes, including their final ends and attachments, and indeed, their character as a whole. But this is an illusion caused by not seeing the original position as a device of representation. The veil of ignorance, to mention one prominent feature of that position, has no metaphysical implications concerning the nature of the self; it does not imply that the self is ontologically prior to the facts about persons that the parties are excluded from knowing. We can, as it were, enter this position any time simply by reasoning for principles of justice in accordance with the enumerated restrictions. When, in this way, we simulate being in this position, our reasoning no more commits us to a metaphysical doctrine about the nature of the self than our playing a game like Monopoly commits us to thinking that we are landlords engaged in a desperate rivalry, winner take all. We must keep in mind that we are trying to show how the idea of society as a fair system of social cooperation can be unfolded so as to specify the most appropriate principles for realizing the institutions of liberty and equality when citizens are regarded as free and equal persons.

V

I just remarked that the idea of the original position and the description of the parties may tempt us to think that a metaphysical doctrine of the person is presupposed. While I said that this interpretation is mistaken, it is not enough simply to disavow reliance on metaphysical doctrines, for despite one's intent they may still be involved. To rebut claims of this nature requires discussing them in detail and showing that they have no foothold. I cannot do that here.

I can, however, sketch a positive account of the political conception of the person, that is, the conception of the person as citizen (discussed in section III), involved in the original position as a device of representation. To explain what is meant by describing a conception of the person as political, let's consider how citizens are represented in the original position as free persons. The representation of their freedom seems to be one source of the idea that some metaphysical doctrine is presupposed. I have said elsewhere that citizens view themselves as free in three respects, so let's survey each of these briefly and indicate the way in which the conception of the person used is political.

First, citizens are free in that they conceive of themselves and of one another as having the moral power to have a conception of the good. This is not to say that, as part of their political conception of themselves, they view themselves as inevitably tied to the pursuit of the particular conception of the good which they affirm at any given time. Instead, as citizens, they are regarded as capable of revising and changing this conception on reasonable and rational grounds, and they may do this if they so desire. Thus, as free persons, citizens claim the right to view their persons as independent from and as not identified with any particular conception of the good, or scheme of final ends. Given their moral power to form, to revise, and rationally to pursue a conception of the good, their public identity as free persons is not affected by changes over time in their conception of the good. For example, when citizens convert from one religion to another, or no longer affirm an established religious faith, they do not cease to be, for questions of political justice, the same persons they were before. There is no loss of what we may call their public identity, their identity as a matter of basic law. In general, they still have the same basic rights and duties; they own the same property and can make the same claims as before, except insofar as these claims were connected with their previous religious affiliation. We can imagine a society (indeed, history offers numerous examples) in which basic rights and recognized claims depend on religious affiliation, social class, and so on. Such a society has a different political conception of the person. It may not have a conception of citizenship at all; for this conception, as we are using it, goes with the conception of society as a fair system of cooperation for mutual advantage between free and equal persons.

It is essential to stress that citizens in their personal affairs, or in the internal life of associations to which they belong, may regard their final ends and attachments in a way very different from the way the political conception involves. Citizens may have, and normally do have at any given time, affections, devotions, and loyalties that they believe they would not, and indeed could and should not, stand apart from and objectively evaluate from the point of view of their purely rational good. They may regard it as simply unthinkable to view themselves apart from certain religious, philosophical, and moral convictions, or from certain enduring attachments and loyalties. These convictions and attachments are part of what we may call their "nonpublic identity." These convictions and attachments help to organize and give shape to a person's way of life, what one sees oneself as doing and trying to accomplish in one's social world. We think that if we were suddenly without these particular convictions and attachments we would be disoriented and unable to carry on. In fact, there would be, we might think, no point in carrying on. But our conceptions of the good may and often do change over time, usually slowly but sometimes rather suddenly. When these changes are sudden, we are particularly likely to say that we are no longer the same person. We know what this means: we refer to a profound and pervasive shift, or reversal, in our final ends and character; we refer to our different nonpublic, and possibly moral or religious, identity. On the road to Damascus Saul of Tarsus becomes Paul the Apostle. There is no change in our public or political identity, nor in our personal identity as this concept is understood by some writers in the philosophy of mind.

The second respect in which citizens view themselves as free is that they regard themselves as self-originating sources of valid claims. They think their claims have weight apart from being derived from duties or obligations specified by the political conception of justice, for example, from duties and obligations owed to society. Claims that citizens regard as founded on duties and obligations based on their conception of the good and the moral doctrine they affirm in their own life are also, for our purposes here, to be counted as self-originating. Doing this is reasonable in a political conception of justice or a constitutional democracy; for provided the conceptions of the good and the moral doctrines citizens affirm are compatible with the public conception of justice, these duties and obligations are self-originating from the political point of view.

When we describe a way in which citizens regard themselves as free, we are describing how citizens actually think of themselves in a democratic society should questions of justice arise. In our conception of a constitutional regime, this is an aspect of how citizens regard themselves. That this aspect of their freedom belongs to a particular political conception is clear from the contrast with a different political conception in which the members of society are not viewed as self-originating sources of valid claims. Rather, their claims have no weight except insofar as they can be derived from their duties and obligations owed to society, or from their ascribed roles in the social hierarchy justified by religious or aristocratic values. Or to take an extreme case, slaves are human beings who are not counted as sources of claims, not even claims based on social duties or obligations, for slaves are not counted as capable of having duties or obligations. Laws that prohibit the abuse and maltreatment of slaves are not founded on claims made by slaves on their own behalf, but on claims originating either from slaveholders, or from the general interests of society (which does not include the interests of slaves). Slaves are, so to speak, socially dead: they are not publicly recognized as persons at all. Thus, the contrast with a political conception which allows slavery makes clear why conceiving of citizens as free persons in virtue of their moral powers and their having a conception of the good, goes with a particular political conception of the person. This conception of persons fits into a political conception of justice founded on the idea of society as a system of cooperation between its members conceived as free and equal.

The third respect in which citizens are regarded as free is that they are regarded as capable of taking responsibility for their ends and this affects how their various claims are assessed. Very roughly, the idea is that, given just background institutions and given for each person a fair index of primary goods (as required by the principles of justice), citizens are thought to be capable of adjusting their aims and aspirations in the light of what they can reasonably expect to provide for. Moreover, they are regarded as capable of restricting their claims in matters of justice to the kinds of things the principles of justice allow. Thus, citizens are to recognize that the weight of their claims is not given by the strength and psychological intensity of their wants and desires (as opposed to their needs and requirements as citizens), even when their wants and desires are rational from their point of view. I cannot pursue these matters here. But the procedure is the same as before: we start with the basic intuitive idea of society as a system of social cooperation. When this idea is developed into a conception of political justice, it implies that, viewing ourselves as persons who can engage in social cooperation over a complete life, we can also take responsibility for our ends, that is, that we can adjust our ends so that they can be pursued by the means we can reasonably expect to acquire given our prospects and situation in society. The idea of responsibility for ends is implicit in the public political culture and discernible in its practices. A political conception of the person articulates this idea and fits it into the idea of society as a system of social cooperation over a complete life.

To sum up, I recapitulate three main points of this and the preceding two sections:

First, in section III persons were regarded as free and equal in virtue of their possessing to the requisite degree the two powers of moral personality (and the powers of reason, thought, and judgment connected with these powers), namely, the capacity for a sense of justice and the capacity for a conception of the good. These powers we associated with two main elements of the idea of cooperation, the idea of fair terms of cooperation and the idea of each participant's rational advantage, or good.

Second, in this section (section V), we have briefly surveyed three respects in which persons are regarded as free, and we have noted that in the public political culture of a constitutional democratic regime citizens conceive of themselves as free in these respects.

Third, since the question of which conception of political justice is most appropriate for realizing in basic institutions the values of liberty and equality has long been deeply controversial within the very democratic tradition in which citizens are regarded as free and equal persons, the aim of justice as fairness is to try to resolve this question by starting from the basic intuitive idea of society as a fair system of social cooperation in which the fair terms of cooperation are agreed upon by citizens themselves so conceived. In section IV, we saw why this approach leads to the idea of the original position as a device of representation.

VI

I now take up a point essential to thinking of justice as fairness as a liberal view. Although this conception is a moral conception, it is not, as I have said, intended as a comprehensive moral doctrine. The conception of the citizen as a free and equal person is not a moral ideal to govern all of life, but is rather an ideal belonging to a conception of political justice which is to apply to the basic structure. I emphasize this point because to think otherwise would be incompatible with liberalism as a political doctrine. Recall that as such a doctrine, liberalism assumes that in a constitutional democratic state under modern

conditions there are bound to exist conflicting and incommensurable conceptions of the good. This feature characterizes modern culture since the Reformation. Any viable political conception of justice that is not to rely on the
autocratic use of state power must recognize this fundamental social fact. This
does not mean, of course, that such a conception cannot impose constraints on
individuals and associations, but that when it does so, these constraints are
accounted for, directly or indirectly, by the requirements of political justice for
the basic structure.

Given this fact, we adopt a conception of the person framed as part of, and
restricted to, an explicitly political conception of justice. In this sense, the
conception of the person is a political one. As I stressed in the previous section,
persons can accept this conception of themselves as citizens and use it when
discussing questions of political justice without being committed in other parts
of their life to comprehensive moral ideals often associated with liberalism, for
example, the ideals of autonomy and individuality. The absence of commitment
to these ideals, and indeed to any particular comprehensive ideal, is essential to
liberalism as a political doctrine. The reason is that any such ideal, when
pursued as a comprehensive ideal, is incompatible with other conceptions of the
good, with forms of personal, moral, and religious life consistent with justice and
which, therefore, have a proper place in a democratic society. As comprehensive moral ideals, autonomy and individuality are unsuited for a political conception of justice. As found in Kant and J. S. Mill, these comprehensive ideals,
despite their very great importance in liberal thought, are extended too far when
presented as the only appropriate foundation for a constitutional regime. So
understood, liberalism becomes but another sectarian doctrine.

This conclusion requires comment: it does not mean, of course, that the
liberalisms of Kant and Mill are not appropriate moral conceptions from which
we can be led to affirm democratic institutions. But they are only two such
conceptions among others, and so but two of the philosophical doctrines likely
to persist and gain adherents in a reasonably just democratic regime. In such a
regime the comprehensive moral views which support its basic institutions may
include the liberalisms of individuality and autonomy; and possibly these liberalisms are among the more prominent doctrines in an overlapping consensus, that
is, in a consensus in which, as noted earlier, different and even conflicting
doctrines affirm the publicly shared basis of political arrangements. The liberalisms of Kant and Mill have a certain historical preeminence as among the first
and most important philosophical views to espouse modern constitutional democracy and to develop its underlying ideas in an influential way; and it may
even turn out that societies in which the ideals of autonomy and individuality
are widely accepted are among the most well-governed and harmonious.

By contrast with liberalism as a comprehensive moral doctrine, justice as
fairness tries to present a conception of political justice rooted in the basic

intuitive ideas found in the public culture of a constitutional democracy. We conjecture that these ideas are likely to be affirmed by each of the opposing comprehensive moral doctrines influential in a reasonably just democratic society. Thus, justice as fairness seeks to identify the kernel of an overlapping consensus, that is, the shared intuitive ideas which when worked up into a political conception of justice turn out to be sufficient to underwrite a just constitutional regime. This is the most we can expect, nor do we need more. We must note, however, that when justice as fairness is fully realized in a well-ordered society, the value of full autonomy is likewise realized. In this way justice as fairness is indeed similar to the liberalisms of Kant and Mill; but in contrast with them, the value of full autonomy is here specified by a political conception of justice, and not by a comprehensive moral doctrine.

It may appear that, so understood, the public acceptance of justice as fairness is no more than prudential; that is, that those who affirm this conception do so simply as a modus vivendi which allows the groups in the overlapping consensus to pursue their own good subject to certain constraints which each thinks to be for its advantage given existing circumstances. The idea of an overlapping consensus may seem essentially Hobbesian. But against this, two remarks: first, justice as fairness is a moral conception: it has conceptions of person and society, and concepts of right and fairness, as well as principles of justice with their complement of the virtues through which those principles are embodied in human character and regulate political and social life. This conception of justice provides an account of the cooperative virtues suitable for a political doctrine in view of the conditions and requirements of a constitutional regime. It is no less a moral conception because it is restricted to the basic structure of society, since this restriction is what enables it to serve as a political conception of justice given our present circumstances. Thus, in an overlapping consensus (as understood here), the conception of justice as fairness is not regarded merely as a modus vivendi.

Second, in such a consensus each of the comprehensive philosophical, religious, and moral doctrines accepts justice as fairness in its own way; that is, each comprehensive doctrine, from within its own point of view, is led to accept the public reasons of justice specified by justice as fairness. We might say that they recognize its concepts, principles, and virtues as theorems, as it were, at which their several views coincide. But this does not make these points of coincidence any less moral or reduce them to mere means. For, in general, these concepts, principles, and virtues are accepted by each as belonging to a more comprehensive philosophical religious, or moral doctrine. Some may even affirm justice as fairness as a natural moral conception that can stand on its own feet. They accept this conception of justice as a reasonable basis for political and social cooperation, and hold that it is as natural and fundamental as the concepts and principles of honesty and mutual trust, and the virtues of cooperation in everyday life. The doctrines in an overlapping consensus differ in how far they maintain a further foundation is necessary and on what that further foundation should be. These differences, however, are compatible with a consensus on justice as fairness as a political conception of justice.

VII

I shall conclude by considering the way in which social unity and stability may be understood by liberalism as a political doctrine (as opposed to a comprehensive moral conception).

One of the deepest distinctions between political conceptions of justice is between those that allow for a plurality of opposing and even incommensurable conceptions of the good and those that hold that there is but one conception of the good which is to be recognized by all persons, so far as they are fully rational. Conceptions of justice which fall on opposite sides of this divide are distinct in many fundamental ways. Plato and Aristotle, and the Christian tradition as represented by Augustine and Aquinas, fall on the side of the one rational good. Such views tend to be teleological and to hold that institutions are just to the extent that they effectively promote this good. Indeed, since classical times the dominant tradition seems to have been that there is but one rational conception of the good, and that the aim of moral philosophy, together with theology and metaphysics, is to determine its nature. Classical utilitarianism belongs to this dominant tradition. By contrast, liberalism as a political doctrine supposes that there are many conflicting and incommensurable conceptions of the good, each compatible with the full rationality of human persons, so far as we can ascertain within a workable political conception of justice. As a consequence of this supposition, liberalism assumes that it is a characteristic feature of a free democratic culture that a plurality of conflicting and incommensurable conceptions of the good are affirmed by its citizens. Liberalism as a political doctrine holds that the question the dominant tradition has tried to answer has no practicable answer; that is, it has no answer suitable for a political conception of justice for a democratic society. In such a society a teleological political conception is out of the question: public agreement on the requisite conception of the good cannot be obtained.

As I have remarked, the historical origin of this liberal supposition is the Reformation and its consequences. Until the Wars of Religion in the sixteenth and seventeenth centuries, the fair terms of social cooperation were narrowly drawn: social cooperation on the basis of mutual respect was regarded as impossible with persons of a different faith; or (in the terminology I have used) with persons who affirm a fundamentally different conception of the good. Thus one of the historical roots of liberalism was the development of various doctrines urging religious toleration. One theme in justice as fairness is to recognize the social conditions that give rise to these doctrines as among the so-called subjective circumstances of justice and then to spell out the implications of the principle of toleration. As liberalism is stated by Constant, de Tocqueville, and Mill in the nineteenth century, it accepts the plurality of incommensurable conceptions of the good as a fact of modern democratic culture, provided, of course, these conceptions respect the limits specified by the appropriate principles of justice. One task of liberalism as a political doctrine is to answer the question: how is social unity to be understood, given that there can be no public agreement on the one rational good, and a plurality of opposing and incommensurable conceptions must be taken as given? And granted that social unity is conceivable in some definite way, under what conditions is it actually possible?

In justice as fairness, social unity is understood by starting with the conception of society as a system of cooperation between free and equal persons. Social unity and the allegiance of citizens to their common institutions are not founded on their all affirming the same conception of the good, but on their publicly accepting a political conception of justice to regulate the basic structure of society. The concept of justice is independent from and prior to the concept of goodness in the sense that its principles limit the conceptions of the good which are permissible. A just basic structure and its background institutions establish a framework within which permissible conceptions can be advanced. Elsewhere I have called this relation between a conception of justice and conceptions of the good the priority of right (since the just falls under the right). I believe this priority is characteristic of liberalism as a political doctrine and something like it seems essential to any conception of justice reasonable for a democratic state. Thus, to understand how social unity is possible given the historical conditions of a democratic society, we start with our basic intuitive idea of social cooperation, an idea present in the public culture of a democratic society, and proceed from there to a public conception of justice as the basis of social unity in the way I have sketched.

As for the question of whether this unity is stable, this importantly depends on the content of the religious, philosophical, and moral doctrines available to constitute an overlapping consensus. For example, assuming the public political conception to be justice as fairness, imagine citizens to affirm one of three views: the first view affirms justice as fairness because its religious beliefs and understanding of faith lead to a principle of toleration and underwrite the fundamental idea of society as a scheme of social cooperation between free and equal persons; the second view affirms it as a consequence of a comprehensive liberal moral conception such as those of Kant and Mill; while the third affirms justice as fairness not as a consequence of any wider doctrine but as in itself sufficient to express values that normally outweigh whatever other values might oppose them, at least under reasonably favorable conditions. This overlapping consensus appears far more stable than one founded on views that express skepticism and indifference to religious, philosophical, and moral values, or that regard the acceptance of the principles of justice simply as a prudent modus vivendi given the existing balance of social forces. Of course, there are many other possibilities.

The strength of a conception like justice as fairness may prove to be that the more comprehensive doctrines that persist and gain adherents in a democratic society regulated by its principles are likely to cohere together into a more or less stable overlapping consensus. But obviously all this is highly speculative and raises questions which are little understood, since doctrines which persist and gain adherents depend in part on social conditions, and in particular, on these conditions when regulated by the public conception of justice. Thus, we are forced to consider at some point the effects of the social conditions required by a conception of political justice on the acceptance of that conception itself. Other things equal, a conception will be more or less stable depending on how far the conditions to which it leads support comprehensive religious, philosophical, and moral doctrines which can constitute a stable overlapping consensus. These questions of stability I cannot discuss here. It suffices to remark that in a society marked by deep divisions between opposing and incommensurable conceptions of the good, justice as fairness enables us at least to conceive how social unity can be both possible and stable.

Membership and Justice *

MICHAEL WALZER

MEMBERS AND STRANGERS

THE IDEA OF DISTRIBUTIVE justice presupposes a bounded world within which distribution takes place: a group of people committed to dividing, exchanging, and sharing social goods, first of all among themselves. That world, as I have already argued, is the political community, whose members distribute power to one another and avoid, if they possibly can, sharing it with anyone else. When we think about distributive justice, we think about independent cities or countries capable of arranging their own patterns of division and exchange, justly or unjustly. We assume an established group and a fixed population, and so we miss the first and most important distributive question: How is that group constituted?

I don't mean, "How *was* it constituted?" I am concerned here not with the historical origins of the different groups, but with the decisions they make in the present about their present and future populations. The primary good that we distribute to one another is membership in some human community. And what we do with regard to membership structures all our other distributive choices: it determines with whom we make those choices, from whom we require obedience and collect taxes, to whom we allocate goods and services. Men and women without membership anywhere are stateless persons. That condition doesn't preclude every sort of distributive relation: markets, for example, are commonly open to all comers. But nonmembers are vulnerable and unprotected in the marketplace. Although they participate freely in the exchange of goods, they have no part in those goods that are shared. They are cut off from the

*Excerpt from *Spheres of Justice* by Michael Walzer. Copyright ©1983 by Basic Books, Inc. Reprinted by permission of Basic Books, a division of HarperCollins Publishers, Inc.

communal provision of security and welfare. Even those aspects of security and welfare that are, like public health, collectively distributed are not guaranteed to nonmembers: for they have no guaranteed place in the collectivity and are always liable to expulsion. Statelessness is a condition of infinite danger.

But membership and nonmembership are not the only—or, for our purposes, the most important—set of possibilities. It is also possible to be a member of a poor or a rich country, to live in a densely crowded or a largely empty country, to be the subject of an authoritarian regime or the citizen of a democracy. Since human beings are highly mobile, large numbers of men and women regularly attempt to change their residence and their membership, moving from unfavored to favored environments. Affluent and free countries are, like elite universities, besieged by applicants. They have to decide on their own size and character. More precisely, as citizens of such a country, we have to decide: Whom should we admit? Ought we to have open admissions? Can we choose among applicants? What are the appropriate criteria for distributing membership?

The plural pronouns that I have used in asking these questions suggest the conventional answer to them: we who are already members do the choosing, in accordance with our own understanding of what membership means in our community and of what sort of a community we want to have. Membership as a social good is constituted by our understanding; its value is fixed by our work and conversation; and then we are in charge (who else could be in charge?) of its distribution. But we don't distribute it among ourselves; it is already ours. We give it out to strangers. Hence the choice is also governed by our relationships with strangers—not only by our understanding of those relationships but also by the actual contacts, connections, alliances we have established and the effects we have had beyond our borders. But I shall focus first on strangers in the literal sense, men and women whom we meet, so to speak, for the first time. We don't know who they are or what they think, yet we recognize them as men and women. Like us but not of us: when we decide on membership, we have to consider them as well as ourselves.

I won't try to recount here the history of Western ideas about strangers. In a number of ancient languages, Latin among them, strangers and enemies were named by a single word. We have come only slowly, through a long process of trial and error, to distinguish the two and to acknowledge that, in certain circumstances, strangers (but not enemies) might be entitled to our hospitality, assistance, and good will. This acknowledgment can be formalized as the principle of mutual aid, which suggests the duties that we owe, as John Rawls has written, "not only to definite individuals, say to those cooperating together in some social arrangement, but to persons generally." Mutual aid extends across political (and also cultural, religious, and linguistic) frontiers. The philosophical grounds of the principle are hard to specify (its history provides its practical ground). I doubt that Rawls is right to argue that we can establish it simply by imagining "what a society would be like if this duty were rejected"—for rejection is not an issue within any particular society; the issue arises only among people who don't share, or don't know themselves to share, a common life. People who do share a common life have much stronger duties.

It is the absence of any cooperative arrangements that sets the context for mutual aid: two strangers meet at sea or in the desert or, as in the Good Samaritan story, by the side of the road. What precisely they owe one another is by no means clear, but we commonly say of such cases that positive assistance is required if (1) it is needed or urgently needed by one of the parties; and (2) if the risks and costs of giving it are relatively low for the other party. Given these conditions, I ought to stop and help the injured stranger, wherever I meet him, whatever his membership or my own. This is our morality; conceivably his, too. It is, moreover, an obligation that can be read out in roughly the same form at the collective level. Groups of people ought to help necessitous strangers whom they somehow discover in their midst or on their path. But the limit on risks and costs in these cases is sharply drawn. I need not take the injured stranger into my home, except briefly, and I certainly need not care for him or even associate with him for the rest of my life. My life cannot be shaped and determined by such chance encounters. Governor John Winthrop, arguing against free immigration to the new Puritan commonwealth of Massachusetts, insisted that this right of refusal applies also to collective mutual aid: "As for hospitality, that rule does not bind further than for some present occasion, not for continual residence." Whether Winthrop's view can be defended is a question that I shall come to only gradually. Here I only want to point to mutual aid as a (possible) external principle for the distribution of membership, a principle that doesn't depend upon the prevailing view of membership within a particular society. The force of the principle is uncertain, in part because of its own vagueness, in part because it sometimes comes up against the internal force of social meanings. And these meanings can be specified, and are specified, through the decision-making processes of the political community.

We might opt for a world without particular meanings and without political communities: where no one was a member or where everyone "belonged" to a single global state. These are the two forms of simple equality with regard to membership. If all human beings were strangers to one another, if all our meetings were like meetings at sea or in the desert or by the side of the road, then there would be no membership to distribute. Admissions policy would never be an issue. Where and how we lived, and with whom we lived, would depend upon our individual desires and then upon our partnerships and affairs. Justice would be nothing more than noncoercion, good faith, and Good Samaritanism—a matter entirely of external principles. If, by contrast, all human beings were members of a global state, membership would already have been distributed, equally; and there would be nothing more to do. The first of these arrangements suggests a kind of global libertarianism; the second, a kind of global socialism. These are the two conditions under which the distribution of membership would never arise. Either there would be no such status to distribute, or it would simply come (to everyone) with birth. But neither of these arrangements is likely to be realized in the foreseeable future; and there are impressive arguments, which I will come to later, against both of them. In any case, so long as members and strangers are, as they are at present, two distinct groups, admissions decisions have to be made, men and women taken in or refused. Given the indeterminate requirements of mutual aid, these decisions are not constrained by any widely accepted standard. That's why the admissions policies of countries are rarely criticized, except in terms suggesting that the only relevant criteria are those of charity, not justice. It is certainly possible that a deeper criticism would lead one to deny the member/stranger distinction. But I shall try, nevertheless, to defend that distinction and then to describe the internal and the external principles that govern the distribution of membership.

The argument will require a careful review of both immigration and naturalization policy. But it is worth noting first, briefly, that there are certain similarities between strangers in political space (immigrants) and descendants in time (children). People enter a country by being born to parents already there as well as, and more often than, by crossing the frontier. Both these processes can be controlled. In the first case, however, unless we practice a selective infanticide, we will be dealing with unborn and hence unknown individuals. Subsidies for large families and programs of birth control determine only the size of the population, not the characteristics of its inhabitants. We might, of course, award the right to give birth differentially to different groups of parents, establishing ethnic quotas (like country-of-origin quotas in immigration policy) or class or intelligence quotas, or allowing right-to-give-birth certificates to be traded on the market. These are ways of regulating who has children and of shaping the character of the future population. They are, however, indirect and inefficient ways, even with regard to ethnicity, unless the state also regulates intermarriage and assimilation. Even well short of that, the policy would require very high, and surely unacceptable, levels, of coercion: the dominance of political power over kinship and love. So the major public policy issue is the size of the population only—its growth, stability, or decline. To how many people do we distribute membership? The larger and philosophically more interesting questions—To what sorts of people? and To what particular people?—are most clearly confronted when we turn to the problems involved in admitting or excluding strangers.

ANALOGIES: NEIGHBORHOODS, CLUBS, AND FAMILIES

. . . It was a common argument in classical political economy that national territory should be as "indifferent" as local space. The same writers who defended free trade in the nineteenth century also defended unrestricted immigration. They argued for perfect freedom of contract, without any political restraint. International society, they thought, should take shape as a world of neighborhoods, with individuals moving freely about, seeking private advancement. In their view, as Henry Sidgwick reported it [in *Elements of Politics*] in the 1890s, the only business of state officials is "to maintain order over [a] particular territory . . . but not in any way to determine who is to inhabit this territory, or to restrict the enjoyment of its natural advantages to any particular portion of the human race." Natural advantages (like markets) are open to all comers, within the limits of private property rights; and if they are used up or devalued by overcrowding, people presumably will move on, into the jurisdiction of new sets of officials.

Sidgwick thought that this is possibly the "ideal of the future," but he offered three arguments against a world of neighborhoods in the present. First of all a world would not allow for patriotic sentiment, and so the "casual aggregates" that would probably result from the free movement of individuals would "lack internal cohesion." Neighbors would be strangers to one another. Second, free movement might interfere with efforts "to raise the standard of living among the poorer classes" of a particular country, since such efforts could not be undertaken with equal energy and success everywhere in the world. And, third, the promotion of moral and intellectual culture and the efficient working of political institutions might be "defeated" by the continual creation of heterogeneous populations. Sidgwick presented these three arguments as a series of utilitarian considerations that weigh against the benefits of labor mobility and contractual freedom. But they seem to me to have a rather different character. The last two arguments draw their force from the first, but only if the first is conceived in nonutilitarian terms. It is only if patriotic sentiment has some moral basis, only if communal cohesion makes for obligations and shared meanings, only if there are members as well as strangers, that state officials would have any reason to worry especially about the welfare of their own people (and of *all* their own people) and the success of their own culture and politics. For it is at least dubious that the average standard of living of the poorer classes throughout the world would decline under conditions of perfect labor mobility. Nor is there firm evidence that a culture cannot thrive in cosmopolitan environments, not that it is impossible to govern casual aggregations of people. As for the last of these, political theorists long ago discovered that certain sorts of regimes—namely, authoritarian regimes—thrive in the absence of communal cohesion. That perfect mobility makes for authoritarianism might suggest a utilitarian argument against mobility; but such an argument would work only if individual men and women, free to come and go, expressed a desire for some other form of government. And that they might not do.

Perfect labor mobility, however, is probably a mirage for it is almost certain to be resisted at the local level. Human beings, as I have said, move about a great deal, but not because they love to move. They are, most of them, inclined to stay where they are unless their life is very difficult there. They experience a tension between love of place and the discomforts of a particular place. While some of them leave their homes and become foreigners in new lands, others stay where they are and resent the foreigners in their own land. Hence, if states ever become large neighborhoods, it is likely that neighborhoods will become little states. Their members will organize to defend the local politics and culture against strangers. Historically, neighborhoods have turned into closed or parochial communities (leaving aside cases of legal coercion) whenever the state was open: in the cosmopolitan cities of multinational empires, for example, where state officials don't foster any particular identity but permit different groups to build their own institutional structures (as in ancient Alexandria), or in the receiving centers of mass immigration movements (early-twentieth-century New York) where the country is an open but also an alien world—or, alternatively, a world full of aliens. The case is similar where the state doesn't exist at all or in areas where it doesn't function. Where welfare monies are raised and spent locally, for example, as in a seventeenth-century English parish, the local people will seek to exclude newcomers who are likely welfare recipients. It is only the nationalization of welfare (or the nationalization of culture and politics) that opens the neighborhood communities to whoever chooses to come in.

Neighborhoods can be open only if countries are at least potentially closed. Only if the state makes a selection among would-be members and guarantees the loyalty, security, and welfare of the individuals it selects, can local communities take shape as "indifferent" associations, determined solely by personal preference and market capacity. Since individual choice is most dependent upon local mobility, this would seem to be the preferred arrangement in a society like our own. The politics and the culture of a modern democracy probably require the kind of largeness, and also the kind of boundedness, that states provide. I don't mean to deny the value of sectional cultures and ethnic communities; I mean only to suggest the rigidities that would be forced upon both in the absence of inclusive and protective states. To tear down the walls of the state is not, as Sidgwick worriedly suggested, to create a world without walls, but rather to create a thousand petty fortresses.

The fortresses, too, could be torn down: all that is necessary is a global state sufficiently powerful to overwhelm the local communities. Then the result would be the world of the political economists, as Sidgwick described it—a world of radically deracinated men and women. Neighborhoods might maintain some cohesive culture for a generation or two on a voluntary basis, but people would move in, people would move out; soon the cohesion would be gone. The distinctiveness of cultures and groups depends upon closure and, without it, cannot be conceived as a stable feature of human life. If this distinctiveness is a value, as most people (though some of them are global pluralists, and others only local loyalists) seem to believe, then closure must be permitted somewhere. At some level of political organization, something like the sovereign state must take shape and claim the authority to make its own admissions policy, to control and sometimes restrain the flow of immigrants.

But this right to control immigration does not include or entail the right to control emigration. The political community can shape its own population in the one way, not in the other: this is a distinction that gets reiterated in different forms throughout the account of membership. The restraint of entry serves to defend the liberty and welfare, the politics and culture of a group of people committed to one another and to their common life. But the restraint of exit replaces commitment with coercion. So far as the coerced members are concerned, there is no longer a community worth defending. A state can, perhaps, banish individual citizens or expel aliens living within its borders (if there is some place ready to receive them). Except in times of national emergency, when everyone is bound to work for the survival of the community, states cannot prevent such people from getting up and leaving. The fact that individuals can rightly leave their own country, however, doesn't generate a right to enter another (any other). Immigration and emigration are morally asymmetrical. Here the appropriate analogy is with the club, for it is a feature of clubs in domestic society—as I have just suggested it is of states in international society—that they can regulate admissions but cannot bar withdrawals.

Like clubs, countries have admissions committees. In the United States, Congress functions as such a committee, though it rarely makes individual selections. Instead, it establishes general qualifications, categories for admission and exclusion, and numerical quotas (limits). Then admissible individuals are taken in, with varying degrees of administrative discretion, mostly on a first-come, first-served basis. This procedure seems eminently defensible, though that does not mean that any particular set of qualifications and categories ought to be defended. To say that states have a right to act in certain areas is not to say that anything they do in those areas is right. One can argue about particular admissions standards by appealing, for example, to the condition and character of the host country and to the shared understandings of those who are already members. Such arguments have to be judged morally and politically as well as factually. The claim of American advocates of restricted immigration (in 1920, say) that they were defending a homogeneous white and Protestant country, can plausibly be called unjust as well as inaccurate: as if nonwhite and non-Protestant citizens were invisible men and women, who didn't have to be counted in the national census! Earlier Americans, seeking the benefits of economic and geographic expansion, had created a pluralist society; and the moral realities of that society ought to have guided the legislators of the 1920s. If we follow the logic of the club analogy, however, we have to say that the earlier decision might have been different, and the United States might have taken shape as a homogeneous community, an Anglo-Saxon nation-state (assuming what happened in any case: the virtual extermination of the Indians who, understanding correctly the dangers of invasion, struggled as best they could to keep foreigners out of their native lands). Decisions of this sort are subject to constraint, but what the constraints are I am not yet ready to say. It is important first to insist that the distribution of membership in American society, and in any ongoing society, is a matter of political decision. The labor market may be given free rein, as it was for many decades in the United States, but that does not happen by an act of nature or of God; it depends upon choices that are ultimately political. What kind of community do the citizens want to create? With what other men and women do they want to share and exchange social goods? . . .

TERRITORY

We might, then, think of countries as national clubs or families. But countries are also territorial states. Although clubs and families own property, they neither require nor (except in feudal systems) possess jurisdiction over territory. Leaving children aside, they do not control the physical location of their members. The state does control physical location—if only for the sake of clubs and families and the individual men and women who make them up; and with this control there come certain obligations. We can best examine these if we consider once again the asymmetry of immigration and emigration.

The nationality principle has one significant limit, commonly accepted in theory, if not always in practice. Though the recognition of national affinity is a reason for permitting immigration, nonrecognition is not a reason for expulsion. This is a major issue in the modern world, for many newly independent states find themselves in control of territory into which alien groups have been admitted under the auspices of the old imperial regime. Sometimes these people are forced to leave, the victims of a popular hostility that the new government cannot restrain. More often the government itself fosters such hostility, and takes positive action to drive out the "alien elements," invoking when it does so some version of the club or the family analogy. Here, however, neither analogy applies: for though no "alien" has a right to be a member of a club or a family, it is possible, I think, to describe a kind of territorial or locational right.

Hobbes made the argument in classical form when he listed those rights that are given up and those that are retained when the social contract is signed. The retained rights include self-defense and then "the use of fire, water, free air, *and a place to live in*, and . . . all things necessary for life" [M. W.'s italics]. The right is not, indeed, to a particular place, but it is enforceable against the state, which exists to protect it; the state's claim to territorial jurisdiction derives ultimately from this individual right to place. Hence the right has a collective as well as an individual form, and these two can come into conflict. But it can't be said that the first always or necessarily supercedes the second, for the first came into existence for the sake of the second. The state owes something to its inhabitants simply, without reference to their collective or national identity. And the first place to which the inhabitants are entitled is surely the place where they and their families have lived and made a life. The attachments and expectations they have formed argue against a forced transfer to another country. If they can't have this particular piece of land (or house or apartment), then some other must be found for them within the same general "place." Initially, at least, the sphere of membership is given: the men and women who determine what membership means, and who shape the admissions policies of the political community, are simply the men and women who are already there. New states and governments must make their peace with the old inhabitants of the land they rule. And countries are likely to take shape as closed territories dominated, perhaps, by particular nations (clubs or families), but always including aliens of one sort or another—whose expulsion would be unjust.

This common arrangement raises one important possibility: that many of the inhabitants of a particular country won't be allowed full membership (citizenship) because of their nationality. I will consider that possibility, and argue for its rejection, when I turn to the specific problems of naturalization. But one might avoid such problems entirely, at least at the level of the state, by opting for a radically different arrangement. Consider once again the neighborhood analogy: perhaps we should deny to national states, as we deny to churches and political parties, the collective right of territorial jurisdiction. Perhaps we should insist upon open countries and permit closure only in nonterritorial groups. Open neighborhoods together with closed clubs and families: that is the structure of domestic society. Why can't it, why shouldn't it be extended to the global society?

An extension of this sort was actually proposed by the Austrian socialist writer Otto Bauer, with reference to the old multinational empires of Central and Eastern Europe. Bauer would have organized nations into autonomous corporations permitted to tax their members for educational and cultural purposes, but denied any territorial dominion. Individuals would be free to move about in political space, within the empire, carrying their national memberships with them, much as individuals move about today in liberal and secular states, carrying their religious memberships and partisan affiliations. Like churches and parties, the corporations could admit or reject new members in accordance with whatever standards their old members thought appropriate.

The major difficulty here is that all the national communities that Bauer wanted to preserve came into existence, and were sustained over the centuries, on the basis of geographical coexistence. It isn't any misunderstanding of their histories that leads nations newly freed from imperial rule to seek a firm territorial status. Nations look for countries because in some deep sense they already have countries: the link between people and land is a crucial feature of national identity. Their leaders understand, moreover, that because so many critical issues (including issues of distributive justice, such as welfare, education, and so on) can best be resolved within geographical units, the focus of political life can never be established elsewhere. "Autonomous" corporations will always be adjuncts, and probably parasitic adjuncts, of territorial states; and to give up the state is to give up any effective self-determination. That's why borders, and the movements of individuals and groups across borders, are bitterly disputed as soon as imperial rule recedes and nations begin the process of "liberation." And, once again, to reserve this process or to repress its effects would require massive coercion on a global scale. There is no easy way to avoid the country (and the proliferation of countries) as we currently know it. Hence the theory of justice must allow for the territorial state, specifying the rights of its inhabitants and recognizing the collective right of admission and refusal.

The argument cannot stop here, however, for the control of territory opens the state to the claim of necessity. Territory is a social good in a double sense. It is living space, earth and water, mineral resources and potential wealth, a resource for the destitute and the hungry. And it is protected living space, with borders and police, a resource for the persecuted and the stateless. These two resources are different, and we might conclude differently with regard to the kinds of claim that can be made on each. But the issue at stake should first be put in general terms. Can a political community exclude destitute and hungry, persecuted and stateless—in a word, necessitous—men and women simply because they are foreigners? Are citizens bound to take in strangers? Let us assume that the citizens have no formal obligations; they are bound by nothing more stringent than the principle of mutual aid. The principle must be applied, however, not to individuals directly but to the citizens as a group, for immigration is a matter of political decision. Individuals participate in the decision making, if the state is democratic; but they decide not for themselves but for the community generally. And this fact has moral implications. It replaces immediacy with distance and the personal expense of time and energy with impersonal bureaucratic costs. Despite John Winthrop's claim, mutual aid is more coercive for political communities than it is for individuals because a wide range of benevolent actions is open to the community which will only marginally affect its present members considered as a body or even, with possible exceptions, one by one or family by family or club by club. (But benevolence will, perhaps, affect the children or grandchildren or great-grandchildren of the present members— in ways not easy to measure or even to make out. I'm not sure to what extent considerations of this sort can be used to narrow the range of required actions.) These actions probably include the admission of strangers, for admission to a country does not entail the kinds of intimacy that could hardly be avoided in the case of clubs and families. Might not admission, then, be morally imperative, at least for *these* strangers, who have no other place to go?

Some such argument, turning mutual aid into a more stringent charge on communities than it can ever be on individuals, probably underlies the common claim that exclusion rights depend upon the territorial extent and the popula-tion density of particular countries. Thus, Sidgwick wrote that he "cannot concede to a state possessing large tracts of unoccupied land an absolute right of excluding alien elements." Perhaps, in his view, the citizens can make some selection among necessitous strangers, but they cannot refuse entirely to take strangers in so long as their state has (a great deal of) available space. A much stronger argument might be made from the other side, so to speak, if we consider the necessitous strangers not as objects of beneficent action but as desperate men and women, capable of acting on their own behalf. In *Leviathan*, Hobbes argued that such people, if they cannot earn a living in their own countries, have a right to move into "countries not sufficiently inhabited: where nevertheless they are not to exterminate those they find there, but constrain them to inhabit closer together and not range a great deal of ground to snatch what they find." Here the "Samaritans" are not themselves active but acted upon and (as we shall see in a moment) charged only with nonresistance. . . .

MEMBERSHIP AND JUSTICE

The distribution of membership is not pervasively subject to the constraints of justice. Across a considerable range of the decisions that are made, states are simply free to take in strangers (or not)—much as they are free, leaving aside the claims of the needy, to share their wealth with foreign friends, to honor the achievements of foreign artists, scholars, and scientists, to choose their trading partners, and to enter into collective security arrangements with foreign states. But the right to choose an admissions policy is more basic than any of these, for it is not merely a matter of acting in the world, exercising sovereignty, and pursuing national interests. At stake here is the shape of the community that acts in the world, exercises sovereignty, and so on. Admission and exclusion are at the core of communal independence. They suggest the deepest meaning of self-determination. Without them, there could not be *communities of char-acter*, historically stable, ongoing associations of men and women with some special commitment to one another and some special sense of their common life.

But self-determination in the sphere of membership is not absolute. It is a right exercised, most often, by national clubs or families, but it is held in principle by territorial states. Hence it is subject both to internal decisions by the members themselves (all the members, including those who hold membership simply by rights of place) and to the external principle of mutual aid. Immigration, then, is both a matter of political choice and moral constraint. Naturalization, by contrast, is entirely constrained; every new immigrant, every refugee taken in, every resident and worker must be offered the opportunities of citizenship. If the community is so radically divided that a single citizenship is impossible, then its territory must be divided, too, before the rights of admission and exclusion can be exercised. For these rights are to be exercised only by the community as a whole (even if, in practice, some national majority dominates the decision making) and only with regard to foreigners, not by some members with regard to others. No community can be half-metric, half-citizen and claim that its admissions policies are acts of self-determination or that its politics is democratic.

The determination of aliens and guests by an exclusive band of citizens (or of slaves by masters, or women by men, or blacks by whites, or conquered peoples by their conquerors) is not communal freedom but oppression. The citizens are free, of course, to set up a club, make membership as exclusive as they like, write a constitution, and govern one another. But they can't claim territorial jurisdiction and rule over the people with whom they share the territory. To do this is to act outside their sphere, beyond their rights. It is a form of tyranny. Indeed, the rule of citizens over noncitizens, of members over strangers, is probably the most common form of tyranny in human history. I won't say much more than this about the special problems of noncitizens and strangers: henceforth, whether I am talking about the distribution of security and welfare or about hard work or power itself, I shall assume that all the eligible men and women hold a single political status. This assumption doesn't exclude other sorts of inequality further down the road, but it does exclude the piling up of inequalities that is characteristic of divided societies. The denial of membership is always the first of a long train of abuses. There is no way to break the train, so we must deny the rightfulness of the denial. The theory of distributive justice begins, then, with an account of membership rights. It must vindicate at one and the same time the (limited) right of closure, without which there could be no communities at all, and the political inclusiveness of the existing communities. For it is only as members somewhere that men and women can hope to share in all the other social goods—security, wealth, honor, office, and power—that communal life makes possible.

MEMBERSHIP AND NEED

Membership is important because of what the members of a political community owe to one another and to no one else or to no one else in the same degree. And the first thing they owe is the communal provision of security and welfare. This claim might be reversed: communal provision is important because it teaches us the value of membership. If we did not provide for one another, if we recognized no distinction between members and strangers, we would have no reason to form and maintain political communities. "How shall men love their country," Rousseau asked, "if it is nothing more for them than for strangers, and bestows on them only that which it can refuse to none?" Rousseau believed that citizens ought to love their country and therefore that their country ought to give them particular reasons to do so. Membership (like kinship) is a special relation. It's not enough to say, as Edmund Burke did, that "to make us love our country, our country ought to be lovely." The crucial thing is that it be lovely for us—though we always hope that it will be lovely for others (we also love its reflected loveliness).

Political community for the sake of provision, provision for the sake of community: the process works both ways, and that is perhaps its crucial feature. Philosophers and political theorists have been too quick to turn it into a simple calculation. Indeed, we are rationalists of everyday life; we come together, we sign the social contract or reiterate the signing of it, in order to provide for our needs. And we value the contract insofar as those needs are met. But one of our needs is community itself: culture, religion, and politics. It is only under the aegis of these three that all the other things we need become *socially recognized needs*, take on historical and determinate form. The social contract is an agreement to reach decisions together about what goods are necessary to our common life, and then to provide those goods for one another. The signers owe one another more than mutual aid, for that they owe or can owe to anyone. They owe mutual provision of all those things for the sake of which they have separated themselves from mankind as a whole and joined forces in a particular community. *Amour social* is one of those things; but though it is a distributed good—often unevenly distributed—it arises only in the course of other distributions (and of the political choices that the other distributions require). Mutual provision breeds mutuality. So the common life is simultaneously the prerequisite of provision and one of its products.

Men and women come together because they literally cannot live apart. But they can live together in many different ways. Their survival and then their well-being require a common effort: against the wrath of the gods, the hostility of other people, the indifference and malevolence of nature (famine, flood, fire, and disease), the brief transit of a human life. Not army camps alone, as David Hume wrote, but temples, storehouses, irrigation works, and burial grounds are the true mothers of cities. As the list suggests, origins are not singular in character. Cities differ from one another, partly because of the natural environments in which they are built and the immediate dangers their builders encounter, partly because of the conceptions of social goods that the builders hold. They recognize but also create one another's needs and so give a particular shape to what I will call the "sphere of security and welfare." The sphere itself is as old as the oldest human community. Indeed, one might say that the original community is a sphere of security and welfare, a system of communal provision, distorted, no doubt, by gross inequalities of strength and cunning. But the system has, in any case, no natural form. Different experiences and different conceptions lead to different patterns of provision. Though there are some goods that are needed absolutely, there is no good such that once we see it, we know how it stands vis-à-vis all other goods and how much of it we owe to one another. The nature of a need is not self-evident.

Communal provision is both general and particular. It is general whenever public funds are spent so as to benefit all or most of the members without any distribution to individuals. It is particular whenever goods are actually handed over to all or any of the members. Water, for example, is one of "the bare requirements of civil life," and the building of reservoirs is a form of general provision. But the delivery of water to one rather than to another neigborhood (where, say, the wealthier citizens live) is particular. The securing of the food supply is general; the distribution of food to widows and orphans is particular. Public health is most often general, the care of the sick, most often particular. Sometimes the criteria for general and particular provision will differ radically. The building of temples and the organization of religious services is an example of general provision designed to meet the needs of the community as a whole, but communion with the gods may be allowed only to particularly meritorious members (or it may be sought privately in secret or in nonconformist sects). The system of justice is a general good, meeting common needs; but the actual distribution of rewards and punishments may serve the particular needs of a ruling class, or it may be organized, as we commonly think it should be, to give to individuals what they individually deserve. Simone Weil has argued that, with regard to justice, need operates at both the general and the particular levels, since criminals need to be punished. But that is an idiosyncratic use of the word *need*. More likely, the punishment of criminals is something only the rest of us need. But need does operate both generally and particularly for other goods: health care is an obvious example that I will later consider in some detail.

Despite the inherent forcefulness of the word, needs are elusive. People don't just have needs, they have ideas about their needs; they have priorities, they have degrees of need; and these priorities and degrees are related not only to their human nature but also to their history and culture. Since resources are always scarce, hard choices have to be made. I suspect that these can only be political choices. They are subject to a certain philosophical elucidation, but the idea of need and the commitment to communal provision do not by themselves yield any clear determination of priorities or degrees. Clearly we can't meet, and we don't have to meet, every need to the same degree or any need to the ultimate degree. The ancient Athenians, for example, provided public baths and gymnasiums for the citizens but never provided anything remotely resembling unemployment insurance or social security. They made a choice about how to spend public funds, a choice shaped presumably by their understanding of what the common life required. It would be hard to argue that they made a mistake. I suppose there are notions of need that would yield such a conclusion, but these would not be notions acceptable to—they might not even be comprehensible to—the Athenians themselves.

The question of degree suggests even more clearly the importance of political choice and the irrelevance of any merely philosophical stipulation. Needs are not only elusive; they are also expansive. In the phrase of the contemporary philosopher Charles Fried, needs are voracious; they eat up resources. But it would be wrong to suggest that therefore need cannot be a distributive principle. It is, rather, a principle subject to political limitation; and the limits (within limits) can be arbitrary, fixed by some temporary coalition of interests or majority of voters. Consider the case of physical security in a modern American city. We could provide absolute security, eliminate every source of violence except domestic violence, if we put a street light every ten yards and stationed a policeman every thirty yards throughout the city. But that would be very expensive, and so we settle for something less. How much less can only be decided politically. One can imagine the sorts of things that would figure in the debates. Above all, I think, there would be a certain understanding—more or less widely shared, controversial only at the margins—of what constitutes "enough" security or of what level of insecurity is simply intolerable. The decision would also be affected by other factors: alternate needs, the state of the economy, the agitation of the policemen's union, and so on. But whatever decision is ultimately reached, for whatever reasons, security is provided because the citizens need it. And because, at some level, they all need it, the criterion of need remains a critical standard (as we shall see) even though it cannot determine priority and degree.

COMMUNAL PROVISION

There has never been a political community that did not provide, or try to provide, or claim to provide, for the needs of its members as its members understood those needs. And there has never been a political community that did not engage its collective strength—its capacity to direct, regulate, pressure, and coerce—in this project. The modes of organization, the levels of taxation, the timing and reach of conscription: these have always been a focus of political controversy. But the use of political power has not, until very recently, been controversial. The building of fortresses, dams, and irrigation works; the mobilization of armies; the securing of the food supply and of trade generally—all these require coercion. The state is a tool that cannot be made without iron. And coercion, in turn, requires agents of coercion. Communal provision is always mediated by a set of officials (priests, soldiers, and bureaucrats) who introduce characteristic distortions into the process, siphoning off money and labor for their own purposes or using provision as a form of control. But these distortions are not my immediate concern. I want to stress instead the sense in which every political community is in principle a "welfare state." Every set of officials is at least putatively committed to the provision of security and welfare; every set of members is committed to bear the necessary burdens (and actually does bear them). The first commitment has to do with the duties of office; the second, with the dues of membership. Without some shared sense of the duty and the dues, there would be no political community at all and no security or welfare—and the life of mankind "solitary, poor, nasty, brutish, and short."

But how much security and welfare is required? Of what sorts? Distributed how? Paid for how? These are the serious issues, and they can be resolved in many different ways. Since every resolution will be appropriate or inappropriate to a particular community, it will be best to turn now to some concrete examples. I have chosen two, from different historical periods, with very different general and particular distributive commitments. The two represent the two strands of our own cultural tradition, Hellenic and Hebraic; but I have not looked for anything like extreme points on the range of possibilities. Rather, I have chosen two communities that are, like our own, relatively democratic and generally respectful of private property. Neither of them, so far as I know, has ever figured significantly in histories of the welfare state; and yet the citizens of both understood well the meaning of communal provision.

ATHENS IN THE FIFTH AND FOURTH CENTURIES

"The Hellenistic city-states were highly sensitive to what may be called the general welfare, that is, they were quite willing to take measures which looked to the benefit of the citizenry as a whole; to social welfare . . . in particular the benefit of the poor as such, they were, on the contrary, largely indifferent." This comment by the contemporary classicist Louis Cohn-Haft occurs in the course of a study of the "public physicians" of ancient Greece, a minor institution but a useful starting point for my own account. In Athens, in the fifth century B.C. (and during the later Hellenistic period in many Greek cities), a small number of doctors were elected to public office, much as generals were elected, and paid a stipend from public funds. It's not clear what their duties were; the surviving evidence is fragmentary. They apparently charged fees for their services much as other doctors did, though it seems likely that "as stipendiaries of the whole citizen body [they] would be under considerable social pressure not to refuse a sick person who could not pay a fee." The purpose of the election and the stipend seems to have been to assure the presence of qualified doctors in the city—in time of plague, for example. The provision was general, not particular; and the city apparently took little interest in the further distribution of medical care. It did honor public physicians who "gave themselves ungrudgingly to all who claimed to need them"; but this suggests that the giving was not a requirement of the office; the doctors were paid for something else.

This was the common pattern at Athens, but the range of general provision was very wide. It began with defense: the fleet, the army, the walls down to Piraeus, were all the work of the citizens themselves under the direction of their magistrates and generals. Or, perhaps it began with food: the Assembly was required, at fixed intervals, to consider an agenda item that had a fixed form—"corn and the defense of the country." Actual distributions of corn occurred only rarely; but the import trade was closely watched, and the internal market regulated, by an impressive array of officials: ten commissioners of trade, superintendents of the markets, ten inspectors of weights and measures, thirty-five "corn guardians" who enforced a just price, and—in moments of crisis—a group of corn buyers "who sought supplies wherever it could find them, raised public subscriptions for the necessary funds, introduced price reductions and rationing." All of these officials were chosen by lot from among the citizens. Or, perhaps it began with religion: the major public buildings of Athens were temples, built with public money; priests were public officials who offered sacrifices on the city's behalf. Or, perhaps it began, as in Locke's account of the origins of the state, with justice: Athens was policed by a band of state slaves (eighteen hundred Scythian archers); the city's courts were intricately organized and always busy. And beyond all this, the city provided a variety of other goods. Five commissioners supervised the building and repair of the roads. A board of ten enforced a rather minimal set of public health measures: "they ensure that the dung collectors do not deposit dung within ten *stados* of the walls." As I have already noted, the city provided baths and gymnasiums, probably more for social than for hygienic reasons. The burial of corpses found lying on the streets was a public charge. So were the funerals of the war dead, like the one at which Pericles spoke in 431. Finally, the great drama festivals were publicly organized and paid for, through a special kind of taxation, by wealthy citizens. Is this last an expense for security and welfare? We might think of it as a central feature of the religious and political education of the Athenian people. By contrast, there was no public expenditure for schools or teachers at any level: no subsidies for reading and writing or for philosophy.

Alongside all this, the particular distributions authorized by the Athenian

Assembly—with one central exception—came to very little. "There is a law," Aristotle reported, "that anyone with property of less than three *minae* who suffers from a physical disability which prevents his undertaking any employment should come before the Council, and if his claim is approved he should receive two *obols* a day subsistence from public funds." These (very small) pensions could be challenged by any citizen, and then the pensioner had to defend himself before a jury. One of the surviving orations of Lycias was written for a crippled pensioner. "All fortune, good and bad," Lycias had the pensioner tell the jury, "is to be shared in common by the community as a whole." This was hardly an accurate decription of the city's practices. But the citizens did recognize their obligations to orphans and also to the widows of fallen soldiers. Beyond that, particular provision was left to the families of those who needed it. The city took an interest but only at a distance: a law of Solon required fathers to teach their sons a trade and sons to maintain their parents in old age.

The central exception, of course, was the distribution of public funds to all those citizens who held an office, served on the Council, attended the Assembly, or sat on a jury. Here a particular distribution served a general purpose: the maintenance of vigorous democracy. The monies paid out were designed to make it possible for artisans and farmers to miss a day's work. Public spirit was still required, for the amounts were small, less than the daily earnings even of an unskilled laborer. But the yearly total was considerable, coming to something like half of the internal revenue of the city in the fifth century and more than that at many points in the fourth. Since the revenue of the city was not raised from taxes on land or income (but from taxes on imports, court fines, rents, the income of the silver mines, and so on), it can't be said that these payments were redistributive. But they did distribute public funds so as to balance somewhat the inequalities of Athenian society. This was particularly the case with regard to payments to elderly citizens who would not have been working anyway. Professor M. I. Finley is inclined to attribute to this distributive effect the virtual absence of civil strife or class war throughout the history of democratic Athens. Perhaps this was an intended result, but it seems more likely that what lay behind the payments was a certain conception of citizenship. To make it possible for each and every citizen to participate in political life, the citizens as a body were prepared to lay out large sums. Obviously, this appropriation benefited the poorest citizens the most, but of poverty itself the city took no direct notice.

A MEDIEVAL JEWISH COMMUNITY

I shall not refer here to any particular Jewish community but shall try to describe a typical community in Christian Europe during the high Middle Ages. I am concerned primarily to produce a list of goods generally or particularly provided;

and the list doesn't vary significantly from one place to another. Jewish communities under Islamic rule, especially as these have been reconstructed in the remarkable books of Professor S. D. Goitein, undertook essentially the same sort of provision though under somewhat different circumstances. In contrast to Athens, all these were autonomous but not sovereign communities. In Europe, they possessed full powers of taxation, though much of the money they raised had to be passed on to the secular—that is, Christian—king, prince, or lord, either in payment of his taxes or as bribes, subsidies, "loans," and so on. This can be thought of as the price of protection. In the Egyptian cities studied by Goitein, the largest part of the communal funds was raised through charitable appeals, but the standardized form of the gifts suggests that social pressure worked very much like political power. It was hardly possible to live in the Jewish community without contributing; and short of conversion to Christianity, a Jew had no alternative; there was no place else to go.

In principle, these were democratic communities, governed by an assembly of male members, meeting in the synagogue. External pressures tended to produce oligarchy or, more precisely, plutocracy—the rule of the heads of the wealthiest families, who were best able to deal with avaricious kings. But the rule of the wealthy was continually challenged by more ordinary members of the religious community, and was balanced by the authority of the rabbinic courts. The rabbis played a crucial role in the apportionment of taxes, a matter of ongoing and frequently bitter controversy. The rich preferred a per capita tax, though in moments of cricis they could hardly avoid contributing what was necessary to their own, as well as the community's, survival. The rabbis seem generally to have favored proportional (a few of them even raised the possibility of progressive) taxation.

As one might expect in communities whose members were at best precariously established, subject to intermittent persecution and constant harassment, a high proportion of public funds was distributed to individuals in trouble. But though it was established early on that the poor of one's own community took precedence over "foreign" Jews, the larger solidarity of a persecuted people is revealed in the very strong commitment to the "ransom of captives"—an absolute obligation on any community to which an appeal was made, and a significant drain on communal resources. "The redemption of captives," wrote Maimonides, "has precedence over the feeding and clothing of the poor." This priority derived from the immediate physical danger in which the captive found himself, but it probably also had to do with the fact that his danger was religious as well as physical. Forced conversion or slavery to a non-Jewish owner were threats to which the organized Jewish communities were especially sensitive; for these were above all religious communities, and their conceptions of public life and of the needs of individual men and women were alike shaped through centuries of religious discussion.

The major forms of general provision—excluding protection money—were religious in character, though these included services that we now think of as secular. The synagogue and its officials, the courts and their officials, were paid for out of public funds. The courts administered Talmudic law, and their jurisdiction was wide (though it did not extend to capital crimes). Economic dealings were closely regulated, especially dealings with non-Jews since these could have implications for the community as a whole. The pervasive sumptuary laws were also designed with non-Jews in mind, so as not to excite envy and resentment. The community provided public baths, more for religious than for hygienic reasons, and supervised the work of the slaughterers. Kosher meat was taxed (in the Egyptian communities, too), so this was both a form of provision and a source of revenue. There was also some effort made to keep the streets clear of rubbish and to avoid overcrowding in Jewish neighborhoods. Toward the end of the medieval period, many communities established hospitals and paid communal midwives and physicians.

Particular distributions commonly took the form of a dole: regular weekly or twice-weekly distributions of food; less frequent distributions of clothing; special allocations for sick people, stranded travelers, widows and orphans, and so on—all this on a remarkable scale given the size and resources of the communities. Maimonides had written that the highest form of charity was the gift or loan or partnership designed to make the recipient self-supporting. These words were often quoted but, as Goitein has argued, they did not shape the structure of social services in the Jewish community. Perhaps the poor were too numerous, the situation of the community itself too precarious, for anything more than relief. Goitein has calculated that among the Jews of Old Cairo, "there was one relief recipient to every four contributors to the charities." The contributors of money also contributed their time and energy: from their ranks came a host of minor officials involved in the endless work of collection and distribution. Hence, the dole was a large and continuous drain, accepted as a religious obligation, with no end in sight until the coming of the messiah. This was divine justice with a touch of Jewish irony: "You must help the poor in proportion to their needs, but you are not obligated to make them rich."

Beyond the dole, there were additional forms of particular provision, most importantly for educational purposes. In fifteenth-century Spain, some sixty years before the expulsion, a remarkable effort was made to establish something like universal and compulsory public education. The Valladolid synod of 1432 established special taxes on meat and wine, and on weddings, circumcisions, and burials, and ordered

> that every community of fifteen householders [or more] shall be obliged to maintain a qualified elementary teacher to instruct their children in Scripture. . . . The parents shall be obliged to send their children to that teacher,

and each shall pay him in accordance with their means. If this revenue should prove inadequate, the community shall be obliged to supplement it.

More advanced schools were required in every community of forty or more householders. The chief rabbi of Castile was authorized to divert money from wealthy to impoverished communities in order to subsidize struggling schools. This was a program considerably more ambitious than anything attempted earlier on. But throughout the Jewish communities a great deal of attention was paid to education: the school fees of poor children were commonly paid; and there were greater or lesser public subsidies, as well as additional charitable support, for religious schools and academies. Jews went to school the way Greeks went to the theater or the assembly—as neither group could have done had these institutions been left entirely to private enterprise.

Together, the Jews and the Greeks suggest not only the range of communal activity but also, and more important, the way in which this activity is structured by collective values and political choices. In any political community where the members have something to say about their government, some such pattern will be worked out: a set of general and particular provisions designed to sustain and enhance a common culture. The point would hardly have to be made were it not for contemporary advocates of a minimal or libertarian state, who argue that all such matters (except for defense) should be left to the voluntary effort of individuals. But individuals left to themselves, if that is a practical possibility, will necessarily seek out other individuals for the sake of collective provision. They need too much from one another—not only material goods, which might be provided through a system of free exchange, but material goods that have, so to speak, a moral and cultural shape. Certainly one can find examples—there are many—of states that failed to provide either the material goods or the morality or that provided them so badly, and did so much else, that ordinary men and women yearned for nothing so much as deliverance from their impositions. Having won deliverance, however, these same men and women don't set out simply to maintain it but go on to elaborate a pattern of provision suited to their own needs (their own conception of their needs). The arguments for a minimal state have never recommended themselves to any significant portion of mankind. Indeed, what is most common in the history of popular struggles is the demand not for deliverance but for performance: that the state actually serve the purposes it claims to serve, and that it do so for all its members. The political community grows by invasion as previously excluded groups, one after another—plebians, slaves, women, minorities of all sorts—demand their share of security and welfare.

Justice and Solidarity*

JÜRGEN HABERMAS

PROCEDURAL EXPLANATIONS OF THE "MORAL POINT OF VIEW"

FORMALIST ETHICS DESIGNATE A rule or a procedure that establishes how a morally relevant action conflict can be judged impartially—that is, from a moral point of view. The prototype is Kant's categorical imperative, understood not as a maxim of action but as a principle of justification. The requirement that valid maxims of action must be able to serve as the basis for a "general legislation" brings to bear both the concept of autonomy (as the freedom to act in accordance with laws one gives oneself) and the correlative concept that the corresponding actions are capable of general consensus: the point of view of impartial judgment is assured through a universalization principle that designates as valid precisely those norms that *everyone* could *will*. The quantifier "every" refers to everyone who could possibly be affected (that is, restricted in the scope of his or her action) if the norm in question were generally followed. The predicate "will" is to be understood in accordance with the Kantian notion of the autonomous will; it means "accept as binding on myself on the basis of my own insight." The fundamental intuition is clear: under the moral point of view, one must be able to test whether a norm or a mode of action could be generally accepted by those affected by it, such that their acceptance would be rationally motivated and hence uncoerced. This intuition has been reformulated in various ways by contemporary philosophers, primarily in such a way, however, that the procedural character of the proposed testing emerges more clearly than it did in Kant. The most illuminating are the

*Excerpt from Jürgen Habermas's "Justice and Solidarity: On the Discussion Concerning 'Stage 6'" in *The Moral Domain: Essays in the Ongoing Discussion between Philosophy and the Social Sciences*, edited by Thomas E. Wren, MIT Press. Copyright ©1990 Massachusetts Institute of Technology. Reprinted by permission of MIT Press.

following four positions, which with varying accentuations are based on social contract or role-taking models, that is, on models that construe the process of reaching agreement in counterfactual terms.

1. The first position makes use of the central thought-motif of social contract theories (as it is commonly found in modern, rational natural-law theory since Hobbes), namely, the motif, derived from civil law, of a contractual agreement between autonomous legal subjects. Both in terms of the history of philosophy and systematically, this represents a return to *pre*-Kantian concepts. In order to bring the contract motif up to the level of the Kantian intuition, certain conditions must be added. For this reason Rawls places his contracting partners—who are to enjoy equal freedom of choice, to make decisions in a purposively rational way, and to pursue only their own interests (that is, not to be interested in their *mutual* welfare)—in an original position. This original position is defined such that rational egoists must make their agreements under certain restrictions. The conditions that establish this framework, especially the "veil of ignorance" (ignorance of one's own status within the future social intercourse that is to be institutionally regulated), require that enlightened self-interest be reoriented toward the perspective of the universalizability of normatively regarded interests. The orientation that Kant built into practical reason through the moral law, and thereby into the motives of autonomously acting subjects themselves, now comes about only as the result of the interplay of rational egoism with the substantive normative conditions of the original position under which that egoism operates.

At first, this seems to relieve the "theory of justice" from the presupposition-laden premises of Kantian moral philosophy. The parties making the contract need only act reasonably, rather than out of duty. To be sure, the theorist still has to check whether his construction of the original position and the principles agreed to in it actually accord with our moral intuitions. His assumptions, which are regulated only by the criterion of "reflective equilibrium," establish "the appropriate initial status quo which insures that the fundamental agreements reached in it are fair" (Rawls, A *Theory of Justice*, 1971). Only the procedure proposed in the theory guarantees the correctness of the results, and does so in such a way that "the parties have no basis for bargaining in the usual sense." Everyone who puts himself in the role of one of the contracting parties in the original position should be able to reach the same conclusions deductively that Rawls (with some obvious additional assumptions concerning life plans, primary goods, and so forth) develops in his theory. Like the categorical imperative, each person must be able to apply Rawls's model for testing on his own, i.e., "in his imagination."

These advantages, however, have their reverse side. Rawls has by no means completely captured the fundamental intuition of Kantian ethics in his model of a contractual agreement supplemented by a framework of conditions. According to Kant, everyone can grasp the moral law by virtue of practical reason; the benefits derived from the moral law satisfy strictly *cognitive* demands. According to Rawls, however, in the role of a contracting party in the original position, only instrumental-rational decisions are required. Here the voluntarism of a contract model tailored to the understanding of private-legal subjects is readily apparent; from the point of view of those involved, the fictive agreement in the original position lacks any moment of insight that would point beyond the calculation of their own interests. Moral-practical knowledge is reserved for the theorist, who has to give a plausible explanation of why he constructed the original position in this way rather than another. If, however, the rationality of the rationally motivated acceptance of principles and rules is not guaranteed by the rational decision of the partners to the contract, but rather results only from an interplay into which they have no subjective insight, with a framework of conditions that are established a priori, then the further question arises: how can Rawls motivate his audience to place themselves in the original position at all?

2. On these and similar grounds, T. M. Scanlon proposes a revision that brings the social contract model closer to Kantian notions. He drops the construct of an original position occupied by rational egoists shrouded with a veil of ignorance, and instead equips each of the contracting parties from the outset with the desire to justify their own practice to all who might possibly be affected, and to justify it so convincingly that the latter could not (whether or not they actually do so) refuse their assent to the universalization of this practice. Scanlon proposes the following test principle for the impartial judgment of moral questions: a mode of action is morally right if it is authorized by any system of universal rules for action that everyone concerned can rationally represent as being the result of an informed, uncoerced, and rational agreement of all concerned. This formulation shifts the meaning of "agreement" from the decision in making a contract toward a rationally motivated understanding (judgmental harmony). With this emphasis on the element of insight or understanding in a process of will formation that is rational from the perspective of the participants themselves, Scanlon also hopes to resolve the question of moral motivation. The desire to justify one's own modes of action to others on the basis of norms that are acceptable or worthy of agreement already provides a motive for avoiding actions that are morally wrong because they cannot be justified.

Through his cognitivistic reinterpretation of the social contract model, Scanlon revokes the distinction that Rawls undertook to make between the preestablished transsubjective, justice-compelling perspective of the original position, on the one hand, and the perspective of the participants, limited to subjective rationality, on the other. The moral philosopher is thereby relieved of the task of justifying a priori the normative construction of the original position. At the same time, the parties themselves, with knowledge of all the circumstances, are required to determine what sort of action could not be rejected on good grounds as a general practice by anyone within the sphere of those concerned—given that all participants are interested in an uncoerced, rationally motivated agreement. This procedure can no longer be applied in a strictly monological manner, as could Rawls's. It is no longer enough for me, in the role of a party in the original position, to determine what admits of universal approval from the perspective of that role (thus, from my perspective); rather, the revised contract model requires me to examine what everyone would, from his own perspective, judge to be capable of universal approval if he were oriented to the goal of reaching an agreement. The additional burden on the subject making the moral judgment is shown by the fact that he must at least imagine, that is, perform virtually, the intersubjective execution of a procedure that cannot be applied monologically at all. According to Scanlon, principles and rules find *general* acceptance only when *all* can be convinced that *each* person could give his well-founded assent from his own perspective:

> To believe that a principle is morally correct one must believe that it is one which all could reasonably agree to. . . . But my belief that this is the case may often be distorted by a tendency to take its advantage to me more seriously than its possible costs to others. For this reason, the idea of "putting myself in another's place" is a useful corrective device.

3. It is no accident that at this point Scanlon has to borrow from another model. Mead's fundamental notion that one participant in a social interaction takes the perspective of the other is not a "useful corrective" to the social contract model; it is rather the alternative that presents itself as soon as it becomes clear that a consistent attempt to reach the level of the fundamental intuition of Kantian ethics under post-Kantian premises (that is, having dispensed with the two-world doctrine) exceeds the capacity of the fundamental notions of the contract model. Thus Lawrence Kohlberg explains [elsewhere in *The Moral Domain*] the moral point of view of impartially judging moral conflicts with the help of the concept of ideal role-taking, which Mead [in G. H. Mead, *Mind, Self, and Society*, 1934] had already used as the correlate of *universal discourse* in reformulating the fundamental idea of Kantian ethics within the framework of his theory of action. Kohlberg develops this concept through a series of steps, beginning with simple interactions between at least two persons engaged in communicative action.

Ego must first fulfill the condition of sympathetic identification with the situation of Alter; he must actually identify with him in order to be able to take the precise perspective from which Alter could bring his expectations, interests, value orientations, and so forth to bear in the case of a moral conflict. Then Ego must be able to assume that the project of perspective-taking is not one-sided but reciprocal. Alter is expected to take Ego's perspective in the same way, so that the contested mode of action can be perceived and thematized in mutual agreement, taking into consideration the interests affected on both sides. In more complex circumstances, this dyadic relationship must be extended to an interlocking of perspectives among members of a particular group. Only under this social cognitive presupposition can each person give equal weight to the interests of the others when it comes to judging whether a general practice could be accepted by each member on good grounds, in the same way that I have accepted it. Finally, Ego must satisfy the condition of universalizability of his reflections, which initially are internal to the group and refer to simple interactions: Ego must disregard the concrete circumstances of a particular interaction and examine abstractly whether a *general* practice could be accepted without constraint under comparable circumstances by each of those affected, from the perspective of his own interests. This requires a universal interchangeability of the perspectives of all concerned; Ego must be able to imagine how each person would put himself in the place of every other person.

What was sympathetic empathy and identification under the concrete initial conditions is sublimated at this level to accomplishments that are purely cognitive: on the one hand, *understanding* for the claims of others that result in each case from particular interest positions; on the other hand, *consciousness* of a prior solidarity of all concerned that is objectively grounded through socialization. At this level of abstraction, sensitivity to individual claims must be detached from contingent personal ties (and identities), just as the feeling of solidarity must be detached from contingent social ties (and collectivities).

All the same, the procedure of ideal role-taking retains a strong emotivistic tinge from its origins in social psychology. Rawls made a procedure taken from the social contract model the basis for judging the capacity of norms to achieve consensus; we have seen that the element of insight then became less significant in comparison to that of decision, specifically, that of calculated agreement among parties capable of deciding. If, instead, a procedure in accordance with the role-taking model is made the basis of this test, practical reason is relegated to a secondary position in a similar way—this time in comparison to empathy, that is, the intuitive understanding that parties capable of empathy bring to one another's situation. The discursive character of rational will formation, which can end in intersubjective recognition of criticizable validity claims only if attitudes are changed through arguments, is here neglected in favor of achievements of empathic understanding. The presentation in this volume [i.e., *The Moral Domain*] by Kohlberg, Boyd, and Levine demonstrates a tendency (which is in any case suggested by the passages from the interview with Joan) to view "dialogue" not as a form of argumentation but as a method from group dynamics for sharpening the capacity for empathy and strengthening social ties. Where this tendency becomes dominant, however, it is to the detriment of the purely cognitive meaning of ideal role-taking as a procedure for the impartial judgment of moral states of affairs.

4. To counter this emotivistic bias, one can, as Apel and I have suggested, interpret the role-taking model from the outset as a discourse model. There is already adequate support for this interpretation in Mead, who introduces ideal role-taking as the quintessential social cognitive presupposition of a universal discourse that extends beyond all purely local states of affairs and traditional arrangements. Mead begins with the idea that what the categorical imperative was supposed to achieve can be accomplished through the projection of a process of will formation under the idealized conditions of a universal discourse. The subject making a moral judgment cannot test for himself alone whether a contested mode of action as a general practice would lie within the common interest; he can do so only socially, with all the rest of those concerned. When one recognizes (with Scanlon) that the goal of this sort of inclusive process of reaching understanding, namely, unconstrained agreement, can be attained only through the vehicle of good reasons, the reflective character of that universal discourse emerges more sharply than in Mead: discourse must be thought of not only as a net of communicative action that takes in all those potentially affected, but as a reflective form of communicative action—in fact, as argumentation.

With this, Mead's construction loses the status of a mere projection: in every argumentation that is actually carried out, the participants themselves cannot avoid making such a projection. In argumentation, the participants have to make the pragmatic presupposition that in principle all those affected participate as free and equal members in a cooperative search for truth in which only the force of the better argument may hold sway. The principle of discourse ethics— that only those norms may claim validity that could find acceptance by all those concerned as participants in a practical discourse—is based on this universal pragmatic state of affairs. It is those idealizing presuppositions, which everyone who engages seriously in argumentation must in fact make, that enable discourse to play the role of a procedure that explains the moral point of view. Practical discourse can be understood as a process of reaching agreement that, through its form, that is, solely on the basis of unavoidable general presuppositions of argumentation, constrains all participants at the same time to ideal role-taking. It transforms ideal role-taking, which in Kohlberg was something to be antici-pated privately and in isolation, into a public event, something practiced, ideally, by all together.

Of course, when it is a question of examining norms with a genuinely universal domain of validity, that is, moral norms in the strict sense, this idea is purely regulative. By the standard of this idea, discourses conducted as advocacy or internalized—set in the "inner life of the psyche"—can serve only as substitutes. Arguments played out in "the internal forum," however, are not equivalents for real discourses that have not been carried out; they are subject to the proviso of being merely virtual events that, in specific circumstances, can simulate a procedure that cannot be carried out. This reservation becomes more acceptable, however, given that discourses that are actually carried out also stand under limitations of time and space and social conditions that permit only an approximate fulfillment of the presuppositions, usually made counterfactually, of argumentation.

IS THERE A PLACE FOR THE GOOD IN THE THEORY OF THE JUST?

From the beginning, deontological approaches in ethics have aroused the suspicion that they are on the wrong track in taking as their point of departure the question of the conditions of impartial moral judgment—and the question of the meaning of the moral point of view that assures impartiality. In particular, they arouse the suspicion that under the compulsion to assimilate practical questions to scientific ones they narrow the concept of morality to questions of justice and distort it by seeing it from the specifically modern perspective of bourgeois commerce carried on by subjects under civil law. There are several aspects to this critique. In part it amounts to a defense of classical ethical theories that emphasize the primacy of questions of the good life, the successful conduct of one's individual life, and harmonious forms of social life—character and ethos. In part it is concerned with defending motifs of modern utilitarianism, which aims at the welfare of all and subsumes the rights of individuals under the notion of distributable goods. In part it has as its goal a defense of ethics of compassion and love, which accord a privileged position to altruistic concern for the welfare of a fellow human being in need of help. It is always a question of welfare and concrete goods—whether of the community, the greatest number, or the weak individual; the appeal is to a dimension of happiness and suffering that does not seem to be touched at all by the deontological question of the intersubjectively accepted justification of norms and modes of action. Is it not the case that one simply passes over the question of morally right action and the good life when one focuses, as Kant did, on the phenomenon of the "ought," i.e., on the obligatory character of commands—and thus on a question that is detached from all concrete life circumstances, all interpersonal relationships and identities, namely, the question of the grounds for the validity of maxims of action? . . .

The concept of ideal role-taking borrowed from Mead provides Kohlberg with a basis from which he can reach the level of Kant's fundamental intuition without possessive-individualistic abridgements. Mead himself already appropriated Kant in this way: "The universality of our judgments, upon which Kant places so much stress, is a universality that arises from the fact that we take the attitude of the entire community, of all rational beings." He then adds the characteristic thesis:

> We are what we are through our relationship to others. Inevitably, then, our [morally justified] end must be a social end, both from the standpoint of its content and from the point of view of form. Sociality gives the universality of ethical judgments and lies back of the popular statement that the voice of all is the universal voice; that is, everyone who can rationally appreciate the situation agrees [to a morally justified end].

Valid norms derive their obligatory character from the fact that they embody a universalizable interest, and the autonomy and welfare of individuals as well as the integration and welfare of the social collective are at stake in the maintenance of this interest. I gather that these thoughts lie behind Kohlberg's attempt to bring to bear the principle of concern for the welfare of the other in addition to the principle of justice. Viewed against the background of the contemporary discussion in moral philosophy, this program, which is not to be confused with the projects discussed under (1) to (3) above, is pioneering. However, I do not find the way the program is carried out to be as convincing as its intention.

Kohlberg sets forth essentially three trains of thought. First, he relativizes the idea of justice derived from the moral point of view of impartial judgment of conflicts; this idea is downgraded to the status of a principle and supplemented by a second principle, the principle of benevolence. That principle, of doing good and avoiding doing harm, refers equally to individual and general welfare. On the level of attitude, this principle corresponds to concern for the welfare of the other, compassion, love of one's fellow man, and willingness to help in the broadest sense, but also to community spirit. The two principles stand in a relationship of tension to one another, but are nevertheless thought to be derivable from a common higher principle.

In a second step, Kohlberg grounds justice and benevolence in a further principle, one that since Kant has been considered the equivalent of the principle of equal treatment and thus of the justice principle. This is the principle of equal respect for the integrity or dignity of each person, which corresponds to the formula of the categorical imperative whereby each person is to be treated as an end in himself. Kohlberg establishes the connection to the principle of benevolence by an equivocation in the concept of the person. Equal respect for each person in *general* as a subject capable of autonomous action means equal treatment; however, equal respect for each person *as an individual* subject individuated through a life history can mean something rather different from equal treatment: instead of protection of the person as a self-determining being, it can mean support for the person as a self-realizing being. In this second variant the meaning of "respect" is quietly altered; strictly speaking, it does not follow from *respect (Achtung)* for the integrity of a vulnerable person that one *cares* for his well-being. Thus Kohlberg cannot accommodate the principle of benevolence under the principle of equal respect for every person without an implicit shift in meaning. A further difficulty is more serious. The principle of equal respect, like the principle of equal treatment in general, refers only to individuals. A principle of benevolence "derived" from it might on that account be able to ground concern for the welfare of one's fellow man (or for one's own welfare), but it could not ground concern for the common welfare, and thus not the corresponding sense of community.

In a third step, Kohlberg has to show how both principles arise from the procedure of ideal role-taking. Up to this point the concepts of "the moral point of view" and "justice" have had equivalent meanings. Thus it was the meaning of justice that was explained with the help of ideal role-taking. Now Kohlberg makes room for the meaning of benevolence by analyzing the concept of ideal role-taking into three moments, as previously indicated. Perspective-taking is linked to two further operations: on the one hand, to empathy or identification with the respective other, and, on the other hand, to universalization. Then sympathy can be brought into at least an associative connection with concern for the welfare of the other, and universalization into a similar connection with justice. This argument, too, which is only suggested, loses much of its power when one reflects that with the transition to universalized, completely reversible perspective-taking, not much more is left of a sympathy that is initially directed to concrete reference persons than a purely cognitive feat of understanding.

THE DISCOURSE ETHICS ALTERNATIVE

Kohlberg formulates a correct intuition with the wrong concepts when he ascribes to the principle of equal respect for every person an expanded meaning that includes both equal treatment and benevolence. His intuition can be explicated through Mead's central insight that persons, as subjects capable of speech and action, can be individuated only via the route of socialization. They are formed as individuals only by growing into a speech community and thus into an intersubjectively shared lifeworld. In these formative processes the identity of the individual and that of the collectivity to which he belongs arise and are maintained with equal primacy. The farther individuation progresses, the more the individual subject is caught up in an ever denser and at the same time ever more subtle network of reciprocal dependencies and explicit needs for protection. Thus the person forms an inner center only to the extent to which he simultaneously externalizes himself in communicatively produced interpersonal relationships. This explains the danger to, and the chronic susceptibility of, a vulnerable identity. Furthermore, moralities are designed to shelter this vulnerable identity. Because moralities are supposed to compensate for the vulnerability of living creatures who through socialization are individuated in such a way that they can never assert their identity for themselves alone, the integrity of individuals cannot be preserved without the integrity of the lifeworld that makes possible their shared interpersonal relationships and relations of mutual recognition. Kohlberg is trying to develop this *double* aspect when he emphasizes the intersubjective conditions for the maintenance of individual integrity. Moral provisions for the protection of individual identity cannot safeguard the integrity of individual persons without at the same time safeguarding the vitally necessary web of relationships of mutual recognition in which individuals can stabilize their fragile identities only mutually and simultaneously with the identity of their group.

Kohlberg cannot do justice to this fundamental pragmatist insight, however, by overextending the concept of equal respect for the dignity of each person and then stopping halfway, i.e., at a notion of benevolence toward one's fellow man (a direction in which Joan's partiality to the use of communicative means, with its overtones of group therapy, does point, albeit misleadingly). From the perspective of communication theory there emerges instead a close connection between concern for the welfare of one's fellow man and interest in the general welfare: the identity of the group is reproduced through intact relationships of mutual recognition. Thus the perspective complementing that of equal treatment of individuals is not benevolence but solidarity. This principle is rooted in the realization that each person must take responsibility for the other because as consociates all must have an interest in the integrity of their shared life context in the same way. Justice conceived deontologically requires solidarity as its reverse side. It is a question not so much of two moments that supplement each other as of two aspects of the same thing. Every autonomous morality has to serve two purposes at once: it brings to bear the inviolability of socialized individuals by requiring equal treatment and thereby equal respect for the dignity of each one; and it protects intersubjective relationships of mutual recognition requiring solidarity of individual members of a community, in which they have been socialized. Justice concerns the equal freedoms of unique and self-determining individuals while solidarity concerns the welfare of consociates who are intimately linked in an intersubjectively shared form of life—and thus also to the maintenance of the integrity of this form of life itself. Moral norms cannot protect one without the other: they cannot protect the equal rights and freedoms of the individual without protecting the welfare of one's fellow man and of the community to which the individuals belong.

As a component of a universalistic morality, of course, solidarity loses its merely particular meaning, in which it is limited to the internal relationships of a collectivity that is ethnocentrically isolated from other groups—that character of forced willingness to sacrifice oneself for a collective system of self-assertion that is always present in premodern forms of solidarity. The formula "Command us, Führer, we will follow you" goes perfectly with the formula "All for one and one for all"—as we saw in the posters of Nazi Germany in my youth—because fellowship is entwined with followership in every traditionalist sense of solidarity. Justice conceived in postconventional terms can converge with solidarity as its reverse side only when solidarity has been transformed in the light of the idea of a general discursive will formation. To be sure, the fundamental notions of equal treatment, solidarity, and the general welfare, which are central to *all* moralities, are (even in premodern societies) built into the conditions of symmetry and the expectations of reciprocity characteristic of every ordinary communicative practice, and, indeed, are present in the form of universal and necessary pragmatic presuppositions of communicative action. Without these idealizing presuppositions, no one, no matter how repressive the social structures under which he lives, can act with an orientation to reaching understanding. The ideas of justice and solidarity are present above all in the mutual recognition of responsible subjects who orient their actions to validity claims. But *of themselves* these normative obligations do not extend beyond the boundaries of a concrete lifeworld of family, tribe, city, or nation. These limits can be broken through only in discourse, to the extent that the latter is institutionalized in modern societies. Arguments extend per se beyond particular lifeworlds, for in the pragmatic presuppositions of argumentation, the normative content of the presuppositions of communicative action is extended—in universalized, abstract form and without limitations—to an ideal communication community (as Apel, following Peirce, calls it) that includes all subjects capable of speech and action.

For this reason discourse ethics, which derives the contents of a universalistic morality from the general presuppositions of argumentation, can also do justice to the common root of morality. Because discourses are a reflective form of understanding-oriented action that, so to speak, sit on top of the latter, their central perspective on moral compensation for the deep-seated weakness of vulnerable individuals can be derived from the very medium of linguistically mediated interactions to which socialized individuals owe that vulnerability. The pragmatic features of discourse make possible a discerning will formation whereby the interests of each individual can be taken into account without destroying the social bonds that link each individual with all others. For as a participant in the practical discourses each person is on his or her own and yet joined in an association that is objectively universal. In this respect the role-taking model used in discourse is not equivalent to the social contract model. Procedural ethics is one-sided as long as the idea of an agreement between subjects who are originally isolated is not replaced by the idea of a rational will formation taking place within a lifeworld of socialized subjects. Both in its argumentative methods and its communicative presuppositions, the procedure of discourse has reference to an existential preunderstanding among participants regarding the most universal structures of a lifeworld that has been shared intersubjectively from the beginning. Even this procedure of discursive will formation can seduce us into the one-sided interpretation that the universalizability of contested interests guarantees only the equal treatment of all concerned. That interpretation overlooks the fact that every requirement of universalization must remain powerless unless there also arises, from membership in an ideal communication community, a consciousness of irrevocable solidarity, the certainty of intimate relatedness in a shared life context.

Justice is inconceivable without at least an element of reconciliation. Even in the cosmopolitan ideas of the close of the eighteenth century, the archaic bonding energies of kinship were not extinguished but only refined into solidarity with everything wearing a human face. "All men become brothers," Schiller could say in his "Ode to Joy." This double aspect also characterizes the communicative form of practical discourse: the bonds of social integration remain intact despite the fact that the agreement required of all transcends the bounds of every natural community. On the one hand, every single participant in argumentation remains with his "yes" and "no" a court of final appeal; no one can replace him in his role of one who pronounces on criticizable claims to validity. On the other hand, even those interpretations in which the individual identifies needs that are most peculiarly his own are open to a revision process in which all participate; the social nature of that which is most individual shows itself here and in the mutuality of a consensus that adds the reciprocity of mutual recognition to the sum of individual voices. Both are accurate: without unrestricted individual freedom to take a position on normative validity claims, the agreement that is actually reached could not be truly universal; but without the empathy of each person in the situation for everyone else, which is derived from solidarity, no resolution capable of consensus could be found. Because argumentation merely extends, using reflective means, action that is oriented to reaching understanding, the consciousness that the egocentric perspective is not something primary, but rather something socially produced, does not disappear. Thus the procedure of discursive will formation takes account of the inner connection of the two aspects: the autonomy of unique individuals and their prior embeddedness in intersubjectively shared forms of life.

This does not amount to a reconciliation of Kant with Aristotle. When it opposes one-sided individualistic conceptions and emphasizes solidarity as the reverse side of justice, discourse ethics draws only on the modern concept of justice. The structural aspects of the "good life," which from the perspective of communicative socialization in general are universally distinguishable from the concrete totalities of particular forms of life (and life histories), are included in its conception. Discourse ethics stands under the premises of postmetaphysical thought and cannot incorporate the full meaning of what classical ethical theories once conceived as cosmic justice or justice in terms of salvation. The solidarity on which discourse ethics builds remains within the bounds of earthly justice. . . .

PART III

State, Law, and Resistance

The Purpose of the State
and the Idea of Justice*

ERNEST BARKER

1. THE STATE AND LAW

IN THE TWO PREVIOUS books of this treatise [i.e., *Principles of Social and Political Theory*] the state and society have both been in question; and the aim of the argument has been to study and define their relations, first in historical terms, and then in terms of contemporary life. The future course of the argument will be directed purely to the state: to the purpose which it serves, and the idea of justice on which it is based; to the rights which it secures, the principles of their distribution, and the methods of their declaration and enforcement; to the grounds of the obligation which it imposes on its members, and the limits of that obligation; to the nature of the functions which its government exercises, and the relation of those functions to the rights of individuals.

The state, on the conception here adopted, is a legal association: a "juridically organized nation, or a nation organized for action under legal rules." It exists *for* law: it exists *in* and through law: we may even say that it exists *as* law, if by law we mean not only a sum of legal rules, but also, and in addition, an operative system of effective rules which are actually valid and regularly enforced. The essence of the state is a living body of effective rules; and in that sense the state is law.

To understand better the terms "state" and "law" we shall do well to study their etymology and history: to discover their original sense, and to trace the connotations and associations which they have gradually acquired in the course

---

*Reprinted from *Principles of Social and Political Theory* by Ernest Barker (1951) by permission of Oxford University Press.

102

of time. The English word "state" comes from the Latin *status*, which has had a curious and checkered history during the centuries of its development. (Words too have their growth and their evolution; and they too may go through curious mutations.) In classical Latin, the word *status* meant generally the "standing"— that is to say, the position—of a person or body of persons: but by Cicero's time it had come to be specially applied to the "standing" or position of the whole community, and Cicero accordingly speaks of the *status civitatis*, or the *status reipublicae*, in the general sense of the constitution and institutions by which, and in which, the *civitas* or *respublice* stands. Traveling through late Latin (in which, like many other words beginning with similar double consonants, it acquired an initial *i* and became *i-status*), and then through the Romance languages, the Latin *status* gave us eventually three English words— (1) "estate," in the sense of a standing or position in regard to some form of property (a "real estate" in land, or a "personal estate" in movables); (2) "estate," as when we speak of the three estates of the realm, using the word in the primary sense of a grade or rank in the system of social standing or position, and thence in the derivative sense of the body of persons belonging to such grade or rank; and, finally, (3) "state." This last derivative, it is important to notice, was not originally used in the Ciceronian sense of *status civitatis* or *status reipublicae*; nor did it mean, as those phrases had meant, the general standing, position, or "polity" of the whole community and all its members. It had another and different connotation which long persisted and may still be traced in modern usage. The word "state," when it came into use in England during the sixteenth century, brought with it from Italy the idea of a high "state" or stateliness (*stato*) vested in some one person or some one body of persons. It meant primarily a peculiar standing, of a kind which was political, and of a degree in that kind which was superior or supreme; and thence, by an easy extension, it came to be used derivatively of the person or body of persons invested with such standing. This was the usage down to 1789, and even later: the "state" meant primarily the position of being the superior or supreme political authority, and thence it came to be applied derivatively to the person or body enjoying that position. It was thus a term very similar to, and practically identical with, the terms "sovereignty" and "sovereign," similarly derived from the Latin (in the late Latin form *superanus*) and similarly transmitted to England through Romance derivatives from the Latin (and especially through the Italian *sovrano*). Bacon, in the beginning of the seventeenth century, uses "state" as a term synonymous with or parallel to "king," as when he speaks of "Kings and States" consulting judges. Louis XIV, in the middle of the seventeenth century, must have thought that he was stating a truism, and not attempting a paradox, when he exclaimed *L'État, c'est moi!* Was he not in his own view, as in that of his subjects, the person who enjoyed the "state" and position of being the supreme political authority, and was he not therefore "the state"?

So far, and so long as these views prevailed, the notion of authority, of a position or "standing" of supreme authority, and of the person or body placed in that position and having that "standing"—this was what formed the connotation of the word "state." Such a connotation belongs to a graded and hierarchical society, in which there are different states or "estates" (or sorts and conditions of men) arranged in ascending degrees, and one of these states or "estates" is *the* state par excellence. But this connotation begins to disappear—or rather to be overlaid—when a graded and hierarchical society yields to a society of equals. After the end of the eighteenth century it may be said, *L'État, c'est nous!* The state is now the whole community: the whole legal association; the whole of the juridical organization. This is democracy, or a result of democracy: we must henceforth think of the state as ourselves (or as the juridical organization which we have given to ourselves, or the legal association into which we have formed ourselves); and we must henceforth give the name of "government" to the authority—before called "state"—which is now seen as exercising on our behalf the powers which it had hitherto claimed as its own. But language is slow in adapting itself to changes of thought; and words may long continue to carry the associations of a vanished past. We still use the term "state" with the connotation—only overlaid, and not yet erased—of earlier centuries. We regard the state still as some sort of being, somehow distinct from ourselves, which still interferes with us (thus we speak of "state-interference"), and against which we still must defend the cause of individualism in the war (as Spencer called it) of "The Man versus the State." It is a sad complication of thinking that we so often think with obsolete words, or rather with words whose connotation, in the sense in which we still use them, is obsolete or obsolescent.

From the etymology and history of the term "state" we may now turn to those of the term "law." The term appears to have been borrowed by the English, about the year 1000, from their Scandinavian invaders: it came to them not from the Latin (the Latin terms *lex* and *legalis* are not cognate in origin or connotation), but from a Teutonic root meaning to "lay," to place, or to set. Law is thus etymologically something *positum*, or, as we should say, "imposed": it is something laid down or set, as one sets a task or lays down a rule; and it is accordingly defined in the *Oxford English Dictionary* as "a rule of conduct imposed by authority." If this definition be accepted, we are carried back to the notion of the state as being, in its nature, a superior or supreme authority: we are led to regard law as a rule, or a body of rules, imposed by that authority; and we are driven in the issue to conclude that the command of the state, regarded as a supreme authority, is ipso facto the law for its members, regarded as the "subjects" of that authority. This indeed is a view which long prevailed. It may be called the Austinian view of law. It is expressed by Austin in the propositions that "law is a command which obliges a person or persons"; that "the term 'superiority' . . . is implied by the term 'command,'" and that accordingly "every law simply and strictly so called is set by a sovereign person or . . . body of persons to a member or members of the independent political society wherein that person or body is superior or supreme."

Upon this view, then, the state is regarded as being in its nature authority—the superior or supreme authority—and law as being a body of commands set by that authority to all the persons who are its subjects. The view has some historical justification, or at any rate explanation; but it does not square with the facts and ideas of contemporary life. We have already seen that the word "state" no longer suggests to our minds the idea of authority, or presents them with a picture of the high "state" and the sovereign status of a person or body of persons enjoying and exercising a right of command over subjects. It rather suggests to our minds the idea of association; it presents them with the image of an associated group, as wide and as multitudinous as the whole of a nation, which lives together by virtue of a constitution which it has made, and lives by the rules of law made for it and on its behalf by a law-making agency which acts as its organ under that constitution. The state is now—though that was not the sense of the word when it was adopted into our language—the *status reipublicae*, the standing or condition of the whole of the legally organized community. It is, in its primary and abstract sense, the status or position, common to us all, of being the members of a legal association: it is, in its derivative and concrete sense, the members themselves—the whole of the members—when regarded as holding, and holding in common, such status or position. Upon this conception of the state there follows a correlative conception of law. Law ceases to be the product of the authority of a person or body of persons conceived as being superior or supreme in the political society in which they act. It becomes the product of the whole of the association, primarily in the form of the constitutive memorandum of association (or, as it is generally termed, the "constitution") made, or at any rate ratified, in the general usage of modern states, by the action of the members themselves, and secondarily in the form of a current system of legal rules made by a body, or bodies (for, as we shall see, there may be more than one body concerned), representative of the members and acting on their behalf under the constitution and in virtue of the authority conferred by the constitution.

That is the line we may follow if we think in terms of the present. But even if we go back to the past, and consider the source and the growth of law in terms of the past, we may find that we are driven to the conclusion that law has always been something more than the simple command of a single person or body of persons possessing authority over all others. That conclusion emerges when we ask and endeavor to answer two questions: The first concerns the way in which the general body of law has been imposed and made binding on a political society. Has it been the way of command, or the way of something other than command? The second question concerns the origin of the various branches of law which go to form the general body. Have they all proceeded from a *single* source; or have some come from one source and some from another, and are there thus *several* sources of law?

The development of Roman law will help us to answer these questions. The Latin word for the general body of law is *jus*, which is something broader and more comprehensive than *lex*, though *lex* is one of its elements. How is this *jus* imposed? Before we return an answer, we shall do well to study the etymology of the word. *Jus* is not connected with the verb *jubeo*: it does not mean what is commanded by authority, or *quod jussum est*. That may be true of *lex*, which has some connotation of command and which is defined by the Roman jurists as "*quod populus* jubet *et constituit.*" But *jus* has a different connotation, and is associated with different ideas. It seems to be connected with the Latin word *jungere*: it means primarily a joining or fitting, a bond or tie; and it readily glides into the sense of binding or obliging. We may define *jus*, in its original form, as "what is fitting" and therefore also "binding"; or in more detail, we may say that "it conveys . . . the idea of valid custom [i.e., the deposited common tradition of the 'fitting'], to which any citizen can appeal, and which is recognized and can be enforced by a human authority." We may then go on to think of *jus*, in its developed form, as a body of binding or obliging rules which—however they have been made, whether by the growth of valid custom or by legislative enactment or otherwise—the courts recognize as binding, and not only recognize but also enforce. We must notice here the importance of the courts. The Romans—at any rate in the period of the Republic—thought less of state authority, making law by command, than they did of the authority of the courts giving effect to law (however made) by recognition and enforcement of its rules and remedies. It is significant that the same word *jus* is used to denote both the body of law and the courts which enforce that body. We may therefore say that what imposed the whole body of law and made it binding on the members of the Roman community, was not the command of a lawgiver (though that, as we shall presently see, played some part and made some contribution): it was rather the recognition given, and the enforcement applied, by a law-court. It is the law-court, and not the lawgiver, which is summoned to the mind by the notion of *jus*; and we may say of the Roman people, what a modern writer has said of the English-speaking peoples, that "to them, whether lawyers or not, law means a body of rules enforced by the courts."

That, for the Romans, was the criterion of law, and that is an answer which may be given to the question, "How and in what way has the general body of law been imposed and made binding on a political society?" We now come to the other question, "What is the origin of the various elements or branches of law which go to form the general body?" Here we have to inquire into the various sources of *jus*, and to consider how its different elements emerged and acquired definition. Custom, or unwritten law, or the *jus consensu receptum*, was one of the sources, and it is still mentioned as such in the *Institutes* of Justinian after a thousand years of legal development. (The *Digest* of Justinian has even preserved a passage of the jurist Julianus, approved and translated by Blackstone in the Introduction to his *Commentaries*, which puts custom on a level with, and bases it on the same foundation as, the declared rules of the written law. "For since the written law binds us for no other reason but because it is approved by the judgment of the people, therefore those laws which the people have approved without writing ought also to bind everybody. For where is the difference whether the people declare their assent to a law by suffrage, or by a uniform course of acting accordingly?") Apart from custom, the two main sources of *jus* (the two sources which formed the *jus scriptum*) were legislative declaration and legal formulation. Legislative declaration itself in turn flowed from a number of different springs: one spring, the original, was the Roman people, from which proceeded *leges*; another spring, of a later date, was the Roman Senate, from which proceeded "senatus consulta"—or senatorial decrees and ordinances hardly to be distinguished from *leges*; still a third, of a still later date, was the Roman *princeps* or emperor, from whom proceeded "constitutions," in a variety of forms (decrees, rescripts, and the like), all possessing *legis vigorem*. If legislative declaration was thus triple, legal formulation was double: it consisted partly of the edicts of the magistrates who sat in the courts (edicts at first issued annually, as each new magistrate took office, but becoming in process of time continuous and traditional), and partly of the "responses" of private persons "skilled in the laws" (*jurisconsulti* or *jurisprudentes*) who gave their opinion as it were "in chambers" when they were consulted, and to some extent represented the view of the legal profession. The whole of this process of legal formulation was a great source of Roman law. The judges, and the legal profession behind them, played no small part in the making of *jus*. We may thus conclude that the sources of Roman law were multiple, and not single. We may also conclude that the judges not only imposed the whole body of law, in the sense that gave it legal effect by recognizing its validity. They, and the jurisconsults behind them, were also the *makers*, or at any rate the original declarers, of much of the law they imposed.

Two results emerge from this summary review of the development of Roman law. In the first place, the "imposing" of law by the state is seen to be, in effect, the recognizing and enforcing of it by the courts. In the second place, the source of the law thus recognized and enforced is seen to be at least twofold, even apart from custom, and to consist not only of legislative declaration, but also of legal formulation by the double agency of the courts and the jurisconsults. The same, or very similar, results emerge from a consideration of the development of English law. In England, too, as well as in Rome, law is the general body of rules recognized and enforced, and in that sense imposed, by the courts. In England, too, as well as in Rome, the sources of law are twofold: in part the judges, with the members of the legal profession behind them, who have made, and continue to make, the "common law"; in part the legislature, which enacts statutes and is thus the maker of statute law, and which, being the immediate sovereign and sitting in constant session, can at any time alter or annul the rules of the "common law" in virtue of such sovereignty. From England, therefore, as well as Rome, we may learn the lessons (1) that the action of making law may proceed from more than one agent, and may involve a number of forces or sources; and (2) that over and above the action of making, and at least as important as that action, there is also the action of imposing the whole of the system of law (however its different parts may be made) by a continuous process of recognition and enforcement applied in and by the courts. But when once it is made, by whatever bodies, and when in addition it is steadily imposed by the recognition and enforcement of the courts, law possesses the attribute of validity and produces the effect of obligation. *Valet*—its injunction avails and prevails: *obligat*—it binds men to an engagement of performing what is enjoined.

2. LAW AND JUSTICE

The law which has hitherto been in question is positive law: law which is declared and "set" (*positum*): law which is recognized by the courts and actively enforced by their action (*impositum*). Positive law is a large term, which embraces many divisions. If you look at its origin, asking yourself how it came to be and in what ways it was made, you will say that some of it is common law and some of it statute law. If you look at the matters with which it deals, and examine its content, you will say that some of it is primary or constitutional law and some of it secondary or ordinary law; and dividing the latter again, according to its subject-matter and content, you will go on to say that some of it is criminal and some of it civil law. But all the divisions, taken together, are one body of positive law, in the sense of a body of legal rules actually "set" and actively enforced.

But is that the whole of the matter? Is the notion of law exhausted by the conception of positive law? Here we are faced by the question whether there does not exist, side by side with the positive law which contains and expresses actual validities, another law which contains and expresses ideal values (values, possibly, none the less real for being ideal): a law which we may call "natural" because it corresponds "to the nature of things" or to the nature of man (as a rational being living, or intended to live, in harmony with the rational nature of things): a law founded on what is right in itself, on what is just everywhere and at all times, on what is valuable whether or not it be valid. The question is as old as the *Antigone* of Sophocles; and Aristotle, in a passage of the *Rhetoric*, already supplied an answer. Distinguishing between "particular law," which is "the law defined and declared by each community for its own members," and the "universal law" of all mankind, he notes that the latter is "the law of nature; for there really exists, as all of us in some measure divine, a natural form of the just and unjust which is common to all men, even when there is no community or contract to bind them to one another." He cites the lines of Sophocles:

> Not of today or yesterday its force:
> It springs eternal: no man knows its birth.

The answer thus suggested by Aristotle was further developed by the Stoic philosopher Zeno and the Stoic school which he founded; and it passed from the philosophy of the Stoics into the jurisprudence of Rome. By the side of the positive law, the *jus civile*, recognized and enforced on Romans by the courts of the *civitas Romana*, the Roman jurists, in process of time, set the conception of *jus naturale*. This *jus naturale* may be defined as a "law imposed on mankind by common human nature, that is by reason in response to human needs and instincts." But it is not "imposed" in the sense that it is an actual body of law, recognized as such and enforced as such in the Roman courts of law. It is a spirit rather than a letter: a spirit of "humane interpretation," present in the minds of jurists and judges, which affects the law that is actually enforced, but does so without being actual law in the strict sense of the word. Yet the fact remains that the Romans cherished the conception of a law distinct from the positive law of the state (even if it was a spirit rather than a written and visible letter); that they regarded this law as universal, because it came from man's common nature and extended its range to all mankind; and that they gave it the name of "natural" in contradistinction to the positive law which was the "artifact" of the civic community.

The distinction drawn by the Roman jurists was sharpened and hardened in the course of the ages. Natural law became something more than a spirit of humane interpretation, subtly penetrating and quietly affecting the administration of positive law. It became a separate and almost rival body of law, claiming recognition and demanding enforcement by itself and in its own virtue. Two different, and indeed opposed, forces, acting at different times, conspired to produce this consummation. On the one hand, the Catholic Church espoused the conception of natural law; and the force of religious faith added majesty to a law which the Church interpreted as drawing its origin, through man's divine faculty of reason, from the very being of God. On the other hand, and at a later date, the secular spirit of rational enlightenment equally adopted the conception; and during the seventeenth and eighteenth centuries the secular force of rationalism, expressed in what may be called the secular school of natural law, brought the principles of philosophy (Cartesian or Leibnizian) and the resources of logic to impress a new stamp of science on a law which was now interpreted in terms of reason and not of faith. Under such different auspices the natural law of mankind was made to confront the positive law of the state as something separate from it, something which might be opposed to it, and something which, in the event of such opposition, ought to be deemed superior to it. Laws became "two and two, one against another"; there was a natural law and a positive law, and the two might fail to meet.

We thus seem driven to ask ourselves, "Are there two separate laws, and is one of them 'against the other'?" To put the question in that way, and to attempt to think in those terms, is to run at once into heavy weather and to steer a difficult course. If the state is a legal association, it must have one law as the condition of being one legal association or state. If there were two laws, there would be two states; or at any rate every member of the state would be torn in two by the question, "Which law am I to obey?" Any theory of two separate laws is at once face to face with the possibility of a conflict between the two, and is thus confronted by the problem of finding a solution of the conflict. Theorists who gave their adhesion to the school of natural law were ready with their answer: in any case of conflict, natural law carried the day. Blackstone himself, in a passage of the Introduction to his *Commentaries* in which he is following, and even copying, a contemporary Swiss theorist of the school of natural law, can lay it down that "the law of nature . . . is of course superior in obligation to any other . . . no human laws are of any validity if contrary to this." The difficulty of such an answer was that there was no certain and known body of natural law; and even if there had been, there was no established system of courts to give it recognition and enforcement. In practice two things happened, which themselves conflicted with one another. In normal times it was allowed that positive law, as being known and enforceable, must necessarily prevail. In revolutionary times, as for instance during the American Revolution and the issue of the Declaration of Independence, an appeal was made from positive law to the "evident truths" contained in "the laws of Nature and of Nature's God"; and popular resistance was used to enforce the appeal to these truths. But a law (or laws) which operates only in revolutionary times, and operates then to overturn the state, can hardly be law in any real sense of the word. Real law must be constantly operative, and it must at once sustain the state and be sustained by the state.

We may therefore put the question which confronts us in a different form. Instead of asking whether there are two laws, "one against another," we may begin by assuming that there is only one law, in any real sense of the word, and that this is the positive law which is actually imposed upon us, as members of a state, by the definite declaration and specific recognition of the organs of that state, legislative and judicial, and by the process of continuous enforcement which they apply. But having made that assumption we may then proceed to ask whether there are not two sources of this one law: (1) the personal source of a human authority (which may, in the last analysis, be the authority of the community itself, acting through organs evolved by it for the purpose of declaring, recognizing, and enforcing its own sense of the necessary rules of its common life); and (2) the impersonal source of an inherent rightness or justice, which adds to a law proceeding from the personal source of a human authority the further strength of a sense that it is right and just in itself, apart from, and over and above, the fact of its being declared to be law. If we make this distinction, we may say that authority gives validity to law, and justice gives it value. A law has validity, and I am legally obliged to obey it, if it is declared, recognized, and enforced as law by the authority of the legally organized community, acting in its capacity of a state. A law has value, and I am bound to obey it not only legally, and not only by an outward compulsion, but also morally and by an inward force, if it has the inherent quality of justice. Ideally law ought to have both validity and value. We may even say that it is only because law, *as a whole and in its general nature*, possesses both attributes, that it actually operates and is actually effective. At the same time we must recognize that, for the purposes of the legal association, it is sufficient that a law has validity, and we are legally bound to obey it if only it has that attribute. Though law as a whole, and in its general nature, has both validity and value, any particular law may have only validity. But that is enough to involve an absolute *legal* obligation.

3. THE MEANING AND ORIGIN OF THE IDEA OF JUSTICE

It has already been noted that the root idea of the word *jus*, and therefore also of the words *justus* and *justitia*, is the idea of joining or fitting, the idea of a bond or tie. Primarily, the joining or fitting implied in this root idea is that between *man and man* in an organized system of human relations. But we may also conceive of the "just" and "justice" as connected with, and expressed in, a joining or fitting between *value and value* in a general sum and synthesis of values. We recognize a number of different values as necessary to an organized system of human relations. There is the value of liberty; there is the value of equality; there is the value of fraternity, or (as it may also be called, and is perhaps better called) cooperation. All these values are present in any system of law; but they are present in different degrees at different periods of time, and there is a constant process of adjustment and readjustment between their claims. The claims of liberty have to be adjusted to those of equality; and the claims of both have also to be adjusted to those of cooperation. From this point of view the function of justice may be said to be that of adjusting, joining, or fitting the different political values. Justice is the reconciler and the synthesis of political values; it is their union in an adjusted and integrated whole; it is, in Aristotle's words, "What answers to the whole of goodness . . . being the exercise of goodness as a whole . . . towards one's neighbour" [*Ethics* 1130b 18–19]. We must presently inquire into each of the values. But before we can do so, it is necessary to inquire into the origin and nature of the general notion of justice—the notion of the "first" or "total" value in which the others are all combined, by which they are all controlled, and in virtue of which their different claims (if and so far as a conflict arises) are reconciled and adjusted.

How do we discover, and from what source do we draw, the total notion of justice—the general and controlling idea of the right and the just—which we feel that the law of the state should express? We acknowledge that justice will justify law to us; we admit that, in virtue of this justification, it finally ties and obliges us to law. But what is the source of its justifying grace and obliging power? . . .

7. ETHICS AS THE ORIGIN OF THE IDEA OF JUSTICE

Can we find this principle [i.e., the origin of the idea of justice] in ethics? If we answer in the affirmative, the moral standard of the community, precipitated in and enforced by the general moral conscience, will be the source of a notion of justice, containing a system or synthesis of values, which will be in its turn the impersonal source of positive law. We shall accordingly hold that if law is to have value as well as validity—value all round, and not some single "broken arc" of value called by the name of "solidarity" or by some other such name—it must satisfy, in the last resort, the demands of the general moral conscience, issuing and expressed in a general all-round notion of what is just and right in the conduct of human relations. In order that law may be valid, it is enough that it should satisfy the canon of declaration, recognition, and enforcement by a constituted authority acting on behalf of the community. In order that it may have value, over and above validity, law must also satisfy—*as much as it can, and so far as its strength avails*—the canon of conformity to the demands of moral conscience as expressed in the general notion of justice. In other words, and in simpler terms, law will have value only if it expresses and realizes—*so far as it can and in such ways as it can*—a rule of right for human relations ultimately derived from ethics. Here we touch a difficulty, which the provisos already stated are meant to meet in advance. Law is not ethics; and legality, or obedience to law, is not the same as morality. Law is concerned with external acts, and its demands are satisfied by such acts because they are all that its sanctions, themselves external acts of physical compulsion, can possibly secure. Ethics is concerned not only with external acts, but also with internal motive: its essence, as Aristotle said, is "a state of character, concerned with choice," which is freely determined in its choice by its own internal motive; and the demands of ethics are not satisfied unless an internal motive is present as well as an external act. An act is legal, whatever its motive, so long as it is the act demanded by the law. An act is not moral, whatever its outward show may be, if it is not inspired by an internal motive and does not proceed from a "state of a character concerned with choice."

But though we must draw a distinction between the nature of ethics and the nature of law, it does not follow that such a distinction abolishes any relation. Law and ethics are both concerned with what should be, and they both speak in the imperative mood: they both deal, in the main, with identical areas of life—marriage and its sanctities, the keeping of faith and the honoring of pledges, the duty of consideration for others, and man's general duty to his neighbor. How shall we express their relation? We may attempt two alternative methods of expression, and seek to discover which of the two expresses the relation best.

The first method of expression is based on the fact that law is a uniform rule of action binding on all men alike. Men in general run through the whole gamut of the moral scale: some act on this, and some on that standard; one standard is lower, and another higher. What law does, it may be argued, is to establish a moral minimum which every man must attain. It establishes, as it were, a lowest common measure of conduct which all can compass and which can therefore be made a uniform rule of action for all. If law bids me attach and keep burning a rear light on my bicycle when I am riding it in the dark, that is a lowest common measure of consideration for others, and it may, as such, be legally imposed. If law proceeds to fine me for riding without a rear light, it stimulates me into a disposition to obey the moral minimum—a disposition which itself is not moral (even though it results in obedience to the moral rule of consideration for others) because it is based on the negative and nonmoral factor of force, and not on the positive and moral factor of an inward motive of spontaneous consideration. Law, when it is so considered, may be regarded as a schoolmaster to bring us to morality, through the enforcement of habits of action by the use of coercive discipline.

But there is an obvious objection to this view of law. A moral minimum, enforced by nonmoral means, may have *some* relation to ethics; but it is not a relation which can stand the test of scrutiny, or prove itself to be anything more than a superficial relation. If law is connected with ethics in the sense that it is meant to enforce the rules of ethics on some sort of common standard, ought not the standard initially to be something higher than a mere minimum, and ought we not to be constantly engaged in screwing the strings tighter and tighter, in order to produce a fuller and truer note? And, even more, ought not the standard, whatever its pitch, to be enforced by means, such as reformatory punishment and moral education, which will themselves have a moral quality because they tend to promote a moral disposition? These questions suggest that if once we adopt the idea that law is a moral minimum, we shall soon be led to seek to obliterate any distinction between law and ethics, and to substitute law for ethics, with the result of eliminating ethics.

We may therefore turn to another method of expressing the relation between law and ethics. This second method, like the first, is based on the fact that law deals only with men in the mass, and is in its nature no more than a uniform rule of action binding equally on all alike. But the corollary which we now draw from that fact is that the only thing which law can get from man in the mass is external conduct, because the only thing which it can apply to men in the mass is external force. From this point of view, and bearing in mind the word "external," we arrive at another method of expressing the relation between law and ethics. We conclude that law is related to ethics in the sense that it seeks to secure the set of external conditions necessary for moral action, or the general framework of external order in which the moral conscience can act and determine itself most easily and most freely. Law, from this point of view, is not the lowest common measure of ethics, or the lowest story in the house of ethics: it is rather the best and highest set of conditions, set round the house and forming, as it were, a fence for its protection, which has to be assembled, and firmly established, before moral action can find a free space for its play and in order that moral development may unfold its energies freely. All moral development is inevitably confronted by external obstacles or hindrances: it is the function of law "to remove the obstacles" or "hinder the hindrances."

The law relating to education, as it has been gradually assembled and established in England since 1870, may be cited as an example. Moral development requires—the more as the world grows older, fuller of accumulated knowledge, and fuller, too, of complications alike in the social structure and the material environment of life—a period of initiation in the fund of accumulated knowledge, and a period of introduction to all the complications of structure and environment. This initiation and introduction is what we call education. But the process of education is confronted by possible obstacles. The state has sought by means of its law to remove those obstacles progressively. First, there is the obstacle that there may not be schools enough to provide education for all. The state, which had already been acting, through the law of the budget, to aid the establishment of voluntary schools, proceeded in 1870 to establish by law an additional and general system of schools provided entirely from its own funds. Next, there is the obstacle that parents may not be willing, if the matter is left to their choice, to send their children to school. The state, which had already enacted in 1870 that the "school boards" charged with the establishment of schools might, if they wished, make attendance at schools compulsory in their area, proceeded by a law of 1880 to make attendance compulsory everywhere up to a given age. Here we may say, from one point of view (the point of view of the parents), that the law established a moral minimum, by making it the legal duty of parents to do for their children, for a prescribed period, what parents are morally bound to do as long as they possibly can; but from another point of view (the point of view of the children), which is the essence of the matter, we have to say that the law removed an obstacle, and hindered a hindrance, by clearing away from their path a hurdle which would have impeded, or even blocked, their development. Finally, there is the obstacle that parents may not have the means to pay for their children's education, even though they are under compulsion to send their children to school. The state, which had already enacted in 1870 that "school boards" might remit fees in cases of poverty, proceeded in 1891 to make remission of fees the general rule, and thus to make the compulsory period of education free and gratuitous as well as compulsory. In effect, it pooled the payment of fees among all the members of the community; it removed the obstacle to a child's development arising from his parents' want of means by making it the legal duty of all to provide the means.

In the whole of this process the driving force and the ultimate purpose is thus the growth of the child, during and through a preliminary period of initiation and introduction, into the stature of a free and responsible moral agent. But if that is the ultimate purpose which is served by law, the fact remains that law serves the purpose only by removing obstacles, and only by securing, in virtue of such removal, the presence of the external conditions which make development possible. The development itself must proceed from within; it must be self-moved and spontaneous; otherwise it will not be moral development. We may thus say of education, when we consider it in its essence as a process of moral development in which teachers and children cooperate that it lies outside the law and is free from the arm of the state. It is not the business of law, or of any legal authority, to control the inner life of the process of education. It is only the business of law, and of any legal authority (even if it be called an education authority), to secure the external conditions of a process which, in itself, is necessarily independent of law and legal authority.

It follows from the course of the argument that if we have to choose between two conceptions of law—the conception which makes the purpose of law consist in the provision of a moral minimum, and the conception which makes it consist in the maximum provision of the external conditions which make moral development possible—we are bound to choose the second, and we are bound to choose it for the simple reason that it connects law and ethics more intimately, and more truly, than the first can ever do. Law which is conceived as a moral minimum suffers itself from being viewed as a minimum; and it makes morality suffer, by appearing to provide in its place a sort of low-grade substitute. Law which is conceived as the maximum provision of the external conditions of morality gains itself by being viewed as a maximum; and it also makes morality gain because it opens a freer field for its exercise, making it able to do its own work with less hindrance and fewer obstacles. It may even be said, in a paradox, that we connect law and ethics the more closely, the more clearly we distinguish their provinces. We separate them clearly if we define the one as the province of voluntary self-determination, with innumerable springs of individual initiative, and the other as the province of obligatory action, governed by uniform rules flowing in their set channels from a single central source. But we also connect the provinces which we have begun by distinguishing, and we connect them closely and intimately, if we add that it is the business of the province of law to defend and extend the province of morality—to defend it, in the present, by providing the conditions now demanded for its free play; to extend it, for the future, by increasing the provision of those conditions as new demands arise both from the development of social structure and from changes of material environment. To stand outside in self-restraint, and yet to defend with power—to be separate and yet connected—such is the relation of law to morality.

On this basis the law of the state will be careful not to diminish the area of moral autonomy in the process of extending the area of legal automatism. If the state attempts to increase the area of the compulsory action—the area of law and coercion—by bringing into it actions which might have been safely left to voluntary self-determination, it is offending against the nature of law and the true relation of law to morality. It is indeed a safe rule for the state that it should always command and enforce by law any act which ought so much to be done that it had better be done under coercion than not be done at all; but it is equally a safe rule for the state that it should not, in seeking to secure the conditions of goodness, diminish the area of goodness itself. On the contrary, an increase of compulsion at one point should always result in a more than proportionate increase of freedom at others; for an increase of freedom which was merely equivalent to the loss involved by the change would merely leave things as they were, and afford no justification for the change which was being made. The law of education may once more be cited in evidence. A law which makes the attendance of children at school compulsory brings their parents, in that respect, into the area of legal coercion, and diminishes, to that extent, the area of free goodness; but the education of the child is so vitally important a condition of his own moral development, and the total area of free goodness may be so much extended by the compulsory provision of the condition, that the price may safely be paid.

8. INDIVIDUAL PERSONALITY AND SOCIAL ORGANIZATION

The course of the argument has led to the conclusion that the idea of justice, which is the impersonal source of law, is an idea which itself has its source in ethics and ethical principles. But the foundation of ethics, and the source of all ethical principles, is the value and the worth of individual personality. The moral world is a world of individual persons, each intrinsically valuable, but all existing in time, and all accordingly subject to the conditions of a time-process. The intrinsic value of each personality is the basis of political thought, just as (and just because) it is the basis of moral thought; and worth of persons—individual persons; *all* individual persons—is the supreme worth in the state. Existing under, and subject to, the conditions of a time process, these persons—not fixed substances, but so many *growing* nuclei—are engaged in a motion of development, which is the turning of capacity into energy or (as we may also say) of "potency" into "act." The end of any national society is to foster and encourage, in and through partnership, the highest possible development of all the capacities of personality in all of its members; and this end is the justice, or "right ordering," of such a society, and may accordingly be called by the name of social justice. Similarly the end of any legal association or state, which is based and superimposed on a national society, is to assemble and establish the external conditions required by every citizen for the development of his capacities; and this end is the justice, or right ordering, of such a legal association, and may accordingly be called legal justice.

The formula here suggested—the highest possible development of all the capacities of personality in all the members of society—was foreshadowed in a formula of the eighteenth century. That formula, which would appear to have been invented by Francis Hutcheson, sometime professor of moral philosophy in the University of Glasgow, but which was afterwards adopted and popularized by Bentham and his disciples, was "the greatest happiness of the greatest number." It is a shadow of the truth; but it is also a dangerous shadow. If happiness, as it readily may be, is identified with pleasure, and thus made to consist in a surplus of sensations of pleasure over sensations of pain, it becomes the end of society and the state to secure for as many persons as possible, and in as great a degree as possible, the presence of a static condition of pleasurable sensation. This is the filling of a sieve with water. Owing to the law of satiety, which means that a continuing pleasure is a continually less pleasure, there will always be a leakage of pleasurable sensation; and the static condition will not even be static. In any case, and even if it were possible to prevent it from deteriorating and running backward, . . . a static condition is not in harmony with the conditions of the time-process to which man is subject; nor does the human faculty of judgment, which recognizes values and applies them *in foro conscientiae*, assign most value to the person most steadily enjoying most pleasure with the minimum of leakage. A personality dynamically developing all its capacities in a constant progression is a better answer to the process of time and a greater satisfaction to our sense of values; and our formula of social and legal justice, or the right ordering of society and the state, will accordingly be the highest possible development of capacity in the greatest possible number of persons. . . .

Inevitability and the Sense of Injustice*

BARRINGTON MOORE, JR.

1. INTRODUCTORY OBSERVATIONS

A S W E A P P R O A C H T H E end of a long journey I would like to return with the reader to concerns that have impelled us to make the journey together. What is moral outrage? Under what conditions does it occur? When and why does it not occur? It is something natural to all human beings? If so, what does "natural" really mean? Is not the apparent absence of a sense of injustice even more significant that its appearance? Though [my] book [*Injustice: The Social Bases of Obedience and Revolt*] has explored these questions, its author does not pretend to have provided definitive answers if definitive implies the kind of answer that will persuade and satisfy everybody. Nor do I intend to present in conventional capsule form here what has been discussed at greater length throughout the book. Instead I propose to explore once again how the sense of injustice does make its appearance, drawing on the material we have covered together and whatever considerations I myself can contribute.

Let us begin by asking if there might be some common themes that appear in the behavior of Hindu Untouchables, steelworkers in the Ruhr before 1914, Ulrich Braker's inability to get angry at the patron who sold him as a mercenary to the armies of Frederick the Great, the awe of the Spartacists before stamps and signatures, the self-inflicted tortures of ascetics, and the reactions of human beings upon whom the Nazis inflicted the trauma of the concentration camps. In varying degrees and in different ways all these people felt that their sufferings were unavoidable. For some victims such suffering appeared to a degree inevitable and legitimate. People are evidently inclined to grant legitimacy to any-thing that is or seems inevitable no matter how painful it may be. Otherwise the pain might be intolerable. The conquest of this sense of inevitability is essential to the development of politically effective moral outrage. For this to happen, people must perceive and define their situation as the consequence of human injustice: a situation that they need not, cannot, and ought not to endure. By itself of course such a perception, be it a novel awakening or the content of hallowed tradition, is no guarantee of political and social changes to come. But without some very considerable surge of moral anger such changes do not occur.

It is tempting to posit a straightforward reaction of pain and anger at the blows inflicted by the physical and social environment, as the beginning of all human attempts to "do something" about whatever hurts. Undoubtedly the pain is there and an indispensable spur to action. There may even be an almost automatic angry response that is independent of whatever cultural conditioning and social standards the individual has acquired. Did anyone have to tell Thersites that soldiering for Agamemnon was no fun? Homer didn't think it was necessary to explain how he came to feel that way. The reaction of a poor foot soldier, dragged into a campaign in which he had no interest, was presumably as understandable to a Greek three thousand years ago as it is to us. What was remarkable to Homer's audience, and to us, is that Thersites had the audacity to stand up before Agamemnon and say to his fellow soldiers "Let us go back home in our ships, and leave this man here by himself in Troy. . . ." Such daring is indeed out of the ordinary.

Essentially our problem is to state what conditions may make such audacity possible—and effective. But we are not even safe in assuming that a person in the boots of Thersites or someone like him will even *feel* the anger, far less speak his mind about it. The notion that there is some indomitable spirit of revolt in all human beings is, I fear, sheer myth. As the material from the concentration camps shows, it is possible to destroy any such spirit and even the will to survive. Admittedly, that is an extreme case, and not all inmates by any means re-sponded in this fashion. Still the evidence there is enough to show that any inclination toward anger, and even the capacity to feel pain, can vary over a wide range to the point of complete extinction.

The most that one can assert with considerable confidence is that suffering in the forms of hunger, physical abuse, or deprivation of the fruits of hard work is indeed objectively painful for human beings. They do not seek suffering for its own sake. Even ascetics impose suffering on themselves for the sake of other goals, such as salvation, release from social obligations, or control of the universe. In the objective quality of suffering our search does reach a point that can serve as a firm basis for departure. If no culture makes suffering an end in itself and all cultures treat certain forms of suffering as inherently painful, we are justified in considering the absence of felt pain as due to some form of moral and psychological anesthesia. From this standpoint the assertion that there is no indomitable spirit of revolt takes on a different meaning. It means that under certain specifiable sociological and psychological conditions the anesthesia can be terribly effective.

How does the introduction of an historical perspective alter our understanding of social anesthesia? Historical analysis brings into the center of our vision the importance of improving capacities to control the natural and social environment along with the apparently endless chain of new causes of human suffering that this improvement produces, and the related changes in the principles of social inequality. It will be necessary to return to these issues again. It is a perspective that raises the question of whether we can legitimately speak of historically necessary forms of anesthesia. These could be connected with aspects of human suffering for which human society generally had not yet developed adequate techniques to control or eliminate. The control of diseases seems to be the clearest example. For historically necessary forms of suffering then there is nothing human beings can do but endure the pain or resort to such forms of cultural anesthesia as magic and religion. At any given stage of human development there would also be historically unnecessary—or historically futile— forms of suffering, that is, those that people could eliminate but fail to do so, presumably due to the opposition of vested interests. Thus in any concrete case we would have to ask, historically necessary for whom and why?

There are potentially dangerous pitfalls in the use of the concept of historical necessity, some of which have turned up in earlier chapters [of Injustice]. Others it will be better to defer to a more appropriate context. By asking to whom the necessity applies and who gets what out of its application, it is possible to avoid the pitfalls and retain the kernel of antiutopian truth: not everything is possible all of the time.

That will do as a preliminary outline of the theoretical dangers. The task at hand is to determine how human beings awake from anesthesia, how they overcome the sense of inevitability and how a sense of injustice may take its place. The situation of the Hindu Untouchables, one of maximum acceptance of servile status with a minimum of force, may serve to illustrate the type of starting point in which we are mainly interested. In milder forms the same feelings and social relationships are quite plain in the case of Ulrich Braker, the steelworkers of the Ruhr, and countless others. On further inspection and reflection they cease to seem in any way bizarre. Instead they are instances of responses to one of the oldest and commonest of human experiences, generalized patriarchal authority. In this prototypical experience the young person *wants* to please the father, even if hatred may also exist. There is an exchange of dependence, services, and childlike trusting adoration in return for care, protection, and another type of affection. In daily life one can see the essence of the relationship in the behavior of a dog toward its master.

I do not know whether dogs can develop a rudimentary sense of injustice if their masters mistreat them. Quite possibly experimental psychologists have demonstrated something of the sort. Quite obviously human beings can and do develop it. In this process of growth and emancipation one can discern three distinguishable but related processes. At the level of the individual human personality it is necessary to overcome certain forms of dependence on others and acquire or strengthen controls over impulses. This dependence and lack of control, to the extent that it actually exists and is not merely a rationalization for the authority of the dominant strata, is likely to be one aspect of psychological adaptation to the fact of subordination and powerlessness. In effect, people have to grow up.

At the level of social organization they also have to overcome dependence. Here the historical component becomes more obvious, due to the ways in which economic and political forms (in Europe, for example: city-state, feudalism, royal absolutism, capitalism, state socialism) have succeeded each other. As part of the process of overcoming dependence there may be the creation of new forms of solidarity and new networks of cooperation if the subordinate group was composed of atomized units. If, on the other hand, it was already a cohesive unit with a high degree of internal cooperation and sentiments of solidarity, this solidarity may require redirection. Instead of working in cooperation with and support of the dominant groups, it will be necessary to find ways to turn it against these groups. Instead of solidarity in adopting heroic gestures that endanger the group, it will be necessary to find ways to support effective resistance. Finally, at the level of cultural norms and shared perceptions, it will be necessary to overcome the illusion that the present state of affairs is just, permanent, and inevitable. The historical component is crucial in this area too. What is an illusion at one point in time will not have been an illusion at an earlier point. Economic and social trends have to develop to a point where the possibilities change, where what was reality becomes illusion. It is vastly easier for historians to explain the illusion convincingly after the event than for social prophets to proclaim the event convincingly before it happens. It is harder still to tell exactly whose reasoning is correct. . . .

3. SOCIAL ASPECTS

Let us now therefore focus on the social and economic aspects of how a social order that appears more or less inevitable to the underlying population may lose all or part of this aura. Once again, but with attention directed to different variables and processes, the task is to understand how standards of condemnation arise and through what kinds of social organization human beings put them into effect. I shall concentrate almost entirely on urban populations, drawing only occasionally on agrarian experiences for comparative purposes.

The first essential ingredient for the whole process is a rather rapid improve-ment in a society's capacity to produce goods and services, enough to make it appear possible to "solve" the problem of poverty as it has been traditionally defined. One could go further and assert that the improvement must be enough to make poverty appear as a *problem* and not part of the natural order of the universe. Such a transformation, it is worth emphasizing again, has occurred only once on this scale in human history and only very recently.

It is possible to imagine an improvement in a society's capacity to produce and exchange goods and services taking place in such a way that all sectors of the population make equal gains and therefore without generating any pressures for institutional changes. Conceivably that could happen somewhere in the future. But it has not happened anywhere yet, and is highly unlikely because any such improvement is almost certain to bring in its train significant changes in the division of labor and hence in systems of authority, as well as in the procedures for distributing goods and services among the population. That is one reason why Marxists regard changes in economic structure as over the long haul the basic causes of other social changes, including moral standards.

There is another good reason behind the Marxist position. Changes in ideas and ideals will not be feasible until and unless there are changes in a society's capacity to reduce its level of socially necessary misery, based on an increase in productivity. Without this increase in economic potential, ideas of liberation can be no more than intellectual dreams and playthings for a limited number of people. The same may not be necessarily true for repressive notions about how to intensify subjection and submission, though on this score too advancing technology has made available new and alarming possibilities.

Nevertheless the Marxist position is open to serious criticism when it asserts, as Marx himself occasionally did, that economic changes necessarily *cause* intellectual and social changes. Sometimes they may and sometimes not, and the causation can also run in the opposite direction. Economic institutions have often been adapted to military, political, and even religious considerations. Systems of ideas and cultural meanings also display a dynamic of change quite on their own that may have very significant consequences for economic institu-tions. That changes in economic arrangements are a necessary condition for successful change in, say, law, morals, and religious beliefs is not the same thing as asserting that economic changes are always the causes for the latter. Universal propositions about the primacy of economic changes, even when qualified by the useful escape clause "in the long run," are to be rejected out of hand.

Granting and even emphasizing that ideas cannot become effective without economic (and other) changes, there is still an important positive point to be made. Without strong moral feelings and indignation, human beings will not act against the social order. In this sense moral convictions become an equally necessary element for changing the social order, along with alterations in the economic structure. The history of every major political struggle reflects the clash of passions, convictions, and systems of belief. That is plain as far back as the historical record will take us, back to the Hebrew prophets, back even to the struggles of Ikhnaton, beyond which the record begins to fade. Convictions are also probably necessary for a society to continue to work along customary lines, though that is harder to demonstrate. People may be able to continue to behave according to familiar routines in a rather cynical and desultory fashion with only small cues from their associates to indicate what is expected from them. In a crisis or novel situation, on the other hand, their reactions are liable to be unpredictable, at which point collapse and chaos may set in.

For reasons mentioned a moment ago it is highly unlikely that the benefits of a rise in productive capacity will benefit all sectors of a society equally. A rise in productive capacity is not the same thing as a change in a society's capacity to solve its own problems—or again more accurately to make long-standing causes of human suffering *become* problems. It is only one indispensable contribution to this capacity. For the desire to make use of this potential, or for standards of condemnation to arise and take hold, other things have to happen, and often do happen.

The next ingredient, which appears to be an indispensable as well as a frequently observed one, is a marked increase in the suffering of the lower strata. For standards of condemnation to take hold, the suffering has to increase rapidly enough so that people do not have time to become accustomed to it. It will be necessary to go into this aspect more thoroughly later. It is important that the apparent causes of the suffering be new and unfamiliar, traceable to the acts of concrete, easily identified persons. That such judgments have often been mistaken goes without saying. It is the consequences that matter from the standpoint of this inquiry.

In this form of suffering the disruption of the social organization is probably more significant in its political consequences than straightforward material deprivation, painful though the latter undoubtedly is. For the individual the disruption means the collapse or at least partial breakdown of familiar daily routines. Artisans and sellers lose their customers; new forms of "unfair" competition appear; others start hoarding; it becomes hard to find food, or to pay for it if it can be found. Crop failures in an economy still vulnerable to them can greatly intensify the disruption. By itself disruption may cause nothing more than apathy, confusion, and despair. If it is liable to make a population more malleable, it can make it malleable to new and oppressive forms of authority. We have seen that happen in the case of the Nazis, and something of the sort apparently played a part in the submission of the German iron and steelworkers to their fate. The destruction of the social framework supporting traditional morality and expectations does not automatically mean that better ones will take their place. In fact the complete destruction of existing institutions and habits of cooperation may make resistance impossible, indeed unthinkable, by destroying the basis from which it can start.

For changes that will reduce human suffering, other things have to happen. The disruption has to spread to the dominant classes and split them in such a way that alliances can be formed between elements in both the dominant and subordinate classes. One reason the Revolution of 1848 in Germany produced so few results is that this realignment did not occur. At the same time, for standards of condemnation to take form, some elements in the dominant classes must appear as parasitic to the lower classes, as making no contribution to the workings of the social order and hence as violating the implicit social contract. In this connection it would be enlightening to investigate more carefully the historical development of popular attitudes toward effort—the intensity of work rather than work itself—to see if there has not been up until quite recent times a steadily increasing value put upon this quality.

Where the causes of misery appear to the sufferers as due to the acts of identifiable superiors, such as employers or prominent officials, in the early stages these acts are likely to appear too as violations of established rights and norms, again a breaking of the established social contract. Petitions for redress, addressed to still higher authority, are therefore a characteristic first response. The supreme authority appears as a benevolent paternal figure who needs only to hear about injustice in order to correct it. This reaction was widespread in Germany, but by no means confined to that country or cultural milieu. In other situations there may be blind outbursts of rage at the violation of norms of conduct and reward that human beings always create in the course of antagonistic cooperation in the place of work. The final cry of poor Karl Fischer, "There is no order here!" comes to mind as a sad, vivid example. For such persons the world has gotten out of joint—it is a cry against essential unfairness.

For large numbers of people the world does get out of joint in the sense that they lose any regular respected and moderately secure status in it, even if their services in the form of brute physical labor power remain necessary. Though it is important to avoid romanticizing the security of the lower classes in premodern times, there is no reason to doubt that this process of atomization and degradation has taken place on a very wide scale. While the process may create some additional raw material for urban riots, its consequences for the social order do not by themselves appear to be very significant. Riots can be controlled by disciplined troops relatively easily. Indeed I would hazard the generalization that the formation of a large body of semi-outsiders, or proletariat, constitutes one of the least politically effective forms of human misery, as well as possibly the most painful. To be sure, the mere presence of this kind of a prefactory proletariat can and did frighten the upper classes all over Europe in the early stages of industrialization. De Tocqueville in his *Souvenirs* reveals the horror and revulsion that many in the upper classes must have felt at this apparition from the depths during the rising in Paris in 1848. That rising on the other hand came to nothing, and General Cavaignac, perhaps the first of a sinister line of modern saviors of civilization, brutally stamped out its last flames a few months later. After 1848 the danger was past. The Russian Revolution was to come from quite a different constellation of forces: the grievances of land-short peasants and industrial workers in big factories in a few key cities.

Once a critical mass of potentially discontented people has come into exis-tence through the working out of large-scale institutional forces the stage is set for the appearance of "outside agitators." It is important to recognize the crucial significance of their role because social critics are inclined to minimize it for fear of carrying water to the mills of conservatism and reaction. Since the time of the Apostles, and perhaps earlier, no social movement has been without its army of preachers and militants to spread the good tidings of escape from the pains and evils of this world. It is always an activist minority that promotes and pro-mulgates new standards of condemnation. They are an indispensable if insuf-ficient cause of major social transformations, peaceful and gradualist as well as violent or revolutionary. Generally they are relatively young and unencumbered by social ties and obligations. That is one more indication of the importance of social and cultural space, to be discussed shortly. Very frequently they are outsiders to the locality in which they serve. Their task is to find and articulate latent grievances, to challenge the dominant mythology, to organize for a contest with the dominant forces around them. The outside agitators do the hard work of undermining the old sense of inevitability. They are also the traveling salesmen for the new inevitability. In human affairs it requires tremendous effort to produce the inevitable, new or old, and no one is quite sure of what the new one will look like until after it has already happened. By then it is, generally too late.

The weakness of any collective consciousness and social organization beyond the narrow confines of neighborhood and occupation in the Paris of 1848 may have contributed to the failure of that uprising. Be that as it may, the point to be emphasized is that the new forms of collective action that grow up in an urban context, revolutionary parties and trade unions, display a strong tendency to come to terms with the status quo.

One clear reason for this widespread turn to a gradualist and reformist strategy is the experience of defeat in revolutionary uprisings. Gradualism, reformism, and the techniques of legitimate opposition do not arise out of some innate process of maturing or even out of situations where there gets to be so much to go around that fighting ceases to be attractive and worthwhile. An increase in the size of the social product to be divided up may indeed be a helpful ingredient in domestic tranquillity. But the historical record shows that even in England, and still more so on the continent, suppression prepared the way for negotiation and bargaining. For the weaker contestants gradualism was not the virtue in its own right that it became for the dominant classes; it was a virtue forced upon them by necessity.

By this observation I do not mean to imply that even in this early stage of development there was among the lower strata in the cities any powerful revolutionary impulse that was somehow stifled and diverted. Both the liberal and the Marxist models of characteristic working-class development seem to me misleading because they are too schematic and fail to capture the most important variables. According to the liberal view, the trauma of industrialization in its early phase is liable to create more or less irrational radical demands. With the passage of time and rising productivity the workers learn the virtue of collective bargaining and democratic pressure-group tactics and thus become peaceably incorporated into a system of liberal capitalism. There follows the demise of ideology. According to the Marxist scheme, the workers start from a generally inert situation, capable at most of occasional acts of instinctive revolt. Through the experience of industrialization, which brings them together in huge factories to impose upon them a common fate, they acquire a revolutionary class consciousness. This form of consciousness amounts to an awareness of their crucial role in the whole historical process as perceived and outlined by Marx, and a willingness to act on this awareness at the crucial historical moment. Though in Lenin's variant the awareness would not come of itself but had to be brought to the workers from the outside by intellectuals who had turned into professional revolutionaries, the experience of factory life under capitalism was a necessary prerequisite for the masses to undergo this *crise de conscience* with the help of the intellectuals.

The German evidence made it necessary to reject both the Leninist interpretation and one that looks toward an independent capacity among industrial workers for general solutions to the problems of industrial society. To the extent that it is possible to discern mass reactions and attitudes, there is very little indication of a desire to overhaul the society. There can be at times a very large stockpile of anger. But this anger will not necessarily, and in fact in Germany did not, turn into a desire to make the world over, even in the form of quite simple egalitarian notions or a desire to have rich and poor change places. Certainly it did not turn into massive support for socialism, even at the height of the revolt in the Ruhr in 1920.

Insofar as the rank-and-file participants were concerned the revolt in the Ruhr was primarily a defensive spasm against the threat from rapidly reviving rightist forces. This strictly defensive aspect has been a major component in popular support for other revolutionary movements. In the Russian Revolution the workers' demands that surfaced after the Tsarist collapse were essentially defensive: they were not for a new social order, even if they helped to bring one about. And in China, in order to mobilize peasant support the Chinese Communists had to soft-pedal their revolutionary objectives and stress limited peasant grievances. These were objections to "bad" landlords, that is, those who failed to adhere to patriarchal standards of behavior and charged rents exceeding traditional norms. Communists generally are likely to claim that more radical demands were stifled under the weight of the traditional village structure dominated by more well-to-do peasants. But that is highly doubtful. In any case it is nonsense to consider modern revolutionary regimes as expressing the spontaneous feelings of the mass of the oppressed population. In both Russia and China the overwhelming mass of the population was, of course, peasants. The really revolutionary changes, the collectivization of agriculture, came about against the will of this mass. On this score the difference between Russia and China is one of degree. It is not a qualitative distinction.

What spontaneous general notions there were about the reordering of German society cropped up mainly among the artisans of 1848. Among the proletariat of that time there appears to have been nothing: they were inarticulate. Among the workers in the latter part of the nineteenth century, and down to the First World War, the reasons they gave for their anger and the remedies they sought were very specific to their own circumstances within specific industries. This industry-specific character and some of the general reasons for it appear very clearly from the contrast between the responses of the coalminers and the steelworkers to the experiences of industrialization. The experiences were broadly similar, the reactions very different and dependent on the social organization in the workplace and traditions about the nature of authority. The miners had their *Gedinge* and their *Berggesetz* and became very active. Lacking the cooperative relationships and norms emerging from teamwork in the *Gedinge*, and lacking the source of traditional legitimation for their grievances in the *Berggesetz*, the iron and steelworkers meekly accepted the authority of the employers. The standards of condemnation that workers develop spontaneously and the means that they use to put them into effect, it appears from this evidence, reflect the structure of cooperation or lack of it in the workplace, together with standards of legitimacy that also derive from experience but are considerably influenced by factors operating outside of the workers' own milieu.

To sum up provisionally, spontaneous conceptions among prefactory workers, factory workers, and modern revolutionary peasants have been mainly backward looking. They have been attempts to revive a social contract that had been violated. Most frequently they were efforts to remedy specific and concrete grievances in their particular occupation. The tremendous diversity in the forms of daily life created through modern industry has almost certainly been a major obstacle to collective action by industrial workers, an obstacle only rarely and briefly overcome during periods of intense crisis, such as defeat in war, that disrupt the daily routines of an entire population. Conceptions of justice and injustice appear as generalizations from daily experience without the features that would be painful for any human being not continually conditioned and reconditioned to put up with them. It is hard to see how people who have to devote most of their time and strength to their work—and on this score industrial society has been changing and promises to change further—could develop very different ideas. In this light the powerful defensive component in insurrection and revolution also becomes quite comprehensible. At the same time these considerations point to the need to be wary about talking in terms of the creation or discovery of new standards of condemnation—within or by the masses—to say nothing of revolutions of rising expectations. What is apparent here is rather the emergence to the surface of latent standards. Some are deeply embedded in a specific historical experience and set of institutions. Others appear to be more pan-human reactions that surface with the prospect that a long familiar system of domination may be breaking up. These latent standards are new only in the sense that human beings have become newly aware of them.

In other contexts, however, experience can lead to new reactions that do amount to novel standards of condemnation. Over time a substantial number of German workers did pass through the stages of appeals to paternalist authority, through organizing to defend and advance their own interests in unions, to participation in revolutionary movements. The key factor here is rather clearly disappointment: as each strategy failed to bring about the hoped-for results, the workers changed their strategy. Meanwhile the context within which they had to apply their strategy was of course changing. There are also changes in standards that come from increasing satisfaction. French nineteenth-century workers had no idea of annual paid vacations. For them such a prospect was almost certainly beyond imagining. Nowadays the sudden cancellation of vacations by the employers would appear as the acme of arbitrary injustice. And what group of workers in modern capitalist industry would put up with the long hours, arbitrary discipline, lack of procedure for the expression and settling of grievances, the absence of provisions for unemployment and other forms of social security, all of which were commonplace before the First World War?

Ideas about a new social order arose mainly among dissident intellectuals. In this sense the evidence, as I read it, fully supports the Leninist thesis that industrial workers on their own do not create anything except pure trade unionism. But it does not support the corollary that a vanguard party based on the workers can bring about either revolution or liberation. German intellectuals did establish a revolutionary party. Then pressure from the workers transformed it into a reformist one. As mentioned above, this happened partly because nothing else seemed possible. But it also happened because there was no pressure, at least none before 1914, from the advanced sector of the industrial proletariat to make it revolutionary. Industrialism killed the kind of revolutionary impetus that had existed in 1848. The miners were militant enough, especially the unorganized sector, but had essentially limited and very concrete demands. The steelworkers were inert. To be sure, the reformist character of other unions can often be traced to the survival of craft traditions and practices and the conservative, small-town atmosphere still widely characteristic of German industry and especially industry where the unions took hold. Nevertheless the situation in the Ruhr constitutes decisive evidence against the thesis that there was a substantial reservoir of revolutionary discontent waiting for the right leaders to tap it.

After the war there were mass uprisings in the more industrialized parts of Germany, as well as in Bavaria, which on the surface do look like massive support for revolutionary socialism. Certainly there were enough vocal spokesmen, enemies and leaders of these movements, who proclaimed that such was the case. Nevertheless the appearance dissolves on closer examination. The uprisings did not start on a wide scale until after January of 1919 and were in large measure a defensive response to justified fears of the return of the bad old days, or worse—a return to the old regime under the auspices of the SPD [Social Democratic Party of Germany] leaders in a de facto coalition with the military and support from right-wing business circles. In this sense the experiences of the war had indeed created, if not a clear desire for a new society, a definite unwillingness to return to the old one. The standards of condemnation had changed, but the change was, however, mainly negatively expressed: the workers knew what they did *not* want far more than what they *did* want. Except for a limited degree of socialization, the demands of rank-and-file workers, so far as they can be ascertained, were mainly defensive in character (such as the disarming of the *Freikorps* [an irregular force created by SPD leaders]) or else had to do with immediate and local grievances.

Looking at the process as a whole, we can see that the workers took what ideas and organizational help they wanted from the intellectuals and turned it to their own purposes. Unions were generally started up with outside help. On the other hand, if unions did not serve the workers' purposes, they soon withered and died. There was a process of interaction between workers and intellectuals in which the ideas of the intellectuals about changing the social order as a whole became transformed. Workers in the course of upward mobility in the unions and the Socialist Party became intellectuals of a new type, essentially pragmatic, bureaucratic politicians. These did develop a vision of society considerably wider than that of the workers at the bench. At the same time this process of organization produced a split between organized and unorganized workers, with the latter a constant danger to the former. In the whole process there was a strong element of straightforward group egoism. The interests of certain workers within the body of those in a particular trade or occupation tended to set the political tone. The political strategy did not reflect the interest of all the workers in the trade, certainly not all industrial workers, and even more certainly not that of society as a whole.

To assert that the workers took over and modified the ideas of the intellectuals is not to minimize the role of the latter. The existence of the SPD and even the unions is hard to imagine without the contribution of the intellectuals. These organizations had an influence on working-class lives far beyond the ways in which they affected dues-paying members. Intellectuals have had a very powerful influence on the standards of condemnation developed within the working class and the ways in which these standards were put into effect, even if this influence has been very different from that hoped for and at times claimed by revolutionary intellectuals. It was the intellectuals who brought to the workers the conception that human society *did* have a capacity to solve its own problems and who suggested the main ways of doing it. If the workers refused some of the suggestions, and by and large displayed a reluctance to become revolutionary cannon fodder for the sake of ideals they had not created out of their own experience, who can blame them for that?

Nor does the fact that factory workers so far have shown little inclination, and perhaps even little capacity, for generating wide-ranging answers for the problems that plague humanity mean that answers or important contributions to the answers can never come from that quarter. Educational levels are rising along with exposure to other currents in modern culture. Workers may become a conservative force similar to nineteenth-century peasants in Western Europe, anxiously clinging to the limited gains they have achieved at great cost, and fearful of forces in the modern world that threaten them. As long as capitalism works tolerably well, that could be the predominant trend. But there is no guarantee that capitalism will continue to work that way. In response to new and severe strains, equipped with a wider cultural horizon, industrial workers could generate a surge of popular inventiveness culminating in a wholly new diagnosis and remedy for social ills. . . .

5. Cultural Definitions of the Inevitable

. . . In the modern world, and apart from any meaning it may have in specialized philosophical and theological discourse, the word "inevitable" generally characterizes something painful or unpleasant like death and taxes about which human beings supposedly can do little or nothing. People put up with the inevitable as best they can, shrugging their shoulders, gritting their teeth, or steeling themselves to face a tragic event. When something is defined as inevitable, such as occasional bouts of bad weather, there may be some sense to making at least limited preparations and taking some precautions. At the same time the definition rules out any serious struggle, or at least any serious struggle with a prospect of victory. The notion of inevitability implies a conception of the universe ruled at least in part by blind forces of fates ultimately not responsive to human will and action.

This attempt to take a detached look at our own cultural definition of inevitability yields two problems worth pursuing here. In the first place it is quite apparent that the concept of inevitability has contained different things for different reasons at different points in history. What then have been the grounds for labeling certain forms of suffering inevitable and how have these grounds and methods of labeling altered? The second query is a more fundamental one. Do all human cultures have the category inevitability, but apply it to different things depending on their capacity to manage their natural and social environment? Or does the concept of inevitability itself, with its overtones of law and regularity, constitute some form of major historical breakthrough and cultural discovery?

In attempting to answer the second question first, let us take hunger and disease as concrete examples of suffering. Modern educated Westerners who possess a secular explanation and remedy for these misfortunes and disasters are disinclined to treat them as inevitable. Early human cultures, so far as we can make legitimate inferences about them from anthropological evidence— something that appears quite safe in this connection though not by any means in all—were much less inclined to use such principles for the simple reason that they had much less in the way of knowledge and resources at their disposal. Simple secular explanations were not of course completely lacking. Nonliterate peoples, for example, know that crops will not grow without planting seeds, that animals they hunt for food can generally be found in some places and seldom or never in others. Such peoples are often extremely acute at observing the natural environment and its meaning. They know that a broken twig means that game or a dangerous animal has passed that way recently, and can make many correct inferences of this sort that escape the literate man. They have to. But the resources for the application of secular rationality even in their own familiar environment are generally meager.

Where these fail them, they resort, as moderns do, to magic, incantation, and religion. Disease is the consequence of sorcery. Crop failure may be due to the inadequacy of the ruler. For that, as Fraser pointed out, it may be necessary and legitimate to kill the ruler. In these circumstances there is reason to doubt that such people had any concept of the inevitable at all. Where there is a magical remedy for every misfortune, it is hard to see how a general conception such as inevitability could arise. Though there might be at least rudimentary notions of cause and effect, the world would appear as subject to a series of ad hoc controls. If one of them fails to work, there is always the excuse that something went wrong in the attempt to apply the magic, or that someone used more powerful countermagic.

Thus it appears that the concept of inevitability is itself the product of a long historical evolution. While there is evidence for a secular and common-sense root at a later point, myth and religion, as Alfred North Whitehead pointed out in *Science and the Modern World*, had earlier made an indispensable contribution. From them came the idea of the working-out of overwhelming forces over long periods of time, though the capricious aspect by no means disappeared. To Whitehead's derivation of the concept of causality from Hebrew religion and Greek mythology one might add that a conception of causality both strengthens and undermines cultural definitions of inevitability: when one can learn about causes, there arises the possibility of changing and mastering trends and events. Myth and religion also seem to have intensified the connection between notions of causality, inevitability, and moral judgments. Here, too, as in the case of causality and inevitability an element of tension remained, insofar as moral condemnation implied the possibility that a human actor could have acted otherwise and therefore somehow had escaped from the chain of causality. These perplexities have by no means altogether vanished today, and the notion of inevitability still carries moral overtones. In their very different ways both conservatives and revolutionaries use the notion to buttress their own hopes for the future.

In preindustrial civilizations the moral aspect has always been decisive. Ordinary suffering of a chronic sort, the kind to which human beings teach themselves to adapt because it does seem unavoidable, is in such societies likely to appear as a fate that the individual deserves, one that is just and proper. At least the dominant strata will try to make it appear that way. In a stratified society the principles of social inequality, generally systematized by priests, explain and justify the more prevalent and routine forms of suffering. Since these principles also constitute the basic terms of the implicit or explicit social contract, there will be certain forms of suffering that both dominant and subordinate strata define as unjust and improper. Even in cases where force and fraud have played a major role in determining the respective roles of ruler and ruled, as in plantation slavery, there is a strong tendency for the social contract to reappear in actual practice. In these situations, therefore, there is a considerable moral component in the explanation of suffering. The challenge to this morality and this inevitability becomes a major political act. As the history of the iron and steelworkers in the Ruhr before 1914 suggests, human beings may have to be taught what their rights are. From this perspective, moral outrage becomes an historically acquired taste, one acquired in severe political struggles. Such struggles have been the major political fact of modern times. Hence it is worthwhile to stand back from the details once more in order to perceive the main features.

In eighteenth-century Europe and Asia social inequality took the form of estates or orders, ranked according to the esteem or social honor attributed to the social function of the males. There were of course many variations. Usually the warriors and the priests were the only ones marked off in a distinct fashion. The rest were mainly a residual category or series of residual categories, though the ranking might be more distinct again at the bottom, as in the outcastes of

Japan. Only in India was there an attempt by the priests to order the whole society by ranks.

Practice did not correspond to this theory; everywhere in Europe and Asia the ranking was hereditary either in practice or in theory. Some degree of mobility was also possible everywhere. In China membership in the mandarinate was theoretically open and achieved by passing the examinations. In practice economic barriers to learning made the mandarinate a hereditary stratum. In Europe the individual was *born* a member of the Church, but one *became* a bishop, or even a parish priest. There too economic barriers to education limited access to the higher ranks. For each estate there was a prescribed style of life, indicated by rules of etiquette, dress, and by other means. The purpose of economic activity was a moral one: to enable each estate to live according to its appropriate style. The lower orders were expected to provide the higher ones with the means for so living, while at the same time retaining enough from their efforts to maintain their own social honor. It is doubtful that this happened very frequently, and the definition of what peasants, the overwhelming majority of the population, ought to have was, to say the least, ambiguous.

For each estate or order the prescribed style of life specified a distinct and appropriate moral code, even in many cases a specific kind of personality. The warrior was expected to be brave and usually generous, the priest gentle, the artisan diligent. Naturally there were in practice many deviations from both the ideal personality and the ideal morality for each order. On the other hand, there were also strong social sanctions to prevent individuals from adopting a way of life inappropriate to their station, either in an upward or downward direction. Morality was explicitly socially determined, and though these systems were by no means totally inflexible, an air of permanence and inevitability did permeate them. Moral anger arose mainly from violations of the social contract, particularly against individuals who did not act in accord with the requirements of their status. But here and there, especially in the European heretical movements that drew on real or alleged memories of equality among the early Christians, there were stirrings of doubt about the terms of the contract itself.

Wherever it became possible to acquire wealth in a novel fashion, the consequence was to undermine the old principles of social inequality and the old assumptions of inevitability. The older elites appropriated wealth, of course, in a variety of ways. But where new methods became possible, at first mainly in commerce, they enabled upstarts to short-circuit the older arrangements. The newly rich could simply buy necessary perquisites for the manner of existence that had been the privilege of the dominant strata. As modernization gathered momentum and turned into the Industrial Revolution, the old principles disintegrated at certain points amid the smoke and fire of revolution. The principles and practices of inequality that had at one time appeared necessary and inevitable became the source of open mockery, first among intellectuals, later among wide sections of the populace. In a famous passage de Tocqueville captured the political meaning of this metamorphosis of the inevitable into a series of abuses:

> Only a great genius could save a ruler who tries to relieve his subjects after a long oppression. The evil suffered patiently as inevitable seems unendurable as soon as one conceives the idea of escaping from it. All of the abuses that have been removed seem only to delineate better those that remain and to make one's feelings more bitter. The evil, it is true, has become less, but one's sensibility is more acute.

The rising commercial and industrial leaders in the towns did not make the series of revolutionary surges, which, beginning with the Revolt of the Netherlands, destroyed the older conception of the inevitable. The economically active sectors of the bourgeoisie were too busy making money, often in a parasitic fashion in the interstices of the old regimes, to "make" a revolution that in fact frequently frightened many of them. By and large they were quite content to let other people do the fighting and thinking for them. Once the dust had settled they were the main beneficiaries of the political changes that were the result of these revolutions. Furthermore, commercial and manufacturing interests were also the main agents of the economic changes without which it would have been impossible to apply the new ideas in practice.

The new principles were egalitarian only in the sense that they were directed against older forms of privilege. Both in their intent and their consequences they were still principles of social inequality. The rewards of society were to be distributed according to "merit," mainly merit as demonstrated by success in the marketplace. No longer was any individual or group supposed to be able to count on a secure economic underpinning appropriate to the function it performed in and for the social order. Theoretically the race was to the swift while few concerned themselves overmuch about straightening out the starting line.

During the nineteenth century the new principles spread unevenly through Europe from West to East, encountering resistance from old elites, as well as those driven from their niches much lower down in the social order. Together the economic and moral changes created new classes and new conflicts over what weights each could throw on the scales of Justice, a goddess who in the form of *Concurrenz* or the automatic workings of the market often appeared more blind than ever before.

In Germany, as mentioned earlier, the industrial workers did not create out of their own experience any new principles of social equality or inequality with which to combat the new ones. It was the intellectuals who brought to the industrial workers diagnoses of their ills and suggested the remedies. Marx was only one of these, and his ideas for a long time made only slow headway against competing products. Much as his name came to dominate the intellectual scenery for the German workers by the late nineteenth century, the working principles and strategy of the German labor movement were hardly his alone.

In the famous principle of to each according to his (now presumably also her) needs, and from each according to his (and again her) abilities, Marxism still allows for human inequalities. But it is a principle that completely rejects the market as a device for measuring human worth. So far of course no society has reached this objective, and there are reasons for continuing skepticism about its feasibility.

Under pressure from their followers in search of more immediate benefits, European labor movements, and not only those in Germany, stopped short of this goal in their working principles, if not always in their rhetoric about the future. But they did take into their working principles at least part of the goal insofar as they rejected the link between merit and the marketplace as the *sole* determinant of human worth. The workers' own experience was probably a more important component in this rejection than what Marx had to say, though Marxism may well have put faith and fire into what workers wanted to believe for other reasons. Conservatives too had rejected this linkage for their own and quite different reasons. They, however, generally proved rare and untrustworthy allies for the workers. With the help of a few dissident intellectuals the workers created their own organizations for collective defense against the unfettered workings of the market.

The general direction of labor-movement pressures as they were shaped by the obstacles they encountered was still toward a society organized in and through the market, that is, still a capitalist society. Meanwhile, even before the First World War the market had begun to show symptoms suggesting that it might not be the most satisfactory all-around device for organizing human society. Even at its height it had scarcely won universal allegiance in practice from those who had the task of seeing that governments actually worked and stayed in power. After the war the troubles became worse instead of better, and the pressures to revise the social contract both in theory and in practice became stronger. These pressures came from many sources besides the industrial working classes and converged on one point: society had a definite responsibility for the welfare of the individual. More concretely, there was an obligation on society to find ways to protect the individual against the ravages of the invisible hand of fate working through the market.

The ways in which different societies tried to respond to the new imperative, the classes and groups they have tried to protect and the ones upon whom the costs of protection have been thrown, have varied enormously over the past half century and more since the issue became acute. Liberal capitalist democracy, fascism, communism, movements of national liberation in the backward countries have all been responses to this issue. In their internal conflicts and conflicts with each other they have been attempts to set the terms of a new social contract rendered necessary by the loosening of tremendous new productive forces. Meanwhile mankind has used these forces for destruction on a scale without parallel in human history. In holding the state responsible for human welfare we seem to be back to killing the king in earnest. That, roughly speaking, is revolutionary violence. But the kings new and old abide by no contract with their subjects. They kill their own subjects, each other's subjects, and on occasion each other. And they all do it in the name of a "public interest," a "welfare" about which there is no agreement and which threatens to turn into a nightmare. One can only hope that the nightmare itself may be part of the universal illusion of a permanent present. . . .

Integrity*

RONALD DWORKIN

AGENDA

WE HAVE TWO PRINCIPLES of political integrity: a legislative principle, which asks lawmakers to try to make the total set of laws morally coherent, and an adjudicative principle, which instructs that the law be seen as coherent in that way, so far as possible. Our main concern is with the adjudicative principle, but not yet. In this chapter I argue that the legislative principle is so much part of our political practice that no competent interpretation of that practice can ignore it. We measure that claim on the two dimensions now familiar. We ask whether the assumption, that integrity is a distinct ideal of politics, fits our politics, and then whether it honors our politics. If the legislative principle of integrity is impressive on both these dimensions, then the case for the adjudicative principle, and for the conception of law it supports, will already be well begun.

DOES INTEGRITY FIT?

INTEGRITY AND COMPROMISE

Integrity would not be needed as a distinct political virtue in a utopian state. Coherence would be guaranteed because officials would always do what was perfectly just and fair. In ordinary politics, however, we must treat integrity as an independent ideal if we accept it at all, because it can conflict with these other ideals. It can require us to support legislation we believe would be

---

*For permission to photocopy this selection please contact Harvard University Press. Reprinted by permission of the publishers from *Law's Empire* by Ronald Dworkin, Cambridge, Mass.: Harvard University Press. Copyright ©1986 by Ronald Dworkin.

inappropriate in the perfectly just and fair society and to recognize rights we do not believe people would have there. We saw an example of this conflict in [chapter 5 of Law's Empire]. A judge deciding McLoughlin might think it unjust to require compensation for any emotional injury. But if he accepts integrity and knows that some victims of emotional injury have already been given a right to compensation, he will have a reason for deciding in favor of Mrs. McLoughlin nevertheless.

Conflicts among ideals are common in politics. Even if we rejected integrity and based our political activity only on fairness, justice, and procedural due process, we would find the first two virtues sometimes pulling in opposite directions. Some philosophers deny the possibility of any fundamental conflict between justice and fairness because they believe that one of these virtues in the end derives from the other. Some say that justice has no meaning apart from fairness, that in politics, as in roulette, whatever happens through fair procedures is just. That is the extreme of the idea called justice as fairness. Others think that the only test of fairness in politics is the test of result, that no procedure is fair unless it is likely to produce political decisions that meet some independent test of justice. That is the opposite extreme, of fairness as justice. Most political philosophers—and I think most people—take the intermediate view that fairness and justice are to some degree independent of one another, so that fair institutions sometimes produce unjust decisions and unfair institutions just ones.

If that is so, then in ordinary politics we must sometimes choose between the two virtues in deciding which political programs to support. We might think that majority rule is the fairest workable decision procedure in politics, but we know that the majority will sometimes, perhaps often, make unjust decisions about the rights of individuals. Should we tamper with majority rule by giving special voting strength to one economic group, beyond what its numbers would justify, because we fear that straight majority rule would assign it less than its just share? Should we accept constitutional constraints on democratic power to prevent the majority from limiting freedom of speech or other important liberties? These difficult questions arise because fairness and justice sometimes conflict. If we believe that integrity is a third and independent ideal, at least when people disagree about one of the first two, then we may well think that fairness or justice must sometimes be sacrificed to integrity.

INTERNAL COMPROMISES

I shall try to show that our political practices accept integrity as a distinct virtue, and I begin with what I hope will strike you as a puzzle. Here are my background assumptions. We all believe in political fairness: we accept that each person or group in the community should have a roughly equal share of control over the decisions made by Parliament or Congress or the state legislature. We know that different people hold different views about moral issues that they all treat as of great importance. It would seem to follow from our convictions about fairness that legislation on these moral issues should be a matter not just of enforcing the will of the numerical majority, as if its view were unanimous, but of trades and compromises so that each body of opinion is represented, to a degree that matches its numbers, in the final result.

We could achieve this compromise in a Solomonic way. Do the people of North Dakota disagree whether justice requires compensation for product defects that manufacturers could not reasonably have prevented? Then why should their legislature not impose this "strict" liability on manufacturers of automobiles but not on manufacturers of washing machines? Do the people of Alabama disagree about the morality of racial discrimination? Why should their legislature not forbid racial discrimination on buses but permit it in restaurants? Do the British divide on the morality of abortion? Why should Parliament not make abortion criminal for pregnant women who were born in even years but not for those born in odd ones? This Solomonic model treats a community's public order as a kind of commodity to be distributed in accordance with distributive justice, a cake to be divided fairly by assigning each group a proper slice.

Most of us, I think, would be dismayed by "checkerboard" laws that treat similar accidents or occasions of racial discrimination or abortion differently on arbitrary grounds. Of course we do accept arbitrary distinctions about some matters: zoning, for example. We accept that shops or factories be forbidden in some zones and not others and that parking be prohibited on alternate sides of the same street on alternate days. But we reject a division between parties of opinion when matters of principle are at stake. We follow a different model: that each point of view must be allowed a voice in the process of deliberation but that the collective decision must nevertheless aim to settle on some coherent principle whose influence then extends to the natural limits of its authority. If there must be compromise because people are divided about justice, then the compromise must be external, not internal; it must be compromise about which scheme of justice to adopt rather than a compromised scheme of justice.

But there lies the puzzle. Why should we turn our back on checkerboard solutions as we do? Why should we not embrace them as a general strategy for legislation whenever the community is divided over some issue of principle? Why is this strategy not fair and reasonable, reflecting political maturity and a finer sense of the political art than other communities have managed to achieve? What is the special defect we find in checkerboard solutions? It cannot be a failure in fairness (in our sense of a fair distribution of political power) because checkerboard laws are by hypothesis fairer than either of the two alternatives. Allowing each of two groups to choose some part of the law of abortion, in proportion to their numbers, is fairer (in our sense) than the winner-take-all scheme our instincts prefer, which denies many people any influence at all over an issue they think desperately important.

Can we defend these instincts on grounds of justice? Justice is a matter of outcomes: a political decision causes injustice, however fair the procedures that produced it, when it denies people some resource, liberty, or opportunity that the best theories of justice entitle them to have. Can we oppose the checkerboard strategy on the ground that it would produce more instances of injustice than it would prevent? We must be careful not to confuse two issues here. Of course any single checkerboard solution of an important issue will produce more instances of injustice than one of the alternatives and fewer than the other. The community can unite over that proposition while disagreeing about which alternative would be more and which less just. Someone who believes that abortion is murder will think that the checkerboard abortion statute produces more injustice than outright prohibition and less than outright license; someone who believes women have a right to abortion reverses these judgments. So both have a reason of justice for preferring some other solution to the checkerboard one. Our question is whether we collectively have a reason of justice for not agreeing, in *advance* of these particular disagreements, to the checkerboard strategy for resolving them. We have a reason of fairness, as we just noticed, for that checkerboard strategy, and if we have no reason of justice against it, our present practice needs a justification we have not yet secured.

We are looking for a reason of justice we all share for rejecting the checkerboard strategy in advance even if we would each prefer a checkerboard solution on some occasions to the one that will be imposed if the strategy is rejected. Shall we just say that a checkerboard solution is unjust by definition because it treats different people differently for no good reason, and justice requires treating like cases alike? This suggestion seems in the right neighborhood, for if checkerboard solutions do have a defect, it must lie in their distinctive feature, that they treat people differently when no principle can justify the distinction. But we cannot explain why this is always objectionable, so long as we remain on the plane of justice as I have defined it. For in the circumstances of ordinary politics the checkerboard strategy will prevent instances of injustice that would otherwise occur, and we cannot say that justice requires not eliminating any injustice unless we can eliminate all.

Suppose we can rescue only some prisoners of tyranny; justice hardly requires rescuing none even when only luck, not any principle, will decide whom we save and whom we leave to torture. Rejecting a checkerboard solution seems perverse in the same way when the alternative will be the general triumph of the principle we oppose. The internal compromise would have rescued some, chosen arbitrarily, from an injustice that others will be left to suffer, but the alternative would have been to rescue none. Someone may now say: nevertheless, though checkerboard solutions may be desirable for that reason on some occasions, we do better to reject their use out of hand in advance, because we have reason to think that in the long run more discrete injustice will be created than avoided through these solutions. But that would be a plausible prediction only for members of a constant and self-conscious majority of opinion, and if such a majority existed so would a self-conscious minority that would have the opposite opinion. So we have no hope of finding here a common reason for rejecting checkerboard solutions.

But perhaps we are looking in the wrong direction. Perhaps our common reason is not any prediction about the number of cases of injustice that the checkerboard strategy would produce or prevent, but our conviction that no one should actively engage in producing what he believes to be injustice. We might say: no checkerboard statute could be enacted unless a majority of the legislators voted for provisions they thought unjust. But this objection begs the main question. If each member of the legislature who votes for a checkerboard compromise does so not because he himself has no principles but because he wants to give the maximum possible effect to the principles he thinks right, then how has anyone behaved irresponsibly? Even if we were to accept that no legislator should vote for the compromise, this would not explain why we should reject the compromise as an *outcome*. For we can easily imagine a legislative structure that would produce compromise statutes mechanically, as a function of the different opinions about strict liability or racial discrimination or abortion among the various legislators, without any legislator being asked or required to vote for the compromise as a package. It might be understood in advance that the proportion of women who would be permitted an abortion would be fixed by the ratio of votes for permitting all abortions to total votes. If we still object, then our objection cannot be based on the principle that no individual should vote against his conscience.

So it seems we have no reason of justice for rejecting the checkerboard strategy in advance, and strong reasons of fairness for endorsing it. Yet our instincts condemn it. Indeed many of us, to different degrees in different situations, would reject the checkerboard solution not only in general and in advance, but even in particular cases if it were available as a possibility. We would prefer either of the alternative solutions to the checkerboard compromise. Even if I thought strict liability for accidents wrong in principle, I would prefer that manufacturers of both washing machines and automobiles be held to that standard than that only one of them be. I would rank the checkerboard solution not intermediate between the other two but third, below both, and so would many other people. In some cases this instinct might be explained as reflecting the unworkability or inefficiency of a particular checkerboard solution. But many of those we can imagine, like the abortion solution, are not particularly inefficient, and in any case our instinct suggests that these compromises are wrong, not merely impractical.

Not everyone would condemn every checkerboard solution. People who believe very strongly that abortion is always murder, for example, may indeed think that the checkerboard abortion statute is better than a wholly permissive law. They think that fewer murders are better than more no matter how incoherent the compromise that produces fewer. If they rank the checkerboard solution last in other circumstances, in the case of strict liability for manufacturers, for example, they nevertheless believe that internal compromise is wrong, though for reasons that yield when the substantive issue is very grave. So they share the instinct that needs explaining. This instinct is likely to be at work, moreover, in other, more complicated rankings they might make. Suppose you think abortion is murder and that it makes no difference whether the pregnancy is the result of rape. Would you not think a statute prohibiting abortion except in the case of rape distinctly better than a statute prohibiting abortion except to women born in one specified decade each century? At least if you had no reason to think either would in fact allow more abortions? You see the first of these statutes as a solution that gives effect to two recognizable principles of justice, ordered in a certain way, even though you reject one of the principles. You cannot treat the second that way; it simply affirms for some people a principle it denies to others. So for many of us, our preferences in particular cases pose the same puzzle as our more comprehensive rejection of the checkerboard solution as a general strategy for resolving differences over principle. We cannot explain our hostility to internal compromise by appeal to principles of either fairness or justice as we have defined those virtues.

Astronomers postulated Neptune before they discovered it. They knew that only another planet, whose orbit lay beyond those already recognized, could explain the behavior of the nearer planets. Our instincts about internal compromise suggest another political ideal standing beside justice and fairness. Integrity is our Neptune. The most natural explanation of why we oppose checkerboard statutes appeals to that ideal: we say that a state that adopts these internal compromises is acting in an unprincipled way, even though no single official who voted for or enforces the compromise has done anything which, judging his individual actions by the ordinary standards of personal morality, he ought not to have done. The state lacks integrity because it must endorse principles to justify part of what it has done that it must reject to justify the rest. That explanation distinguishes integrity from the perverse consistency of someone who refuses to rescue some prisoners because he cannot save all. If he had saved some, selected arbitrarily, he would not have violated any principle he needs to justify other acts. But a state does act that way when it accepts a Solomonic checkerboard solution; it is inconsistency in principle among the acts of the state personified that integrity condemns.

INTEGRITY AND THE CONSTITUTION

Checkerboard statutes are the most dramatic violations of the ideal of integrity, and they are not unknown to our political history. The United States Constitution contained at its birth particularly hideous examples: the problem of slavery was compromised by counting three-fifths of a state's slaves in determining the state's representation in Congress and forbidding Congress to limit the original states' power to import slaves, but only before 1808. Integrity is flouted not only in specific compromises of that character, however, but whenever a community enacts and enforces different laws each of which is coherent in itself, but which cannot be defended together as expressing a coherent ranking of different principles of justice or fairness or procedural due process. We know that our own legal structure constantly violates integrity in this less dramatic way. We cannot bring all the various statutory and common-law rules our judges enforce under a single coherent scheme of principle. (I discuss some consequences of that fact in chapter 11 [of *Law's Empire*].) But we nevertheless accept integrity as a political ideal. It is part of our collective political morality that such compromises are wrong, that the community as a whole and not just individual officials one by one must act in a principled way.

In the United States this ideal is to some extent a matter of constitutional law, for the equal protection clause of the Fourteenth Amendment is now understood to outlaw internal compromises over important matters of principle. The Supreme Court relies on the language of equal protection to strike down state legislation that recognizes fundamental rights for some and not others. The Constitution requires states to extend to all citizens certain rights—the right to free speech, for example—but leaves them free to recognize other, nonconstitutionally required rights if they wish. If a state accepts one of these nonconstitutionally required rights for one class of citizens, however, it must do so for all. The Supreme Court's controversial 1973 abortion ruling, for example, allows states to prohibit abortions altogether in the last trimester of pregnancy. But the Court would not allow a state to prohibit an abortion in the last trimester only to women born in even years.

This connection between integrity and the rhetoric of equal protection is revealing. We insist on integrity because we believe that internal compromises would deny what is often called "equality before the law" and sometimes "formal equality." It has become fashionable to say that this kind of equality is unimportant because it offers little protection against tyranny. This denigration assumes, however, that formal equality is only a matter of enforcing the rules, whatever they are, that have been laid down in legislation, in the spirit of conventionalism. The equal protection cases show how important formal equality becomes when it is understood to require integrity as well as bare logical consistency, when it demands fidelity not just to rules but to the theories of fairness and justice that these rules presuppose by way of justification.

We can find another lesson about the dimensions of integrity in the constitutional system of the United States, a lesson that will prove important later in this chapter. Integrity holds within political communities, not among them, so any opinion we have about the scope of the requirement of coherence makes assumptions about the size and character of these communities. The American Constitution provides a federal system: it recognizes states as distinct political communities and assigns them sovereignty over many issues of principle. So there is no violation of political integrity in the fact that the tort laws of some states differ from those of others even over matters of principle. Each sovereign speaks with a single voice, though not in harmony with other sovereigns. But in a federal system integrity makes demands on the higher-order decisions, taken at the constitutional level, about the division of power between the national and the more local levels. Some scholars and politicians opposed to the Supreme Court's 1973 abortion decision now argue that the Constitution should be understood to leave decisions about abortion to the various states, so that some could permit abortion on demand, others prohibit it in all circumstances, and others adopt intermediate regimes. That suggestion is not itself a checkerboard solution: each state would retain a constitutional duty that its own abortion statute be coherent in principle, and the suggestion offers itself as recognizing independent sovereigns rather than speaking for all together. But a question of integrity remains: whether leaving the abortion issue to individual states to decide differently if they wish is coherent in principle with the rest of the American constitutional scheme, which makes other important rights national in scope and enforcement.

IS INTEGRITY ATTRACTIVE?

I shall offer no further argument for my claim that our political life recognizes integrity as a political virtue. The case is now strong enough for the weight of interest to shift to the other dimension of interpretation. Do we do well to interpret our politics that way? Is our political culture more attractive if seen as accepting that virtue? I have already described, in chapter 5 [of *Law's Empire*], an obvious challenge to integrity. A pragmatist anxious to reject integrity would attack the deep, working personification we use to define the ideal. We say that the state as a whole does wrong in accepting an internal compromise because "it" then compromises "its" principles. The pragmatist will insist that the state is not an entity that can have principles to compromise. Neither the state nor its government is a person; they are collections of people, and if none of these separate people has acted in any way inconsistently with his or her own principles, what sense can it make to say that the state they represent has done this?

The pragmatist who makes this argument tries to build political responsibility out of ordinary, nonpolitical principles of morality. He proceeds in the fashion of our first argument, in chapter 5 [of *Law's Empire*], about the responsibility of shareholders for defective automobiles, applying ordinary principles about the responsibility of one person for injury to another. He asks what each legislator might do, in the position he happens to occupy, to reduce the total number of incidents of injustice or unfairness according to his own views of what justice and fairness require. If we follow the pragmatist in this order of argument—if we begin with individual official responsibility—we will reach his conclusion because we will then lack any appropriate explanation of why a vote for a checkerboard solution is wrong, any explanation of why a particular official should regard the compromise as a worse outcome than the outcome he regards as more uniformly unjust. If, on the other hand, we insist on treating internally compromised statutes as the acts of a single distinct moral agent, then we can condemn them as unprincipled, and we then have a reason for arguing that no official should contribute to his state's unprincipled acts. In order to defend the legislative principle of integrity, therefore, we must defend the general style of argument that takes the community itself as a moral agent.

Our argument must be drawn from political virtue, not, so far as this is supposed to be different, from metaphysics. We must not say that integrity is a special virtue of politics because the state or community is a distinct entity, but that the community should be seen as a distinct moral agent because the social and intellectual practices that treat community in this way should be protected. Now we confront an obvious and deep difficulty. We have grown accustomed in political life to arguing about social and political institutions in a certain way: by attacking or defending them on grounds of justice or fairness. But we cannot hope to defend integrity in this normal way because we know that integrity will sometimes conflict with what fairness and justice recommend. We must expand the breadth of political argument if we are to claim political integrity as a distinct ideal on its own. But how? Here is one suggestion, though not the only possibility. French revolutionary rhetoric recognized a political ideal we have not yet considered. We should look for our defense of integrity in the neighborhood of fraternity or, to use its more fashionable name, community.

I shall argue that a political society that accepts integrity as a political virtue thereby becomes a special form of community, special in a way that promotes its moral authority to assume and deploy a monopoly of coercive force. This is not the only argument for integrity, or the only consequence of recognizing it that citizens might value. Integrity provides protection against partiality or deceit or other forms of official corruption, for example. There is more room for favoritism or vindictiveness in a system that permits manufacturers of automobiles and of washing machines to be governed by different and contradictory principles of liability. Integrity also contributes to the efficiency of law in the way we noticed earlier. If people accept that they are governed not only by explicit rules laid down in past political decisions but by whatever other standards flow from the principles these decisions assume, then the set of recognized public standards can expand and contract organically, as people become more sophisticated in sensing and exploring what these principles require in new circumstances, without the need for detailed legislation or adjudication on each possible point of conflict. This process works less effectively, to be sure, when people disagree, as inevitably they sometimes will, about which principles are in fact assumed by the explicit rules and other standards of their community. But a community that accepts integrity has a vehicle for organic change, even if it is not always wholly effective, that it would not otherwise have at all.

These consequences of integrity are practical. Others are moral and expressive. We noticed in our initial, cursory discussion of integrity [in chapter 5 of Law's Empire] that many of our political attitudes, collected in our instinct of group responsibility, assume that we are in some sense the authors of the political decisions made by our governors, or at least that we have reason to think of ourselves that way. Kant and Rousseau based their conceptions of freedom on this ideal of self-legislation. The ideal needs integrity, however, for a citizen cannot treat himself as the author of a collection of laws that are inconsistent in principle, nor can he see that collection as sponsored by any Rousseauian general will.

The ideal of self-government has a special aspect that integrity promotes directly, and noticing this will lead us into our main discussion of legitimacy and political obligation. Integrity expands and deepens the role individual citizens can play in developing the public standards of their community because it requires them to treat relations among themselves as characteristically, not just spasmodically, governed by these standards. If people understood formal legislation as only a matter of negotiated solutions to discrete problems, with no underlying commitment to any more fundamental public conception of justice, they would draw a sharp distinction between two kinds of encounters with fellow citizens: those that fall within and those that fall outside the scope of some past political decision. Integrity, in contrast, insists that each citizen must accept demands on him, and may make demands on others, that share and extend the moral dimension of any explicit political decisions. Integrity therefore fuses citizens' moral and political lives: it asks the good citizen, deciding how to treat his neighbor when their interests conflict, to interpret the common scheme of justice to which they are both committed just in virtue of citizenship.

Integrity infuses political and private occasions each with the spirit of the other to the benefit of both. This continuity has practical as well as expressive value, because it facilitates the organic style of change I mentioned a moment ago as a practical advantage. But its expressive value is not exhausted, as its practical value might be, when citizens disagree about which scheme of justice is in fact embedded in the community's explicit political decisions. For the expressive value is confirmed when people in good faith try to treat one another in a way appropriate to common membership in a community governed by political integrity and to see each other as making this attempt, even when they disagree about exactly what integrity requires in particular circumstances. Political obligation is then not just a matter of obeying the discrete political decisions of the community one by one, as political philosophers usually represent it. It becomes a more protestant idea: fidelity to a scheme of principle each citizen has a responsibility to identify, ultimately for himself, as his community's scheme.

THE PUZZLE OF LEGITIMACY

We now turn to the direct connection between integrity and the moral authority of the law, and this bends our study back toward the main argument of [*Law's Empire*]. I said that the concept of law—the plateau where argument among conceptions is most useful—connects law with the justification of official coercion. A conception of law must explain how what it takes to be law provides a general justification for the exercise of coercive power by the state, a justification that holds except in special cases when some competing argument is specially powerful. Each conception's organizing center is the explanation if offers of this justifying force. Every conception therefore faces the same threshold problem. How can *anything* provide even that general form of justification for coercion in ordinary politics? What can ever give anyone the kind of authorized power over another that politics supposes governors have over the governed? Why does the fact that a majority elects a particular regime, for example, give that regime legitimate power over those who voted against it?

This is the classical problem of the legitimacy of coercive power. It rides on the back of another classical problem: that of political obligation. Do citizens have genuine moral obligations just in virtue of law? Does the fact that a legislature has enacted some requirement in itself give citizens a moral as well as a practical reason to obey? Does that moral reason hold even for those citizens who disapprove of the legislation or think it wrong in principle? If citizens do not have moral obligations of that character, then the state's warrant for coercion is seriously, perhaps fatally, undermined. These two issues—whether the state is morally legitimate, in the sense that it is justified in using force against its citizens, and whether the state's decisions impose genuine obligations on them—are not identical. No state should enforce all of a citizen's obligations. But though obligation is not a sufficient condition for coercion, it is close to a necessary one. A state may have good grounds in some special circumstances for coercing those who have no duty to obey. But no general policy of upholding the law with steel could be justified if the law were not, in general, a source of genuine obligations.

A state is legitimate if its constitutional structure and practices are such that its citizens have a general obligation to obey political decisions that purport to impose duties on them. An argument for legitimacy need only provide reasons for that general situation. It need not show that a government, legitimate in that sense, therefore has moral authority to do anything it wants to its citizens, or that they are obligated to obey every decision it makes. I shall argue that a state that accepts integrity as a political ideal has a better case for legitimacy than one that does not. If that is so, it provides a strong reason of the sort we have just now been seeking, a reason why we would do well to see our political practices as grounded in that virtue. It provides, in particular, a strong argument for a conception of law that takes integrity to be fundamental, because any conception must explain why law is legitimate authority for coercion. Our claims for integrity are thus tied into our main project of finding an attractive conception of law.

TACIT CONSENT

Philosophers make several kinds of arguments for the legitimacy of modern democracies. One argument uses the idea of a social contract, but we must not confuse it with arguments that use that idea to establish the character or content of justice. John Rawls, for example, proposes an imaginary social contract as a device for selecting the best conception of justice in the circumstances of utopian political theory. He argues that under specified conditions of uncertainty everyone would choose certain principles of justice as in his interests, properly understood, and he says that these principles are therefore the right principles for us. Whatever we may think of his suggestion, it has no direct connection to our present problem of legitimacy in the circumstances of ordinary politics where Rawls's principles of justice are very far from dominion. It would be very different, of course, if every citizen were a party to an actual, historical agreement to accept and obey political decisions taken in the way his community's political decisions are in fact taken. Then the historical fact of agreement would provide at least a good prima facie case for coercion even in ordinary politics. So some political philosophers have been tempted to say that we have in fact agreed to a social contract of that kind tacitly, by just not emigrating when we reach the age of consent. But no one can argue that very long with a straight face. Consent cannot be binding on people, in the way this argument requires, unless it is given more freely, and with more genuine alternate choice, than just by declining to build a life from nothing under a foreign flag. And even if the consent were genuine, the argument would fail as an argument for legitimacy, because a person leaves one sovereign only to join another; he has no choice to be free from sovereigns altogether.

THE DUTY TO BE JUST

Rawls argues that people in his original position would recognize a natural duty to support institutions that meet the tests of abstract justice and that they would extend this duty to the support of institutions not perfectly just, at least when the sporadic injustice lay in decisions reached by fair, majoritarian institutions. Even those who reject Rawls's general method might accept the duty to support just or nearly just institutions. That duty, however, does not provide a good explanation of legitimacy, because it does not tie political obligation sufficiently tightly to the particular community to which those who have the obligation belong; it does not show why Britons have any special duty to support the institutions of Britain. We can construct a practical, contingent argument for the special duty. Britons have more opportunity to aid British institutions than those of other nations whose institutions they also think mainly just. But this practical argument fails to capture the intimacy of the special duty. It fails to show how legitimacy flows from and defines citizenship. This objection points away from justice, which is conceptually universalistic, and toward integrity, which is already more personal in its different demands on different communities, as the parent of legitimacy.

FAIR PLAY

The most popular defense of legitimacy is the argument from fair play: if someone has received benefits under a standing political organization, then he has an obligation to bear the burdens of that organization as well, including an obligation to accept its political decisions, whether or not he has solicited these benefits or has in any more active way consented to these burdens. This argument avoids the fantasy of the argument from consent and the universality and other defects of the argument from a natural duty of justice and might therefore seem a stronger rival to my suggestion that legitimacy is best grounded in integrity. But it is vulnerable to two counterarguments that have frequently been noticed. First, the fair play argument assumes that people can incur obligations simply by receiving what they do not seek and would reject if they had the chance. This seems unreasonable. Suppose a philosopher broadcasts a stunning and valuable lecture from a sound truck. Do all those who hear it—even all those who enjoy and profit by it—owe him a lecture fee?

Second, the fair play argument is ambiguous in a crucial respect. In what sense does it suppose that people benefit from political organization? The most natural answer is this: someone benefits from a political organization if his overall situation—his "welfare" in the way economists use that phrase—is superior under that organization to what it would otherwise be. But everything then turns on the benchmark to be used, on what "otherwise" means, and when we try to specify the benchmark we reach a dead end. The principle is plainly too strong—it justifies nothing—if it requires showing that each citizen is better off under the standing political system than he would be under any other system that might have developed in its place. For that can never be shown for all the citizens the principle is meant to embrace. And it is plainly too weak—it is too easy to satisfy and therefore justifies too much—if it requires showing only that each citizen is better off under the standing organization than he would be with no social or political organization at all, that is, under a Hobbesian state of nature.

We can deflect this second objection if we reject the "natural" interpretation I described of the crucial idea of benefit. Suppose we understand the argument in a different way: it assumes not that each citizen's welfare, judged in some politically neutral way, has been improved by a particular social or political organization, but that each has received the benefits of that organization. That is, that he has actually received what is due him according to the standards of justice and fairness on which it is constructed. The principle of fair play, understood that way, states at least a condition necessary to legitimacy. If a community does not aim to treat someone as an equal, even according to its own lights, then its claim to his political obligation is fatally compromised. But it remains unclear how the negative fact that society has not discriminated against someone in this way, according to its own standards, could supply any positive reason why he should accept its laws as obligations. Indeed, the first objection I described becomes more powerful yet if we make this response to the second. For now the argument from fair play must be understood as claiming, not that someone incurs an obligation when his welfare is improved in a way he did not seek, but that he incurs an obligation by being treated in a way that might not even improve his welfare over any appropriate benchmark. For there is nothing in the fact that some individual has been treated fairly by his community according to its own standards that guarantees him any further, more material advantage.

OBLIGATIONS OF COMMUNITY

CIRCUMSTANCES AND CONDITIONS

Is it true that no one can be morally affected by being given what he does not ask or choose to have? We will think so if we consider only cases of benefits thrust upon us by strangers like philosophers in sound trucks. Our convictions are quite different, however, when we have in mind obligations that are often called obligations of role but that I shall call, generically, associative or communal obligations. I mean the special responsibilities social practice attaches to membership in some biological or social group, like the responsibilities of family or friends or neighbors. Most people think that they have associative obligations just by belonging to groups defined by social practice, which is not necessarily a matter of choice or consent, but that they can lose these obligations if other members of the group do not extend them the benefits of belonging to the group. These common assumptions about associative responsibilities suggest that political obligation might be counted among them, in which case the two objections to the argument from fair play would no longer be pertinent. On the whole, however, philosophers have ignored this possibility, I believe for two reasons. First, communal obligations are widely thought to depend upon emotional bonds that presuppose that each member of the group has personal acquaintance of all others, which of course cannot be true in large political communities. Second, the idea of special communal responsibilities holding within a large, anonymous community smacks of nationalism, or even racism, both of which have been sources of very great suffering and injustice.

We should therefore reflect on the character of familiar associative obligations to see how far these apparent objections actually hold. Associative obligations are complex, and much less studied by philosophers than the kinds of personal obligations we incur through discrete promises and other deliberate acts. But they are an important part of the moral landscape: for most people, responsibilities to family and lovers and friends and union or office colleagues are the most important, the most consequential obligations of all. The history of social practice defines the communal groups to which we belong and the obligations that attach to these. It defines what a family or a neighborhood or a professional colleague is, and what one member of these groups or holder of these titles owes to another. But social practice defines groups and obligations not by the fiat of ritual, not through the explicit extension of conventions, but in the more complex way brought in with the interpretive attitude. The concepts we use to describe these groups and to claim or reject these obligations are interpretive concepts; people can sensibly argue in the interpretive way about what friendship really is and about what children really owe their parents in old age. The raw data of how friends typically treat one another are no more conclusive of an argument about the obligations of friendship than raw data were conclusive for arguments about courtesy in the community I imagined or for arguments about law for us.

Suppose we tried to compose, not just an interpretation of a single associative practice, like family or friendship or neighborhood, but a more abstract interpretation of the yet more general practice of associative obligation itself. I cannot carry that project very far here or develop any deep and thorough study of that abstract practice. But even a quick survey shows that we cannot account for the general practice if we accept the principle many philosophers have found so appealing, that no one can have special obligations to particular people except by choosing to accept these. The connection we recognize between communal obligation and choice is much more complex and more a matter of degree that varies from one form of communal association to another. Even associations we consider mainly consensual, like friendship, are not formed in one act of deliberate contractual commitment, the way one joins a club, but instead develop through a series of choices and events that are never seen, one by one, as carrying a commitment of that kind.

We have friends to whom we owe obligations in virtue of a shared history, but it would be perverse to describe this as a history of *assuming* obligations. On the contrary, it is a history of events and acts that *attract* obligations, and we are rarely even aware that we are entering upon any special status as the story unfolds. People become self-conscious about the obligations of friendship in the normal case only when some situation requires them to honor these obligations, or when they have grown weary of or embarrassed by the friendship, and then it is too late to reject them without betrayal. Other forms of association that carry special responsibilities—of academic colleagueship, for example—are even less a matter of free choice: someone can become my colleague even though I voted against his appointment. And the obligations some members of a family owe to others, which many people count among the strongest fraternal obligations of all, are matters of the least choice.

We must therefore account for associative obligations, if we accept these at all, in the different way I suggested a moment ago in describing how most people think of them. We have a duty to honor our responsibilities under social practices that define groups and attach special responsibilities to membership, but this natural duty holds only when certain other conditions are met or sustained. Reciprocity is prominent among these other conditions. I have special responsibilities to my brother in virtue of our brotherhood, but these are sensitive to the degree to which he accepts such responsibilities toward me; my responsibilities to those who claim that we are friends or lovers or neighbors or colleagues or countrymen are equally contingent on reciprocity. But we must be careful here: if associative concepts are interpretive—if it can be an open question among friends what friendship requires—then the reciprocity we demand cannot be a matter of each doing for the other what the latter thinks friendship concretely requires. Then friendship would be possible only between people who shared a detailed conception of friendship and would become automatically more contractual and deliberative than it is, more a matter of people checking in advance to see whether their conceptions matched well enough to allow them to be friends.

The reciprocity we require for associative obligations must be more abstract, more a question of accepting a kind of responsibility we need the companion ideas of integrity and interpretation to explain. Friends have a responsibility to treat one another as friends, and that means, put subjectively, that each must act out of a conception of friendship he is ready to recognize as vulnerable to an interpretive test, as open to the objection that this is not a plausible account of what friendship means in our culture. Friends or family or neighbors need not agree in detail about the responsibilities attached to these forms of organization. Associative obligations can be sustained among people who share a general and diffuse sense of members' special rights and responsibilities from or toward one another, a sense of what sort and level of sacrifice one may be expected to make for another. I may think friendship, properly understood, requires that I break promises to others to help a friend in need, and I will not refuse to do this for a friend just because he does not share this conviction and would not do it for me. But I will count him a friend and feel this obligation only if I believe he has roughly the same concern for me as I thereby show for him, that he would make important sacrifices for me of some other sort.

Nevertheless, the members of a group must by and large hold certain attitudes about the responsibilities they owe one another if these responsibilities are to count as genuine fraternal obligations. First, they must regard the group's obligations as *special*, holding distinctly within the group, rather than as general duties its members owe equally to persons outside it. Second, they must accept that these responsibilities are *personal*: that they run directly from each member to each other member, not just to the group as a whole in some collective sense. My brother or my colleague may think he has responsibilities to the reputation of the family or the university he best acquits by concentrating on his own career and thus denying me help when I need it or company when I want it. He may be right about the best use of his time overall from the standpoint of the general good of these particular communities. But his conduct does not form the necessary basis for my continuing to recognize fraternal obligations toward him.

Third, members must see these responsibilities as flowing from a more general responsibility each has of *concern* for the well-being of others in the group; they must treat discrete obligations that arise only under special circumstances, like the obligation to help a friend who is in great financial need, as derivative from and expressing a more general responsibility active throughout the association in different ways. A commercial partnership or joint enterprise, conceived as a fraternal association, is in that way different from even a long-standing contractual relationship. The former has a life of its own: each partner is concerned not just to keep explicit agreements hammered out at arm's length but to approach each issue that arises in their joint commercial life in a manner reflecting special concern for his partner as partner. Different forms of association presuppose different kinds of general concern each member is assumed to have for others. The level of concern is different—I need not act toward my partner as if I thought his welfare as important as my son's—and also its range: my concern for my union "brother" is general across the economic and productive life we share but does not extend to his success in social life, as my concern for my biological brother does. (Of course my union colleague may be my friend as well, in which case my overall responsibilities to him will be aggregative and complex.) But within the form or mode of life constituted by a communal practice, the concern must be general and must provide the foundation for the more discrete responsibilities.

Fourth, members must suppose that the group's practices show not only concern but an *equal* concern for all members. Fraternal associations are in that sense conceptually egalitarian. They may be structured, even hierarchical, in the way a family is, but the structure and hierarchy must reflect the group's assumption that its roles and rules are equally in the interests of all, that no one's life is more important than anyone else's. Armies may be fraternal organizations if that condition is met. But caste systems that count some members as inherently less worthy than others are not fraternal and yield no communal responsibilities.

We must be careful to distinguish, then, between a "bare" community, a community that meets the genetic or geographical or other historical conditions identified by social practice as capable of constituting a fraternal community, and a "true" community, a bare community whose practices of group responsibility meet the four conditions just identified. The responsibilities a true community deploys are special and individualized and display a pervasive mutual concern that fits a plausible conception of equal concern. These are not psychological conditions. Though a group will rarely meet or long sustain them unless its members by and large actually feel some emotional bond with one another, the conditions do not themselves demand this. The concern they require is an interpretive property of the group's practices of asserting and acknowledging responsibilities these must be practices that people with the right level of concern would adopt — not a psychological property of some fixed number of the actual members. So, contrary to the assumption that seemed to argue against assimilating political to associative obligations, associative communities can be larger and more anonymous than they could be if it were a necessary condition that each member love all others, or even that they know them or know who they are.

Nor does anything in the four conditions contradict our initial premise that obligations of fraternity need not be fully voluntary. If the conditions are met, people in the bare community have the obligations of a true community whether or not they want them, though of course the conditions will not be met unless most members recognize and honor these obligations. It is therefore essential to insist that true communities must be bare communities as well. People cannot be made involuntary "honorary" members of a community to which they do not even "barely" belong just because other members are disposed to treat them as such. I would not become a citizen of Fiji if people there decided for some reason to treat me as one of them. Nor am I the friend of a stranger sitting next to me on a plane just because he decides he is a friend of mine.

CONFLICTS WITH JUSTICE

An important reservation must be made to the argument so far. Even genuine communities that meet the several conditions just described may be unjust or promote injustice and so produce the conflict we have already noticed in different ways, between the integrity and justice of an institution. Genuine communal obligations may be unjust in two ways. First, they may be unjust to the members of the group: the conception of equal concern they reflect, though sincere, may be defective. It may be a firm tradition of family organization in some community, for example, that equal concern for daughters and sons requires parents to exercise a kind of dominion over one relaxed for the other. Second, they may be unjust to people who are not members of the group. Social practice may define a racial or religious group as associative, and that group may require its members to discriminate against nonmembers socially or in employment or generally. If the consequences for strangers to the group are grave, as they will be if the discriminating group is large or powerful within a larger community, this will be unjust. In many cases, requiring that sort of discrimination will conflict, not just with duties of abstract justice the group's members owe everyone else, but also with associative obligations they have because they belong to larger or different associative communities. For if those who do not belong to my race or religion are my neighbors or colleagues or (now I anticipate the argument to follow) my fellow citizens, the question arises whether I do not have responsibilities to them, flowing from those associations, that I ignore in deferring to the responsibilities claimed by my racial or religious group.

We must not forget, in puzzling about these various conflicts, that associative responsibilities are subject to interpretation, and that justice will play its normal interpretive role in deciding for any person what his associative responsibilities, properly understood, really are. If the bare facts of social practice are indecisive, my belief that it is unjust for parents to exercise absolute dominion over their children will influence my convictions about whether the institution of family really has that feature, just as a citizen's beliefs about the justice of social rank influences his beliefs about courtesy in the imaginary community [discussed in] chapter 2 [of *Law's Empire*]. Even if the practice of dominion is settled and unquestioned, the interpretive attitude may isolate it as a mistake because it is condemned by principles necessary to justify the rest of the institution. There is no guarantee, however, that the interpretive attitude will always justify reading some apparently unjust feature of an associative institution out of it. We may have to concede that unjust dominion lies at the heart of some culture's practices of family, or that indefensible discrimination is at the heart of its practices of racial or religious cohesion. Then we will be aware of another possibility we have also noticed before, in other contexts. The best interpretation may be a deeply skeptical one: that no competent account of the institution can fail to show it as thoroughly and pervasively unjust, and that it should therefore be abandoned. Someone who reaches that conclusion will deny that the practice can impose genuine obligations at all. He thinks the obligations it purports to impose are wholly canceled by competing moral principle.

So our account of associative obligation now has the following rather complex structure. It combines matters of social practice and matters of critical inter-pretation in the following way. The question of communal obligation does not arise except for groups defined by practice as carrying such obligations: associa-tive communities must be bare communities first. But not every group estab-lished by social practice counts as associative: a bare community must meet the four conditions of a true community before the responsibilities it declares become genuine. Interpretation is needed at this stage, because the question whether the practice meets the conditions of genuine community depends on how the practice is properly understood, and that is an interpretive question. Since interpretation is in part a matter of justice, this stage may show that apparently unjust responsibilities are not really part of the practice after all, because they are condemned by principles needed to justify other responsibilities the practice imposes. But we cannot count on this: the best interpretation available may show that its unjust features are compatible with the rest of its structure. Then, though the obligations it imposes are prima facie genuine, the question arises whether the injustice is so severe and deep that these obligations are canceled. That is one possibility, and practices of racial unity and dis-crimination seem likely examples. But sometimes the injustice will not be that great; dilemmas are then posed because the unjust obligations the practice creates are not entirely erased.

I can illustrate this complex structure by expanding an example already used. Does a daughter have an obligation to defer to her father's wishes in cultures that give parents power to choose spouses for daughters but not sons? We ask first whether the four conditions are met that transform the bare institution of family, in the form this has taken there, into a true community, and that raises a nest of interpretive questions in which our convictions about justice will figure. Does the culture genuinely accept that women are as important as men? Does it see the special parental power over daughters as genuinely in the daughters' interest? If not, if the discriminatory treatment of daughters is grounded in some more general assumption that they are less worthy than sons, the association is not genuine, and no distinctly associative responsibilities, of any character, arise from it. If the culture does accept the equality of the sexes, on the other hand, the discrimination against daughters may be so inconsistent with the rest of the institution of family that it may be seen as a mistake within it and so not a real requirement even if the institution is accepted. Then the conflict disappears for that reason.

But suppose the culture accepts the equality of sexes but in good faith thinks that equality of concern requires paternalistic protection for women in all aspects of family life, and that parental control over a daughter's marriage is consistent with the rest of the institution of family. If that institution is otherwise seriously unjust—if it forces family members to commit crimes in the interest of the family, for example—we will think it cannot be justified in any way that recommends continuing it. Our attitude is fully skeptical, and again we deny any genuine associative responsibilities and so deny any conflict. Suppose, on the other hand, that the institution's paternalism is the only feature we are disposed to regard as unjust. Now the conflict is genuine. The other responsibilities of family membership thrive as genuine responsibilities. So does the responsibility of a daughter to defer to parental choice in marriage, but this may be overridden by appeal to freedom or some other ground of rights. The difference is important: a daughter who marries against her father's wishes, in this version of the story, has something to regret. She owes him at least an accounting, and perhaps an apology, and should in other ways strive to continue her standing as a member of the community she otherwise has a duty to honor.

I have paid such great attention to the structure of associative obligation, and to the character and occasions of its conflict with other responsibilities and rights, because my aim is to show how political obligation can be seen as associative, and this can be plausible only if the general structure of associative obligations allows us to account for the conditions we feel must be met before political obligation arise, and the circumstances we believe must either defeat it or show it in conflict with other kinds of obligations. The discussion just concluded echoes our first discussion, in chapter 3 [of *Law's Empire*], about the kinds of conflict citizens and judges might discover between the law of their community and more abstract justice. We used, there, much the same structure and many of the same distinctions to disentangle the moral and legal issues posed by law in wicked places. That echo supports our present hypothesis that political obligation—including an obligation to obey the law—is a form of associative obligation. Our study of conflict within associative obligation is important, too, in responding to an objection to that hypothesis I noticed briefly earlier. The objection complains that treating political obligation as associative supports the more unattractive aspects of nationalism, including its strident approval of war for national self-interest. We can now reply that the best interpretation of our own political practices disavows that feature, which is anyway no longer explicitly endorsed even by bare practice. When and where it is endorsed any conflict between militant nationalism and standards of justice must be resolved in favor of the latter. Neither of these claims threatens the more wholesome ideals of national community and the special responsibilities these support, which we are about to consider.

FRATERNITY AND POLITICAL COMMUNITY

We are at last able to consider our hypothesis directly: that the best defense of political legitimacy—the right of a political community to treat its members as having obligations in virtue of collective community decisions—is to be found not in the hard terrain of contracts or duties of justice or obligations of fair play that might hold among strangers, where philosophers have hoped to find it, but in the more fertile ground of fraternity, community, and their attendant obligations. Political association, like family and friendship and other forms of association more local and intimate, is in itself pregnant of obligation. It is no objection to that claim that most people do not choose their political communities but are born into them or brought there in childhood. If we arrange familiar fraternal communities along a spectrum ranging from full choice to no choice in membership, political communities fall somewhere in the center. Political obligations are less involuntary than many obligations of family, because political communities do allow people to emigrate, and though the practical value of this choice is often very small the choice itself is important, as we know when we contemplate tyrannies that deny it. So people who are members of bare political communities have political obligations, provided the other conditions necessary to obligations of fraternity, appropriately defined for a political community, are met.

We must therefore ask what account of these conditions is appropriate for a political community, but first we should pause to consider the following complaint about this "solution" of the problem of legitimacy. "It does not solve the problem but evades it by denying there is any problem at all." There is some justice in this complaint, but not enough to be damaging here. The new approach, it is true, relocates the problem of legitimacy and so hopes to change the character of the argument. It asks those who challenge the very possibility of political legitimacy to broaden their attack and either deny all associative obligations or show why political obligation cannot be associative. It asks those who defend legitimacy to test their claims on a new and expanded field of argument. It invites political philosophers of either disposition to consider what a bare political community must be like before it can claim to be a true community where communal obligations flourish.

We have no difficulty finding in political practice the conditions of bare community. People disagree about the boundaries of political communities, particularly in colonial circumstances or when standing divisions among nations ignore important historical or ethnic or religious identities. But these can be treated as problems of interpretation, and anyway they do not arise in the countries of our present main concern. Practice defines the boundaries of Great Britain and of the several states of the United States well enough for these to be eligible as bare political communities. We have noticed this already: we noticed that our most widespread political convictions suppose the officials of these communities to have special responsibilities within and toward their distinct communities. We also have no difficulty in describing the main obligations associated with political communities. The central obligation is that of general fidelity to law, the obligation political philosophy has found so problematic. So our main interest lies in the four conditions we identified. What form would these take in a political community? What must politics be like for a bare political society to become a true fraternal mode of association?

THREE MODELS OF COMMUNITY

We are able to imagine political society as associative only because our ordinary political attitudes seem to satisfy the first of our four conditions. We suppose that we have special interests in and obligations toward other members of our own nation. Americans address their political appeals, their demands, visions, and ideals, in the first instance to other Americans; Britons to other Britons; and so forth. We treat community as prior to justice and fairness in the sense that questions of justice and fairness are regarded as questions of what would be fair or just within a particular political group. In that way we treat political communities as true associative communities. What further assumptions about the obligations and responsibilities that flow from citizenship could justify that attitude by satisfying its other conditions? This is not a question of descriptive sociology, though that discipline may have a part to play in answering it. We are not concerned, that is, with the empirical question of which attitudes or institutions or traditions are needed to create and protect political stability, but with the interpretive question of what character of mutual concern and responsibility our political practices must express in order to justify the assumption of true community we seem to make.

A community's political practices might aim to express one of three general models of political association. Each model describes the attitudes members of a political community would self-consciously take toward one another if they held the view of community the model expresses. The first supposes that members of a community treat their association as only a de facto accident of history and geography, among other things, and so as not a true associative community at all. People who think of their community this way will not necessarily treat others only as means to their own personal ends. That is one possibility: imagine two strangers from nations that despise each other's morals and religion are washed up on a desert island after a naval battle between the two countries. The strangers are thrown together initially by circumstance and nothing more. Each may need the other and may refrain from killing him for that reason. They may work out some division of labor, and each may hold to the agreement so long as he thinks it is to his advantage to do so, but not beyond that point or for any other reason. But there are other possibilities for de facto association. People might regard their political community as merely de facto, not because they are selfish but because they are driven by a passion for justice in the world as a whole and see no distinction between their community and others. A political official who takes that view will think of his constituents as people he is in a position to help because he has special means—those of his office—for helping them that are not, regrettably, available for helping other groups. He will think his responsibilities to his own community special in no other way, and therefore not greater in principle. So when he can improve justice overall by subordinating the interests of his own constituents, he will think it right to do so.

I call the second model of community the "rulebook" model. It supposes that members of a political community accept a general commitment to obey rules established in a certain way that is special to that community. Imagine self-interested but wholly honest people who are competitors in a game with fixed rules or who are parties to a limited and transient commercial arrangement. They obey the rules they have accepted or negotiated as a matter of obligation and not merely strategy, but they assume that the content of these rules exhausts their obligation. They have no sense that the rules were negotiated out of common commitment to underlying principles that are themselves a source of further obligation; on the contrary, they take these rules to represent a compromise between antagonistic interests or points of view. If the rules are the product of special negotiation, as in the contract case, each side has tried to give up as little in return for as much as possible, and it would therefore be unfair and not merely mistaken for either to claim that their agreement embraces anything not explicitly agreed.

The conventionalist's conception of law is a natural mate to this rulebook model of community. Conventionalism suits people each trying to advance his or her own conception of justice and fairness in the right relation through negotiation and compromise, subject only to the single overriding stipulation that once a compromise has been reached in the appropriate way, the rules that form its content will be respected until they are changed by a fresh compromise. A conventionalist philosophy coupled to a rulebook model of community would accept the internal compromises of our checkerboard statutes, as compromises reached through negotiation that ought to be respected as much as any other bargain. The first two models of community—community as a matter of circumstance and as a matter of rules—agree in rejecting the only basis we might have for opposing checkerboard compromises, which is the idea of integrity, that the community must respect principles necessary to justify one part of the law in other parts as well.

The third model of community is the model of principle. It agrees with the rulebook model that political community requires a shared understanding, but it takes a more generous and comprehensive view of what that understanding is. It insists that people are members of a genuine political community only when they accept that their fates are linked in the following strong way: they accept that they are governed by common principles, not just by rules hammered out in political compromise. Politics has a different character for such people. It is a theater of debate about which principles the community should adopt as a system, which view it should take of justice, fairness, and due process, not the different story, appropriate to the other models, in which each person tries to plant the flag of his convictions over as large a domain of power or rules as possible. Members of a society of principle accept that their political rights and duties are not exhausted by the particular decisions their political institutions have reached, but depend, more generally, on the scheme of principles those decisions presuppose and endorse. So each member accepts that others have rights and that he has duties flowing from that scheme, even though these have never been formally identified or declared. Nor does he suppose that these further rights and duties are conditional on his wholehearted approval of that scheme; these obligations arise from the historical fact that his community has adopted that scheme, which is then special to it, not the assumption that he would have chosen it were the choice entirely his. In short, each accepts political integrity as a distinct political ideal and treats the general acceptance of that ideal, even among people who otherwise disagree about political morality, as constitutive of political community.

Now our stage is properly set (or rather managed) for the crucial question. Each of these three models of community describes a general attitude that members of a political community take toward one another. Would political practices expressing one or another of these attitudes satisfy the conditions of true associative community we identified? We need not pause long over the de facto model of circumstance. It violates even the first condition: it adds nothing, by way of any special attitudes of concern, to the circumstances that define a bare political community. It admits community among people who have no interest in one another except as means to their own selfish ends. Even when this form of community holds among selfless people who act only to secure justice and fairness in the world as they understand these virtues, they have no special concern for justice and fairness toward fellow members of their own community. (Indeed, since their only concern is abstract justice, which is universalistic in its character, they can have no basis for special concern.)

The rulebook model of community might seem more promising. For its members do show a special concern for one another beyond each person's general concern that justice be done according to his lights, a special concern that each other person receive the full benefit of whatever political decisions have in fact been taken under the standing political arrangements. That concern has the necessary individualized character to satisfy the second condition: it runs separately from each person directly to everyone else. But it cannot satisfy the third, for the concern it displays is too shallow and attenuated to count as pervasive, indeed to count as genuine concern at all. People in a rulebook community are free to act in politics almost as selfishly as people in a community of circumstances can. Each one can use the standing political machinery to advance his own interests or ideals. True, once that machinery has generated a discrete decision in the form of a rule of law or a judicial decision, they will accept a special obligation to secure the enforcement of that decision for everyone whom it happens to benefit. But that commitment is too formal, too disconnected from the actual circumstances it will promote, to count as expressing much by way of genuine concern, and that is why it rings hollow as an expression of fraternity. It takes hold too late in the political process; it permits someone to act as the crucial legislative stage with no sense of responsibility or concern for those whom he pretends, once every possible advantage has been secured at their expense, to count as brothers. The familiar version of the argument from fair play—these are the rules under which you have benefited and you must play by them—is particularly appropriate to a rulebook community, which takes politics, as I said, to be a kind of game. But that is the version of the argument most vulnerable to all the objections we began by noticing.

The model of principle satisfies all our conditions, at least as well as any model could in a morally pluralistic society. It makes the responsibilities of citizenship special: each citizen respects the principles of fairness and justice instinct in the standing political arrangement of his particular community, which may be different from those of other communities, whether or not he thinks these the best principles from a utopian standpoint. It makes these responsibilities fully personal: it commands that no one be left out, that we are all in politics together for better or worse, that no one may be sacrificed, like wounded left on the battlefield, to the crusade for justice overall. The concern it expresses is not shallow, like the crocodile concern of the rulebook model, but genuine and pervasive. It takes hold immediately politics begins and is sustained through legislation to adjudication and enforcement. Everyone's political acts express on every occasion, in arguing about what the rules should be as well as how they should be enforced, a deep and constant commitment commanding sacrifice, not just by losers but also by the powerful who would gain by the kind of log-rolling and checkerboard solutions integrity forbids. Its rationale tends toward equality in the way our fourth condition requires: its command of integrity assumes that each person is as worthy as any other, that each must be treated with equal concern according to some coherent conception of what that means. An association of principle is not automatically a just community; its conception of equal concern may be defective or it may violate rights of its citizens or citizens of other nations in the way we just saw any true associative community might. But the model of principle satisfies the conditions of true community better than any other model of community that it is possible for people who disagree about justice and fairness to adopt.

Here, then, is our case for integrity, our reason for striving to see, so far as we can, both its legislative and adjudicative principles vivid in our political life. A community of principle accepts integrity. It condemns checkerboard statutes and less dramatic violations of that ideal as violating the associative character of its deep organization. Internally compromised statutes cannot be seen as flowing from any single coherent scheme of principle; on the contrary, they serve the incompatible aim of a rulebook community, which is to compromise convictions along lines of power. They contradict rather than confirm the commitment necessary to make a large and diverse political society a genuine rather than a bare community: the promise that law will be chosen, changed, developed, and interpreted in an overall principled way. A community of principle, faithful to that promise, can claim the authority of a genuine associative community and can therefore claim moral legitimacy—that its collective decisions are matters obligation and not bare power—in the name of fraternity. These claims may be defeated, for even genuine associative obligations may conflict with, and must sometimes yield to, demands of justice. But any other form of community, whose officials rejected that commitment, would from the outset forfeit any claim to legitimacy under a fraternal ideal.

The models of community used in this argument are ideal in several ways. We cannot suppose that most people in our own political societies self-consciously accept the attitudes of any of them. I constructed them so that we could decide which attitudes we should try to interpret our political practices to express, which is a different matter, and the exercise warrants the following conclusion. If we can understand our practices as appropriate to the model of principle, we can support the legitimacy of our institutions, and the political obligations they assume, as a matter of fraternity, and we should therefore strive to improve our institutions in that direction. It bears repeating that nothing in this argument suggests that the citizens of a nation-state, or even a smaller political community, either do or should feel for one another any emotion that can usefully be called love. Some theories of ideal community hold out that possibility: they yearn for each citizen to embrace all others in emotions as profound, and with an equivalent merger of personality, as those of lovers or the most intimate friends or the members of an intensely devoted family. Of course we could not interpret the politics of any political community as expressing that level of mutual concern, nor is this ideal attractive. The general surrender of personality and autonomy it contemplates would leave people too little room for leading their own lives rather than being led along them; it would destroy the very emotions it celebrates. Our lives are rich because they are complex in the layers and character of the communities we inhabit. If we felt nothing more for lovers or friends or colleagues than the most intense concern we could possibly feel for all fellow citizens, this would mean the extinction not the universality of love. . . .

PART IV

Exploitation and Environment

The Marxian Critique
of Justice*

ALLEN WOOD

WHEN WE READ KARL MARX'S descriptions of the capitalist mode of production in *Capital* and other writings, all our instincts tell us that these are descriptions of an unjust social system. Marx describes a society in which one small class of persons lives in comfort and idleness while another class, in ever-increasing numbers, lives in want and wretchedness, laboring to produce the wealth enjoyed by the first. Marx speaks constantly of capitalist "exploitation" of the worker, and refers to the creation of surplus value as the appropriation of his "unpaid labor" by capital. Not only does capitalist society, as Marx describes it, strike us as unjust, but his own descriptions of it themselves seem to connote injustice.

When we look in the writings of Marx and Engels for a detailed account of the injustices of capitalism, however, we discover at once that not only is there no attempt at all in their writings to provide an argument that capitalism is unjust, but there is not even the explicit claim that capitalism is unjust or inequitable, or that it violates anyone's rights. We find, in fact, explicit denunciations and sustained criticisms of social thinkers (such as Pierre Proudhon and Ferdinand Lassalle) who did condemn capitalism for its injustices or advocated some form of socialism as a means of securing justice, equality, or the rights of man. We even find, perhaps to our surprise, some fairly explicit statements to the effect that capitalism, with all its manifold defects, cannot be faulted as far as justice is concerned. Whatever else capitalism may be for Marx, it does not seem that it is unjust.

*Excerpt from Wood, Allen, "The Marxian Critique of Justice," *Philosophy and Public Affairs* 1, no. 3 (1972). Copyright ©1972 by Princeton University Press. Reprinted by permission of Princeton University Press.

The fact that Marx does not regard capitalism as unjust has been noted before. But Marx's reasons for holding this view, and the concept of justice on which it rests, have been less frequently understood. It is of course true that Marx and Engels do not say much about the manner in which social or economic justice may be actualized, and that they do not concern themselves greatly with the ways in which just social institutions may be distinguished from unjust ones. And if, as I wish to argue, the attainment of justice does not, in itself, play a significant role in either Marxian theory or Marxist practice, these omissions are neither serious nor surprising. Nevertheless, Marx and Engels did take seriously the concept of justice and did have a place for it in their conception of society and society practice. Both were in fact highly critical of what they took to be the misuse of this concept in social thought, its "mystification" and ideological "glorification." This Marxian critique of justice may be viewed as an attempt to clarify the role of the concept of justice in social life and to prevent its ideological abuse. Much can be learned, I think, by tracing this critique to its roots in the Marxian conceptions of society and social practice, and viewing it in relation to Marx's own reasons for denying that capitalism is unjust while at the same time calling for its revolutionary overthrow.

I

The concept of justice has traditionally played an important role in theories of the rational assessment of social institutions. It is commonly felt that justice is the highest merit any social institution can possess, while injustice is the gravest charge which could ever be lodged against it. It seems to be no exaggeration to say that to both the philosopher and the common man justice has often appeared, as Engels once put it, "the fundamental principle of all society, . . . the standard by which to measure all human things, . . . the final judge to be appealed to in all conflicts." Why is such importance attached to the concept of justice? "Justice" (*Gerechtigkeit*), according to Marx and Engels, is fundamentally a juridical or legal (*rechtlich*) concept, a concept related to the law (*Recht*) and to the rights (*Rechte*) men have under it. The concepts of rights and justice are for them the highest rational standards by which laws, social institutions, and human actions may be judged from a juridical point of view. This point of view has long been regarded as being of particular importance for the understanding and assessment of social facts. It is not too much to say that the traditional Western conception of society is itself a fundamentally juridical conception. The social whole, according to this tradition, is the "state" or "body politic," the framework within which human actions are regulated by legal and political processes. The study of society in this tradition has been, above all, the study of these processes; the ideal society, since Plato's time, has been conceived of as the ideal *state*; and social practice, in its highest form, has been thought to be the skillful fashioning of a state through the giving of just laws, or the regulation of the actions of citizens by a wise government. The social life of man, according to this tradition, is his life in relation to the political state; man as a social being is man in relation to those powers which promulgate laws, guarantee rights, and issue juridical commands. Granted this conception of society, it is quite understandable that right and justice should be taken as the fundamental social principles, the highest measure of all social things.

The source not only of Marx's critique of justice, but also of the fundamental originality of his social thought, is his rejection of this political or juridical conception of society. Marx tells us in his preface to A Contribution to the Critique of Political Economy that the origins of his social thought lay in the discontent he felt with this conception as a student of law and the philosophy of law, and particularly of Hegel's Philosophy of Right. His critical reflections, he tells us—and we can see it for ourselves in the articles and manuscripts produced by Marx in the course of the year 1843—"led to the result that juridical relations [Rechtsverhaltnisse], like forms of the state, are to be grasped neither through themselves nor through the so-called universal development of the human spirit, but rather are rooted in the material relations of life, whose totality Hegel . . . comprehended under the term 'civil society.'" The social whole, the fully concrete unity of social life was, in Hegel's view, to be found in the political state; the sphere of men's material activities and interests, civil society, was treated by Hegel as a system of social processes taking place within the political whole and dependent on it. Marx reversed this relationship. Human society, he maintained, is a developing system of collective productive activity, aimed at the satisfaction of historically conditioned human needs; its institutions, including juridical and political ones, are all aspects of this productive activity. As early as 1844 Marx tells us that "Religion, the family, the state, the law [Recht], morality, science, art, etc., are only particular modes of production and fall under its general law." And in the German Ideology Marx and Engels reject "the old conception of history which neglects real relationships and restricts itself to high-sounding dramas of princes and states."

The key to Marx's transformation of Hegel's concept of society is found in the Marxian conception of human practice. Human society, according to the Marxian view, is a fact of nature. But it is nevertheless characterized throughout by the essential quality of man as a natural phenomenon, by productive activity or labor, which distinguishes man from the rest of the natural world. . . .

II

. . . For all his detailed study of social reality and his profound concern with the rational assessment of it, we find no real attempts in Marx's writings to provide a clear and positive conception of right or justice. This relative neglect of juridical concepts and principles does not derive from a personal aversion to "moral preaching" or from an "amoral" attitude toward social reality, as some have suggested. It is due rather to Marx's assessment of the role of juridical conceptions in social life. Because Marx regarded juridical institutions as playing only a supporting role in social life, he attached considerably less importance to juridical conceptions as measures of social rationality than most previous social thinkers were inclined to do. The juridical point of view, for Marx, is essentially one-sided, and to adopt it as the fundamental standpoint from which to judge all social reality is to adopt a distorted conception of that reality. But it is not true that Marx tells us nothing about justice as a rational social norm. In *Capital* he says

> The justice of transactions which go on between agents of production rests on the fact that these transactions arise as natural consequences from the relations of production. The juristic forms in which these economic transactions appear as voluntary actions of the participants, as expressions of their common will and as contracts that may be enforced by the state against a single party, cannot, being mere forms, determine this content. They merely express it. This content is just whenever it corresponds to the mode of production, is adequate to it. It is unjust whenever it contradicts that mode. Slavery, on the basis of the capitalist mode of production, is unjust; so is fraud in the quality of commodities.

This passage by no means amounts to a clear statement of a Marxian "theory of justice," but it is nevertheless quite illuminating. For although Marx speaks in the passage only of the justice of "transactions," the account he gives is general enough to apply to actions, social institutions, even to legal and political structures. And what he says about the justice of transactions does suggest several important theses regarding the concept of justice and its proper function in social theory and practice.

First, as we should expect, Marx views the concept of justice in terms of its function within a given mode of production. The employment of this concept by human thought and its application to social practice are always dependent moments of the process of production. The rational validity of any such employment is, for Marx, always measured in terms of the prevailing mode of production. The political state and the concepts of law and right associated with the public regulation of society are for Marx both determinations of the prevailing mode of production and alienated projections of it. They mirror or reflect production, but in a distorted and mystified way. The state gives itself out as the true representative of society, and *Rechtsbegriffe* pretend to constitute the foundation for the rationality of social practice, based either on the autonomous rationality of the state or on unconditioned rational principles of "right" or "justice" beyond which no rational appeal can be made. But in Marx's view the real raison d'être of juridical institutions and concepts can be understood only from the more comprehensive vantage point of the historical mode of production they both participate in and portray. Justice, therefore, as a *Rechtsbegriffe*, always requires explication from beyond "juristic forms." A determination of the justice of transactions or institutions demands, rather, an appreciation of their function in production. When Marx says that a just transaction is one that corresponds to the prevailing mode of production, he means, I think, that it is one which plays a concrete role in this mode, one which functions as an actual moment in the productive process. Just transactions "fit" the prevailing mode, they serve a purpose relative to it, they concretely carry forward and bring to actuality the process of collective productive activity of human individuals in a concrete historical situation. The judgment whether a social institution is just or unjust depends, then, on the concrete comprehension of the mode of production as a whole, and on an appreciation of the connection between this whole and the institution in question. This is perhaps why Engels says that "social justice or injustice is decided by the science which deals with the material facts of production and exchange, the science of political economy."

Secondly, then, justice is not a standard by which human reason in the abstract measures human actions, institutions, or other social facts. It is rather a standard by which each mode of production measures *itself*. It is a standard present to human thought only in the context of a specific mode of production. Hence there are no general rules or precepts of "natural justice" applicable to any and all forms of society. The ownership of one man by another, for example, or the charging of interest on borrowed money are not in themselves just or unjust. Under the ancient mode of production, the holding of slaves was, as Aristotle argued, both right and expedient. Usury, on the other hand, was essentially foreign for the most part to this mode of production; and where it involved simply making a profit on the momentary distress of another, it was certainly unjust. Under capitalist production, however, direct slavery is unjust; while the charging of interest on borrowed capital is perfectly just.

Thirdly, it is clear that Marx followed Hegel in rejecting a formal conception of justice. For Marx, the justice or injustice of an action or institution does not consist in its exemplification of a juridical form or its conformity to a universal principle. Justice is not determined by the universal compatibility of human acts and interests, but by the concrete requirements of a historically conditioned mode of production. There *are* rational assessments of the justice of specific acts and institutions, based on their concrete function within a specific mode of production. But these assessments are not founded on abstract or formal principles of justice, good for all times and places, or on implicit or hypothetical contracts or agreements used to determine the justice of institutions or actions formally and abstractly. Abstracted from a concrete historical context, all formal philosophical principles of justice are empty and useless; when applied to such a context, they are misleading and distorting, since they encourage us to treat the concrete context of an act or institution as accidental, inessential, a mere occasion for the pure rational form to manifest itself. But the justice of the act or institution is its concrete fittingness to *this* situation, in *this* productive mode. The justice of transactions, Marx says, is not a matter of form, but a matter of content. The justice of an institution depends on the particular institution and the particular mode of production of which it is a part. All juridical forms and principles of justice are therefore meaningless unless applied to a specific mode of production, and they retain their rational validity only as long as the content they possess and the particular actions to which they apply arise naturally out of and correspond concretely to this productive mode.

Finally, the justice of acts or institutions does not depend for Marx on their results or consequences. We might think, for instance, that just acts and institutions would tend to make people happier than unjust ones. But this is by no means necessary. For if a mode of production rests on the exploitation of one class by another, then it seems likely that just institutions under that mode will tend in general to satisfy the needs of the oppressors at the expense of the oppressed. But if this is Marx's view, we might at least be tempted to think that he would agree with Thrasymachus that justice is what is in the interest of the stronger, i.e., of the ruling class. And we may be inclined to think also that he would agree with Hume that those acts and institutions are just which contribute to the preservation, stability, and smooth functioning of society, i.e., of the prevailing mode of production. For, we might argue, if a transaction is to arise naturally out of the existing production relations, to correspond to the prevailing mode of production and play a concrete role in it, then it must serve, or tend to serve, the interests of the ruling class under that mode, and it must contribute, or tend to contribute, to the security and stability of the existing order of things. Now in the short run this may very well be so, and just transactions may even be carried on in many cases with the conscious intention of furthering the interests of a certain class or maintaining the stability of the existing order. But if, as Marx believes, there is an inherent tendency in each mode of production itself toward mounting instability, increasing social antagonism and conflict, and ultimately toward its own eventual overthrow and abolition, then in the long run those very transactions which are most just, which are most intimately a part of a specific mode of production, must also contribute in an essential way to its instability and eventual destruction. For Marx, a transaction is just on account of its function within the whole, and not on account of its consequences for the whole. . . .

III

. . . When capitalist exploitation is described as an "injustice," the implication is that what is wrong with capitalism is its mode of *distribution*. When the appropriation by capital of the worker's unpaid labor is thought of as "unjust," the claim being made is that the worker is being given a smaller (and the capitalist a larger) share of the collective product of society than he deserves, according to the juridical or moral rules and practices which govern distribution, or at least, which *should* govern it. It is therefore being suggested that the answer to capitalist exploitation is to be found in the proper regulation of distribution by means of the promulgation and enforcement of laws, the taking of political decisions, and the stricter adherence by individuals to correct and appropriate moral precepts.

Such a conception of what is wrong with capitalist exploitation is, however, entirely mistaken according to Marx. Distribution, he argues, is not something which exists alongside production, indifferent to it, and subject to whatever modifications individuals in their collective moral and political wisdom should choose to make in it. Any mode of distribution is determined by the mode of production of which it is a functional part. The appropriation of surplus value and the exploitation of labor are not *abuses* of capitalist production, or arbitrary and unfair practices which happen accidentally to be carried on within it (like fraud, for instance, or smuggling, or protection rackets). Exploitation of the worker belongs to the essence of capitalism, and as the capitalist mode of production progresses to later and later stages of its development, this exploitation must in Marx's view grow worse and worse as a result of the laws of this development itself. It cannot be removed by the passage or enforcement of laws regulating distribution, or by any moral or political reforms which capitalist political institutions could bring about. Moreover, any "reforms" of capitalist production which proposed to take surplus value away from capital and put an end to the exploitation of the worker would themselves be injustices of a most straightforward and unambiguous kind. They would violate in the most obvious way the fundamental property rights derived from the capitalist mode of production, and constitute the imposition on it of a system of distribution essentially incompatible with it. It is a mystery how such well-meaning reformers could expect to keep their scheme of "just" distribution working once it had been set up. (One is reminded of Aristotle's remark that any system, no matter how misconceived, can be made to work for a day or two.)

But this is not all. Even if revolutionary practice should put an end to capitalist exploitation, and even if an important aspect of this practice should consist in a change in the juridical rules governing distribution, it would still be wrong to say that the end of exploitation constitutes the rectification of "injustice." Revolutionary politics does not consist, for Marx, in the imposition on society of whatever moral or juridical rules or "principles of justice" the revolutionary politician should find most commendable. It consists rather in the adjustment of the political or juridical institutions of society to a new mode of production, of a determinate form and character, which has already taken shape in society. Unless a fundamental change of this kind in the mode of man's productive activity is already taking place in society of its own accord, any attempt at a truly revolutionary politics would be irrational, futile, and, to use Marx's own word, mere "Donquichoterie." This is what Marx and Engels mean when they say in the *German Ideology* that "Communism is for us not a *state of affairs* to be brought about, an *ideal* to which reality must somehow adjust itself. We call communism the actual movement which is transcending [*aufhebt*] the present state of affairs. The conditions of this movement result from presuppositions already existing."

Political action, therefore, is for Marx one subordinate moment of revolutionary practice. Political institutions do not and cannot create a new mode of production, but can only be brought into harmony with a mode of production that men themselves are already bringing to birth. They can only set the juridical stamp of approval, so to speak, on whatever form of productive activity historical individuals are creating and living. If revolutionary institutions mean new laws, new standards of juridical regulation, new forms of property and distribution, this is not a sign that "justice" is at last being done where it was not done before; it is instead a sign that a new mode of production, with its own characteristic juridical forms, has been born from the old one. This new mode of production will not be "more just" than the old, it will only be just in its own way. . . .

IV

. . . Within Marx's account of the essential irrationality and eventual breakdown of capitalism, the concept of the "exploitation" of labor by capital plays an important role. And since it is the Marxian charge that capitalism is essentially a system of exploitation which has done most to create the impression that Marx condemned capitalism for injustice, I would like to try briefly to explain what role I think this charge actually plays in Marx's critique of capitalism.

Human society, according to some philosophers, is founded on the harmony of human interests, the fact that social relationships are of mutual benefit to those participating in them. In the Marxian view, however, past societies have equally been founded on conflicts of interest, and on the forced labor of one class for the benefit of another. All society, Marx believes, involves an "exchange of human activity" between agents of production; but one of the essential forms of such exchanges is the social relation of dominion and servitude. This relation, in Marx's view, constitutes the foundation of class conflicts and of the historical changes wrought by them.

The essence of servitude for Marx consists in the fact that servitude is a specific form of human productive activity: it is, namely, productive activity which, by means of the loss and renunciation of its products, is itself alienated from the producer and appropriated by someone or something external to him, standing over against him as the independent aim and object of his production. Dominion, as Marx points out, involves not merely the appropriation and enjoyment of things, but "the appropriation of another's will." When the master enjoys the slave's services or the fruits of his labor, he enjoys them as the result of the slave's productive activity, as something into which the slave has put his will and realized his purposes. The appropriation of the slave's products by the master, therefore, necessarily involves for the slave their renunciation, the alienation of the slave's own life-activity and the immediate frustration of his productive will. The labor of servitude is, as Hegel said, essentially "inhibited desire." In its essence, such labor is, in Marx's words, "not voluntary but coerced, it is *forced* labor, . . . a labor of self-sacrifice, of mortification."

In capitalist production, according to Marx, these relations of dominion and servitude are disguised. The capitalist and the worker appear to be independent owners of commodities, exchanging their goods as free individuals. The exchanges between them are entirely just and their equal rights as property owners are strictly respected throughout capitalist production relations, thus giving rise to the illusion that these relations themselves are entirely the result of a voluntary contact between independent persons. In fact, however, since the capitalist mode of production is founded on the sale of labor power by one class to another, capitalist production rests essentially on the appropriation by capital of a part of the worker's product in the form of surplus value. Capital, by its very nature as capital, that is, by its function in capitalist production relations, necessarily exploits the worker by appropriating and accumulating his unpaid labor. And as Marx argues in *Capital*, the end result of the wage laborer's activity is always the further accumulation of capital, of his own product in an alien and autonomous form, which becomes both the necessary condition and the independent aim of his labor, of his life-activity itself.

This exploitation of the laborer by capital is not a form of injustice, but it is a form of servitude. "Capital obtains surplus labor," according to Marx, "without an equivalent, and in essence it always remains forced labor, however much it appears to result from a free contractual agreement." Capitalist exploitation is not a form of fraudulent exchange or economic injustice, but it is a form of concealed dominion over the worker. Capitalism is a system of slavery, and a slavery the more insidious because the relations of dominion and servitude are *experienced* as such without being *understood* as such. The fundamental character of the capitalist relation is even hidden from political economy, in Marx's view, so long as it fails to solve the riddle of surplus value. By solving this riddle, Marx believes he has unmasked the capitalist relation and made it possible for the workers to understand their condition of poverty, frustration, and discontent for what it is: a condition of servitude to their own product in the form of capital.

It bears repeating that although this servitude is a source of misery, degradation, and discontent to the worker, it is *not a form of injustice*. Those who believe that the notion of servitude necessarily "connotes" injustice are the victims of prejudices which many men of less enlightened ages (Aristotle, for example) did not share. And for Marx the appearance of such prejudices in capitalist society is largely the result of the bourgeois ideology which praises capitalism for having done away with direct slavery and feudal serfdom, and for having replaced these "injustices" and "human indignities" with an open society of free men meeting in a free market. The actual servitude which hides behind this mask of universal liberty is, however, neither more nor less just than its predecessors in Marx's view. The servitude of the wage laborer to capital is rather an essential and indispensable part of the capitalist mode of production, which neither the passage of liberal legislation nor the sincere resolve by bourgeois society to respect the "human rights" of all its members can do anything to remove. Nor is the mere fact that capitalism involves servitude a sufficient ground for the workers to rise against it. It is not Marx's belief that servitude as such is an unqualified wrong, an evil to be abolished at all cost with an attitude of *fiat justitia, pereat mundi*. The servitude of capitalism, according to Marx, and even the direct slavery involved in capitalist colonies, have been necessary conditions for the development of modern productive forces. To condemn this servitude unqualifiedly would be to condemn all the productive advances of modern society, which Marx was not about to do. Condemning a relation of servitude when it results from historical limitations on productive forces is for Marx about as rational as condemning medical science because there are some diseases it cannot cure.

A historically potent demand, a genuine and effective *need* for emancipation arises in an oppressed class only under certain conditions. This need does not appear merely as a social ideal, but always as an actual movement within the existing production relations toward concrete historical possibilities transcending them. And it arises, according to Marx's theory, only where there is a disharmony or antagonism between the productive forces and the existing production relations. Within a given mode of production, men develop and change the forces of production. In this way they bring about new historical possibilities, and with them new human desires and needs. These new possibilities cannot be actualized, however, and these new needs satisfied, within the existing production relations. The productive forces have, so to speak, outgrown the production relations and have become antagonistic to them. It is this antagonism which, in Marx's view, supplies the conditions for an epoch of social revolution. And it is only in terms of this antagonism that an effective need for emancipation on the part of an oppressed class can take shape. "Humanity," says Marx, "only sets itself tasks it can solve": "A form of society never perishes before all the productive forces for which there is room in it have developed; and new, higher relations of production never come forth before the material conditions for their existence have taken shape in the womb of the old society itself."

Capitalism itself, Marx believed, systematically creates the forces which will eventuate in its revolutionary overthrow and historical transcendence. It is the inherent tendency of capitalist production to increase the rate of surplus value, to accumulate an ever-larger supply of social wealth in the form of capital. This historical tendency of capitalism leads, as Marx argues in *Capital*, to the mounting instability of capitalist production in a number of different but related ways. Prominent among these tendencies to instability is the increasing burden of servitude placed on the workers by capitalist accumulation. Marx does not think that as capital accumulates, the wages of the worker will necessarily decrease. Indeed, he holds that in general those conditions under which capital expands most rapidly relative to labor are likely to be the most favorable for the worker's material situation. But the accumulation of capital does mean that the *dominion* of capital over the worker, and the "golden chain" the worker forges for himself, which fetters him to capital, tend to grow heavier and heavier. The slave's peculium may possibly increase, but his servitude necessarily grows more and more burdensome.

According to the Marxian theory, then, capitalist production accumulates on the one side an ever-growing supply of social wealth, an ever-expanding set of productive forces; but on the other side it creates at the same time a class of restless slaves, constantly growing in numbers and in discontent. It expands the capacities for the satisfaction of human needs, while at the same time cutting men off in steadily increasing numbers from the means of appropriating and making use of these capacities. And it expands the forces of production by means of the forced labor of precisely those who are alienated from them. Thus capitalism itself produces both the need on the part of the workers to overcome and abolish capitalist production and the material forces which make the abolition of capitalism a genuine historical possibility. It produces at once an ever-growing burden of servitude and an ever-greater capacity for emancipation. In this way, the productive forces it has created become increasingly antagonistic to the production relations by means of which it has created them. This does not mean, however, that for Marx capitalism is bad or irrational *because* its downfall is inevitable. On the contrary, Marx thought that its perpetuation of a condition of unnecessary servitude, its extension of this condition to the great majority of men, and its creation of human desires and opportunities which cannot be satisfied within a capitalist framework were precisely the sorts of defects which would bring about its downfall. Capitalism, in Marx's view, was breaking down because it was irrational, and not the reverse. The irrationalities in capitalism were for Marx at once causes of its downfall and reasons for its abolition.

But if Marx viewed the workers' desire for emancipation as an important reason why capitalism should be abolished, it still seems to me almost as mistaken to say that Marx's critique of capitalism is founded on a "principle of freedom" as it is to say that it is founded on a "principle of justice." I think it would be wrong, in fact, to suppose that Marx's critique of capitalism is necessarily rooted in *any* particular moral or social ideal or principle. It has sometimes been claimed that Marx was fundamentally a utilitarian, because he believed the overthrow of capitalism would bring about greater human happiness. Others have argued that Marx was really a Kantian, since the servitude and exploitation of capitalism to which he objected involve the treatment of men as means only, rather than as ends in themselves. Still others have seen in Marx's hope for an expansion of man's powers under socialism an implicit "self-realization" theory. But of course it is quite possible for someone to value human happiness without being a utilitarian, to object to the treatment of men as mere means without being a Kantian, and to favor the development of human powers and capacities without subscribing to any particular moral philosophy. So there is no good reason, it seems to me, for the adherents of any particular position in moral philosophy to claim that Marx is one of their number. At any rate, Marx seems to me no more a subscriber to any particular moral philosophy than is the "common man" with whose moral views nearly every moral philosopher claims to be in agreement.

Marx's own reasons for condemning capitalism are contained in his comprehensive theory of the historical genesis, the organic functioning, and the prognosis of the capitalist mode of production. And this is not itself a *moral* theory, nor does it include any particular moral principles as such. But neither is it "merely descriptive," in the tedious philosophical sense which is supposed to make it seem problematic how anything of that sort could ever be a reason for condemning what is so "described." There is nothing problematic about saying that disguised exploitation, unnecessary servitude, economic instability, and declining productivity are features of a productive system which constitute good reasons for condemning it. Marx's theory of the functioning and development of capitalism does argue that capitalism possesses these features (among others), but Marx never tried to give any philosophical account of why these features would constitute good reasons for condemning a system that possesses them. He was doubtless convinced that the reasons for condemning capitalism provided by his theory were good ones, and that whatever information moral philosophers might or might not be able to give us about the nature of condemnations of social systems and the nature of reasons for them, no special appeal to

philosophical principles, moral imperatives, or evaluative modes of consciousness would be needed to show that his own reasons for condemning capitalism
were good and sufficient ones. That he was correct in these convictions is
indicated by the fact that no serious defender of capitalism has ever disputed his
critique solely on the grounds of moral philosophy. It has been argued in defense
of capitalism that Marx's theory of capitalist production rests on unsound
economic principles, that it distorts or misinterprets the relation between capital
and labor, and that it gives an inaccurate, one-sided, or incomplete picture of
capitalism. It has also been claimed that Marx's account of the genesis of
capitalist production is historically inaccurate, and that his predictions about its
future have been largely falsified by events which have happened since his time.
But no one has ever denied that capitalism, understood as Marx's theory
understands it, is a system of unnecessary servitude, replete with irrationalities
and ripe for destruction. Still less has anyone defended capitalism by claiming
that a system of this sort might after all be good or desirable, and it is doubtful
that any moral philosophy which could support such a claim would deserve
serious consideration.

Exploitation*

NANCY HOLMSTROM

ACCORDING TO MARX ONE of the primary evils of capitalism (and any other class society) is that it is exploitative—and necessarily so. Socialist and communist societies will (necessarily) not be exploitative and this is one of the reasons why they will in some sense be better. To understand such claims we have to determine exactly what Marx means by "exploitation" and what it is about exploitation that Marx finds to be bad. Neither of these questions is as simple as it might seem. A common misunderstanding of Marx is this: exploitation consists simply in an unequal distribution of social wealth. Workers are exploited because they get so much less of the pie than do capitalists. Another interpretation of Marx's concept is that exploitation consists in the fact that workers do not get the whole pie. They produce all value and, therefore, deserve to get it all back. I will show that both of these interpretations are inadequate or simply mistaken. An error common to both is an overemphasis on distribution. Let someone ask: why is exploitation under capitalism (or any other economic formation) bad? The answer we are strongly inclined to give is: because it is unfair or unjust. But some have argued—among them, Allen Wood—that this obvious answer is not Marx's answer, and indeed it is wrong given Marx's specific theory of capitalist exploitation. But then why is exploitation an evil?

I will first explain Marx's theory of exploitation in capitalism and his general concept. We will then be able to see in what ways exploitation is an evil for Marx, whether or not it is unfair or unjust. I will, however, contend that the arguments purporting to show that exploitation, as conceived by Marx, is not unjust are not conclusive. However, I will also contend that, for Marx, what primarily makes exploitation an evil is not its injustice.

*Reprinted with permission from Nancy Holmstrom's "Exploitation" in *Canadian Journal of Philosophy* 3, no. 2 (1977).

I

In order to elucidate Marx's concept of exploitation, it will help first to explain what Marx means by *necessary, surplus,* and *free labor*. The force of my explanation will be limited at this point and should become clearer as we go on. Necessary labor is that labor—and no more—which will satisfy the subsistence needs of the workers and of their dependents. In Marx's view there will always be some necessary labor even under socialism and communism. "Just as the savage must wrestle with Nature to satisfy his wants, to maintain and reproduce life, so must civilized man, and he must do so under all social formations and under all possible modes of production." Now in class societies (societies not controlled by the working class), workers are required to do more than necessary labor. "Surplus labor," as Marx uses the term, means all labor over and above subsistence labor. In socialist and communist societies, there will be no surplus labor required. Marx believed that there would be surplus labor in socialism and communism, but only because people would desire to do it. In fact, he believed that the primary distinguishing property of human beings was the capacity and need to do creative work. However, given that the goal of production in socialism and communism is simply the satisfaction of needs, no one will be required to do any labor that is not necessary. The only labor required will be some necessary labor, the amount of which will be greatly reduced because of increased productivity.

The idea that there are degrees of freedom and lack of freedom is implicit in Marx's discussions of these points. Labor that is necessary (required by nature) is not free in the fullest sense possible. However, this does not doom it to being unfree or forced labor. Speaking about the realm of necessity, Marx says [in *Grundrisse*]:

> Freedom in this field can only consist in socialized man, the associated producers, rationally regulating their interchange with Nature, bringing it under their common control, instead of being ruled by it as by the blind forces of Nature; and achieving this with the least possible expenditure of energy and under conditions most favorable to, and worthy of their human nature.

Necessary labor, then, can be free or unfree. There is a freedom that is compatible with necessity, which requires control over the activity by the agents and the absence of control by others. Necessary labor in socialist and communist societies will meet this condition. Necessary labor that is not under the control of those doing it, but under alien control, is unfree.

Marx makes it clear that freedom which is compatible with necessity is not the fullest kind of freedom possible. It remains necessary. "Beyond it begins that development of human energy which is an end in itself, the true realm of freedom, which, however, can blossom forth only with the realm of necessity as its basis. The shortening of the work day is its basic prerequisite." Let us call the labor that is free, though necessary, "relatively free" labor, as opposed to "really free" labor, which is not necessary. This kind of surplus labor which is really free labor will only be possible for the majority of people in socialist and communist society. More on this later.

II

The first time that the word "exploitation" appears in *Capital* I is in chapter 9, "The Rate of Surplus Value," in the title of section 1, "The Degree of Exploitation of Labor Power." It first occurs in the text when he says: "The rate of surplus value is therefore an exact expression for the degree of exploitation of labor power by capital, or of the laborer by the capitalist." We have to determine, then, why Marx first introduces the term "exploitation" in this context and exactly what the rate of surplus value is.

Marx's theory of surplus value is his explanation of the origins of profits in capitalism. Capitalism is a system of commodity production. It is a system in which things are bought and sold on a market, in which labor power is a commodity. The production of profit is the purpose of production for the capitalist. What the capitalist produces always has some use; it satisfies some want or other. In Marx's terminology, this is to say that all commodities have some use value. But this is not the reason why the capitalist produces what he does. What the capitalist produces must also have some value for exchange, which Marx calls *exchange value*. A capitalist will not produce something that has use value but no exchange value, such as unsubsidized housing of good quality for poor people. The exchange value (usually abbreviated as "value"), at which the capitalist aims, must, moreover, be greater than the value of the means of production and the labor power that went into its production, or else there would be no point to the process for the capitalist. The capitalist pays out money for the means of production, which Marx calls *constant capital* or c, and for labor power, which Marx calls *variable capital* or v. The *value* of the product, then, must be *greater* than c plus v. The additional value has its source in the peculiar nature of the commodity labor power. Like any other commodity, labor power is assumed to be sold at its value most of the time. The (exchange) value of a commodity, according to the Marxist theory, is the simple, abstract, socially necessary labor time required to produce it. This is the labor theory of (exchange) value. In the case of labor power, its value includes the necessities of life not only for the worker, but also for the worker's family, so as to ensure the future supply of labor power. The workers produce this value in only a portion of the time that they work: the labor done during this time is necessary labor. The value that they produce during the rest of the time, during surplus labor time, is surplus value, which we will call s. This is the source of profit. It creates value greater than its own value, which is the reason why labor power is called variable capital.

The ratio of surplus value to the value of labor power, s/v, is the rate of surplus value. When we understand how the value of labor power is determined, we can see that this ratio is equivalent to the ratio of surplus labor to necessary labor. Since the wage that the worker receives is for the necessary labor time and only for necessary labor time (assuming labor power is sold at its value), this same ratio is also equivalent to the ratio of unpaid to paid labor. This division of the work day under capitalism into necessary and surplus labor time, with the latter unpaid, is concealed by the wage relationship. The worker receives a wage and works a full day, which suggests that the wage is payment for a day's labor. However, what workers really sell to the capitalists, according to Marx, is not labor, but the capacity to labor or labor power, which capitalists then use as they wish for the day. It was this discovery of Marx's that enables one to discern the division of the work day under capitalism into necessary and surplus labor time.

Let us turn now to the question of the freedom of labor under capitalism. Labor under capitalism would appear to be free. This appearance, however, according to Marx, is an illusion, which results from several facts. The individual laborer is not tied to any particular capitalist, as is a slave or a serf, but can work for various different capitalists and usually does so. There are no chains and no laws that force workers to work for a particular boss or even to work at all. It appears that what makes them work is their desire to satisfy certain needs, so that they choose the capitalist who offers them the best deal. Sometimes they get a better deal than at other times. Thus the relationship appears to be a free exchange between equals, one buying and the other selling. In fact, Marx believes, the exchange is an unfree one, because it is based on force. Although they are not tied to any particular capitalist, workers under capitalism are tied to the class of capitalists. The laborer under capitalism who is free of feudal bonds is also "free" from ownership of the means of production. Persons who have no access to the means of production other than their own capacity to labor do not need to be forced to work by chains or by laws. The "freedom" they have compels them to sell their labor power to those who own the means of production and to put themselves under their dominion. Workers who have once sold their labor power to the owners of the means of production are then forced by them to do non-necessary surplus labor during part of the work day. This surplus labor is, by definition, unnecessary to them and they are uncompensated for it. Hence Marx says that surplus labor "in essence . . . always remains forced labor no matter how much it may seem to result from free contractual agreement." The source of the capitalists' dominion over unpaid labor is the separation of most of the population from the means of production and the accumulation of those means by a few. This was originally accomplished for the most part by "conquest, enslavement, robbery, murder, briefly, force."

The labor that workers do during the rest of the day is necessary and is compensated in the form of the necessities of life. In a sense they are working for themselves during this time. Hence, necessary labor has less of a forced nature than surplus labor. Nevertheless, it is unfree. As explained earlier, necessary labor can be (relatively) free for Marx only if it is under the control of those who are doing it. In capitalism, however, workers are under the dominion of capitalists who, Marx says, are merely the personifications of capital (the capitalist mode of production). Production is not brought under the conscious collective control of all members of society. Instead "anarchy reigns in the field of production." The market is seen as functioning according to natural necessity, beyond human control. Inside the factory, workers work under the despotism of capital during necessary labor as well as surplus labor time. So both necessary and surplus labor are unfree under capitalism, but the latter has an additional element of compulsion. The same ratio of surplus value to the value of labor power can, therefore, also be expressed as the ratio of forced labor to labor that is relatively unforced but still unfree.

The product of the workers' surplus, unpaid and forced labor, is then appropriated by the owner of labor power and the means of production, the capitalist. This surplus value is the source of their profits. The actual producers have no control over the surplus. The profits of capitalists, then, according to Marx's theory, are generated by surplus, unpaid and forced labor, the product of which the producers do not control. This is exploitation as Marx uses the term.

We can see then why Marx introduced the term "exploitation" in the context of discussing the origin of capitalist profits. Profits come from surplus value and the extraction of surplus value involves the appropriation of the product of forced, unpaid, surplus labor. It is not the fact that capitalists have some, or even a very large income that is exploitative. It is the fact that the income is derived through forced unpaid, surplus labor, the product of which the producers do not control, which makes it exploitative.

Although the concept is first explained with reference to capitalism, Marx did not think that exploitation was unique to capitalism. In fact, he says that "The essential difference, between, for instance, a society based on slave labor, and one based on wage labor, lies only in the mode in which this surplus is in each case extracted from the actual producers, the laborer." While the existence of exploitation in capitalism had to be discovered by science, and specifically through the discovery of surplus value, the discovery of exploitation in feudal society requires no deep analysis. The division of a serf's labor into necessary and surplus labor is quite apparent. Serfs worked part of the time on their own land and kept the product of that labor. This was necessary labor, which is essentially labor for themselves. During that time, however, they were subject to all sorts of constraints set by the lord, which made their necessary labor unfree. To be allowed to do this necessary labor, they had, moreover, to work on the lord's land as well, and the product of this labor went to the lord. That serfs were forced to do this non-necessary labor for the lord was made brutally apparent to any serf who failed to do it. In the feudal mode of production, then, it is quite clear that workers were forced to do unpaid surplus labor the product of which they did not control, hence that they were exploited.

In a system of production based on slavery, the despotism exerted over the slaves in all their labor is very apparent. That the product of slave labor is appropriated by the persons forcing them to work is also clear. What is concealed by the relationship between the slaves and their masters is that part of the slaves' labor is for themselves in that part of the product is returned to them in the form of all or some of the necessities of life. This labor is certainly unfree, although there is a sense in which it is less compelled than the non-necessary, uncompensated labor they do the rest of the time. Slavery thus also involves exploitation: part of the labor that is done is forced unpaid surplus labor the product of which is under the control of nonproducers.

The features common to exploitation, as I have explained it, that it involves forced, surplus, and unpaid labor, the product of which is not under the producers' control, are not four unconnected features. While not logically connected, perhaps, they can be seen to imply one another given Marx's empirical assumptions. If the producers receive merely the necessities of life, then what they produce beyond that is surplus and is uncompensated or unpaid. To be paid or compensated does not simply mean getting a certain amount of money or material goods. A large stockholder in a corporation does not necessarily directly get any more money or material goods if the value of his stock goes up. Nevertheless, he profits, he is compensated, because he has (partial) control over something that has increased in value. If the producers are not compensated for their surplus labor, then it follows both that they do not receive the surplus they have produced and that they have no control over the surplus product. People will seldom knowingly produce more than they need if they have no control over it and are not otherwise compensated. Therefore, labor which has these three features will also, most probably, be forced labor. Thus in speaking about exploitation in general, Marx said that the essential difference between different exploitative systems lay only in the mode in which the surplus was extracted from the producers. This description implies all four features of exploitation: that it is the production of a surplus, appropriated from the producers, uncompensated for, and forced.

Exploitation will occur in all societies in which a minority controls the means of production, in other words, all class societies. This is the basic cause of exploitation. According to Marx, a ruling class developed as soon as it became possible to produce more than was needed for subsistence, to produce a surplus. The ruling class is the class the controls the means of production. This control enables them to force the producers to produce more than they receive. Controlling the means of production, including the producers, the ruling class also controls and lives off the product of the surplus, unpaid and forced labor of the producers. The mode in which this surplus is extracted differs from one class society to another.

III

Marx's theory of exploitation in capitalism and his general concept of exploitation have been explained. I would like now to go into further clarifications of the concept and show why certain alternative interpretations are mistaken.

In our interpretation of Marx's concept of exploitation, little importance has been given to the distribution of income. To do otherwise would be inconsistent with Marx's emphasis on the sphere of production as opposed to the sphere of circulation. It would also be inconsistent with his explicit statement that principles of distribution will always be consequences of a given mode of production. It is true that in an exploitative society nonproducers appropriate the product of producers and also that workers who are exploited do unpaid labor. It is also true that the relationship between profits and wages is connected with the degree of exploitation. However, these facts do not support an analysis of exploitation that makes distribution of income central to the concept.

High wages do not mean that workers are not exploited or even that they are exploited to a lesser degree. However, the ratio of capitalist profits to workers' wages (relative wages) may be seen to be connected with the rate of exploitation, if we accept a key assumption. If labor power is sold at its value (which is the key assumption), the ratio of surplus to necessary labor is equivalent to the ratio of unpaid to paid labor. Since profits come out of surplus value, and since wages are the value of labor power, the ratio of profits to wages will be equivalent to the rate of surplus value or the rate of exploitation. Marx assumed that the ratios of surplus to necessary labor, surplus value to the value of labor power, unpaid to paid labor, and forced to less forced labor were all equivalent because he assumed that labor power, like other commodities, would generally be sold at its value, an assumption shared by almost all economists. However, although there will always be a portion of labor that is unpaid, these ratios will not all be equivalent if labor power is not sold at its value. Neither the fact of exploitation nor its rate would be affected. If wages were to do the unlikely thing and go above the value of labor power, this would not make the worker less exploited, and if, more likely, it went below its value, this would not make the worker more exploited. Although the ratio of profits to wages is connected with the rate of exploitation, this is due to its connection with the ratio of surplus labor to necessary labor and of forced unpaid labor to paid labor. The high relative income of capitalists to that of workers is not definitive of exploitation.

The degree of exploitation is determined by the ratio of surplus to necessary labor. The greater the proportion of time that the worker is forced to work to produce a surplus for the capitalist, the greater the rate of exploitation. Workers who work a six-hour day and produce their own value in one hour, are more exploited than workers who work a twelve-hour day and produce their own value in eight hours. Both the rate of exploitation and the absolute amount of exploitation are greater in the former case. The decrease of the amount of surplus labor down to zero, or down close to zero, is ruled out by the needs of the system. There would be no production if there were no profit derived from production. Thus exploitation can never be eliminated in capitalism. Furthermore, it will always be in the interests of capitalists to try to increase the ratio of surplus to necessary labor, the ratio of profit to investment, and in the interests of workers to decrease it. Hence, the inevitability of class antagonism. This consequence of my interpretation of what it is for one person to exploit others makes it clear why Marx believed in the necessity of a revolution. On many other interpretations, it is less clear why Marx was a revolutionary.

Exploitation is inevitable not only in capitalism but in any class society, including a society ruled by a bureaucracy. The question of whether the bureaucrats' material conditions are better or worse is irrelevant to questions of whether the workers are exploited. It is also irrelevant to study the nature of those in control. So long as workers do not control the means of production they will be exploited, they will be forced to work part of the time for no return, and they will not have control over the surplus they produce.

The reality of exploitation is also not affected by how the surplus is used by those who appropriate it. Under feudalism most of the surplus was directly consumed by the individual feudal lords who appropriated it. Under capitalism most of the surplus goes to maintaining and developing the means of production and buying labor power. Only a small portion is directly consumed by the capitalist class. *Even if some fledgling capitalist reinvested so much of the surplus that his standard of living was no higher than that of his employees, this would not change the fact that he was exploiting them.* They would still be forced to work and produce a surplus that he then appropriates.

Another interpretation of exploitation that makes distribution central is the interpretation which takes exploitation to consist in the fact that workers do not receive back all the wealth that is produced. Behind this interpretation is the idea that, according to Marx, labor is the source of all wealth and hence, workers should get back all the wealth that is produced. Marx, however, directly contradicts both these views in The Critique of the Gotha Program. He says that nature, as much as labor, is the source of wealth, and he makes clear that the elimination of exploitation would not mean returning to workers all the wealth they produce. In a socialist society, Marx explains, before workers receive back the proceeds of their labor, deductions have to be made for a number of social needs and for the maintenance and development of the means of production.

Since these social needs include the care of those unable to work, the producers do not receive it all back indirectly either. Nor does the producing class receive it all back, since Marx does not limit support of those unable to work to members of the producing class. The principle of distribution that will be operative in socialism is "to each according to his labor." The principle that will be operative in a communist society is "to each according to his needs." Neither of these principles implies that workers receive back all the wealth that they produce.

This raises the question of whether some labor in socialism and communism will be unpaid. To the extent that workers do not receive as disposable income all the wealth that they produce, then some of their labor will be unpaid. One of the conditions of exploitation, unpaid labor, would then be a feature of socialism and communism as well as of class societies. Yet Marx did not think that socialism and communism were exploitative societies. This is because being unpaid is not a sufficient condition of exploitation. The other conditions of exploitation are necessary and they are not fulfilled in socialist and communist societies. There is no forced labor. The surplus is under the control of those who produce it. There is no class of nonproducers who appropriate what workers have produced. Workers do not consume it all, directly or indirectly, but they control it as a class. This point suggests another interpretation of what it is to be paid. Earlier in the paper I pointed out that the wealth of stockholders in a corporation is not simply equal to their immediate disposable income. They have wealth in the corporation. This does not imply, however, that they would be permitted to walk off with some of the machinery that belonged to the corporation, the value of which was somehow calculated to be equal to their share in the corporation. They are considered to have wealth in the corporation where wealth means command over resources. In this sense, because workers in socialist and communist societies have control over all the wealth that is produced, they can be said to be fully paid. To conclude this point, we can say that whether or not workers in socialist and communist societies do any unpaid labor depends on what it means to be paid. In one sense, they are fully paid, in another, they are not. Since being unpaid in the narrow sense is not sufficient for exploitation, it does not matter which interpretation of being paid is correct. On either one, it follows that socialist and communist societies are nonexploitative. Since this is clearly what Marx thought, any other implication should raise doubts about itself.

IV

We turn now to the question of why Marx thought exploitation an evil. This question is easy to answer now that the concept of exploitation has been clarified. When x exploits y, y is forced to do unnecessary, unpaid labor and does not control the product of that labor. Force, domination, unequal power and control are involved in exploitation both as preconditions and as consequences. This is why Marx thinks exploitation an evil. And, as Wood says, this servitude is "the more insidious because it is experienced as such without being understood as such."

Those who control the means of production appropriate the product of forced labor. [Lawrence] Crocker calls this undemocratic control of production and says that this is why Marx condemned exploitation. This explanation is inadequate because it obscures the connection that exploitation has to the labor theory of value and to alienation. Although it is true that the majority does not have control of production in class societies, more to the point is the fact that producers do not have control. The labor theory of value says the value of a product is a function of the labor that went into it. Being congealed labor, the product is in some sense part of the producers. When it is taken away from them, they are thereby diminished, impoverished, denuded. The connections with Marx's theory of alienation are obvious, but are not obvious if we describe exploitation simply as undemocratic control of production. This characterization of exploitation is also one-sided in that it fails to bring out the fact that workers who are exploited are themselves under the control of nonproducers. Because they must sell their labor power to the capitalist, their productive activity, their very capacity for life activity comes under the control of the capitalist. Again we see the systematic connection between exploitation and alienation.

Now in addition to involving force and domination, isn't exploitation also unjust? Wood has argued quite persuasively [in his "The Marxian Critique of Justice"] that Marx did not think so. According to Wood, Marx held justice to be a juridical concept which only makes sense in terms of its function within a given mode of production. In what is probably the most important passage from Marx that Wood uses to support his interpretation, Marx says [in *Capital* III], "The justice of transactions arise as natural consequences from the relations of production. . . . This content is just whenever it corresponds to the mode of production, is adequate to it. It is unjust whenever it contradicts that mode." The transaction that goes on between capitalist and worker is the buying of the worker's labor power by the capitalist, usually at its full value. "This is," says Wood, "according to the Ricardian formula and the strictest rules of commodity exchange, a just transaction exchange of equivalent for equivalent. Surplus value, to be sure, is appropriated by the capitalist without an equivalent. But there is nothing in the exchange requiring him to pay any equivalent for it." If the capitalist receives more value from this commodity than he started with, Marx calls this "peculiar good fortune for the buyer (of labor power) but no injustice at all to the seller." Such statements are usually ignored by interpreters who claim that Marx thought exploitation to be unjust. Wood suggests that what they often have in mind is that it is unjust if workers do not receive back all the value that they produce, and, as we have seen, this is a mistake. Wood also argues correctly that "for Marx justice is not and cannot be a genuinely revolutionary notion." An interpretation which construes Marx to base his critique of capitalism on its injustice would most likely lead to reformist conclusions, since the emphasis would tend to be on enlightening people to its injustice. It does not follow, however, as Wood seems to think, that merely to hold exploitation to be unjust has reformist consequences.

An initial problem with Wood's interpretation is that it is not clear that the transaction between worker and capitalist should be looked at in the way Wood does. Allen and Fried both point out that the worker is not paid what he is supposed to be paid according to bourgeois ideology. The transaction that is supposed to be going on is not just by capitalist standards. So there is an inevitable gap between principle and practice in bourgeois society.

The main problem with the interpretation, however, in my opinion, is that Wood views the exchange between capitalist and worker too narrowly, abstracted totally from its background. Some of the key passages that Wood cites in support of his interpretation of the exchange between capitalist and worker as just, do not, upon careful inspection, support his interpretation. One of the most important of these is to be found at *Capital* I, [chapter 6], where Marx talks of the exchange between capitalist and worker as an exchange of equivalent for equivalent which is just, according to the standards of commodity production. Now Marx also says in the same paragraph that workers freely sell their labor power to the capitalist. I think that a useful analogy can be drawn between Marx's views about the freedom of the transaction and the equivalence of the exchange. As for the freedom of the transaction, Marx says, "the 'free' laborer . . . agrees, i.e., *is compelled* by social-conditions, to sell the whole of his active life, his very capacity to work, for the price of the necessities of life, his birthright for a mess of pottage," and also that "surplus labor always remains forced labor—no matter how much it may *appear* to result from free contractual agreement." According to Marx, the exchange between capitalist and worker appears free only if we take a narrow look just at the exchange itself as occurring between an individual worker and capitalist. Looking at the social background of the exchange, and looking at the relationship, not between an individual worker and an individual capitalist, but between the working class and the capitalist class, we get a very different picture. What looks free and independent is in reality totally dependent and unfree.

Applying this point to the question of whether capitalists and workers exchange equivalents, we also get a different answer if we look at the background of the exchange and at the relationship between classes rather than between individuals. This is suggested by Marx when he says "only buyer and seller, mutually dependent, face each other in commodity production." However, he says, the matter looks quite different if we consider capitalist production in the uninterrupted flow of its renewal and if, in place of the individual capitalist and the individual worker, we view them in their totality, the capitalist class and the working class confronting each other. But in doing so, we should be applying standards quite foreign to commodity production.

If matters are looked at in that way we would understand why Marx refers to the surplus product as "the tribute annually exacted from the working class by the capitalist class," and goes on to say that, "though the latter with a portion of that tribute purchases the additional labor power even at its full price, so that equivalent is exchanged for equivalent, the transaction is for all that only the old dodge of every conqueror who buys commodities with the money he has robbed them of." We would hardly call such a transaction just even if equivalent is exchanged for equivalent. But is equivalent exchanged for equivalent? Marx says elsewhere that "capital retains this surplus labor without an equivalent." Looking at the exchange between individual members of the conquered and conquering groups, one might say yes. However, looking at the "exchange" between the conquered and conquering groups as a whole, it is clear that equivalent is not exchanged for equivalent. In fact, it is not really an exchange at all!

Going back to the passage Wood cites, where Marx says that equivalent is exchanged for equivalent, these points suggest that Marx is there describing how matters superficially appear, but not how they really are. This suggestion is confirmed later, on the same page, when Marx describes the sphere where transactions take place as the sphere "which furnishes the 'Free Trader Vulgaris' with . . . the standard by which he judges a society based on capital and wages. . . . This sphere is a very Eden of the innate rights of man. There alone rule Freedom, Equality, Property and Bentham." So the context of the passage that Wood cites in isolation is one of ridiculing such ideas as illusions of bourgeois ideology. Having surveyed the background of this so-called exchange as Marx sees it, we now see that calling it a just exchange could only be done tongue-in-cheek, or to mean: "This is *taken* to be just."

Another questionable interpretation has been placed on Marx's criticism of the demand for and even the notion of a fair day's wage in *The Critique of the Gotha Program*. Wood holds that Marx's criticism was due to the fact that workers were already receiving a fair day's wage, and yet were still exploited. Another, at least equally plausible interpretation, is that the notion of a fair day's wage is a contradiction in terms, since all wages involve unpaid labor, based on force, and hence, are all unfair.

Wood interprets such statements as "right can never be higher than the economic structure of society and the cultural development conditioned by it," as well as the statement from *Capital* III quoted earlier [in this section], to mean that it is inappropriate to use the standards of one mode of production to criticize another mode of production. However, it can also be interpreted as Fried does, to mean that what standards of right can actually be exemplified depends on the mode of production. It is all right, she says, to use the standards of one to criticize another, but only in combination with the struggle to change the mode of production to one where the other standard could be put into practice.

A provocative consequence of Wood's interpretation is that, according to Marx, reforms that would take away surplus value would be "injustices of the most straightforward and unambiguous kind." But surely Marx would never have said this. In fact, he would have considered it just the sort of ideological mystification that lie was concerned to expose and to ridicule.

I conclude that whether Marx thought exploitation to be an evil because it was unjust, as well as for different reasons, is not clear. However, there were other independent reasons why Marx considered exploitation an evil. It is evil, Marx held, because it involves force and domination in manifold ways and because it deprives workers of control that should be theirs. Socialist and communist societies as conceived by Marx will necessarily exclude exploitation. This is one of the reasons why they will be better than any class society.

Why Marxists Should Still Be Interested in Exploitation*

PAUL WARREN

INTRODUCTION

"EXPLOITATION" IS ONE OF Marxism's most salient concepts, figuring importantly in its theory of history, its analysis and critique of capitalism, and its account of possible socialist futures to capitalism.

But the definition of exploitation remains vigorously debated within Marxism. This is no doubt owing to its political and theoretical centrality, but also to its close relation to the problematical labor theory of value. It has been maintained by some that because the labor theory of value is false, the Marxian theory of exploitation is thereby undermined.[1] Sensitive to this objection, as well as to the important place of exploitation within Marxism more generally, a number of economists and philosophers sympathetic to Marxism have sought to elaborate an account of exploitation that would be independent of the labor theory of value, yet consistent with the central thrust of Marx's thought. One of the most important of these reconstructions is John Roemer's property relations theory of exploitation. Roemer aims not only to separate the Marxian concept of exploitation from the labor theory of value, but also to clarify its ethical content and at the same time develop a more general concept of exploitation that would be useful in analyzing contemporary socialism.

Although it contains many valuable insights, in my view Roemer's property relations account of exploitation is inadequate. The main defect of Roemer's account is that it doesn't adequately focus on the differential power that unequal ownership of productive assets confers on the owners of larger shares of those

---

*Printed with the author's permission.

assets. One consequence is that Roemer's theory marginalizes the role that unequal labor exchanges and unequal relations of power have in a normative account of exploitation, focusing instead on injustice in the processes through which unequal distributions of assets arise. Although Roemer is right that exploitation is objectionable on the grounds of its injustice, because the specific approach to justice he proposes neglects both power and labor contribution, it saps much of the normative interest from the Marxian concept of exploitation. Thus, his conclusion that Marxists "shouldn't be interested in exploitation" should be rejected because it rests on an inadequate account of the nature of exploitation.

I will use my criticisms of Roemer to sketch an alternative "power inclusive" definition of exploitation. In my alternative account, "exploitation" refers to the complex process through which differential economic power brings about unequal labor transfers. Accordingly, the unequal control of productive assets is not unjustly exploitative because it arises in an ethically objectionable manner (contra Roemer), but because in a forward-looking way it enables some agents to gain from the labor of others simply in virtue of that unequal control. The ethical objectionability of exploitation so understood stems in part from its being a process that generates outcomes that violate the *labor contribution* principle (i.e., rewards should be proportional to labor contribution) Marx mentions in the *Critique of the Gotha Program*. But the normative significance of exploitation also includes the two additional features that exploiters use their *power* to generate unequal outcomes and they *appropriate the labor* of others in the process. While this "power inclusive" alternative requires more defense than I am able to provide below, I hope to show that it is more promising than Roemer's property relations definition and consequently that Roemer's obituary of the Marxian theory of exploitation is premature.

ROEMER'S CONCEPT OF EXPLOITATION

Roemer discusses at least three different Marxian conceptions of exploitation in his various writings.[2] One is the classical Marxian conception in which exploitation is linked to the labor theory of surplus value, the separation of workers from the means of production, and the domination of workers at the point of production. Although capitalism eliminates the system of coercive labor transfer characteristic of feudal production relations and replaces it with a system of production relations in which individuals control their own labor power, Marx believed the "free" wage-labor made possible by such relations masked the continued exploitation of society's direct producers. Using the labor theory of value and the distinction between labor power and labor activity, Marx argued that labor power is a unique commodity because, in being put to use in production, it generates more value than is required to produce it. For Marx, the process through which surplus labor is extracted from direct producers within capitalism is central to understanding the logic of the capitalist system as a whole and thus fundamental to his scientific enterprise. Furthermore, recognition of this extraction of surplus labor within capitalism provides the basis for the moral charge that capitalism is an inherently exploitative economic system.

A second conception of exploitation is a generalization of the classical Marxian account that Roemer calls the unequal exchange definition. According to this conception, a person is exploited if he or she spends more hours of labor in production than are embodied in the goods that person can purchase with revenues from production; a person who can purchase goods embodying more labor time than spent in production is an exploiter. This definition is more general than the traditional Marxian definition because it omits reference to labor markets, the forced selling of labor power, the domination of workers at the workplace, and the labor theory of value.

A third definition of exploitation is Roemer's own property relations definition, according to which a group of people S is exploited by its complement S' in a society with the private ownership of the means of production if (1) S would benefit and S' would suffer from a redistribution of the means of production in which each owned an equal share, and (2) S' gains by virtue of the labor of S.[3] The first clause tells us that in order to test whether a distribution of assets is exploitative we should consider the welfare consequences of an equal redistribution of those assets for their respective owners. The fundamental idea is that exploiters gain and exploited lose in virtue of exploitation and, conversely, that exploiters should lose and exploited gain by an equal redistribution. Roemer introduces the second clause to capture the idea that exploiters benefit not simply from being unfairly rich, but from the labor of those whom they exploit.[4]

In his book *A General Theory of Exploitation and Class*, Roemer argues that exploitation in the unequal exchange sense can arise in the absence of markets on which labor power is bought and sold, without surplus labor being extracted in the production process, and without direct producers being separated from the means of production. Using a number of general equilibrium models, Roemer demonstrates that the requirements for the unequal exchange of labor are a market in either credit or independently produced commodities and the unequal ownership of the means of production. Consequently, the unequal exchange of labor can occur without the additional institutional specifications required by the traditional Marxian conception of exploitation. Roemer further defends the "Class-Exploitation" and "Wealth-Class Correspondence" principles. The former says that there is a correspondence between class and exploitation (i.e., those who sell their labor power will be exploited and those who buy labor power will be exploiters) and the latter says that relations of both class and exploitation arise endogenously from individuals optimizing under constraints imposed by their respective ownership of productive assets. While the property relations and unequal exchange definitions render the same verdicts about the existence of exploitation, Roemer views the property relations definition as superior. This is not only because it identifies the source of unequal labor exchanges in the unequal ownership of productive assets, but also because it makes explicit the ethical assumptions of Marxian exploitation, viz., that unequal exchanges are bad because they arise from unjust property relations.

In subsequent work Roemer has further extended the case for the superiority of the property relations conception over both the unequal exchange and classical Marxian conceptions.[5] His case is based primarily on three examples. The first is his Adam-Karl model, in which each agent has the very same endowment of capital goods (which can also be used for consumption purposes), but different preferences for leisure and consumption. Karl desires to work little in his youth, preferring to trade future leisure for present leisure. Adam has the opposite preference and is willing to work in the present in order to have future leisure. In the first production period it is possible for each to build up his stock of assets. Given their respective preferences, in the first period Adam accumulates a sizable stock, whereas Karl consumes his. The result is that at the beginning of the second production period Adam proposes an arrangement where Karl works for him, using his (Adam's) assets. On the other hand, Adam would not work at all, but would live off of Karl's labor. Karl is exploited according to both the unequal exchange and classical Marxian conceptions because Karl is forced to accept Adam's offer (i.e., starvation is not an acceptable alternative) and Karl transfers his labor to Adam. Karl is also exploited according to Roemer's own property relations definition because he would benefit and Adam would suffer from an equal redistribution of assets (clause [1]) and Adam would gain in virtue of Karl's labor (clause [2]). But Roemer argues that although *technically* exploitation exists according to all three definitions, this exploitation is not normatively objectionable. He writes in *Free to Lose*,

> The conclusion to be drawn from the example, then, is this: when exploitation is an injustice, it is not because it is exploitation as such, but because the distribution of labor expended and income rewarded in an exploitative situation are consequences of an initial distribution of assets that is unjust. The injustice of an exploitative allocation depends upon the injustice of the initial assets.

If the original distribution of assets arose in an unjust way, then the transfer of labor that ensues from that distribution would be ethically exploitative. However, because in the case described Karl's fate is self-inflicted and not the result of any prior injustice, Roemer concludes that the initial unequal distribution of assets is not unjust and, therefore, that the resulting unequal exchange of labor is not exploitative in any ethically meaningful sense.

Roemer's second model is that of Maggie and Ron, who have different endowments of productive assets and different preferences. Maggie is rich in productive assets, while Ron is poor. Maggie prefers to have more consumption goods than leisure time, whereas Ron prefers leisure time to consumption goods. After having worked her assets Maggie rents some of Ron's, the latter paying her a wage for that labor. The result of this arrangement is an unequal exchange of labor from Maggie to Ron. In this case the unequal exchange and property relations conceptions of exploitation issue different judgments about the existence of exploitation. According to the unequal exchange conception, Ron exploits Maggie because her working more time enables him to work less. But because the unequal exchange of labor results from Ron's and Maggie's different preferences, there is nothing objectionable about it. Hence, the unequal exchange definition gives the wrong verdict if we are concerned with exploitation in the normative sense. On the other hand, with respect to the property relations definition, although clause (1) is satisfied because Ron would gain and Maggie would lose from an equal redistribution of assets, clause (2) isn't satisfied because Maggie doesn't benefit from Ron's labor; conversely, although Ron benefits from Maggie's labor, Ron would not lose from an equal redistribution of assets, hence he is not an exploiter. Thus, there is no exploitation in this case according to the property relations conception. According to Roemer, this is the intuitively correct verdict.

Roemer's third model is that of Andrea and Bob. Andrea owns a large, productive machine and Bob owns a smaller, less productive machine. Additionally, Andrea has come to possess her superior technology through an unjust process. Although Bob could produce goods that would satisfy his subsistence needs by working on his own small machine, Andrea makes a job offer to him that would permit him to earn the same bundle of goods while performing less labor. The profits Andrea gains from this arrangement finance her consumption. Thus, although Bob is not forced to work for Andrea, he is ethically exploited by her. Roemer intends the example to show that the key to the ethical objectionability of exploitation is not the presence of force, but rather a distribution of assets that has arisen through an unjust process. According to Roemer, the reason why we intuitively judge Andrea as an exploiter and Bob as exploited is that Andrea came to possess her machine through an unjust process. The example of Andrea and Bob shows that those such as Jeffrey Reiman who include force in their definition of exploitation are mistaken.[6] The property relations definition renders the correct verdict about the existence of exploitation as long as it can be shown that the original distribution of assets arose through an unjust process.

To summarize, Roemer believes that his Karl-Adam, Ron-Maggie, and Andrea-Bob models provide arguments against the classical Marxian and unequal exchange accounts of exploitation and support for his property relations alternative. These models also show, Roemer contends, that Marxists should reorient their normative focus away from a concern with unequal labor exchanges and toward an examination of the various paths through which the unequal possession of productive assets arise. In the best-case scenario labor transfers are only a "surrogate" for the normative interests of Marxists, which should be directed at questions concerning the legitimacy of different types of property systems. But because exploitation in the sense of the unequal exchange of labor can be misleading, there is no reason for Marxists to be interested in it. This result has the salutary effect of clearing the decks, releasing Marxists from the burden of having to tie their moral concerns to traditional exploitation theory, and enabling them to directly engage liberal arguments concerning the distributive justice of different systems of property relations. Capitalism may indeed be unjust, but exploitation theory is of no help in making that case. Another implication of Roemer's property relations account is that it is not private ownership, but rather the unequal distribution of privately owned assets that is exploitative. The property relations conception of exploitation supports people's capitalism and not the more traditional Marxian commitment to socialism.

CRITIQUE OF ROEMER

Roemer interprets the Karl-Adam model as showing both (1) that unequal labor exchanges are objectionable only if the initial distribution of assets is unjust, and (2) that when unequal labor exchanges are objectionable it is because they stem from an unjust distribution of assets. But there are two problems with this interpretation. First, Roemer is wrong in holding that a necessary condition for the ethical objectionability of unequal labor transfers is that they arise from a prior unjust distribution. Exploitation in the ethical sense can exist even if the original distribution of assets came about justly. Second, even if Roemer is right about the previous point concerning the *existence* of exploitation, the approach he recommends fails to adequately account for judgments about the *intensity* of exploitation. These judgments require that we attend to processes determining the transfer of labor and not only to those determining the original distribution of assets.

Let me first explain the point about the intensity of exploitation. Imagine two societies, S and T, each of which has two economic actors between whom productive assets are unequally divided. Suppose further that the unequal division of assets has arisen through an identical unjust process in each case (e.g., suppose that the asset-rich stole their greater share). Roemer's view is that any unequal labor exchanges that result from such an unjust distribution of assets will be not only technically exploitative, but ethically exploitative, and that the normative content of this ethical exploitation will stem from the original unjust distribution of assets of which it is a consequence. But suppose we assume further that the transfer of labor is greater in S than in T. While the labor transfers in both S and T are exploitative because they stem from a distribution of assets that itself came about unjustly, it is also true that the exploitation in S is ethically worse than in T because the transfer of labor is greater in S than in T.

But if it is solely the justice or injustice of the process determining the initial distribution of assets that explains why labor transfers are exploitative, as Roemer maintains, then these two cases should be judged as equally exploitative from an ethical standpoint because the processes determining the initial distribution are the same in each case. In other words, given Roemer's account of what makes unequal labor exchanges ethically exploitative, one would expect that his account of what makes one unequal labor exchange ethically worse than another would have something to do with why they count as unjust and hence as instances of exploitation. That is, Roemer should presumably say that if one inequality-generating process is worse than another, then the unequal labor transfers that result from the former would be worse than those that result from the latter. But *ex hypothesis* the processes through which the initial distribution of assets result are the same and hence equally objectionable.

Therefore, simply knowing how an unequal distribution of assets arises isn't sufficient for an adequate moral assessment of the labor exchanges that result from that initial distribution. Although Roemer can say that there is more technical exploitation in S than in T, he cannot say this exploitation is morally worse in S than in T without amending his account of what makes exploitation objectionable. There is an additional injustice involved here that he fails to explain.

In specific cases it may be difficult to determine the amount of labor that is transferred from one party to another. But it is nevertheless reasonable to suppose that a theory of exploitation, at least in principle, should be able to accommodate judgments about the intensity of exploitation. We should not only want a theory that supports the view that capitalism as a system is exploitative, but which also could support judgments that specific capitalists, or forms of capitalism, are more exploitative than others. However, it is unclear how Roemer could account for judgments about the intensity of exploitation given his position that labor transfers lack moral significance apart from that conferred by the process through which the initial distribution of assets originates.

If, on the other hand, we recognize that unequal labor exchanges have independent moral significance, even though they are not sufficient for the charge of exploitation, then we will be able to explain one situation as more exploitative than another. It is not simply that there are unequal flows of labor that are significant on their own account, but that these labor flows result from relations of unequal economic power. To go back to the example above, one possible reason the exploitation is morally worse in S than in T is because the exploiter in S uses his economic power to generate a greater unequal exchange than does the exploiter in T. By economic power I mean, roughly, the capacity to shape the economic choices and fates of other people, including both the nature and amount of work they perform as well as the size of their consumption bundle. The distribution of economic power is shaped by a number of factors including, most importantly, the distribution of productive assets. But there are other factors that can influence the nature of this power: the structure of the workplace, the bargaining skill of the relevant economic actors, levels of political organization of workers and capitalists respectively, and market conditions (e.g., the relative scarcity of labor power and capital respectively). All these factors influence the nature of economic power and, consequently, the intensity of exploitation.

Going back to my example, it is possible that the exploited parties in S are less well organized or less skillful bargainers than those in T. Or the exploiters might be better organized in S. Or perhaps in S there is a reserve army of labor power that enables exploiters to bid down the wage of those they exploit, whereas in T this isn't possible. As a consequence of domination at the point of production, one employer may extract more surplus labor from his workers than another employer who allows his workers more autonomy. Even if these employers came to control productive assets through identical processes, it doesn't follow that ethical judgments about their exploitation should be the same. The point is that in addition to the processes determining the original distribution of assets, the unequal power that the unequal distribution of assets confers and the amount of labor transferred to exploiters are both relevant to normative judgments about exploitation.

In light of this criticism it might seem plausible to propose an account of exploitation that supposes the normative significance of exploitation to involve both injustice in the initial distribution of assets and unjust labor transfers—without the second injustice being reducible to the first. Such an account of exploitation would have the virtue of according independent moral weight to real transfers of labor and their sources in unequal power and would thus seem to meet the above criticism. However, contrary to what Roemer claims on the basis of the Adam-Karl model, injustice in the initial distribution of assets is not a necessary condition for subsequent unequal labor exchanges to be ethically exploitative. Consequently, even this suggested composite definition of exploitation fails. To see why, it is necessary to examine not only whether our intuitions about the Adam-Karl model agree with Roemer's, but also whether his explanation of those intuitions is satisfactory.

Recall that the initial situation between Karl and Adam is one in which they have an equal share of assets. In the first production period Karl consumes his assets and Adam increases his through hard work; thus Adam ends up asset-rich while Karl has no assets at all. This sets the stage for the second production period. Notice that there are three alternatives at this stage: (1) Karl accepts Adam's work offer, receives a subsistence wage, and transfers part of his labor to Adam; (2) no agreement is reached and Karl starves; or (3) there is a forcible transfer of Adam's wealth to Karl to prevent the latter from starvation. Roemer argues that as long as we postulate that Karl's preferences are autonomously formed and his fate self-inflicted, alternative (1) best accords with our ethical intuitions, even though it involves technical exploitation. His explanation of these intuitions is that Adam accumulated his larger share of assets justly and thus any technical exploitation that may result from subsequent transactions between Adam and Karl will necessarily be unobjectionable. It is also important to recognize that the agreement reached between Adam and Karl will not simply be a one-shot deal, after which Karl will work by himself, but instead will be repeated in future production periods. Karl will have to work for Adam in perpetuity. But for Roemer, because the original distribution was just, these subsequent transactions are ethically unexploitative regardless of how much labor is transferred from Karl to Adam.

There is a problem with this argument. First, Roemer fails to consider what is surely true, which is that our intuitions about repeated transactions in which Karl transfers his labor to Adam for a wage are, at the very least, less firm than our intuitions about the transaction viewed as a one-shot arrangement. Roemer seems to argue that we are compelled to render the same intuitive judgment about subsequent labor transactions because we are committed to the principle that transactions arising from a just process are necessarily just. But why should we be committed to this principle? Apparently, Roemer thinks, because this principle explains our intuitive judgment that Adam would not be exploiting Karl if the latter worked for him after having consumed his own assets. But notice that it is possible to account for the intuition that the initial transaction between Karl and Adam is nonexploitative without also going on to affirm that all subsequent transactions between them are necessarily nonexploitative. That is, we should not agree with Roemer's general normative principle that "exploitation" is unobjectionable if it arises from unequal distributions that came about justly. Nor, contrary to Roemer, do our intuitions in the case of Adam-Karl support such a general principle.

An alternative explanation of our intuitions in the Adam-Karl case could appeal to the labor contribution principle. It is plausible to argue that the reason there is nothing ethically exploitative about Karl's initial transfer of labor to Adam is that its net result is an equalization (or at least a tendency toward the equalization) of their respective labor contributions. By the same token, to require a forcible transfer of assets to Karl from Adam (3) would violate the labor contribution principle, allowing Karl to benefit from Adam's labor. Such an alternative explanation of our intuitions is important because it yields a different—and I believe a more intuitively correct—judgment in answer to the question concerning the repeated transfer of labor from Karl to Adam than does Roemer's normative principle. If our concern is with labor contribution, then our intuition would be that Karl shouldn't be stuck with working for Adam in perpetuity simply because of his initial myopia. Instead, it would be reasonable to suppose that there is an upper limit on the extent to which Karl should have to labor to support Adam to make up for his initial consumption. After this limit is reached Adam would be not only technically exploiting Karl, but also ethically exploiting him as the arrangement extends into the future. One way the proper limit could be determined is by examining Adam's initial labor contributions and balancing them against Karl's subsequent contributions. This principle of reward proportional to labor contribution seeks to prevent distributive outcomes from reflecting morally arbitrary factors such as differential asset possession and differential economic power. The mere fact that someone owns a greater share of productive assets should not enable them to require those who happen to own fewer assets to work for them.

These considerations concerning power and labor expenditure provide a more likely moral basis for a Marxian conception of exploitation than Roemer's rather narrow focus on those processes governing the origin of the initial distribution of assets. What Roemer fails to countenance is that it is possible for ethically exploitative conditions to be created through a just process that violates no one's rights.

CONCLUSION: TOWARD A POWER INCLUSIVE ALTERNATIVE

If the above criticisms are on target, it means Roemer's contention that Marxists should not be interested in exploitation is mistaken because it rests upon an inadequate account of Marxian exploitation. But what would be a more adequate conception of exploitation? In conclusion I will try to sketch out an answer to this question that is suggested by my criticisms of Roemer. What those criticisms suggest is a "power inclusive" conception of exploitation that includes the notions of labor contribution, unequal power, and labor appropriation. Capitalist exploitation is a complex process in which each of these components has a role to play.

A reconsideration of the Andrea-Bob example will help to clarify the power inclusive alternative. Recall that Andrea's having a more productive machine enables her to make Bob an offer that, although in his interest, would allow her to live off his labor. Thus, there would be a transfer of labor from Bob to Andrea. Roemer uses this example to argue against those such as Jeffrey Reiman who would require that we include force in our definition of exploitation. According to Reiman's force inclusive definition of exploitation, a society is exploitative when its social structure is organized so that unpaid labor is systematically forced from one class and put at the disposal of another. Roemer points out that although Andrea doesn't force Bob to work for her, our intuitions are that she does exploit him. Roemer's punchline is that the reason we have such an intuitive response is that Andrea came to own her machine through an unjust process—hence she is now taking unfair advantage of Bob. But contrary to what Roemer argues, the injustice through which Andrea takes advantage of Bob is importantly different from the injustice through which she came to possess her technologically superior machine. According to the power inclusive definition, Andrea exploits Bob in the conditions described because her ownership of a more productive machine grants her economic power over Bob. In virtue of this power Bob transfers his labor to her and thus is exploited by her. Therefore, the power inclusive definition gives the intuitively correct verdict, unlike the force inclusive definition. But the rationale for this verdict differs from that given by the property relations account. It is not because Andrea came to own her machine through illicit means that she exploits Bob, but because now owning that machine she is able to command Bob's labor.

It might be objected that there is no additional injustice in the Andrea-Bob example because Bob has other acceptable alternatives to Andrea's offer. But although it is true that Bob has other alternatives, it is also true that Andrea has power over Bob because in the situation described he can advance his interests and improve his situation only if he accepts her offer. This is to say that Andrea's control over the more productive technology creates a situation in which her interests are *hegemonic* over Bob's within existing relations of ownership. Thus, though Bob is not forced to transfer his labor to Andrea, his choices are structured in such a way that he can only advance his interests by doing so. Paradoxically, then, Bob improves his situation by agreeing to be exploited by Andrea. It seems paradoxical to say that Bob is exploited by Andrea because it is natural to think exploitation is incompatible both with Bob's voluntariness and his improved welfare position. But this way of thinking misses the point that I have been urging: exploitation involves unequal power creating a situation where a person can both voluntarily consent to being exploited and also improve his or her welfare in the process. Exploitation in the ethical sense still exists because there is a transfer of labor that results from unequal power.

Jeffrey Reiman has recently agreed, for reasons similar to those I have given, that Andrea exploits Bob in the case described.[7] However, he argues that this example says nothing important about the specifically Marxian concept of exploitation. That concept of exploitation, Reiman argues, must include force. Reiman argues that so construed the Marxian concept of exploitation is sharpened and its critical power is enhanced. Such a force inclusive definition enables us to stress the ways in which capitalism is like classical slavery and feudalism.

I think Reiman is wrong for insisting that Marxists include force within their definition of power. To be sure, there are plainly important ethical differences between a situation in which an agent is forced to accept an offer because he or she has no acceptable alternative and one where acceptable alternatives exist, such as in the Andrea-Bob story, and we should want our theory of exploitation to account for those differences. But there is no reason for requiring that only severe cases of exploitation—ones that involve force—should count as exploitation for Marxists. Furthermore, it is important to recognize that the source of exploitation in the Andrea-Bob case stems from the control that Andrea exercises over the more productive means of production. In other words, she is *capitalistically* exploiting Bob because it is her control over the means of production that enables her to appropriate labor from Bob. Marxists should not simply be interested in eliminating those forms of capitalist exploitation that involve force, but capitalist exploitation of all varieties.

Far from being anomalous, the exploitation in the case of Andrea-Bob is precisely the sort that a Marxian theory of exploitation should capture. In requiring that exploitation include force Reiman contracts the scope of the Marxian concept of exploitation. As I argued earlier in criticism of Roemer, questions of the severity or intensity of exploitation are important. But it isn't clear how restricting the scope of the concept of exploitation, as Reiman proposes, helps to answer those questions.

To conclude, Roemer's Adam-Karl model shows that unequal economic power can arise from an initially fair situation without anyone's rights being violated. But it is important to recognize that this doesn't mean such an exercise of power is thereby rendered morally unobjectionable. To be sure, Marx directed attention at those historical processes that brought about capitalism, and he vividly described the injustice involved in the "primitive accumulation" that made it possible. Nevertheless, for Marx exploitation was a dynamic feature of the capitalist system, not a feature of the historical process that made that system possible. I have argued that Roemer's account of the nature and ethical significance of exploitation is inadequate because it neglects to focus on how inequalities in economic power lead to unequal labor exchanges. The result is that his conception of exploitation impoverishes the Marxian critique of capitalism because it fails to recognize the exploitation that is a feature of capitalism as an ongoing system. A power inclusive conception is a more promising alternative.

Notes

1. See for example Robert Nozick, *Anarchy, State, and Utopia* (New York: Basic Books Inc., 1974).
2. John Roemer, "What Is Exploitation? A Reply to Jeffrey Reiman," *Philosophy and Public Affairs* 18, no. 2 (1989): 91–97.
3. Ibid., and John Roemer, "Second Thoughts on Property Relations and Exploitation," in *Analyzing Marxism*, ed. Robert Ware and Kai Nielsen, supplementary volume 15 of *Canadian Journal of Philosophy* (Calgary: University of Calgary Press, 1989).
4. Roemer's property relations definition of exploitation has evolved over the years since the publication of *A General Theory of Exploitation and Class* (Cambridge, MA:

Harvard University Press, 1982). His original definition of exploitation did not include clause (2), but rather a clause that said that the members of S would be worse off if they were to withdraw with their own productive assets. But Roemer now thinks that the original clause does not adequately capture the relation of dependency that exists between exploiter and exploited. See his "What Is Exploitation" and his "Second Thoughts."

5. John Roemer, "Should Marxists Be Interested in Exploitation?" *Philosophy and Public Affairs* 14, no. 1 (1985): 30–65. See also, Roemer's *Free to Lose: An Introduction to Marxist Economic Philosophy* (Cambridge, MA: Harvard University Press, 1988).

6. Jeffrey Reiman, "Exploitation, Force, and the Moral Assessment of Capitalism: Thoughts on Roemer and Cohen," *Philosophy and Public Affairs* 16, no. 1 (1987): 3–41.

7. Jeffrey Reiman, "Why Worry about How Exploitation Is Defined?: Reply to John Roemer," *Social Theory and Practice* 16, no. 1 (1990): 101–13.

Population and Poverty*

BARRY COMMONER

ONE OF THE VIRTUES of the environmental point of view is that we see the planet as a harmonious whole, a global system of water, soil, and living things bounded by the thin skin of air. However, when we look at the planet with an eye on human manifestations—the technosphere and the social systems that create it—it is split in two. The northern hemisphere contains most of the modern technosphere—its factories, power plants, automotive vehicles, and petrochemical plants—and the wealth that it generates. The southern hemisphere contains most of the people, nearly all of them desperately poor. The result of this division is a painful global irony: the poor countries of the south, while deprived of an equitable share of the world's wealth, suffer the environmental hazards generated by the creation of that wealth in the north. The developing countries of the south will not only experience the impact of global warming and ozone depletion, which are now chiefly due to the industrialized countries, but are also victimized by the north's toxic exports. For example, as bans have been imposed on particularly dangerous pesticides in industrialized countries, manufacturers have marketed them in developing countries instead. There, poorly regulated, they have created in the bodies of local populations the world's highest concentrations of pesticides. Similarly, as environmental concerns have limited disposal sites for trash and the toxic ash from trash-burning incinerators in the United States, efforts have been made to get rid of these pollutants—not always successfully—in developing countries.

Yet the gravest threat of the environmental crisis to developing countries comes, not from the pollutants so generously imposed on them by their wealthy planetary neighbors, but from a more subtle source. This threat arises from a serious, frequently voiced misconception about the origin of the environmental crisis. In this and earlier analyses, I have argued that the environmental crisis originates, not in the natural ecosphere, but in the man-made technosphere. The data about both the development of the post-1950 assault on the environment and the effort since 1970 to reduce it support this conclusion. There is, however, another view of the environmental crisis that turns these relationships upside down. This view holds that the problem is ecological; that environmental degradation originates in an imbalance between the earth's limited resources and the rapidly growing human population, which stresses the environment and also causes social problems such as poverty and hunger.

This position had a popular following in the early days of the environmental movement, based on unequivocal assertions by some well-known environmentalists. In a widely quoted article, "The Tragedy of the Commons," Garrett Hardin put it this way:

> The pollution problem is a consequence of population. It did not matter much how a lonely American frontiersman disposed of his waste. . . . But as population became denser, the natural chemical and biological recycling processes became overloaded. . . . Freedom to breed will bring ruin to all.

Paul Ehrlich's best-seller, *The Population Bomb*, was even more explicit about the origin of the environmental crisis:

> The causal chain of the deterioration [of the environment] is easily followed to its source. Too many cars, too many factories, too much detergent, too much pesticide, multiplying contrails, inadequate sewage treatment plants, too little water, too much carbon dioxide—all can be traced easily to too many people.

In the early 1970s, such statements encouraged the view that population control is the only practical way to reduce pollution, a notion that some environmentalists took personally. I recall a conversation I had with a pregnant faculty member while I was visiting a midwestern university in the early 1970s; she had received anonymous letters condemning her for contributing to the environmental crisis. Enthusiasm for contraception as an environmental strategy has faded considerably, although recently the head of the National Organization for Women (NOW), desperate for allies in the fight against the Supreme Court's invitation to state control of abortions, sought to enlist environmentalists on these same grounds. This basic position is still held by a number of leaders of the environmental organizations that have grown to prominence since the early 1970s. Russell W. Peterson, the former president of the National Audubon Society, a major environmental organization, expressed it this way a few years ago:

Almost every environmental problem, almost every social and political problem as well, either stems from or is exacerbated by the growth of human population. . . . As any wildlife biologist knows, once a species reproduces itself beyond the carrying capacity of its habitat, natural checks and balances come into play. . . . The human species is governed by this same natural law. And there are signs in many parts of the world today—Ethiopia is only one of many places, a tip of the iceberg—that we *Homo sapiens* are beginning to exceed the carrying capacity of the planet.

Such statements send a chilling message to developing countries. They are in a desperate struggle to improve living standards, and—in violation of Mr. Peterson's dictum—are eager to use *more* resources to support their rapidly growing populations. Surely sweeping prescriptions such as those just cited, which affect the destiny of most of the world's people, ought to be solidly founded in fact. Are they?

The chief source of these views is a fundamental ecological concept regarding the relationship between the eater and the eaten. In a normal ecological system, there is a balance between a species' population and its food supply. If rabbits reproduce at the rate at which they are eaten by wolves and the wolves reproduce at the rate at which they die or are killed by hunters, both populations will be stable in size. Suppose, however, that some outside influence on the wolves' death rate is eased—fewer hunters, perhaps—so that their population rises above the equilibrium size. Now the rabbits are likely to be eaten faster than they can reproduce, and their population will decline, reducing the "carrying capacity" of the ecosystem for wolves. The wolf population will then be short of food, die off faster, and become smaller until it is once more in balance with the rabbits. Applied to human beings, this concept suggests that in a country like Ethiopia, devastated by repeated famines, starvation is a symptom of overpopulation, and—in the absence of outside intervention—a precursor to a catastrophic population decline that will restore the balance between its size and the country's limited food supply. Relying on this concept, some environmentalists urge population reduction and oppose famine relief as a misguided, futile gesture. Thus, Garrett Hardin provides this explanation of why he is opposed to feeding hungry countries:

> When we send food to a starving population that has already grown beyond the environment's carrying capacity we become a partner in the devastation of their land. Food from the outside keeps more natives alive; these demand more food and fuel; greater demand causes the community to transgress the carrying capacity more, and transgression results in lowering the carrying capacity in the future. The deficit grows exponentially. Gifts of food to an overpopulated country boomerang, increasing starvation over the long run. Our choice is really between letting some die this year and letting more die in

the following years. . . . Only one thing can really help a poor country: population control.

Apart from humane considerations, there is a ready response to this position: if the necessary funds were available, by applying modern production processes, Ethiopia could increase food production and if need be use its increased wealth to import it. But such reliance on economic growth and development is also regarded as ecologically unsound by population-minded environmentalists, for in Paul Ehrlich's terms, it would only lead to "too many cars, too many factories, too much detergent, too much pesticide" and the inevitable deterioration of the environment.

This approach has been elaborated on a global scale by means of computer models that purport to show, mathematically, that the interaction between a growing world population, the economic growth impelled by it, and the resultant environmental degradation and food shortages leads inevitably to the kind of population crash experienced by wolves in an ecosystem of too few rabbits. This conclusion was reached by the Club of Rome (a self-appointed organization of industrialists and environmentalists) in a report that was widely publicized, but less widely acclaimed for its scientific soundness, *The Limits to Growth*.

The "limits to growth" approach is based on a serious misconception about the global ecosystem. It depends upon the idea that the earth is like a spaceship, a closed system isolated from all outside sources of support and necessarily sustained only by its own limited resources. But the ecosphere is not in fact a closed, isolated system, for it is totally dependent on the huge influx of energy from an outside source—the sun. Living things must be provided with energy to sustain their vital processes, in particular growth, development, and reproduction. That energy is derived from the sun. Sunlight, absorbed by plants, drives the energy-requiring chemical reactions that synthesize the complex organic compounds characteristic of life, such as protein, carbohydrates, fat, and nucleic acids. This process, photosynthesis, is the gateway that brings solar energy into the ecosphere: the rabbit, nibbling vegetation, derives its energy from the plant's organic compounds; the wolf obtains its energy by devouring the rabbit. Such food chains transmit the solar energy initially captured by plants throughout the ecosphere.

Thus, solar energy, captured by photosynthesis, sustains every form of life and drives the ecological cycles in which they participate. If an ecological cycle is viewed only as a static array of animals, plants, and microorganisms linked through the physical environment into a circular system, it appears to be closed, like a ring. But this image is misleading, for without the energy that it receives, externally, from the sun, the plants and animals would die and the circular system would disintegrate.

Solar energy also creates the weather: the seasonal temperature changes; the moisture that the sun lifts from the oceans; the wind and the storms that carry rain and snow to the soil and replenish the lakes and rivers that feed the oceans. In turn, the weather molds the physical features of the earth's surface, creating the ecological niches that living things occupy. In sum, the global ecosystem is not, in the basic thermodynamic sense, an isolated, self-sufficient system. In fact, neither is a spaceship, which after all depends for the energy that operates it on electricity generated by photovoltaic cells—from the sun.

In the abstract sense, there is a global "limit to growth," but this is determined not by the present availability of resources but by a distant limit to the availability of solar energy. It is true, of course, that the ecosystem that occupies the earth's thin skin, and the underlying mineral deposits, are essential both to population growth and economic production. It is also true that there is a potential limit to economic growth due to the finite amounts of these essential resources. However, since matter is, after all, indestructible, the chemical elements that comprise the planet's resources can be recycled and reused indefinitely, as long as the energy necessary to collect and refine them is available. This is precisely what is done when the resource is sufficiently valuable; despite its extensive dispersion, well over half of all the gold ever mined is still in hand today, regathered when necessary by expending energy. Hence, the ultimate limit on economic growth is imposed by the rate at which renewable, solar energy can be captured and used. If we ignore the exceedingly slow extinction of the sun, this limit is governed only by the finite surface of the earth, which determines how much of the energy radiated by the sun is actually intercepted and is therefore capable of being used.

Thus, the theoretical limit to the growth of the global economy is determined by the rate at which the earth receives solar energy. How close is this limit at present? It has been estimated that the solar energy that falls annually only on the earth's *land* surface is more than a thousand times the amount of energy (almost entirely from fuels, hydroelectric and nuclear power) now being used each year to support the global economy. Of course, because some parts of the land are difficult to reach or otherwise unsuitable, not all of the solar energy that falls on it could be used. If, let us say, only 10 percent of the total solar energy falling on land could be captured, it would still be possible to expand our present rate of using energy a hundredfold before encountering the theoretical limit to growth. Even if this figure should turn out to be somewhat optimistic, it seems clear that we are at present nowhere near the limit that the availability of solar energy will eventually impose on production and economic growth. That distant limit is irrelevant to current policy.

The issue we face, then, is not how to facilitate environmental quality by limiting economic development and population growth, but how to create a system of production that can grow and develop in harmony with the environment. The question is whether we can produce bountiful harvests, productive machinery, rapid transportation, and decent human dwellings sufficient to support the world population without despoiling the environment.

It is useful, at this point, to turn to the data that relate environmental deterioration to the factors that influence it. As we have seen, production technologies differ considerably in their tendency to pollute the environment. Consider, for example, the different environmental impacts of two alternative technologies of beer distribution: the throwaway bottles, and the returnable bottles that are likely to be used forty times before being broken or discarded. Each bottle contains an economic good—twelve ounces of beer—and the production of that good is associated with a pollutant: the bottle discarded as trash. We can compare the pollution-generating potential of the two technologies by computing the number of beer bottles used to deliver each twelve ounces of beer. In the case of the throwaway bottles, the figure is one bottle per twelve ounces of beer; for returnable bottles, the figure is one-fortieth of a bottle per twelve ounces of beer. Thus, the pollution-generating tendency of a technology can be expressed numerically as the amount of pollution generated in producing a unit amount of economic good.

The total amount of pollution generated can then be expressed by multiplying this "technology factor" (pollution per unit good) by the total amount of good produced. Finally, the latter figure can be broken down into the product of two factors: good produced per capita (the "affluence factor") multiplied by the size of the population. In this way, the total amount of pollution can be expressed numerically in the form of an equation:

$$\text{total pollution} = \text{pollution per unit good} \times \text{good per capita} \times \text{population}$$

This relationship shows that the total amount of pollution generated will increase if any of the three factors increases. Thus, it is possible to say with equal validity that environmental deterioration—say, the number of beer bottles—is exacerbated by "too many people" as Paul Ehrlich claims, or, in keeping with my own analysis, by a change in the technology of production that increases the number of bottles used to deliver twelve ounces of beer. And it is equally possible that the number of discarded beer bottles will increase because of greater beer consumption per capita. What is at issue is the relative impact of each of these factors on environmental pollution. Such an evaluation will indicate which factor, if reduced, provides the most effective means of improving environmental quality.

In the United States, data are readily available to evaluate the relative effect of the three factors on a number of pollutants. In the case of beer bottles, they show, for example, that between 1950 and 1967, as the number produced annually increased by 593 percent, the population increased by 30 percent, per capita beer consumption (the affluence factor) rose by 5 percent, and the number of bottles used per unit of beer shipped (the technology factor) increased by 408 percent. Clearly, the largest impact on the amount of beer bottle trash was due to the technology factor: the introduction of nonreturnable bottles, which sharply increased the number of bottles needed to ship a unit amount of beer.

The relative impact of the three factors in reducing the environmental impact of beer bottle trash between 1950 and 1967 is indicated by the following: if there had been no change in the technology of beer distribution, the number of beer bottles would have increased by 37 percent; if only population had remained constant, the number of beer bottles would have increased by 433 percent; if only the affluence factor had remained constant, the number of beer bottles would have increased by 560 percent. Clearly, an effort to change the technology of beer distribution will result in the greatest reduction in environmental impact.

The pattern revealed by the beer bottle data is typical of the new post-1950 production technologies. For example, between 1950 and 1967, when pesticide use for crop production increased by 266 percent, the population increased by 30 percent, crop production per capita (the affluence factor) by 5 percent, and the amount of pesticide used per unit of crop production (the technology factor) by 168 percent. In the case of phosphate, an important water pollutant, emissions into surface waters increased by 1,845 percent between 1946 and 1968, while population rose by 42 percent, the amount of cleansers per capita remained constant, and the amount of phosphate per unit amount of cleansers increased by 1,270 percent due to the technology factor: the introduction of phosphate-containing detergents in place of soap. Similarly, between 1946 and 1967, when nitrogen oxides emitted by cars increased by 628 percent, population rose by 41 percent, vehicle miles per capita doubled, and nitrogen oxides emitted per mile increased by 158 percent.

It is apparent, then, that in the United States the factor most responsible for the sharp increases in pollutants since World War II—and the factor most capable of reducing pollution—is production technology: the new methods used to produce vehicular travel, cleansers, crops, beer, and many other goods. It can be argued, of course, that in developing countries the situation is different and that their impact on the environment is in fact largely due to what many people regard as their most prominent feature—rapid population growth. Unfortunately, the available data on pollutant levels in developing countries are scanty and incomplete, so that a numerical analysis such as that described for the United States is impossible. However, the problem can be approached indirectly, based on what is already known about the relation between certain pollutants and the production processes that generate them.

For example, it has been established that the rising level of nitrate—a pollutant that contributes to eutrophication and to health problems in drinking-water supplies—in U.S. and European surface waters is largely due to the application of nitrogen fertilizer to crops. Where such data have been obtained, about 20 to 25 percent of the applied nitrogen reaches surface waters. Hence, subject to this range of uncertainty, the amount of nitrogen fertilizer applied to crops can be used, as a proxy, to represent the resultant level of nitrate in surface waters. Thus, the relative effects of the population, affluence, and technology factors on the pollutant, nitrate, can be estimated if, for a given country or area, changes over time in the following factors can be computed: population, crop production per capita, and nitrogen fertilizer used per unit crop.

Data on these factors for the period 1970–1980 are available for most developing countries; they are conveniently expressed as the annual rate of change. In ninety developing countries, nitrogen fertilizer use (a proxy for nitrate pollution) increased by an average of 8.6 percent per year, while the rise in population averaged 2.5 percent per year, crop production per capita (affluence) decreased by 0.06 percent annually, and fertilizer use per unit of crop production (the technology factor) increased by 6.6 percent. The impact of the technology factor on the amount of nitrogen fertilizer used, and hence on the level of nitrate pollution, considerably outweighs the effect of both the rapidly rising population and "affluence." Similar analyses show that the introduction of automotive vehicles and power plants in developing countries has had a significantly greater impact on the resultant pollution levels than either population or "affluence."

In sum, the data both from an industrial country like the United States and from developing countries show that the largest influence on pollution levels is the pollution-generating tendency of the system of industrial and agricultural production, and the transportation and power systems. In all countries, the environmental impact of the technology factor is significantly greater than the influence of population size or of affluence.

What does this mean for developing countries, where increased production is the engine of economic progress? At present, developing countries usually introduce those technologies that have proven to be both highly productive and ecologically unsound in industrial countries—nitrogen fertilizer, for example. As pointed out in the recent Bruntland report, the upshot is that "the industries most heavily reliant on environmental resources and most heavily polluting are growing most rapidly in the developing world, where there is more urgency for growth and less capacity to minimize damaging side effects."

Thus, especially in developing countries, the question of environmental quality is an inseparable component of the issue of economic development. To claim that the two are in conflict and that environmental quality can only be achieved at the expense of development ignores the dominant role of production technologies in determining environmental impact. Economic development can proceed without a concomitant decrease in environmental quality if it is based on an appropriate, ecologically benign production technology. For example, crop production can be increased without incurring the environmental hazards of conventional chemical agriculture by practicing organic farming instead. The apparent conflict between environmental quality and economic development that motivates proposals to limit the growth of population and/or production can be largely eliminated by the proper choice of production technologies.

What, next, is the evidence that overpopulation is responsible for famine? Hunger is widespread in the world and those who believe that the world's resources are already insufficient to support the world population cite this fact as evidence that the world is overpopulated. Once more, it is revealing to examine the actual data regarding the incidence of malnutrition. It is useful to remember that people in other countries did not go hungry because they sent food to Ethiopia to relieve the famine there—that what was sent to Ethiopia was *surplus* food. In fact, the world produces more than enough food to feed the total world population. Total world production of food, equally distributed to the global population, would today provide everyone with more than enough for the physiologically required diet. According to a recent estimate by the United Nations Food and Agriculture Organization, the world produces enough grain alone to provide every person on earth with 3,600 calories a day—more than one-and-a-half times the calories required in a normal diet. Enough grain is produced to give everyone on earth two daily loaves of bread.

Famine is caused, not by a global food shortage, but by the grossly uneven distribution of the global food supply. This is not an ecological phenomenon but a political and economic one. Neither England nor Haiti produces enough food for its own population, but hunger is much more prevalent in Haiti than it is in England, because Haiti cannot afford to import enough food to make up the deficit, while England can.

Hunger and malnutrition are also a consequence of maldistribution of food *within* a country. From a detailed study of nutritional levels among various populations in India in 1967, we learn, for example, that in Madras State more than one-half the population consumed significantly less than the physiologically required calories and protein in their diet. However, the *average* values for all residents of the state represented 99 percent of the calorie requirement and 98 percent of the protein requirement. What this means, of course, is that a significant part of the population received more than the required dietary intake. About one-third of the population received 106 percent of the required calories and 104 percent of the required protein; about 8 percent of the population received 122 percent of the calorie requirement and 117 percent or more of the protein requirement. These dietary differences were determined by income. The more than one-half of the population that received significantly less than the physiologically required diet earned less than $21 per capita per year, as compared with the statewide average of $33. What these data indicate is that hunger in Madras State, defined simply in terms of a significantly inadequate intake of calories and protein, was not the result of too many people and not enough food. Rather, it resulted from the social factors that govern the distribution of available food—and income—among the population.

Thus, the available data about both hunger and environmental quality in developing countries show that they have been governed less by population size than by the countries' economic status and the kinds of production technology employed. It remains true, nevertheless, as shown by the multiplicative relation among the three factors that govern pollution, that, other things being equal, a rising population will contribute to the demand for food and to environmental stress. Even though the impact of population on environmental quality is less than the effect of the technology of production, in developing countries it is not negligible, and must be taken into account. It is of interest, therefore, to consider what is known about the stabilization of human populations and how that demographic process is related to biological factors such as birth and death rates, and social factors such as economic development.

Like all living things, people have an inherent tendency to multiply geometrically—that is, the more people there are the more people they tend to produce. In contrast, the supply of food rises more slowly, for unlike people it does not increase in proportion to the existing rate of food production. This is, of course, the familiar relationship described by Malthus that led him to conclude that the population will eventually outgrow the food supply (and other needed resources), leading to famine and mass death. The problem is whether other countervailing forces will intervene to limit population growth and to increase food production.

When we turn from merely stating the problem to analyzing and attempting to solve it, the issue becomes much more complex. The simple statement that there is a limit to the growth of the human population, imposed on it by the limited availability of the necessary resources, is a useful but abstract idea. In order to reduce it to the level of reality in which the problem must be solved, we need to analyze the actual relationship between population growth and resources. Current views on this question are neither simple nor unanimous.

One view is that the cause of the population problem is uncontrolled fertility, the countervailing force, the death rate, having been weakened by medical advances. According to this view, given the freedom to do so, people will inevitably produce children faster than the goods needed to support them. It follows, then, that the birth rate must be deliberately reduced to the point of "zero population growth."

The methods that have been proposed to achieve this kind of direct reduction in birth rate vary considerably. One method is family planning: providing people with effective contraception and access to abortion facilities and educating them about the value of having fewer children. Another suggestion, sometimes called the "lifeboat ethic," is to withhold food from the people of starving developing countries which, having failed to limit their birth rate sufficiently, are deemed to be too far gone or too unworthy to be saved. The author of this so-called ethic, Garrett Hardin, stated it this way:

> So long as we nations multiply at different rates, survival requires that we adopt the ethic of the lifeboat. A lifeboat can hold only so many people. There are more than two billion wretched people in the world—ten times as many as in the United States. It is literally beyond our ability to save them all. . . . Both international granaries and lax immigration policies must be rejected if we are to save something for our grandchildren.

But there is another view of population that is much more complex. It is based on the evidence, amassed by demographers, that the birth rate is not only affected by biological factors, such as fertility and contraception, but also by equally powerful social and economic influences. Demographers have delineated a complex network of interactions among the various biological and social factors. It shows that population growth is not the consequence of a simple arithmetic relationship between birth rate and death rate. Instead, there are circular relationships in which, as in an ecological cycle, every step is connected to several others.

Thus, while a reduced death rate does, of course, increase the rate of population growth, it can also have the opposite effect, since families usually respond to a reduced rate of infant mortality by opting for fewer children. This negative feedback modulates the effect of a decreased death rate on population size. Similarly, although a rising population increases the demand on resources, it also stimulates economic activity, which in turn improves educational levels. This tends to raise the average age at marriage and to facilitate contraceptive practices, leading to a reduced birth rate, which mitigates the pressure on resources.

In these processes, there is a powerful social force that reduces the death rate (thereby stimulating population growth) and leads people voluntarily to restrict the production of children (thereby reducing population growth). That force, simply stated, is the quality of life: a high standard of living, a sense of well-being, security in the future. When and how the two opposite effects of this force are felt differs with the stages in a country's economic development. In a premodern society, such as England before the Industrial Revolution or India before the advent of the English, both death rates and birth rates were high. But they were in balance and population size was stable. Then, as agricultural and industrial production began to increase and living conditions improved, the death rate began to fall. With the birth rate remaining high, the population grew rapidly. However, some thirty to forty years later, as living standards continued to improve, the decline in the death rate persisted, but the birth rate began to decline as well, reducing the rate of population growth.

Swedish demographic data, which are particularly detailed, provide a good example of this process. In around 1800, Sweden had a high birth rate, about 33 per 1,000 population, but since the death rate was equally high, the population was in balance. Then as agriculture and, later, industrial production advanced, the death rate dropped until, by the mid-nineteenth century, it stood at about 20 per 1,000. Since the birth rate remained virtually constant during that period, there was a large excess of births over deaths and the population increased rapidly—an early version of the "population explosion." Then the birth rate began to drop, until in the mid-twentieth century it reached about 14 per 1,000, when the death rate was about 10 per 1,000. Thus, under the influence of a constantly rising standard of living, the population moved, with time, from a position of balance at high birth and death rates to a new position of near balance at low birth and death rates. But in between, the population increased considerably.

This process, the demographic transition, has been characteristic of all industrialized countries. In these countries, the death rate began to decline in the mid-eighteenth century, reaching an average of 30 per 1,000 in 1850, 24 per 1,000 in 1900, 16 per 1,000 in 1950, and 9 per 1,000 in 1985. In contrast, the birth rate remained constant at about 40 per 1,000 until 1850, then dropping rapidly, reaching 32 per 1,000 in 1900, 23 per 1,000 in 1950, and 14 per 1,000 in 1985. As a result, populations grew considerably, especially in the nineteenth century, then slowed to the present net rate of growth of 0.4 percent per year.

The same process has been under way in developing countries, but with a longer time lag between the declines in death rate and birth rate. In developing countries, the average death rate was more or less constant, at about 38 per 1,000 until 1850, then declining to 33 per 1,000 in 1900, 23 per 1,000 in 1950, and 10 per 1,000 in 1985. The average birth rate, on the other hand, remained at a constant high level, 43 per 1,000, until about 1925; it has since declined at an increasing rate, reaching 37 per 1,000 in 1950, and 30 per 1,000 in 1985. As a result, the increase in the population of the developing countries that began around 1850 has started to slow down and those countries' populations are now growing at an average rate of about 1.74 percent annually. It is important to note that the *death rates* of developed and developing countries are now nearly the same and, given the inherent biological limits, are not likely to decline much further. Thus, in developing countries the progressively rapid drop in birth rate will accelerate progress toward populations that, like those of developed countries, are approximately in balance.

One indicator of the quality of life—infant mortality—is especially decisive in this process. Couples respond to a low rate of infant mortality by realizing that they no longer need to have more children to replace the ones that die. Birth control is, of course, an essential part of this process; but it can succeed—

barring compulsion—only in the presence of a rising standard of living, which generates the necessary motivation. There is a critical point in the rate of infant mortality below which the birth rate begins to drop sharply, creating the conditions for a balanced population. This process appears to be just as characteristic of developing countries as of developed ones. Thus, where infant mortality is particularly high, as in African countries, the birth rate is also very high. Infant mortality is always very responsive to improved living conditions, especially with respect to nutrition. Consequently, there is a kind of critical standard of living which, if achieved, can lead to a rapid reduction in birth rate and an approach to a balanced population.

Thus, in human societies, there is a built-in process that regulates population size: if the standard of living, which initiates the rise in population, continues to increase, the population eventually begins to level off. The chief reason that populations in developing countries have not yet leveled off is that this basic condition has not yet been met. The explanation is a fact about developing countries that is often forgotten: they once were, and in the economic sense often still remain, colonies of more developed countries. In the colonial period, Western nations introduced improved living conditions (roads, communications, engineering, agricultural and medical services) as part of their campaign to increase the labor force needed to exploit the colony's natural resources. (The anthropologist Clifford Geertz has pointed out, for example, that in Indonesia Dutch colonists imposed a tax on the Indonesian population that could only be paid in labor.) This increase in living standards initiates the first phase of the demographic transition; death rates fall, but with birth rates remaining high, there is a rapid increase in population. However, since most of the resultant wealth does not remain in the colony, the second (or population-balancing) phase of the demographic transition is hindered. Instead, the wealth produced in the colony is largely diverted to the advanced country—where it helps that country achieve for itself the second phase of the demographic transition. Thus, colonialism is a kind of demographic parasitism: the second, population-balancing phase of the demographic transition in the colonialist country is fed by the suppression of that same phase in the colony.

The colonies, whether governed legally (albeit after military conquest) or—as in the case of the U.S. control of Latin American countries—by extralegal and economic means, have now become the developing countries of the Third World. Their characteristic condition—large and rapidly growing populations; grinding poverty; desperate efforts for economic development, now hampered by huge debts—is not the outcome of a "primitive" past. The Eskimo peoples are an illuminating test case, for like African countries, let us say, they are "undeveloped" by modern industrial standards. Yet having never been colonized, the Eskimo lands, unlike Africa, show no signs of a "population explosion."

In sum, as the demographer Nathan Keyfitz has concluded, in the period 1800–1950 colonialism resulted in the development of an excess of one billion in the world population, largely in the tropics.

Given this background, what can be said about the various alternative methods of achieving a stable world population? In India there has been an interesting, if partially inadvertent, comparative test of two possible approaches: family-planning programs, and efforts, also on a family basis, to elevate the living standard. The results of this test show that while the family-planning effort itself failed to reduce the birth rate, improved living standards succeeded.

In 1954 a Harvard team undertook the first major field study of birth control in India. The population of a number of test villages was provided with contraceptives and suitable educational programs. Over a six-year period, 1954–60, birth rates, death rates, and health status in this population were compared with the rates found in an equivalent population in villages not provided with the birth control program. A follow-up in 1969 showed that the population control program had failed. Although in the test population the birth rate dropped from 40 per 1,000 in 1957 to 35 per 1,000 in 1968, a similar reduction also occurred in the comparison population. The birth control program had no measurable effect on the birth rate.

We now know why the study failed, thanks to a remarkable book by Mahmood Mamdani, *The Myth of Population Control*. He investigated in detail the impact of the study on one of the test villages, Manupur. What Mamdani discovered confirms the view that population control in a country like India depends on the *economic* factors that indirectly limit fertility. Talking with the Manupur villagers, he discovered why, despite the study's statistics regarding ready "acceptance" of the offered contraceptives, the birth rate was not affected:

> One such "acceptance" case was Asa Singh, a sometime land laborer who is now a watchman at the village high school. I questioned him as to whether he used the [birth control] tablets or not: "Certainly I did. You can read it in their books. From 1957 to 1960, I never failed." Asa Singh, however, had a son who had been born sometime in "late 1958 or 1959." At our third meeting I pointed this out to him. . . . Finally he looked at me and responded. "Babuji, someday you'll understand. It is sometimes better to lie. It stops you from hurting people, does no harm, and might even help them." The next day Asa Singh took me to a friend's house . . . and I saw small rectangular boxes and bottles, one piled on top of the other, all arranged as a tiny sculpture in a corner of the room. This man had made a sculpture of birth control devices. Asa Singh said: "Most of us threw the tablets away. But my brother here, he makes use of everything."

Such stories have been reported before and are often taken to indicate how much "ignorance" has to be overcome before birth control can be effective in countries like India. But Mamdani takes us much deeper into the problem, by asking why the villagers preferred not to use the contraceptives. In one interview after another, he discovered a simple, decisive reason: in order to advance their economic condition, to take advantage of the opportunities newly created by the development of independent India, *children were essential*. Mamdani makes this very explicit:

> To begin with, most families have either little or no savings, and they can earn too little to be able to finance the education of *any* children, even through high school. Another source of income must be found, and the only solution is, as one tailor told me, "to have enough children so that there are at least three or four sons in the family." Then each son can finish high school by spending part of the afternoon working. . . . After high school, one son is sent on to college while the others work to save and pay the necessary fees. . . . Once his education is completed, he will use his increased earnings to put his brother through college. He will not marry until the second brother has finished his college education and can carry the burden of educating the third brother.

Mamdani points out that "it was the rise in the age of marriage—from 17.5 years in 1956 to 20 in 1969—and not the birth control program that was responsible for the decrease in the birth rate in the village from 40 per 1,000 in 1967 to 35 per 1,000 in 1968. While the birth control program was a failure, the net result of the technological and social change in Manupur was to bring down the birth rate."

Here, then, in the simple realities of an Indian village are the principles of the demographic transition at work. There is a way to control the rapid growth of populations in developing countries. It is to help them develop, and to achieve more rapidly the level of welfare that everywhere in the world is the real motivation for reducing the birth rate.

Against this conclusion it will be argued, to quote Hardin, that "it is literally beyond our ability to save them all." This reflects the view that there is simply insufficient food and other resources in the world to support the present world population at the standard of living required to motivate the demographic transition. It is sometimes pointed out, for example, that the United States consumes about one-third of the world's resources to support only 6 percent of the world's population, the inference being that there are simply not enough resources in the world to permit the rest of the world to achieve the standard of living and low birth rate characteristic of the United States. The fault in this reasoning is readily apparent from the actual relationship between the birth rates and living standards in different countries. The only available comparative measure of standard of living is the gross national product (GNP) per capita. Neglecting for this purpose the faults inherent in GNP as a measure of the quality of life, a plot of birth rate against GNP per capita is very revealing. For example, in 1984 in the United States GNP per capita was $15,541 and the birth rate was 16 per 1,000. In the poorest countries (GNP per capita less than $500 per year), the birth rates were 32 to 55 per 1,000. In those countries where GNP per capita was $4,000 to $5,000 (for example, Greece), the birth rate ranged from 15 to 19 per 1,000. Thus, in order to bring the birth rates of the poor countries down to the low levels characteristic of the richer ones, the poor countries do not need to become as affluent (at least as measured by GNP per capita) as the United States. By achieving a per capita GNP only, let us say, one-third of that of the United States, these countries could reach birth rates almost as low as those of the European and North American countries.

In a sense, the demographic transition is a means of translating the availability of a decent level of resources, especially food, into a voluntary reduction in birth rate. The per capita cost, in GNP, of increasing the standard of living of developing countries to the point that would motivate a voluntary reduction in birth rate is small, compared to the wealth of the rich, developed countries—a much neglected, global bargain.

I have tried, thus far, to analyze the Third-World problem based on data about the demographic changes that have already taken place. The data confirm what the world already painfully knows: that in comparison to developed countries, the Third World is terribly impoverished; that it is struggling, against great odds, to develop and to increase its peoples' standard of living; that because the rate of economic development has barely kept up with the rapidly rising population, the standard of living (as measured by GNP per capita) has remained essentially the same in recent years.

Proposals on how to resolve this network of intransigent problems are heavily conditioned by fear of the future. What will the world be like fifty or a hundred years from now if Third-World populations continue to grow rapidly, vastly increasing the ranks of the poor and intensifying the environmental impact of our ecologically unsound technologies? Present demographic trends indicate that developing countries as a whole will reach the death rate now characteristic of developed countries in about 2000; about thirty or forty years later, they will reach the birth rate now characteristic of developed countries. This suggests that perhaps four to five decades from now, developing countries, on the average, will have achieved the sort of demographic stability now found in developed countries. An estimate by the World Bank, based on earlier trends, is less optimistic: approximate stability will be reached about a hundred years from now, when the world population will be about ten billion, or about twice its present size.

World food production is now well above the minimum requirement of the present world population, and growing about 30 percent faster than the population. If present trends continue, there will be more than enough food to support a world population of ten billion when that relatively stable size is reached. At least in these rudimentary terms, the developing countries could traverse the demographic transition without encountering the massive famines predicted by the adherents of the "carrying capacity" hypothesis. But if nothing is done to realign the distribution of food and economic resources, the world will then have twice as many poor and hungry people as it does now. And in that time total production in developing countries will have quadrupled or more so that they, rather than the countries of the north, will then account for most of the world's pollution. Thus, if the world continues on its present path, the moral concerns engendered by massive poverty, and the practical concerns about the degradation of the environment, will only intensify. In sum, the Third-World problem will still be with us, only larger and more devastating than before.

Clearly, something more must be done. The pressure on food supplies, resources, and the environment would be reduced if birth rates were to decline faster than they are at present. Improvement in the standard of living—and hence a faster decline in the birth rate—would be hastened if the rate of economic development could be accelerated. Increased impact on resources and the environment could be avoided if development were based on ecologically sound technologies of production.

All of these problems have a common solution: the elimination of poverty. Poverty is the reason for the failure thus far of developing countries to stabilize their populations. Poverty is the reason why their peoples are malnourished, sick, and hungry. Poverty is the reason why they experience such difficulty in applying the remedy: ecologically sound economic development. Poverty engenders poverty, holding the efforts of developing countries to overcome its tragic effects in a tight, nearly incapacitating embrace.

This is the distant outcome of colonial exploitation. Colonialism has determined the distribution of both the world's wealth and its human population, accumulating most of the wealth north of the equator and most of the people below it. The only remedy, I am convinced, is to return some of the world's wealth to the countries whose resources and peoples have borne so much of the burden of producing it—the developing nations. Such colonial reparations ought to be paid not only in goods but, more usefully, in the means of producing them. And the productive processes should be those that correct both the environmental and economic defects of the technologies that have enveloped the global ecosphere in pollution. Obviously, this proposal would involve exceedingly difficult economic, social, and political problems, especially for the rich countries. But the alternative solutions thus far advanced are at least as difficult and socially stressful; and some are morally repugnant.

A major source of confusion is that the diverse proposed solutions to the population problem, which differ so sharply in their moral postulates and their political effects, appear to have a common base in scientific fact. It is, after all, equally true that the size of the population can be reduced by promulgating contraceptive practices (providing they are used), by elevating living standards, or by withholding food from starving nations. But what I find particularly disturbing is that behind the screen of confusion between scientific fact and political intent there has developed an escalating series of what can be only regarded as inhumane, abhorrent political schemes put forward in the guise of science. There have been "triage" proposals that would condemn whole nations to death through some species of global "benign neglect." There have been schemes for coercing people to curtail their fertility, by physical and legal means that are ominously left unspecified. Now we are told that we must curtail rather than extend our efforts to feed the hungry peoples of the world. Where will it end? Is it conceivable that the proponents of coercive population control will be guided by one of Garrett Hardin's earlier, astonishing proposals?:

> How can we help a foreign country to escape overpopulation? Clearly the worst thing we can do is send food. . . . Atomic bombs would be kinder. For a few moments the misery would be acute, but it would soon come to an end for most of the people, leaving a few survivors to suffer thereafter.

The present confusion can be remedied by recognizing all of the proposals for what they are—not scientific observations but value judgments that reflect sharply differing ethical views and political intentions. The family-planning approach, if applied as the exclusive solution to the population problem, would put the burden of remedying a fault created by a social and political evil—colonialism—solely on the individual victims of that evil. The so-called "lifeboat ethic" would compound the original malevolence of colonialism by forcing its victims to forgo the humane course toward a balanced population—improvement of living standards—or, if they refuse, to abandon them to destruction, or even to thrust them toward it.

My own purely personal conclusion is, like all of these, not scientific but political: the world population crisis, which is the ultimate outcome of the exploitation of poor nations by rich ones, ought to be remedied by returning to the poor countries enough of the wealth taken from them to give their peoples both the reason and the resources voluntarily to limit their own fertility. In sum, I believe that if the root cause of the world population crisis is poverty, then to end it we must abolish poverty. And if the cause of poverty is the grossly unequal distribution of the world's wealth, then to end poverty, and with it the population crisis, we must redistribute that wealth, among nations and within them.

Intergenerational Justice
in Energy Policy*

BRIAN BARRY

THE PROBLEM THAT I shall address in this chapter is as follows. How are we to deal with the fact that the energy resources that at present provide the bulk of our supply, namely fossil fuels, are in practical terms nonrenewable? At best they are renewable only over geological time-spans, while we are exhausting them at rates measured in decades, or at most centuries. Is it possible to define a criterion such that, if we meet it, we will be behaving justly toward later generations? In answer I shall define precisely wherein the morally significant problem lies; propose and defend, in outline terms, a solution; and consider several practical problems of interpretation and implementation.

I. THE NATURE OF THE PROBLEM

The characteristic of fossil fuels that raises problems of justice between generations is that their quantity is finite. This is, indeed, true of all mineral resources, but fossil fuels are special in two ways. (1) Once a fossil fuel has been used, it cannot be reused: there is no possibility of recycling (which in the case of other mineral resources can be done, if the economic incentives exist), to provide a considerable proportion of what is used in the world economy. And (2), while enormous quantities of most minerals are estimated to be in the top mile of the earth's crust, much of the supply is difficult and expensive to get at and is located inconveniently in relation to sources of demand. Therefore, winning these

*Reprinted by permission of the publisher from Brian Barry's "Intergenerational Justice in Energy Policy" in *Energy and the Future*, edited by Douglas MacLean and Peter G. Brown and published by Rowman and Littlefield in 1983.

minerals will incur steadily increasing costs over a time-span measured in centuries.

Of course, as the marginal cost of obtaining a mineral increases, the economic rents that can be realized by those who control the better deposits will also increase. The total cost to consumers will therefore tend to increase more than the total cost of actually extracting, refining, and transporting the minerals. But from the point of view of the world as a whole, this part of the cost is simply a transfer, although it will have distributive implications unless these are neutralized by global policies. The only factor that will make future generations collectively worse off is the additional real cost of minerals. Since at present the total cost of minerals (other than those producing energy) in the world economy is less than 3 percent, it seems clear that, over time, even a doubling or a quadrupling of the real cost of mineral resources could be accommodated without enormous strain.

As far as fossil fuels are concerned, there are already large proved reserves of coal, and there is every reason to believe that there is much more, as well. The immediate impediments to expanding its use are ecological: the damage caused by open-cast mining, and the possible "greenhouse effect" of an increase in the proportion of carbon dioxide in the atmosphere. (I shall return to these matters in section III.) With oil, however, the situation is quite different. It is, of course, dangerous to take too seriously industry estimates of world oil reserves, since these are employed as bargaining counters to obtain better terms from governments, and governments have not yet spent enough on research to be in a position to make entirely independent estimates. But although much of the land surface of the world (let alone the continental shelf) has not yet had a proper geological survey, and although new discoveries, such as the recent Mexican one, are continually being made, almost no one with any degree of expertise will predict that the world can continue to consume oil at the current rate—much less at a continuously increasing rate for centuries.

Of course, tar sands and oil shales do approach the quantities of coal deposits. But even if we waive the ecological problems of processing them, it seems unlikely that any technology will be created that does not make a barrel of oil derived from these sources far more expensive than a barrel of oil from Saudi Arabia or Kuwait, which still costs less than a dollar to pump out and pipe into a tanker. Future generations who relied on such sources for oil in the same amounts as we now use it would therefore be worse off than we are, all else remaining the same; that is, if the capital stock and the technology it embodied were what they are now.

Therefore, the context within which energy policy raises issues of fairness toward future generations, while not different in kind, is different in degree from those raised by other nonrenewable resources. What precisely is the problem of fairness? That some natural resources are finite in quantity would not matter if the supply were so huge that we and succeeding generations could use as much of them as necessary and still leave adequate quantities as easily obtainable and as usefully located as those we now use. It is because that condition does not hold that nonrenewable resources raise a problem of fairness. It is not simply that the more we use the less they will have—which is a tautology, given the definition of "nonrenewable"—but that the more we use the fewer options they will have, other things being equal. They will not be able to produce as much with the same technology, the same amount of capital, the same amount of personal effort, or the same degree of environmental degradation as we now can.

We might, of course, say that the only fair thing to do in the circumstances is to pass on the natural resource base that we—the present generation—inherit. But this would exhibit in a more extreme form the same logic as the town council which passed an ordinance to the effect that there should always be at least one taxi waiting at the station to ensure that taxis would be available for arriving passengers. We must come up with a criterion that allows for some exploitation of nonrenewable resources even when that is going to mean that, other things being equal, future generations will be put at a relative disadvantage compared with us.

II. A Solution and Its Defense

Once the problem has been set up in this way, my solution will, I hope, appear quite natural. I propose that future generations are owed compensation in other ways for our reducing their access to easily extracted and conveniently located natural resources. In practice, this entails that the combination of improved technology and increased capital investment should be such as to offset the effects of depletion.

What, precisely, constitutes "offsetting"? There are two possible interpretations. The one that would naturally occur to economists—and not only to economists—would be to define offsetting in terms of utility: we should do whatever is necessary to provide future generations with the same level of utility as they would have had if we had not depleted the natural resources. There are all kinds of difficulties in drawing practical implications from this idea, but the objection that I shall put is pitched at a level of principle and would still be relevant even if all the practical problems could be swept away.

The alternative that I wish to defend is that what constitutes offsetting the depletion of natural resources is the replacement of the productive opportunities we have destroyed by the creation of alternative ones. In other words, when we say that resource depletion makes future generations "worse off" than we are, this should be taken to mean that they will be worse off in terms of productive potential; and it is that loss of productive potential for which justice requires us to compensate. (The notion of productive potential will be explained below.)

Questions immediately arise, of course. What is an acceptable "alternative," and what happens if future people have different tastes from ours (as seems a priori very likely)? I shall discuss these and other problems in the next section.

First, I want to offer a general argument for defining the criterion in terms of opportunities rather than utilities.

My answer is that this is true of justice in all contexts, so intergenerational justice is simply an application of the general idea. We therefore need a discussion of the broad thesis rather than one confined to future generations, for the conclusion will surely be stronger for the rather strange case of future generations if it can be shown to be plausible in more familiar cases. To this end, let me return to the alternative interpretation of the criterion of compensation for resource depletion, that it should be defined in terms of utility. This idea stems from a general conception of what should be the subject matter of moral assessment: that, although we perforce distribute rights, opportunities, or material goods rather than utility, the ultimate standard of judgment should be the utility to people that arises from them.

Utilitarianism, understood as the theory that the aggregate amount of utility should be maximized, is the best-known example of a theory that takes utility as the only thing that matters, in the last analysis. Thus, as Sidgwick put it, utilitarianism is concerned with "the distribution of Happiness, not the means of happiness." Recently Ted Honderich has advanced a "Principle of Equality," defined not in terms of equal treatment, but in terms of "the qualities of the experience of individuals." The principle is then "that things should be so arranged that we approach as close as we can, which may not be all that close, to equality in satisfaction and distress." Again, Amartya Sen began a recent article by saying: "Usual measures of economic inequality concentrate on income, but frequently one's interest may lie in the inequality of welfare rather than of income as such." And he went on to say that this raises problems not only of "interpersonal comparisons of welfare, but also those arising from differences in non-income circumstances, e.g., age, the state of one's health, the pattern of love, friendship, concern and hatred surrounding a person."

Of course, it is generally agreed that there are, in practice, severe limits to the extent to which distribution can be individuated so as to take account of the way in which different people either get different amounts of happiness from some baseline amount of the means of happiness, or gain unequal amounts of happiness from the same increments in the means of happiness. The relevant information is difficult to come by—some would say that the problem is not even well defined. Collecting the information would in any case intrude on personal privacy. The policy would place a premium on dissimulation, as people would try to give the appearance of having a utility function of a kind that would provide them with a large allocation of income or other means of happiness. And the implementation of a program of adapting distribution to individual psychological characteristics would obviously place vast powers in the hands of those doing the allocating—powers to make decisions on a largely discretionary basis, because of the lack of precisely defined objective criteria for establishing the susceptibility of different people to external advantages or disadvantages.

For all these reasons it might be admitted that in practice idiosyncratic differences in the way people convert the means of happiness into happiness itself should be disregarded for purposes of public policy. And it might plausibly be added that the case for disregarding idiosyncrasies becomes overwhelming when we don't know anything definite about the people concerned—as must be the case with people as yet unborn. We could therefore, by invoking ignorance, get from the premise that the ultimate object of distribution is utility to the conclusion that justice between generations should be defined in terms of resources: in the absence of the appropriate information we must fall back on distributing resources without looking beyond resources to utilities. Instead, however, I want to suggest that the whole idea of treating utility as the object of distribution is wrong.

To strip away the practical complications, imagine that by some incredible advance in psychometric technology it became possible to fit people with tiny, tamper-proof "black boxes" implanted under the skin, and that these "black boxes" measured (and somehow could be shown to measure to the satisfaction of anyone with enough training in neurophysiology and electronics) the amount of utility received by the recipient within, say, a period of a year. I don't think that the availability of this kind of publicly verifiable information would eliminate the case against allocating the means of happiness so as to achieve a certain distribution of happiness. For my view is that such information is in principle irrelevant when it comes to determining a just distribution.

Suppose we believe that two people should be paid the same amount: they do the same work equally well, have equal seniority in the same firm, and so on. What this means is that they have an equal claim on the resources of society to do what they like with that chunk of resources. (Taking account of market distortions, we can say that prices do roughly correspond to the real claim on resources at the margin represented by alternative purchases.) Justice consists in their getting an equal crack at society's resources, without any mention of comparative utility. If we discover that one of them gets more fun out of spending his income than does the other, this is no reason for transferring income from the one who derives more utility to the one who derives less. Similarly, if the price of something one of them enjoys goes up (e.g., because of an increased demand for it), this is no reason for increasing his income in compensation. For he had no special claim on the amount of utility he was getting before. All he had a claim on was the share of resources.

The argument as applied to future generations is, then, that we should not hold ourselves responsible for the satisfaction they derive from their opportunities.

What is important from the point of view of justice is the range of choice open to them, rather than what they get out of it. But choice of what? The range of choice I have so far discussed has been the range of consumption choices. Broadly speaking, I have been making the case for defining justice in terms of income rather than utility.

But this is not the whole story. For we obviously cannot literally provide people not yet born with income, any more than we can provide them with utility. The question is, in either case, whether we need to predict how much they will actually get, if we do one thing rather than another. Even if this were feasible (which it is not), it would still be beside the point.

The important thing is that we should compensate for the reduction in opportunities to produce brought about by our depleting the supply of natural resources, and that compensation should be defined in terms of productive potential. If we could somehow predict that there would be a general decline in working hours or in the amount of effort people put into work, this would be no reason to say that we must hand over additional productive resources to future generations. This notion of productive potential will be analyzed below. For the present, all we need to grasp is that productive potential is equal in two situations if the same effort would produce the same output.

Two questions follow from this. First, why should future generations be left not worse off (in opportunity terms) than they would have been in the absence of our having depleted the resources? To the second and much more difficult question, I shall not be able to give a wholly satisfactory answer. In order to say that our depletion of resources should not leave future generations with a smaller range of opportunities than they would otherwise have had, we must have some standard on the basis of which we can establish what opportunities they would otherwise have had. What is the appropriate standard?

Let me begin with the first point. The basic argument for an equal claim on natural resources is that none of the usual justifications for an unequal claim— special relationships arising in virtue of past services, promises, etc.—applies here. From an atemporal perspective, no one generation has a better or worse claim than any other to enjoy the earth's resources. In the absence of any powerful argument to the contrary, there would seem to be a strong presumption in favor of arranging things so that, as far as possible, each generation faces the same range of opportunities with respect to natural resources. I must confess that I can see no further positive argument to be made at this point. All I can do is counter what may be arguments on the other side. Is there any way in which the present generation can claim that it is entitled to a larger share of the goods supplied by nature than its successors? If not, then equal shares is the only solution compatible with justice.

The only theory of distributive justice that might appear to have implications inconsistent with the equality of generations is the Lockean one of a "natural right" to appropriate by "mixing one's labor" with natural resources. This might be taken to imply that there is no criterion by which the collective exploitation of natural resources by a generation can be judged, as long as the individualistic requirements of the Lockean theory are met. However, even taking that theory seriously for a moment, we should bear in mind that Locke said that legitimate appropriation was limited by the proviso that "enough and as good" should be left for others. If we interpret "others" to include later generations as well as contemporaries, we get the notion of equality between generations. And Locke's unconvincing attempt to fudge the application of the proviso once people have "consented to the use of money" cannot get a foothold in the intergenerational case, since future generations are obviously in no position to consent to our exploitation of natural resources in a way that fails to leave "as good" for them.

Clearly, if each generation has an equal right to enjoy the productive opportunities provided by natural resources, it does not necessarily follow that compensation for violating that right is acceptable. We all will agree that doing harm is in general not canceled out by doing good, and conversely that doing some good does not license one to do harm, provided it doesn't exceed the amount of good. For example, if you paid for the realignment of a dangerous highway intersection and saved an average of two lives a year, that wouldn't mean that you could shoot one motorist per year and simply reckon on coming out ahead.

Here, however, the example involves gratuitous infliction of harm. In the case of resources and future generations, the crucial feature is that we can't possibly avoid harming them by using up some nonrenewable resources, given the existing population level and the technology that has developed to sustain that level. So the choice is not between reducing the resource base for future generations and keeping it intact, but between depletion with compensation and depletion without compensation. The analogy is therefore with the traveler caught in a blizzard who, in order to survive, breaks into somebody's empty weekend cottage, builds a fire, and helps himself to food. Not even Robert Nozick (I think) would deny that this is a legitimate use of another's property without his permission. It will be generally agreed, also, that while the unauthorized taking of another's property was entirely justifiable in the circumstances, the traveler is not absolved from making restitution for whatever he damaged or consumed.

The second problem arises in this way. Suppose we say that justice requires us to compensate future generations for depleted resources, so that they have as much productive potential as they would have inherited had the resources not been depleted. To give this criterion any operational significance, we obviously must give some definite content to the notion of the amount of productive potential that future generations would have enjoyed in the absence of resource depletion; or we have no means of deciding what is required by justice in the way of compensation.

We cannot say that "the productive potential that future generations would otherwise have enjoyed" is to be settled by predicting. Perhaps, in the absence of resource depletion, we would in fact be inclined to leave future generations with far less productive potential than, as a matter of justice, we ought to leave them with. If we were to leave them an inadequate amount plus an amount calculated to compensate for resource depletion, we would then be behaving unjustly. Conversely, in the absence of resource depletion, maybe we would leave future generations with far more productive potential than is required by justice whatever that is. In that case, even when resource depletion is taken into account, the same amount would still more than satisfy the requirements of justice.

It is apparent, therefore, that "the productive potential that future generations would otherwise have enjoyed" must be defined in terms of justice. We must understand the following: what future generations would justly have enjoyed in the absence of resource depletion. But how much is that? The answer is critical in determining the whole outcome of our enquiry. To make the most extreme case, suppose we said the only things we owe to future generations are whatever natural resources we inherited plus due compensation (measured in terms of productive capacity) for what we depleted. If we left anything more than a few picks and shovels they would be ahead, since they would then be in a better position to exploit natural resources than if they had to use their bare hands. Anything more than that would go beyond the demands of justice. But human generations do not succeed one another with one generation marching off the stage as another marches on, so self-interest on the part of the living will ensure that far more than that is handed on. However selfishly those alive at any given time behave, they can scarcely avoid passing on to their successors a pretty large capital stock that embodies thousands of years of technological development. Hence, the principle of compensation for the depletion of natural resources could be accepted without the slightest implication that more should be done to protect the interests of future generations than would inevitably be done as a by-product of the pursuit of self-interest by the current generation.

I imagine that few would really want to say that we would be beyond criticism on grounds of justice if we ran down capital and used up natural resources in whatever way best suited us, as long as we left our successors somewhat better equipped than people were in the Stone Age. But it is hard to come up with a clear-cut principle to say exactly how far the bounds of justice extend. I believe, however, that there are some leading ideas which can guide us.

Most of our technology and the capital stock embodying it are not by any stretch of the imagination the sole creation of the present generation; we cannot therefore claim exclusive credit for it. The whole process of capital formation presupposes an inheritance of capital and technology. To a considerable extent, then, we can say that, from the standpoint of the current generation, natural resources are not really as sharply distinguished from capital and technology as might at first appear. Both are originally inherited, and thus fall outside any special claims based on the present generation's having done something to deserve them. We therefore can make no special claim on our side. But can others (those who did create them) claim that they can endow us with exclusive control over what we inherit? This raises complicated issues.

It seems to me that inherited capital can be looked at from two standpoints, that of the creators and that of the receivers, and that the trick is to give weight to both perspectives. From the side of the recipients, inherited capital is exactly like inherited natural resources—the present generation can claim credit for neither. From the side of the earlier generations, on the other hand, accumulated capital and natural resources that are handed on have different statuses, in that capital is created and natural resources are not. Yet no generation creates from scratch all the capital it hands on. It seems reasonable to suggest that it should get credit only for the capital it adds.

This, then, gives us a rough basis for proceeding. Let us say that, as a reasonable reconciliation of the two perspectives, each generation's sacrifices (if any) to increase the capital stock it passes on give it a claim to some consideration by the following generation of its objectives in making these sacrifices. Beyond one generation, its specific wishes for the disposition of the increment become progressively less significant as constituting claims on the decisions of the living.

We can now venture a statement of what is required by justice toward future generations. As far as natural resources are concerned, depletion should be compensated for in the sense that later generations should be left no worse off (in terms of productive capacity) than they would have been without the depletion. And how well off they would have been is to be determined by applying the principles that have been worked out above. As a starting point, we may say that the capital stock inherited should be passed on without diminution, but this can be modified somewhat to accommodate the claims of past generations. If we suppose, for example, that the previous generation made sacrifices to permit the present generation a higher standard of living without any expectation that this generation would pass it on, it would seem legitimate for the present generation to pass on slightly less. On the other hand, if one believes that successive past generations made sacrifices in the (no doubt vague) expectation that each generation would pass on more than it inherited, this would constitute a prima facie case for saying that the present generation has a certain obligation to continue with this process. The whole notion of obligations to continue the undertakings of past generations, however, raises difficulties that need further work. I do not think we should go far wrong here if we set it aside and simply say that compensation should be reckoned as what is required to maintain productive potential.

III. Practical Problems

Three practical problems arise in any attempt to apply the conclusions of the abstract discussion so far. The first is whether the compensation criterion can be given a workable significance. The second is where issues of intragenerational distribution fit in. And the third is how to deal with the difficulty that alternative policies have results in the future that are associated with varying degrees of uncertainty.

On the feasibility of the compensation criterion, the apparent problem is this: oil is oil is oil. How do we decide what is adequate compensation for running down the world's reserves of oil? In the most favorable case, it may be possible to compensate in a quite direct way. If we run down the oil by 10 percent but develop technology that makes it possible to extract 10 percent more oil from any given deposit, we have in effect left future generations with as much (exploitable) oil as we found. Or if we develop internal combustion engines that produce more power per gallon of gasoline used, we have made the remaining stock of oil go further, measured in output terms—which is what counts—than it would otherwise have done. And so on.

I do not want to suggest that this will solve all the problems of implementation; where it is not applicable, we have to fall back on the more general idea of maintaining productive capacity. Within limits, which over a long time period may be very wide, it is always possible to substitute capital for raw materials by recycling, cutting down waste, and making things get results by being complicated and well engineered, rather than big and heavy. Energy may appear unamenable to this treatment, since, as I noted at the outset, once it has been used it cannot be recovered. But it can still be economized by a greater expenditure of capital, and the performance of the U.S. economy in recent years has illustrated the way in which, with the right incentives, capital expenditure will be substituted for energy.

The second practical problem is this: What happens when the principles for justice between generations are combined with moral principles governing distribution among people who are contemporaries, whether they live now or in the future? One reason for confronting the question of intragenerational distribution is that there are some who profess impatience with a concern for the interests of unborn generations when there are so many existing people now starving or suffering from preventable malnutrition and disease. I must admit to some sympathy with this impatience. I have a possibly prejudiced idea that one could run in Marin County more successfully on a platform of doing good things for future generations than of transferring money to poor people now, either domestically or internationally. Being in favor of future generations is somehow more antiseptically apolitical than being in favor of contemporaries, and also, in an odd way, gives an impression of being more high-minded.

If it were really necessary to make a choice between intragenerational and intergenerational justice, it would be a tough one. But in my view there is no such dilemma, because I do not believe that there will turn out to be any inconsistency between the requirements of each. In the absence of a full theory of both, I cannot show this. But I predict that whatever redistribution among contemporaries is required by justice will also be able to observe the constraints that the interests of future generations be protected.

Of course, if citizens and governments in the rich countries are willing to make only token sacrifices to meet the demands of either intragenerational or intergenerational justice, a choice will have to be made. But we ought then to be clear that the necessity for choice arises not from any real incompatibility, but simply from the not unusual phenomenon that people are not prepared to behave justly when it is contrary to their immediate interests, unless they are somehow coerced into doing so. And while poor countries have a certain amount of ability to cause trouble to rich ones, future generations obviously have no way of enforcing a fair deal on the present generation.

It will be apparent that the principles already enunciated for justice among generations may be applied equally well to relations among contemporaries. Thus, the argument that there is no act by which the value of natural resources may be regarded as earned or deserved by whoever happens to find them suggests an equal claim of all contemporaries on that value. Similarly, the idea that inherited capital and technology gradually merge into the "common heritage of mankind" clearly implies a just claim by poor countries on rich ones.

Intragenerational justice would best be met by a combination of a self-balancing, shadow (positive and negative) income tax on countries and a severance tax on the exploitation of natural resources, the proceeds being transferred to resource-poor countries such as India, Bangladesh, or some central African countries. This would, in an admittedly rough and ready way (but no other is to be expected), make tax liability depend on both the special advantages arising from possession of rich natural resources and the more general advantages that make for high per capita income. Intergenerational justice requires, as we have seen, maintenance of capital (with certain modest exceptions) plus the creation of additional technology and capital to compensate for resource depletion. Yet this has an intragenerational aspect, too. To say that "the present generation" should pass on certain productive capabilities to "future generations" leaves open the question of how the burdens and the benefits should be distributed among contemporaries, now and in the future. What can be said about this?

It is legitimate for those who form the current generation in a country to make special efforts to provide extra benefits for their own descendants if they choose to do so, since this is more than is called for by justice anyway. This is in effect an intergenerational gift of resources whose disposition the people in that country have a just claim to control. But the mere passing along of the amount of capital inherited draws no credit. And, as I have suggested, the wishes of those who originally made the sacrifices to accumulate it should be regarded as fading out over the course of a few generations. This implies that some of the capital stock should be diffused as claims to special benefits run out, in the same way as patents and copyrights expire with time.

The problem of resource depletion by those living in the country can be divided into two parts: who should provide the compensation, and who should receive it? I suggest that those countries which consume the largest quantities of nonrenewable natural resources should be responsible for the bulk of the effort to provide the technology and capital formation to substitute for them.

On the other hand, I wish to argue that it would be extremely inequitable if the compensatory technology and capital were passed on for the exclusive benefit of the successors of those in the countries who depleted the natural resources. Since running down of any natural resources deprives all future inhabitants of the world of the production from any given combination of capital and labor, the compensation is owed not to descendants of the current heavy users only, but to all in the future who are disadvantaged by that use—in fact, everybody.

The redistributive case is even stronger than this. For industrial countries have achieved their present prosperity by first using their own natural resources and then, when these began to get scarce, by using those of the rest of the world at relatively low cost to themselves—in the case of oil, for example, for a few cents per gallon through the 1950s and 1960s. In effect, this bonanza has been turned into accumulated capital that is regarded by these countries as their private property to do with as they choose. But it is obviously harder for countries that missed out on this era of cheap resources to undertake a similar course of economic development in the future. (The effect of oil price increases on Indian economic planning is a dramatic illustration, and many others could be offered.) The poor countries, therefore, have been especially disadvantaged because, unlike the rich countries, they have nothing to show for the past depletion of world resources except perhaps in free access to some unpatented technology that was part and parcel of Western development.

The upshot of this discussion is that, generally speaking, the countries with the highest per capita production and the highest use of nonrenewable natural resources (the two are highly correlated) should be making transfers, to meet the requirements of intergenerational justice, to the poor countries. This clearly overlaps with the requirements of purely intragenerational justice that were outlined earlier. An across-the-board international income tax (levied on countries, to be raised through their own domestic tax systems), whether or not supplemented by a severance tax on the extraction of mineral resources, would meet all the requirements, as long as part of the proceeds of the tax were devoted to the building up of technology and capital in the recipient countries, and as long as those in the rich countries did not treat payment of the tax as an alternative to accumulating capital domestically to enable their own descendants to offset the effects of resource depletion.

The final problem is that of uncertainty. It cannot be avoided because, in deciding what technologies we ought to develop to compensate future generations for the depletion of resources, we must somehow deal with the fact that the risks and benefits are, to some degree, speculative. Suppose most competent authorities agree that there is a possibility (i.e., it cannot be excluded on the basis of existing scientific knowledge) that some action taken now (e.g., burying nuclear wastes deep underground, releasing fluorocarbons into the atmosphere, or carrying out experiments on recombinant DNA) will have serious and irreversible (or only doubtfully/expensively/gradually reversible) adverse consequences in the long term; and suppose further that either there is disagreement on the likelihood of these adverse consequences coming to pass or agreement on the impossibility, in the present state of knowledge, of quantifying the risk (or some mixture of the two). The question, then, is how we should react to this state of affairs. Should we say that the profound uncertainty makes it unreasonable (or "premature," if one is optimistic about the prospects for finding out more in the future) to decide against taking the action? Or should we say that, in the absence of better information, the possibility of disastrous consequences is a decisive reason for not acting? *Ex hypothesi*, methods of decision making that discount alternative outcomes by their probabilities of occurrence are not available here.

The simplest argument for giving the second answer rather than the first is a two-part one: (1) in the case of an individual making a choice that affects only himself, we should regard anyone who acted on the basis of the first alternative as crazy; and (2) when we change the case to one that involves millions of people and extends over many centuries, the same reasoning applies, with increased force. The best way to establish (1) is by means of an example. Imagine that your dentist were to say: "The only way of saving this tooth is by means of a new procedure. There is every reason to believe that the procedure will succeed in saving the tooth, but it's conceivable that it will kill you. It may be that, however many times it were done, nobody would ever be killed by it. But it can't be ruled out on the basis of anything we currently know about physiology that it's highly lethal. It's not impossible that it has one chance in a hundred of killing you. Since we have no idea of the magnitude of the risks involved, I draw two conclusions: more research is needed, and in the meantime you should undergo the procedure." I predict that not only would you decline his suggestion, but you'd also think he should have his license withdrawn for professional incompetence.

As far as (2) is concerned, I need only say that there is no prima facie reason for supposing that changing the case so that the numbers involved are larger and extend over a longer time is going to make the choice associated with an uncertain potential for catastrophe more palatable rather than less. If anything, the argument is even strengthened. Let me conclude by offering three considerations.

First, we might ask whether genocide is universally abhorred for no other reason than that it entails killing a large number of individual human beings. Or is it worse to wipe out an entire people than to kill an equal number of individuals scattered throughout the world? One answer might be that genocide is worse because it is the expression of an evil theory—that of racial superiority and inferiority. But genocidal attempts antedated the Nazis (e.g., the "Armenian massacres" and the hunting to extinction of the native populations of Tasmania and California in the nineteenth century), yet those cases were no less terrible.

We can approach what I consider the critical point by discussing what has been called "cultural genocide"—the practice of systematically exterminating the intelligentsia: the professionals, writers, journalists, students, and anyone with an above-average level of education. Those with greater knowledge of history than I can no doubt cite examples going back thousands of years, but the recent examples with which I am familiar are Pakistan (the early stages of the civil war that led to the creation of Bangladesh) and Burundi. (Cambodia may be another case, but I don't know enough to say—maybe nobody does.) These examples of "cultural genocide" seem to me less terrible than the destruction of the entire Bengali or Hutu populations would have been—numbers obviously do make a difference. At the same time, they are, in my view, worse than random killing of the same numbers of the same populations.

My point is that the destruction of cultures is a bad over and above the physical destruction of its bearers. This, then, gives us a reason for holding that destroying a large population is more serious than killing the same number of random individuals. And this in turn is another reason why remote possibilities of catastrophic accidents (e.g., in nuclear reactors) should be treated as especially grave threats, and not simply balanced against the number of deaths from bronchitis or lung cancer that can be associated with the use of fossil fuel as an alternative. One chance in a million per annum of wiping out New York simply is not the same as having ten more people die each year in the United States (or in New York).

Risk may be acceptable if it is accepted voluntarily in the pursuit of something that seems valuable to the person who chooses it. If somebody wishes to risk his or her life gratuitously by rock climbing or white-water canoeing, one might say that there is no case for preventing or discouraging these freely chosen activities.

But the risks of, say, nuclear power generation are not at all plausibly construed on that model. The risk cannot be confined to the beneficiaries. We have a public good and a public bad; people who use the electricity get the good, and those who live near the plant get the bad, irrespective of whether they would prefer to do without both. If we were to respond that in the nature of the case consent cannot be obtained from everyone affected before any piece of collective action is undertaken, I would of course agree. But then the question of distributive equity arises. The canoeist gets the risk, and the benefit. But with larger-scale projects, it is unlikely that the risks and the benefits will be distributed to each person in the same proportions. If nuclear plants are located in the country and mainly supply the cities, the rural people get a disproportionate share of the risks, while the city people benefit.

These problems are exacerbated across generations. First, cultural impoverishment is irreversible and continues to impoverish all successive generations. Second, if we do things now that impose risks on future people, there is clearly no way of getting their consent. And, finally, with some examples such as nuclear power plants, the benefits and risks are asymmetrically distributed across time: the benefits disproportionately occur while the plant is producing electricity, and the risks continue in some form for thousands of years, until the radioactivity of the waste decays to a safe level.

PART V

Race and Gender

Race-Specific Policies
and the Truly Disadvantaged*

WILLIAM JULIUS WILSON

IN THE PERIOD FOLLOWING the thirtieth anniversary of the 1954 Supreme Court decision against racial separation, *Brown v. the Board of Education of Topeka, Kansas*, and the twentieth anniversary of the 1964 Civil Rights Act, a troubling dilemma confronts proponents of racial equality and social justice. The dilemma is that while the socioeconomic status of the most disadvantaged members of the minority population has deteriorated rapidly since 1970, that of advantaged members has significantly improved. This is perhaps most clearly seen in the changes that have occurred within the American black population in recent years.

In several areas, blacks have not only improved their social and economic positions in recent years, but have made those improvements at a relatively faster rate than the reported progress of comparable whites. The most notable gains have occurred in professional employment, income of married-couple families, higher education, and home ownership. The number of blacks in professional, technical, managerial, and administrative positions increased by 57 percent (from 974,000 to 1,533,000) from 1973 to 1982, while the number of whites in such positions increased by only 36 percent. The median annual income for black married-couple families in 1982 was $20,586, compared to $26,443 for white married-couple families. The gap was even narrower in households where both husband and wife were employed; this was especially true for couples between the ages of twenty-four and thirty-five, where the difference

*Reprinted from *The Truly Disadvantaged: The Inner City, the Underclass, and Public Policy* by William Julius Wilson. Copyright ©1987 by the University of Chicago. Reprinted with permission of the University of Chicago Press.

in annual income between blacks and whites was less than $3,000. And the fraction of black families earning $25,000 or more (in 1982 dollars) increased from 10.4 percent in 1960 to 24.5 percent in 1982. Meanwhile, the number of blacks enrolled full time at American colleges and universities nearly doubled between 1970 and 1980 (going from 522,000 to over 1 million). Blacks recorded a 47 percent increase in home ownership during the 1970s (from 2.57 million to 3.78 million), compared to a 30 percent increase for whites.

But for millions of other blacks, most of them concentrated in the ghettos of American cities, the past three decades have been a time of regression, not progress. These low-income families and individuals are, in several important respects, more socially and economically isolated than before the great civil rights victories, particularly in terms of high joblessness and the related problems of poverty, family instability, and welfare dependency. These changes are reflected in a growing economic schism between lower-income and higher-income black families. As shown in table 1, the percentage of total black family income attributable to the lowest two-fifths of black families declined from 15.8 percent in 1966 to 13.4 percent by 1981; the upper two-fifths of black families contributed 67.3 percent of the total in 1966, but 70.6 percent in 1981. The lowest two-fifths of white families, on the other hand, contributed 18.2 percent to the total white family income in 1966, and 17.1 percent in 1981; the upper two-fifths of white families contributed 64 percent in 1966, and 65.4 percent in 1981. The index of income concentration (a statistical measure of income inequality ranging from zero, which indicates perfect equality, to one, which reveals perfect inequality) reveals that income inequality is greater and has increased at a faster rate among black families than among white families from 1966 to 1981.

The factors associated with the growing woes of low-income blacks are exceedingly complex and go beyond the narrow issue of contemporary discrimination. Indeed, it would not be unreasonable to contend that the race-specific policies emanating from the civil rights revolution, although beneficial to more advantaged blacks (i.e., those with higher income, greater education and training, and more prestigious occupations), do little for those who are truly disadvantaged. The Harvard black economist Glenn Loury has argued in this connection that

> It is clear from extensive empirical research on the effect of affirmative action standards for federal contractors, that the positive impact on blacks which this program has had accrues mainly to those in the higher occupations. If one examines the figures on relative earnings of young black and white men by educational class, by far the greater progress has been made among those blacks with the most education. If one looks at relative earnings of black and white workers by occupation going back to 1950, one finds that the most dramatic earning gains for blacks have taken place in the professional,

technical, and managerial occupations, while the least significant gains have come in the lowest occupations, like laborer and service worker. Thus a broad array of evidence suggests, at least to this observer, that better placed blacks have simply been able to take more advantage of the opportunities created in the last twenty years than have those mired in the underclass.

TABLE 1   Share of Aggregate Income by Each Fifth of Families, by Percentage of Distribution of Aggregate Income by Race

Selected Family Positions	1966	1976	1981
Blacks and other races			
Lowest fifth	4.9	4.4	4.0
Second fifth	10.9	9.6	9.4
Middle fifth	16.9	15.9	16.0
Fourth fifth	25.0	25.2	25.5
Highest fifth	42.3	44.9	45.1
Top 5%	14.6	16.1	16.0
Index of Income Concentration	.377	.411	.418
White			
Lowest fifth	5.6	5.8	5.4
Second fifth	12.6	12.1	11.7
Middle fifth	17.8	17.7	19.5
Fourth fifth	23.7	23.9	24.2
Highest fifth	40.3	40.6	41.2
Top 5%	15.4	15.4	15.1
Index of Income Concentration	.346	.349	.359

Source: U.S. Bureau of the Census, *Current Population Reports*, series P-60, no. 137, "Money Income of Households, Families, and Persons in the United States, 1981" (Washington, DC: Government Printing Office, 1983).

The crucial point is not that the deteriorating plight of the ghetto underclass is associated with the greater success enjoyed by advantaged blacks as a result of race-specific programs, but rather that these programs are mistakenly presumed to be the most appropriate solution to the problems of all blacks regardless of economic class. In the following sections this argument is explored in some detail, beginning with a critical discussion of the basic assumptions associated with two liberal principles that underlie recent, but entirely different, policy approaches to problems of race—namely, equality of individual opportunity, which stresses the rights of minority individuals, and equality of group opportunity, which embodies the idea of preferential treatment for minority groups.

EGALITARIAN PRINCIPLES OF RACE AND DISADVANTAGED MEMBERS OF MINORITIES

The goals of the civil rights movement have changed considerably in the last fifteen to twenty years. This change has been reflected in the shift in emphasis from the rights of minority individuals to the preferential treatment of minority groups. The implementation of the principle of equality of group rights results in the formal recognition of racial and ethnic groups by the state, as well as economic, educational, and political rewards based on formulas of group membership. Although many of the proponents of this principle argue that preferential treatment is only a temporary device to overcoming the effects of previous discrimination, this shift in precepts has long divided the civil rights movement, which, in the early 1960s, was unified behind the principle of equality of individual opportunity.

However, neither programs based on equality of individual opportunity nor those organized in terms of preferential group treatment are sufficient to address the problems of truly disadvantaged minority group members. Let us consider, first of all, the principle of equality of individual rights which dominated the early phases of the civil rights movement.

At mid-twentieth century, liberal black and white leaders of the movement for racial equality agreed that the conditions of racial and ethnic minorities could best be improved by an appeal to the conscience of white Americans to uphold the American creed of egalitarianism and democracy. These leaders directed their efforts to eliminating Jim Crow segregation statutes through Supreme Court litigation, pressing for national legislation to outlaw discrimination in employment and housing, and breaking down the extralegal obstacles to black voting in the South.

It was assumed that the government could best protect the rights of individual members of minority groups not by formally bestowing rewards and punishments based on racial or ethnic categories, but by using antidiscrimination legislation to enhance individual freedom of choice in education, employment, voting, and public accommodations. The individual, therefore, was "the unit of attribution for equity considerations," and the ultimate goal was to reward each citizen based on his or her merits and accomplishments. In short, equality of opportunity meant equality for citizens.

Thus, from the 1950s to 1970, emphasis was on the equality of individual opportunity, or freedom of choice; the approved role of government was to ensure that people were not formally categorized on the basis of race.

Antidiscrimination legislation was designed to eliminate racial bias without considering the actual percentage of minorities in certain positions. These actions upheld the underlying principle of equality of individual rights, namely, that candidates for positions stratified in terms of prestige or other social criteria should be judged solely on individual merit and therefore ought not be discriminated against on the basis of race or ethnic origin.

It would be ideal if programs based on this principle were sufficient to address problems of inequality in our society because they are consistent with the prevailing ideals of democracy and freedom of choice, do not call for major sacrifices on the part of the larger population, and are not perceived as benefiting certain groups at the expense of others. The "old" goals of the civil rights movement, in other words, were more in keeping with "traditional" American values, and thus more politically acceptable than the "new" goals of equal opportunity for groups through a system of collective racial and ethnic entitlements. However, programs based solely on the principle of equality of individual opportunity are inadequate to address the complex problems of group inequality in America.

More specifically, as James Fishkin appropriately points out, this principle does not address the substantive inequality that exists at the time the bias is removed. In other words, centuries or even decades of racial subjugation can result in a system of racial inequality that may linger on for indefinite periods of time after racial barriers are eliminated. This is because the most disadvantaged minority group members, who have been crippled or victimized by the cumulative effects of both race and class subordination (including those effects passed on from generation to generation), are disproportionately represented among that segment of the total population that lacks the resources to compete effectively in a free and open market. The black columnist William Raspberry recognized this problem when he stated:

> There are some blacks for whom it is enough to remove the artificial barriers of race. After that, their entry into the American mainstream is virtually automatic. There are others for whom hardly anything would change if, by some magical stroke, racism disappeared from America. Everyone knows this of course. And yet hardly anyone is willing to say it. And because we don't say it, we wind up confused about how to deal with the explosive problems confronting the American society, confused about what the problem really is.

It is important to recognize that in modern industrial society the removal of racial barriers creates the greatest opportunities for the better-trained, talented, and educated segments of the minority population—those who have been crippled the least by the weight of past discrimination. This is because they possess the resources that allow them to compete freely with dominant group members for valued positions. In this connection, as Leroy D. Clark and Judy Trent Ellis have noted, there must be a recognition that civil rights legislation can only benefit those in a position to take advantage of it. To the extent that some members of minority groups have been denied education and certain work experience, they will be able to compete for only a limited number of jobs. Certain disabilities traceable in general to racism may deprive some minority members of the qualifications for particular jobs. Title VII, however, protects only against arbitrary use of race or its equivalents as a barrier to work; it does not assure one of employment or promotion if legitimate qualifications are lacking.

In short, the competitive resources developed by the advantaged minority members—resources "resulting from the income, family stability, peer groups, and schooling that their parents can make available to them"—result in their benefiting disproportionately from policies that promote the rights of minority individuals, policies that remove artificial barriers and thereby enable individuals to compete freely and openly for the more desirable and prestigious positions in American society.

However, since 1970, government policy has tended to focus on the equitable distribution of *group* rights, so that people have been formally categorized or recognized on the basis of race or ethnicity. Formal programs have been designed and created not only to prevent discrimination, but also to ensure that minorities are adequately represented in certain positions. Thus emphasis has shifted from equality of opportunity, stressing individual rights, to equality of condition, emphasizing group rights. Between the mid-1950s and 1970, the elimination of existing discrimination was the sole concern of liberal policymakers; since 1970, however, serious attention has also been given to negating the effects of past discrimination. This has resulted in a move from the simple investigation and adjudication of complaints of racial discrimination by fair employment practices commissions and civil rights commissions to government-mandated affirmative action programs designed to ensure minority representation in employment, in public programs, and in education.

Nonetheless, if the more advantaged minority members profit disproportionately from policies built on the principle of equality of individual opportunity, they also reap disproportionate benefits from policies of preferential treatment based solely on their group membership. I say this because minority individuals from the most advantaged families are likely to be disproportionately represented among the minority members most qualified for preferred positions—such as higher-paying jobs, college admissions, promotions, and so forth. Accordingly, if policies of preferential treatment for such positions are conceived not in terms of the actual disadvantages suffered by individuals but rather in terms of race or ethnic group membership, then these policies will further enhance the opportunities of the more advantaged without addressing the problems of the truly disadvantaged. In other words, programs such as affirmative action "can be very effective in increasing the rate of progress for minorities who are doing reasonably well." Special admission programs that enlarge the number of minorities in law schools and medical schools, and special programs that increase minority representation in high-level government jobs, in the foreign service, and on university faculties not only favor minorities from advantaged backgrounds but require a college education to begin with. To repeat: programs of preferential treatment applied merely according to racial or ethnic group membership tend to benefit the relatively advantaged segments of the designated groups. The truly deprived members may not be helped by such programs.

Nonetheless, as William L. Taylor has argued, "the focus of much of the [affirmative action] effort has been not just on white collar jobs, but also on law enforcement, construction work, and craft and production jobs in large companies—all areas in which the extension of new opportunities has provided upward mobility for less advantaged minority workers." Taylor also notes that "studies show that of the increased enrollment of minority students in medical schools during the 1970s, significant numbers were from families of low income and job status, indicating that the rising enrollments of minorities in professional schools stemming from affirmative action policies reflects increased mobility, not simply changing occupational preferences among middleclass minority families." However, although affirmative action programs do in fact create opportunities for some less advantaged minority individuals, ghetto underclass individuals are severely underrepresented among those who have actually benefited from such programs. In other words, upon close examination what we really see is a "creaming" process in the sense that those with the greatest economic, educational, and social resources among the less advantaged individuals are the ones who are actually tapped for higher paying jobs and higher education through affirmative action.

It has been argued, however, that group preferential treatment based on race, although more directly beneficial to advantaged minority members, will "trickle down" to the minority poor. Thus, a government policy favoring minority business would ultimately lead to greater employment opportunities for the black poor. Affirmative action programs designed to increase the number of blacks in medical schools would thus ultimately result in improved medical care for low-income blacks. Indeed, these programs are often justified on the ground that they would improve the black poor's chances in life. "The question should be raised though as to how the black poor are to be benefited by the policy actions extracted from the system in their name," observes Glenn Loury. "The evidence of which I am aware suggests that, for many of the most hotly contested public policies advocated by black spokesmen, not much of the benefit 'trickles down' to the black poor. There is no study, of which I am aware, supporting the claim that set-asides for minority businesses have led to a significant increase in the level of employment among lower class blacks."

But what about the argument, often heard during the heated debate over the *Bakke* decision, that increasing the percentage of blacks in medical schools will result in improvements in medical care for lower-income blacks? Although there is virtually no definitive research on this question, I believe that we would not improve the health of the ghetto underclass, in either the long or the short run, even if we tripled the number of black physicians in our large central cities.

This is not to say that a sharp increase in the number of black physicians would have no impact in the black community. Blacks who can afford to pay for adequate medical care would certainly have more black physicians to choose from, and poor blacks would undoubtedly witness the opening of more clinics, staffed by black physicians, in their neighborhoods. But the ultimate determinant of black access to medical care is not the supply of black physicians, even if an overwhelming majority choose to practice in the black community, but the availability of programs such as Medicaid, Medicare, National Health Insurance, or other benefits designed, regardless of race, to give people who lack economic resources access to expensive medical care. There are plenty of doctors for those who can afford them.

However, there does exist a third liberal philosophy concerned with equality and social justice, namely, what Fishkin has called the principle of equality of life chances. According to this principle, if we can predict with a high degree of accuracy where individuals will end up in the competition for preferred positions in society "merely by knowing their race, sex, or family background, then the conditions under which their talents and motivations have developed must be grossly unequal." Supporters of this principle believe that a person "should not be able to enter a hospital ward of healthy newborn babies and, on the basis of class, race, sex, or other arbitrary native characteristics, predict the eventual positions in society of those children." In other words, it is unfair that some individuals "are given every conceivable advantage while others never really have a chance, in the first place, to develop their talents."

Proponents of equality of life chances recognize not only that those from higher social strata have greater life chances or more-than-equal opportunities, but that "they also have greater than equal influence on the political process and greater than equal consideration from the health care and legal systems." The major factor that distinguishes the principle of equality of life chances from the principles of equality of individual opportunity and equality of group opportunity is the recognition that the problems of truly disadvantaged individuals—class background, low income, a broken home, inadequate housing, poor education, or cultural or linguistic differences—may not be clearly related to the issue of previous discrimination. Nevertheless, "children growing up in homes affected by these disadvantages may be deprived of an equal life chance because their environments effectively inhibit the development of their talents or aspirations."

Accordingly, programs based on this principle would not be restrictively applied to members of certain racial or ethnic groups but would be targeted to truly disadvantaged individuals regardless of their race or ethnicity. Thus, whereas poor whites are ignored in programs of reverse discrimination based on the desire to overcome the effects of past discrimination, they would be targeted along with the truly disadvantaged minorities for preferential treatment under programs to equalize life chances by overcoming present class disadvantages.

Under the principle of equality of life chances, efforts to correct family background disadvantages through such programs as income redistribution, compensatory job training, compensatory schooling, special medical services and the like would not "require any reference to past discrimination as the basis for justification." All that would be required is that the individuals targeted for preferred treatment be objectively classified as disadvantaged in terms of the competitive resources associated with their economic-class background.

Ironically, the shift from preferential treatment for those with certain racial or ethnic characteristics to those who are truly disadvantaged in terms of their life chances would not only help the white poor, but would also address more effectively the problems of the minority poor. If the life chances of the ghetto underclass are largely untouched by programs of preferential treatment based on race, the gap between the haves and have-nots in the black community will widen, and the disproportionate concentration of blacks within the most impoverished segments of our population will remain. As Fishkin appropriately points out, programs based on the principle of equality of life chances would not be mistargeted to those who are already relatively affluent.

TARGETED PROGRAMS AND THE PROBLEMS
OF POLITICAL SUPPORT

Despite the emphasis placed on helping disadvantaged members of minority groups through programs based on the principle of equality of individual opportunity and those based on the principle of equality of group opportunity (as brought out in the previous section), only programs based on the principle of equality of life chances are capable of substantially helping the truly disadvantaged. Nonetheless, even these, however comprehensive and carefully constructed, may not represent the most efficacious or viable way to lift the truly disadvantaged from the depths of poverty today. In the next section of this chapter, I discuss the effectiveness of targeted programs in a stagnant economy. For now let me focus on the problem of generating and sustaining public support for such programs.

An important consideration in assessing public programs targeted at particular groups (whether these groups are defined in terms of race, ethnicity, or class) is the degree of political support those programs receive, especially when the national economy is in a period of little growth, no growth, or decline. Under such economic conditions, the more the public programs are perceived by members of the wider society as benefiting only certain groups, the less support those programs receive. I should like to deal with the implications of this argument by briefly contrasting the institutionalization of the programs that emanated from the New Deal legislation of the Roosevelt administration with the demise of the Great Society programs of the Johnson administration, bearing in mind that Johnson's Great Society program was the most ambitious effort in our nation's history to implement the principle of equality of life chances.

In 1932 Franklin D. Roosevelt received a popular mandate to attack the catastrophic economic problems created by the Great Depression. He then launched a series of programs—such as Social Security and unemployment compensation—designed to protect all citizens against sudden impoverishment. One of these programs was Aid to Families with Dependent Children (AFDC), the current symbol of income-tested public welfare programs. Aid to Families with Dependent Children, however, was conceived not as a permanent alternative to working but as a temporary means of support for families that were, at the time they applied for aid, clearly unemployable. Indeed, the "safety net" of Roosevelt's New Deal emphatically included the creation of public works projects designed to forestall the formation of a permanent welfare class. It was not necessary to satisfy a means test to work in these projects; the only requirement was that the applicant be unemployed, want a job, and be able to work. Furthermore, no one was denied eligibility for these jobs as a result of being either overskilled or underskilled; the programs attempted to match jobs with individual abilities.

Thus, jobs for able individuals, Social Security, and unemployment compensation for the unemployed were to provide a modicum of security for all. Economic stability was not tied to the dole. By contrast, nearly all of the Great Society programs *were* tied to the dole. Job training, legal aid, and Medicaid levied income tests. In effect, one had to be on welfare to be eligible. Unlike the New Deal programs, the Great Society programs were modeled on the English poor laws. Although these programs improved the life chances of many of their recipients—because job-training programs enabled many long-term welfare recipients to find their first jobs, Medicaid enabled many to receive decent medical care for the first time, and legal aid gave many access to capable lawyers—the programs were increasingly perceived in narrow terms as intended for poor blacks. In the cities, especially, the Great Society programs established what amounted to separate legal and medical systems—one public and predominantly black, the other private and predominantly white. The real problem, however, was that the taxpayers were required to pay for legal and medical services that were provided to welfare recipients but not to the taxpayers—services many taxpayers could not afford to buy for themselves. In other words, this system amounted to taxation to pay for programs that were perceived to benefit mostly minorities, programs that excluded taxpayers perceived to be mostly white. Thus, these programs were cut back or phased out during the recent periods of recession and economic stagnation because they could not sustain sufficient political support.

From the New Deal to the 1970s, the Democrats were able to combine Keynesian economics and prosperity for the middle class with social welfare programs and pressures for integrating the poor and minorities into the mainstream of American economic life. The MIT economist Lester Thurow reminds us that "in periods of great economic progress when [the incomes of the middle classes] are rising rapidly, they are willing to share some of their income and jobs with those less fortunate than themselves, but they are not willing to reduce their real standard of living to help either minorities or the poor."

In the face of hard economic times, President Ronald Reagan was able to persuade the middle classes that the drop in their living standards was attributable to the poor (and implicitly, minorities), and that he could restore those standards with sweeping tax and budget cuts. In short, the New Deal coalition collapsed when Reagan was elected. In 1980 the only groups that did not leave the Democratic party in significant numbers were blacks, Hispanics, and the poor—groups that constitute only a quarter of the American population, hardly enough to win a national election, and certainly not enough to sustain programs, incorrectly perceived as benefiting only the minority poor, based on the principle of equality of life chances. What is interesting, however, is that the Reagan administration has shown far less willingness to cut significantly the much more expensive universal programs such as Social Security and Medicare, programs that are not income tested and therefore are available to people across class lines. In this connection, one of the reasons why western European social welfare programs enjoy wide political support (especially in countries such as the Federal Republic of Germany, France, Austria, Sweden, the Netherlands, Belgium, and Norway) is that they tend to be universal—applied across class and racial/ethnic lines—and therefore are not seen as being targeted for narrow class or racially identifiable segments of the population.

I am convinced that, in the last few years of the twentieth century, the problems of the truly disadvantaged in the United States will have to be attacked primarily through universal programs that enjoy the support and commitment of a broad constituency. Under this approach, targeted programs (whether based on the principle of equality of group opportunity or that of equality of life chances) would not necessarily be eliminated, but would rather be deemphasized—considered only as offshoots of, and indeed secondary to, the universal programs. *The hidden agenda is to improve the life chances of groups such as the ghetto underclass by emphasizing programs in which the more advantaged groups of all races can positively relate.*

In the final section of this chapter, I should like to amplify and support this position by focusing on what I consider to be one of the most important universal programs of equality—an economic policy to address the problems of American economic organization.

THE CASE FOR A UNIVERSAL PROGRAM

I believe that many of the problems plaguing the truly disadvantaged minorities in American society can be alleviated by a program of economic reform characterized by rational government involvement in the economy. I have in mind a general economic policy that would involve long-term planning to promote both economic growth and sustained full employment, not only in higher-income areas but in areas where the poor are concentrated as well. Such a policy would be designated to promote wage and price stability, favorable employment conditions, and the development and integration of manpower training programs with educational programs. As I see it, the questions usually ignored when ad hoc strategies to promote employment are discussed and proposed should be systematically addressed. These questions include the relative impact of proposed strategies on labor markets in different areas of the country; the type, variety, and volume of jobs to be generated; the extent to which residents in low-income neighborhoods will have access to these jobs; the quality of these jobs in terms of stability and pay; the extent to which proposed strategies enhance the employment opportunities of both new entrants into the labor market and the currently unemployed; and whether the benefits from economic development and employment provide reasonable returns on public investment.

Although the basic features of such a program are designed to benefit all segments of society, I believe the groups that have been plagued by severe problems of economic dislocation, such as the ghetto underclass, would be helped the most. I say this because the low-income minority community is disadvantaged not simply by cyclical economic stagnation but by profound structural economic changes. The widely heralded shift from goods-producing to service-producing industries is polarizing the labor market into high-wage and low-wage sectors. Technological innovations in industry are affecting the number and types of jobs available. Manufacturing industries are relocating from the central city to the suburbs, to other parts of the country, and even to foreign countries. While these changes adversely affect segments of the poor and working classes in general, they have been especially devastating for low-income blacks and other minorities because these groups are concentrated in the central areas that have been hardest hit by economic dislocation.

Accordingly, those who argue that the deteriorating economic plight of the truly disadvantaged minorities can be satisfactorily addressed simply by confronting the problems of current racial bias fail to recognize how the fate of these minorities is inextricably connected with the structure and function of the modern American economy. The net effect is the recommendation of programs that do not confront the fundamental causes of poverty, underemployment, and unemployment. In other words, policies that do not take into account the changing nature of the national economy—including its rate of growth and the nature of its variable demand for labor; the factors that affect industrial employment, such as profit rates, technology, and unionization; and patterns of institutional and individual migration that result from industrial transformation and shifts—will not effectively handle the economic dislocation of low-income minorities.

But it is not only disadvantaged minorities who would benefit from a program of economic reform designed to promote full employment and balanced economic growth. Even the trained, talented, and educated minorities could not really benefit from the removal of racial barriers if the economy lacked sufficient positions to absorb either them or any new entrants into higher-paying or valued positions. In other words, deracialization, or the removal of racial barriers, has far greater meaning when positions are available or become available to enhance social mobility. Indeed, the significant movement of blacks into higher-paying manufacturing positions from 1940 to the 1960s had much more to do with fairly even and steady economic growth in the manufacturing sector than with equal employment legislation. It is noteworthy, however, that the uneven economic growth since the latter half of the 1960s resulted in a much more rapid rate of social mobility for trained and educated blacks than for the untrained and uneducated. While deindustrialization was subjecting the latter to the gradual reduction of the more desirable blue-collar positions into which workers can enter without special skills or higher education, the former, that is, trained and educated blacks, were experiencing increasing job opportunities in the expanding corporate and government sectors.

Thus, the necessary factor for minority mobility is the availability of positions. For example, affirmative action programs have had little impact in a slack labor market where the labor supply is greater than the labor demand. This has been the case with higher-paying blue-collar positions in which employment opportunities for the lesser-trained and less-experienced blacks remain restricted due to increases in plant closings, labor-saving technology, and the efforts of unions to protect remaining jobs. On the other hand, the impact of antibias programs to enhance minority jobs tends to be greater in a tight labor market. This argument should come as no surprise.

In a tight labor market, job vacancies are numerous, unemployment is of short duration, and wages are higher. Moreover, the labor force becomes larger because increased job opportunities not only reduce unemployment but also draw into the labor force those workers who, in periods when the labor market is slack, respond to fading job prospects by dropping out of the labor force altogether. Thus, the status of minority workers improves in a tight labor market because unemployment is reduced and better jobs are available.

Affirmative action and other antibias programs are accordingly more successful in tight labor markets than in slack ones. Not only are there sufficient positions for many qualified workers, but also employers faced with a labor shortage are not as resistant to affirmative action. Furthermore, in a favorable economic climate, those who support affirmative action are encouraged to push such programs because they perceive greater chances for success. Finally, nonminority employees are less likely to oppose affirmative action when there are sufficient jobs available because they are less likely to see minorities as a threat to their own employment.

In a slack labor market, on the other hand, employers tend to be more selective in recruiting and in promoting; they can afford to demand greater experience, skills, and education than a job actually requires. They are thus more resistant to affirmative action pressures. And the longer the labor market is slack, the less pressure they receive from supporters of affirmative action, who become increasingly discouraged in the face of shrinking resources. The situation is exacerbated by increased hostility to affirmative action by dominant-group workers who fear the loss of their own jobs to minority competition. In short, the success of affirmative action and other antidiscrimination programs is in no small measure related to the state of the economy.

Thus, unlike programs based on equality of individual opportunity and equality of group opportunity, a universal program of economic reform would benefit both advantaged and disadvantaged minority members as well as nonminority groups, including women.

However, to embrace the idea of a universal program of reform does not mean a shift in focus away from the current suffering of racial minorities. Many of their problems, especially those of the truly disadvantaged among them, call for immediate attention and therefore cannot wait for the launching of long-term programs. Short-term programs consistent with the principle of equality of life chances (such as manpower job training and education for the disadvantaged, and public assistance) are needed now. But such programs are hardly a solution to the current woes of groups such as the ghetto underclass. Although they provide some short-term relief, these programs do not address problems of economic organization (e.g., plant closings and layoffs due to deindustrialization), that impact heavily on disadvantaged groups in society. Moreover, as I have tried to show in the previous section, without a tight labor market or a full-employment situation the very survival of targeted programs for low-income groups is threatened. To repeat: income-tested programs are much less likely to be introduced or to receive continuing support in a stagnant economy.

Although sustained full employment and balanced economic growth would ultimately render targeted programs for the able-bodied superfluous, they would create the economic climate to help preserve such programs when they are needed in the short run.

Moreover, without full employment it is much more difficult to shift from income-tested and stigmatized public assistance programs to the kinds of universal programs of social welfare (e.g., family allowances) found in Western European democracies. Universal welfare programs, usually tied to employment and labor market policies, depend on conditions approximating full employment so that workers can combine their income from transfers with income from employment, maximize tax revenues, and thereby reduce the strain on the welfare budget inflated by the broad coverage of transfer payments.

In short, to speak of the need for long-term economic reform in the United States is not to disregard the need for short-term targeted programs for the disadvantaged. Rather, it is to recognize that the more effective the universal program of reform, the less targeted programs are required.

In the final analysis, the question of reform is a political one. Accordingly, if the issues are couched in terms of promoting economic security for all Americans, if the essential political message underscores the need for economic and social reform that benefits all groups in society, not just poor minorities, a basis for generating a broad-based political coalition to achieve such reform would be created. Minority leaders could play an important role in this coalition once they fully recognize the need to shift or expand their definition of racial problems in America and to broaden the scope of suggested policy programs to address them. This would certainly not mean the abandonment of race-specific policies that embody either the principle of equality of individual rights or that of group rights. It would simply mean that such programs are no longer central to advancing the cause of minorities, especially the cause of the truly disadvantaged such as the ghetto underclass.

Black Progress and
the Free Market*

BERNARD BOXILL

THE LEGACY OF BOOKER T. WASHINGTON

BOOKER T. WASHINGTON ONCE told the story of an old colored doctor who employed somewhat peculiar methods of treatment. One of the doctor's patients was a rich old lady who thought she had cancer, and who for twenty years had enjoyed the luxury of being treated by the doctor. As the doctor became—mainly thanks to the cancer—pretty rich himself, he decided to send one of his boys to medical school. After graduating the young doctor returned home, and his father took a vacation. While he was away, the old lady called in the young doctor. He treated her, and within a few weeks the "cancer" was cured. When the old doctor returned and found his patient well, he was outraged. He reminded his son that he had put him through high school, college, and medical school on that cancer. "Let me tell you, son," the old man concluded, "you have started all wrong. How do you expect to make a living practicing medicine in that way?"

Now Booker T. was not in the habit of telling amusing stories just for the fun of it. He always told them to make a point. The point he was making in this case was, as he went on to put it, "there is a certain class of race-problem solvers who don't want the patient to get well, because as long as the disease holds out they have not only an easy means of making a living, but also an easy medium through which to make themselves prominent before the public." The worst offenders, Washington thought, were certain colored people. These people, he charged, make "a business of keeping the troubles, the wrongs and the hardships

*Reprinted from *Blacks and Social Justice* by Bernard R. Boxill. Copyright ©1984 by Rowman and Allanheld. Reprinted with the permission of the publisher.

of the Negro race before the public . . . partly because they want sympathy, and
partly because it pays. [They] do not want the Negro to lose his grievances
because they do not want to lose their jobs."

This barbed observation, the result of Washington's philosophy of stoicism
and self-help, suitably coarsened for late twentieth-century wrangles, continues
to be the weapon of choice in the armory of his contemporary representatives.
Walter E. Williams, one-time student of Thomas Sowell's and now professor of
economics at George Mason University, recently swung this roundhouse:

> a whole lot of people have their livelihoods staked on the existence of a
> so-called "disadvantaged" class of people. I'm not only talking about the
> "poverty pimps" who administer and manage these programs. I'm also talking
> about professors who get federal grants to study poverty, and then meet in
> Miami in the winter to discuss the problems of the poor.

This outburst was ignited by a theory about racial subordination and racial
progress, shared by Sowell and Williams, that is virtually identical to Washington's. The centerpiece of that theory is the proposition that the free market
system is the only sure road to black elevation, and correspondingly, that governmental interference in the free market is the chief cause of black subordination.
Williams puts this most clearly: The "basic problem of blacks in America," he
writes, is "severe government-imposed restraints on voluntary exchange. Or put
another way: the diminution of free markets in the United States."

Surrounding this fundamental proposition are various other propositions of a
consequential, ancillary, and supportive nature. Perhaps the most provocative
of these is that racial discrimination does not explain, and is not even an
important part of the explanation, of black subordination; according to this
theory, after governmental interference in the economy, the most important
explanation of black subordination is that black people lack those valuable
personal qualities the economy demands. This has the corollary that, if blacks
are subordinated, it is because of their own inadequacies. While this inference
does not blame the victim, as some have misleadingly charged, it does succeed
in absolving everyone from blame. Washington expressed his allegiance to this
view as well as his faith in the free market eloquently, if obliquely, in his famous
"Atlanta Exposition Address": "No race that has anything to contribute to the
markets of the world," he declared, "is long in any degree ostracized." And even
Thomas Sowell, who is not noted for his delicacy, hides the unpleasant truth in
a bland generality: "What determines how rapidly a group moves ahead," he
writes, "is not discrimination but the fit between the elements of its culture and
the requirements of the economy."

If this proposition is true, it follows at once that an essential condition of
black progress is that blacks acquire what the market demands. When he wanted
to, Washington could strip away the frills as well as anybody: "Harmony will

come," he observed, "in proportion as the black man gets something the white man wants." Sowell, the professional economist, makes the same point less trenchantly: "To get ahead," he writes, "you have to have some ability to work, some ability at entrepreneurship or something else that the society values."

Now, among the things the "white man wants," or, if you will, "the society values," will be certain skills, and accordingly, Washington and Sowell both stress the need for blacks to acquire such skills. But, they explicitly deny that blacks must have a *high level* of skills in order to progress. According to them, even a low level of saleable skills—or incompetence—cannot explain black unemployment. Competence and incompetence are relative matters. Hardly anyone is so incompetent that there is no work he can do, and no one ready to pay him to do it. Consequently, even assuming black incompetence, black advocates of the free market must still explain the disproportionately high rate of black unemployment. Part of their explanation is that it is the fault of government interference. For example, Williams accuses the government, through its minimum-wage laws (and these are, perhaps, the chief bugbear of black free market supporters), of interfering with the freedom of blacks to work for wages employers are prepared to pay for the use of their skills. They admit, of course, that these wages will be low. But this dovetails neatly with their partiality for the rags-to-riches approach to life. Low-paying jobs, they argue, are the bottom rung of the ladder on which countless European and Asian immigrants have climbed out of poverty.

Washington first outlined the essentials of this theory of progress. It was one of his favorite themes that the acquisition of basic, humble skills would be sufficient to start blacks on the road to elevation. Black radicals, usually from a relatively safe berth in the North, accused him of "accommodating" his theory to white prejudice, but the fact that Sowell, who accommodates no one, makes the same claim shows that they were mistaken. While Washington evidently arrived at this view intuitively, Sowell comes to it via the study of history. According to Sowell, history reveals that a high level of education is not a necessary condition of progress. Even the immigrant Jews, he argues, who did arrive in the country with a long tradition of learning, did not rise from poverty because of that learning. And, he continues, since education, past a basic minimum, is unnecessary to social elevation, much compulsory education is unjustified. "Everyone recognizes," he writes, "the need for literacy and other educational basics. But compulsory attendance laws have been applied to keep youths in school long past the time necessary to learn these things." Their effect, he asserts, is simply to keep black youths out of the labor force, and blacks as a whole from starting the long march to affluence.

But although higher education and greater skills may not be necessary to advancement, it does not follow that they cannot accelerate it. Why then, the skeptic may ask, cannot black youths use compulsory secondary education and the opportunities for higher education, to acquire skills which will enable them to steal a march on history? Sowell's negative response to this idea reveals the most dismaying aspect of his theory. Most black youths, he argues, do not and cannot use their years in school to acquire exceptional skills and learning. They simply lack the discipline for it. Learning "many of the most valuable intellectual skills," he writes, is "dry, tedious, frustrating" and a cause of "headaches." "How many black students are prepared to accept headaches after twelve years of coasting through inferior public schools?" he asks, and he thinks that the question "answers itself." Moreover, he believes, the universities know this very well. They recruit black students only to "keep government money coming in" and with no real hope of educating them. At many universities which have drives to recruit more minority students, those students "are flunking out in droves," or else special easy courses are cooked up for them. The result: "Never has it been easier to graduate from college as a complete ignoramus." Moreover, he opines, basically the same process occurs during secondary education.

Sowell believes that this problem of attitude and discipline has hampered black education since emancipation. Though the newly freed slaves eagerly sought education, teaching them was a "trial." They were convinced that "education was a good thing" but they had no conception of the "disciplined work" it required. If Sowell's theory of what hinders black progress is sound, there is no question of their stealing a march on history. Blacks as a group must start at the bottom. As Washington had warned prophetically: "it is at the bottom of life we must begin and not at the top." Opportunities for education can speed a group's progress, but education cannot allow them to skip a stage of that progression. What a generation can learn in school is limited by the attitude to education it has absorbed from its parents. There is hope, for the "first generation to break out of the vicious cycle of undereducation tends to raise the next generation to still higher levels," but the process, which is thus cumulative, is also gradual. Sowell aptly describes it as an "intergenerational relay race," and, like a die-hard Marxist denying that the "stages of society" can be skipped, he is consistently emphatic about his law of history.

But as Sowell realizes, minimum-wage laws, compulsory school attendance, and other policies through which do-gooders in government try, and predictably fail, to circumvent history, cannot explain black backwardness. Since these laws did not always exist, why, unlike other groups, did not blacks climb the free market ladder when it was there? Part of Sowell's answer is that many blacks *did* climb the ladder when it was there. Their descendants are most of the middle-class blacks of today. The majority of blacks did not climb the ladder because they lived in the rural South, and only relatively recently migrated to the great urban centers in the North. The chance to get on the ladder used to be found there, but after the great wave of European immigrants the government had taken away the ladder. The rest of Sowell's answer is, however, at a more fundamental level and involves blacks' attitudes to menial jobs.

And, as always, Washington said it first. Because of two hundred years of slavery, he lamented, for generations the "Negro's idea of freedom" was "freedom from restraint and work." We must learn, he resolved, "to dignify and glorify common labor." Sowell adds little to Washington's diagnosis: "blacks who suffered from slavery," he writes, "also suffered from its aftermath in that many became hypersensitized against menial jobs. That's tragic because most of the groups in America that started out destitute and rose to affluence began in menial jobs."

BLACK LIBERTARIANISM

There are, of course, differences between Washington and his disciples. The one which emerges most clearly in Sowell's work is his belief that it is wrong for government to interfere in the liberties of its citizens, even when this may seem the way to secure some valuable end. This fundamental view is obscured because Sowell usually advances empirically based arguments to the effect that the end in question will best be secured by policies which do not interfere with citizens' liberties. But when these empirical arguments are challenged, he invariably falls back on the moral argument that it is morally wrong to interfere with citizens' liberties. For example, Sowell is a strong advocate of the voucher system, an idea originally popularized by economist Milton Friedman, one of Sowell's mentors. The system is one whereby, for each school-age child, parents receive a voucher worth the average cost to the taxpayer of educating a child, and use these vouchers to pay for the education of their children at any school that is willing to accept them, public or private, and at any location. Advocates of this scheme defend it both on the moral ground that it breaks the monopoly of the public school system, thus widening the range of choices open to parents and increasing their liberty, and on the empirical ground that it makes schooling more effective. Sowell, at least, seems to feel that the moral justification alone is sufficient. Thus, when Hugh Price of the *New York Times* opposed the voucher system, arguing that management improvements could make public schools more effective, Sowell conceded the point, but fell back on the idea of liberty as the basis of his defense of the system. "I am not sure," he responded to Price, "whether that's an argument against vouchers versus compelling people to go to a particular monopoly."

What is so controversial about this? It is part of conventional wisdom, seemingly enshrined, moreover, in the U.S. Constitution, that a government ought not to transgress on individual liberties for utilitarian advantages. But before anyone thinks of invoking this truism in order to render Sowell's view comfortably commonplace, he should be clear of the nature and extent of the individual liberties Sowell believes in.

These liberties are the liberties of a night-watchman state. Walter Williams puts this clearly: "I would confine government to performing only its legitimate function," he notes, "namely defending us against foreign and domestic adversaries who would like to take our lives and our private property." In this view, the right to private property, in particular the right to keep what one has, as Locke put it, "mixed one's labor with," becomes the main concern of justice. No one could have put this better than Williams, when, for all the world like Thrasymachus showing Socrates the plain truth about justice, he stunned a panel on social justice held in New York by the Manhattan Institute for Policy Research with this blunt definition of justice: "I keep what I produce, and you keep what you produce."

Given this account of the nature of individual rights, many of the functions people have become used to government performing, and ostensibly performing to secure their rights—to education and welfare, for example—are really instances of transgression, for utilitarian purposes, against individual liberties. Again I quote from Williams, who has, more than Sowell, inherited Washington's gift for the earthy example:

> Here is a poor lady that needs teeth. I could walk up to you with a gun and say, "Give me your money so I can give this old lady some teeth." That is robbery and it's unjust. It doesn't change anything when, poof! the government comes to me and says, "Mr. Williams that money you were going to spend to plant trees you will now give to me and it will go to that toothless old lady"—it's pretty callous to forcibly deprive me of the fruits of my labor for the benefit of some other individual who didn't sweat my sweat. I don't consider that social justice.

What is more, argue Sowell and Williams—and here both their moral and their economic arguments against governmental intervention in the economy happily coincide—even when government transgresses against individual rights from benevolent motives, it is usually not successful in delivering the utilitarian advantages it has transgressed against rights to secure. And, they remind us—who should not need reminding—as often as not government transgresses against rights, or permits transgression, from malevolent motives. "Black people were enslaved in the United States," Williams notes, "because government did not do its proper job of protecting their individual rights." On these grounds Sowell and Williams echo what is perhaps the most characteristic aspect of Washington's social program—his opposition to political activism and to enlisting government help for black progress. "I would urge people not to look at government as the benefactor of blacks," Williams warns. But he cannot resist a dig at the "poverty pimps." Government, he allows, is "the benefactor of elite blacks who get jobs controlling other blacks." But, these opportunists apart: "for blacks in particular, and Americans in general, what is needed is less government and more freedom."

Now, since governmental enforcement of color-conscious policies interferes with the free market, when Sowell and Williams attack governmental interference on the grounds that it transgresses rights and is counterproductive, they are, by inference, attacking the enforcement of color-conscious policies. And, indeed, they are among the most potent forces against special treatment for blacks. Their views have received enormous attention in newspapers and magazines and they have become pundits of race relations and racial policies. Sowell, in particular, has become the most quoted man in America on racial issues, with white conservatives using his candid words about black laziness and incompetence to tell the kind of harsh truth delicacy forbids them from telling themselves.

Of course, all this is part of an intellectual and popular revival of conservative and libertarian philosophies. The election of Ronald Reagan made unmistakable the fact that the revival was on a popular level, but more significant was the publication in 1975 of Robert Nozick's *Anarchy, State, and Utopia*, which made the intellectual respectability of the revival equally unmistakable. In this book, Nozick, a professor of philosophy at Harvard, presents a series of brilliant and sophisticated arguments in defense of the once disdained libertarian philosophy, of a minimal state—one in which government is limited to protecting its citizens from fraud, force, and violence, and to securing contracts—and by implication of Williams's "I keep what I produce and you keep what you produce" definition of social justice. As Randall Rothenberg observed in *Esquire*, Nozick is "the intellectual bedrock behind latter-day libertarianism, a do-your-own-thing, laissez-faire capitalist darling of the Right."

However, there is a fundamental difference between Nozick's projects, on the one hand, and those of Sowell and Williams on the other. Nozick can respond to certain objections to his libertarianism with sangfroid. When, for example, opponents ask what his minimal state would do about poor people, Nozick answers comfortably, "charity." But Sowell and Williams cannot give this answer. They are proud men and they scorn the idea of charity for blacks. Indeed, their most vehement denunciations of color-conscious policies are based on the conviction that they are charity. Accordingly, the task they have set themselves is different, and in many ways more difficult, than the task Nozick set himself. Nozick is concerned with demonstrating that "the minimal state is the most extensive state that can be justified. Any state more extensive violates people's rights." He does not have to demonstrate that the minimal state provides the best opportunity for a subordinated minority like blacks to progress. Sowell and Williams, however, have to demonstrate just that. I believe that this task is too much for even their considerable powers. They are not able to prove their empirical claims, they do not adhere to their moral claims, and their moral claims—both those they hold ostensibly and those they retreat to—are unacceptable. My object, in this chapter, is to confute black conservativism and the whole Booker T. Washington philosophy of racial uplift, once and for all.

DISCRIMINATION AND BLACK SUBORDINATION

As I noted earlier, perhaps the most provocative of the claims Sowell and Williams make in support of their theory that the free market system is the only sure path to black advancement, is that racial discrimination is not a decisive cause of black subordination. But although this is their official view, the one trumpeted to the press, it is not their real view. Their real view, at least the view for which they provide argument, is that in a free market, racial discrimination is not a decisive cause of black subordination. And this shows how careless—and misleading—their official view is. For since, as they frequently insist and lament, markets have rarely been free, their real view provides absolutely no support for their official view. On the contrary, it suggests that their official view is false.

Sowell and Williams imply that it is the absence of free markets that permits racial discrimination to have its effects, and, consequently, that it is the absence of a free market that is the real cause of black subordination in this country. But, even if it is true that a free market tends to eliminate the effects of discrimination, as they say, it does not follow that the absence of a free market is the cause of black subordination, since rigidly enforced equal opportunity laws might, equally, tend to eliminate the effects of discrimination. Ideology, not logic, seems to determine Sowell's and Williams's choice of the main cause of black subordination.

Consider the pièce de résistance of their argument: the free market tends to eliminate the effects of discrimination. Sowell distinguishes two main kinds of discrimination. In the first—pure discrimination—"people are treated differently because of group membership as such." This is the kind of discrimination in which blacks are not hired because, although they are the most qualified, employers view them with "antipathy or hostility." Williams, in a more perspicuous discussion of the same phenomenon, calls it "racial preference." In the second kind of discrimination Sowell distinguishes—perceptual discrimination—people are treated differently because "the group is perceived as less capable or less responsible by employers, landlords or other potential transactors." This is the kind of discrimination which results in blacks not being hired because, although they may be the most qualified, and although employers may not view them with antipathy or hostility, they are considered generally less capable or less responsible than whites. Williams calls this kind of discrimination racial prejudice, using the word "prejudice" to stress that this kind of discrimination involves essentially an "attempt to minimize information costs," that is, to minimize the cost of actually obtaining information about individuals.

Sowell and Williams have no difficulty in demonstrating that the free market tends to eliminate pure discrimination and some kinds of perceptual discrimination. If an employer engages in these kinds of discrimination, he hires inferior workers for the same wage he would pay superior workers. If all employers do this, none gains an edge on the others. But if some don't, even if for no better reason than that their greed outweighs their prejudice, they, by hiring the superior workers other employers reject, gain a considerable edge over the others. These will either have to change their policies or drop out of business. Since few employers want to discriminate more than they want to stay in business, most come to their senses. In this way the competitive free market functions to remove the effects of discrimination.

This argument, as Sowell observes, "assumes that (1) employers are attracted by prospects of unusually high profits and that (2) there is no effective collusion against a particular group." Objections can hardly be raised to either assumption. The first is obviously true, and the second is part of the definition of a free market. Moreover, Sowell argues, attempted collusions are not likely to be effective for long. It is costly to police a hiring system so it is certain to exclude the unwanted group, though Sowell allows that these costs would be relatively low for blacks because their color makes them easy to identify; and there are temptations to break such agreements, for profits can be made by hiring the superior workers of the excluded group.

Sowell and Williams believe, however, that government interference in the free market, even with the best of intentions, is likely to be far more effective than collusion in suppressing the beneficient effect of the market in eliminating discrimination, and is for that reason much more to be feared. Their favorite example is a government-imposed minimum wage. "A higher wage rate," Sowell writes, "simultaneously attracts more job applicants and reduces the number of persons whom it is profitable to hire. . . . The net result is that the number of jobs decreases as the number of applicants increases. One consequence of this is that ethnic discrimination becomes less costly—perhaps free—to the employer, even in a profit-seeking business."

These arguments are supposed to have the sort of effect on common sense that so many arguments in physical science have. Common sense gives its verdict on a particular phenomenon, but science magisterially controverts that verdict, and, bowing before its logic, ordinary mortals must abandon their belief in common sense. However, unfortunately for Sowell and Williams, we do not have to give up the common-sensical view that discrimination is an important cause of black subordination, because their logic is not the logic of science. There are instances and kinds of discrimination which are not likely to be cured by the panacea of the free market.

The first and most obvious is discrimination in the nonprofit sector, which includes universities and government-regulated industries, and most important, government itself, both local and national. Sowell is, of course, aware of this case. For government, he observes, "racial discrimination is free." Indeed this fact is his coup de grace against advocates of government regulation of industry and a more than minimal state. But it does not support his conclusion. There are reasons for expanding government regulation of industry and government itself, in particular reasons that stem from moral principles to which he ostensibly holds allegiance, for example, taking citizens' liberties seriously. I hope to demonstrate that, as a result, even if Sowell is right that discrimination is free in government, he still cannot consistently urge the abolishment of government regulation of industry and the idea of a minimal state. On the contrary, I will argue that the principles he ostensibly holds imply that there should be an increase in government regulation of industry, and a more than minimal state, and that we should depend on methods other than those of the free market, perhaps even the hated color-conscious policies, to eliminate discrimination.

Another kind of discrimination that is resistant to the influence of the free market is discrimination—either pure or perceptual—against highly trained blacks. Sowell also acknowledges this. He writes,

> In situations where long and costly preparations are necessary to be able to enter an excluded area [or] years of training to become a skilled craftsman or a classical musician—the very fact that the exclusion exists tends to prevent any backlog of qualified people from building up, and therefore reduces the cost of those who maintain the exclusion.

What is more, he admits that this consideration, which gains in importance in "blue-collar skills which are highly specific," may also explain why "Negroes have had far less success in breaking into skilled blue-collar fields." How anyone can make these admissions, and simultaneously proclaim that "culture, not discrimination decides who gets ahead," boggles the mind. One's equanimity returns only after one reminds oneself of the power of an ideology to confuse thought.

Sowell and Williams focus their gaze, unaccountably, on the tendency of the employer to discriminate. But what of the tendency of the public to discriminate? The idea that employers may be racially prejudiced but that the public is color-blind is perfectly ludicrous. As anyone knows, who has even the slightest acquaintance with the significance of race in America, the public is as prone to pure or perceptual discrimination as the employers. Because of this the employer may have to engage in a type of discrimination which has not, so far, been defined. An employer may decide that he had better not hire blacks, even if he neither dislikes them nor believes them to be incompetent, because he perceives that the public would rather not be served by blacks, either because it dislikes them (pure discrimination) or thinks them incompetent (perceptual discrimination). What is worse, precisely the same argument that Sowell and Williams use to show that the free market compels employers not to discriminate can be used to show instead that the free market compels employers to discriminate. For, just as there are situations in which the free market makes it costly to discriminate, in the situation cited the free market makes it costly not to discriminate.

It could be objected that discrimination is not as widespread among the public as this argument assumes. But, whether or not this is true, it is not an option available to Sowell and Williams, because they insist that discrimination *is* widespread. In fact, confusingly, they see its prevalence as the cornerstone of their case against the efficacy of discrimination. "Oxygen is so pervasive in the world," Williams observes, "that it alone cannot explain very much. Similarly with discrimination. Discrimination is so pervasive that it alone cannot explain much."

Given the pervasiveness of discrimination—a point on which, as I noted, Sowell and Williams are consistently emphatic—the situation outlined above is more crucial to the issue than the cases of employer discrimination that Sowell focuses on. He ignores it in *Markets and Minorities*, but does note it in his earlier book, *Race and Economics*. "If a group is paid less, or employed or promoted less often, because it is disliked by employers, co-workers and customers," he writes there, "then it may continue to suffer low wages and higher unemployment rates even if its current capabilities are equal to those of others." And how does the champion of the free market deal with this most pertinent point? I will let him rebut his own views: "The functioning of the market," Sowell admits, "will not tend to eliminate such differentials."

Less ideologically laced arguments for the harmlessness of discrimination are no more persuasive. Consider for example the views of William Julius Wilson in his book *The Declining Significance of Race* (1978), which, for a brief time, stole the limelight from Sowell. According to Wilson, because of recent complex changes in government, the economy, and society, racial discrimination is not now an obstacle to black progress. His view must not be identified or confused with that of Sowell and Williams. Wilson does not share Sowell's and Williams's faith in the free market. In particular, he does not believe that the market eliminates discrimination, nor, accordingly, that government intervention in the market is always counterproductive. Indeed, he believes that sometimes government intervention in the market decisively enhances a group's progress. Thus, while Wilson shares Sowell's view that it is "class-related disabilities," that is, lack of skills and poor attitudes to work, not race, which hold back blacks, and that special treatment for blacks is mistaken and wrong, he does not share Sowell's view that the best policy is for the government to step back and let the market work its magic. On the contrary, he calls for massive government intervention in the market. Sowell is the darling of the color-blind right, and Wilson is the darling of the color-blind left.

What then are the arguments Wilson uses to support his view? He admits that racial discrimination persists unabated in the sociopolitical system—that is, in the competition for "public schools, municipal political systems and residential areas"—but he thinks that it is harmless because it has virtually disappeared in the economic order, that is, in the competition for jobs, and discrimination in the sociopolitical order "has far less effect on individual or group access to those opportunities and resources that are centrally important to life survival than antagonism in the economic order."

This is a terrible argument. From the assumption that discrimination in the sociopolitical order is less important than discrimination in the economic order, it cannot be inferred that discrimination in the sociopolitical order is not important. Further, the implication that school and residential segregation, though persistent, is harmless is contradicted by Wilson's own view. Even if he is right in his belief that job discrimination harms more than school or residential discrimination, if black children are restricted to poor schools and ghettos, where they are poorly educated and exposed to bad influences, they will not acquire the skills or attitudes which would enable them to get and hold jobs. Hence, if, as Wilson seems to believe, it is not having decent jobs which fundamentally destroys the black members of the underclass, then school and residential discrimination is—indirectly—just as harmful as job discrimination.

JUSTICE AND DISCRIMINATION

We have seen that there are numerous gaps, often admitted, as well as flaws and contradictions, in the arguments Sowell, Williams, and Wilson make in support of the claim that discrimination is not an important cause of black subordination. And a closer study of their account of discrimination reveals subtler confusions in their discussion of discrimination and the inconsistency of their moral position.

We recall that, in "perceptual discrimination," or "prejudice" to use Williams's preferred term, persons perceive the group discriminated against as "less capable or less responsible." This perception could be mistaken. It might be that the group discriminated against is as capable and responsible as other groups. But we cannot assume that it is. As Sowell notes, "There is too much evidence of group differences . . . to arbitrarily assume that they are homogenous in all the relevant variables when they transact in labor, housing or other markets. It is an empirical question not an axiom."

And we know, of course, how Sowell answers the empirical question about black group differences. Blacks, he maintains, are, as a group, not as capable and responsible as other groups. They earn low wages because "their share of the human capital of the country" is "desperately small," not only in saleable skills and formal education, but, more importantly, in "basic traits" such as "punctuality, efficiency and long term planning" which are valued by the economy. Blacks lack these traits in the first place because of the effects of slavery, and second because of being "limited to menial jobs for generations." In many if not all cases of perceptual discrimination against blacks, therefore, the discrimination is based, as Williams puts it, on "the recognition of real differences."

Much perceptual discrimination is immune to free market pressures. Indeed, according to the account of Sowell and Williams, it is the market which often engenders this kind of discrimination. This is because of the cost, to a potential employer, of acquiring knowledge of any individual's productivity level. Since, by assumption, blacks are on the average less productive than whites, it may pay employers not to consider blacks for employment. As Williams observes, "physical attributes are easily observed and hence constitute a cheap form of information." And, on the other hand, employers who take the trouble to acquire knowledge of individual productivity incur costs the others avoid, and put themselves at a competitive disadvantage. Hence, on precisely the same basis on which Sowell concludes that the market eliminates discrimination— the economic considerations of the employers—in this case, the market engenders discrimination.

Sowell tries to camouflage this further gap in his argument by maintaining that, although discrimination may be deleterious to exceptional blacks, it does not harm blacks as a group. "Where employment, renting, lending, or other transactions decisions are based on assessments that are accurate for the group average but inaccurate for the individual under consideration," he writes, "the windfall losses of those individuals underestimated by applying the group average are offset by windfall gains by those individuals over-estimated by applying the group average." In this way Sowell hopes to bolster his claim that discrimination is not a barrier to black progress. But what of justice? Isn't the individual black who is excluded by this kind of discrimination unjustly treated? Significantly, Sowell agrees. "Choosing cost bearers on the basis of race or ethnicity," he concedes, "goes counter to general conceptions of justice." Yet, he resists suggesting that employers bear the costs of acquiring the knowledge of individuals which would preclude this injustice. "No one does that in real life," he notes, "because costs of knowledge make it prohibitive."

Now this is a fine thing for the senior partner of black libertarianism's dynamic duo to be saying! One would have expected Sowell to insist on the primacy of rights, and let efficiency go to the wall. But no, he insists on efficiency, and lets rights—black rights—go to the wall.

Consequently, Sowell's position on this issue is, simply, that utility outweighs justice, and sometimes he makes the point explicitly. Thus, he thinks that John Rawls, a professor of philosophy at Harvard and author of the influential book *A Theory of Justice*, exaggerates the importance of justice. The proper attitude to justice, Sowell believes, is that of Adam Smith, whose *Wealth of Nations* spawned modern economics. "To Smith," Sowell observes, "some amount of justice was a prerequisite for any of the other features of society to exist." But Smith did not, in Sowell's view, countenance the "doctrinaire" view suggested by Rawls that "all increments of justice invariably outweighed increments of other things." Sowell postulates an extreme case to show that sometimes utility outweighs justice and tries to use it to discredit Rawls. According to Rawls, he notes, "a policy that benefitted all of the human race except one person should not be adopted" because it would be unjust. But the extreme and farfetched nature of such arguments is their weakness. They cannot show that in less extreme cases utility outweighs justice. And the case of discrimination is among the less extreme cases. Surely, even if legislation compelling employers to be fairer does reduce efficiency, it does not spell disaster. On the contrary, by giving incentives to blacks to become productive—a possibility Sowell notes—it may in the long run increase efficiency.

It may be objected that since by assumption most blacks are unproductive relative to whites, perceptual discrimination only risks not employing the most productive, and so only risks being unfair. One response to this objection is that, in terms of decency, it is unfair not to treat a person as an individual. But Sowell's argument can be undone even if we concede that it is only unfair to deny the most productive employment. Let us look at how a fairly consistent libertarian treats the question of policies that risk unfairness of this kind.

Robert Nozick believes that it is not enough that those who engage in risky behavior compensate those whose rights they violate. A system which allows this still "has a cost in the uncompensated for fear of those potential victims who were not actual victims." Because he takes rights seriously, as a libertarian should, Nozick thinks that people have a right to be free from fear that their rights will be transgressed against, and to protect that right Nozick argues that the state may prohibit behavior which risks violating rights. Now, employers who engage in the kind of discrimination which Sowell approves of on utilitarian grounds are certainly engaged in behavior which risks violating blacks' rights—even if we concede for the moment that no one can expect to be treated as an individual when he is looking for a job. For, since the correlation between blackness and low productivity is not exact, discrimination on those grounds risks violating the right of the black who happens to be the most productive person in a pool of applicants. Nor, since the average productivity of different pools of applicants varies, does it risk violating the rights only of truly "exceptional" blacks. Every black would be subject to the possibility that, no matter how poor his competition, his rights might be violated. And this means, in Nozick's terms, the right of every black not to fear that his rights are going to be violated would be traduced. This result doesn't even depend on the assumption that all employers practice discrimination. As Nozick acknowledges, for the general case the fact that society permits it at all is enough. Every black person would have to live with the fear that his rights might be violated. (However, as I point out later in this chapter, Nozick's libertarian conception of "rights" may still be invidious to the idea of justice for blacks.)

Now this fear, and the violation of rights it involves, are, of course, the sources of that loss of self-confidence which advocates of preferential treatment have noted and tried to combat. To deal with these effects one of two alternative policies—both of which are suggested by Nozick—is necessary. On the one hand, discrimination could be prohibited. On the other hand, if discrimination results in great savings for employers and industry, it could be permitted if its beneficiaries pay compensation to those whose rights they have violated. A libertarian who takes rights seriously must adopt either one of these alternatives. But black libertarians adopt neither, and so we must conclude that they do not take rights—especially black rights—seriously. They are ready to sacrifice black rights on the altar of efficiency, and they do not even ask for compensation. Furthermore, if they did adopt one of the alternatives they would seriously undermine their position on free market efficacy. For either alternative would require government expansion, the first by increasing government's regulation of industry, and the second by requiring the creation of a government department to oversee the payment of compensation. This would also mean that Sowell and Williams would have to withdraw their contention that discrimination in government is unimportant. Their support for this view was their thesis that, although discrimination in government is unchecked by the market, government ought, in any case, to be minimal. But we have seen that even if government sticks to the libertarian definition of its function as protector of rights it is still apt to expand.

However, it will surely be objected that the whole of my attempt to show black libertarianism as contradictory rests on the assumption that libertarianism allows that blacks—and people in general—have the right to be considered for positions on the basis of their individual merits, or that the best candidate has a right to a position. This, it may be pointed out, is utterly false. The libertarian view rejects the idea that applicants for jobs have rights to be considered. These merit-based rights are liberal rights. But they are not libertarian rights. They conflict with the rights libertarianism holds sacrosanct—property rights—and hence do not exist for libertarians. The property owner, and therefore the employer, says the libertarian, has a right to hire whom he pleases. In this particular case he has a right to hire—deliberately—unproductive whites instead of productive blacks if he so wishes. If Sowell is right, if he does this he will bankrupt himself. But this too, libertarians say, is his right. Thus, it may seem that what I have shown is that libertarianism does not take liberal rights seriously but that I have not shown that libertarianism does not take libertarian rights seriously. . . .

The Alleged Disutility of Color-Conscious Policies

One of Sowell's deepest misgivings about color-conscious policies, and in this he is joined by Wilson, is that they will exacerbate racial conflict. Sowell, for example, has warned in the popular press that if the "government continues to hand out goodies on a racial or ethnic basis" it may not take long for "people to be at each other's throats—and for blood to be in the streets." And Wilson writes that "if there is an imminent potential for racial conflict in the industrial order it would most probably be related to the affirmative action program." However, even if these warnings are well-founded, they cannot, on Sowell's and Wilson's own accounts, be the basis of an independent argument against color-conscious policies. Suppose that color-conscious policies are just and useful to black progress. Then, if we refrain from implementing them because of fear of racial conflict, racism *would* be an important barrier to justice and to black progress—contrary to the class theory to which Sowell and Wilson adhere. Consequently, they cannot, on pain of self-contradiction, use predictions about racial conflict as independent arguments against color-conscious policies. They must first prove such policies pernicious.

Wilson's argument, in brief, is this: there is no competition for jobs in the underclass. Jobs exist, but because they are low-paying and menial, blacks and whites don't compete for them. (They are taken by illegal aliens.) Consequently, since there is no racial competition for jobs, and therefore no opportunity for racial discrimination over jobs, racial discrimination cannot be the factor keeping blacks in the underclass from getting jobs. Finally, he concludes, because racial discrimination is not the factor keeping these blacks from getting jobs, color-conscious policies are irrelevant to their ability to get jobs, and hence irrelevant to their progress.

The final step in this argument is a giant non sequitur. From the claim that racial discrimination is not what keeps blacks in the underclass from getting jobs, it does not follow that color-conscious policies are not necessary for the progress of these blacks. The inference is as faulty as would be the argument that, since no one unfairly discriminates against the musically gifted, or the artistically or mathematically gifted, special programs for them are irrelevant to their progress. Yet, Wilson's opposition to color-conscious policies in this area is adamant. He concludes *The Declining Significance of Race* with the observation that the problems of the underclass must be tackled "on a broad class front" which goes "beyond the limits of ethnic and racial discrimination."

But, as I observed, not only is Wilson's dismissive attitude toward color-conscious policies unjustified, his own class theory suggests that his advocacy of color-blind policies is ill-considered.

Wilson suggests a color-blind policy which will make available to the black and white underclass "jobs that pay decent wages and that provide opportunities of advancement—jobs that will enhance an individual's self-respect and feelings of self-worth," and he properly stresses that this is in "sharp contrast" to Sowell's suggested policy which would create low-paying, menial jobs—jobs which already exist. But if, as Wilson assumes, this kind of color-blind policy will solve the problems of the black and white underclass, there is a large gap in his argument—implied by his own theory. According to Wilson's theory "jobs that pay decent wages" already exist, just like low-paying, menial jobs. The problem is that these decently paying jobs are not within the reach of the underclass. As he himself repeatedly stresses, decently paying jobs "are decreasing in the central cities of our nation" and exist more in the suburbs. The solution to the problem then would seem to be to move blacks to the suburbs. But Wilson also repeatedly stresses that opposition to residential integration in the country continues unabated. Consequently, given that residential integration would require a deliberate color-conscious policy, it would seem that if Wilson's proposal is to succeed, it cannot, after all, be color-blind.

This conclusion blunts the point of Wilson's version of Washington's attack on "race-problem solvers." The black intelligentsia, Wilson charges, "has a vested interest in keeping race as the single most important issue in developing policies to promote black progress." This is because it achieved, and maintains, its present comfortable position largely through color-conscious policies like affirmative action which are based on the assumption that race *is* the most important issue. Consequently, in pursuit of what Wilson perceives as self-interest, the black middle class advertises the miseries of the black underclass while promoting and sustaining the illusion that these miseries are due to racism. In this way it hopes to expand color-conscious programs which create more opportunities for itself. Carl Gershman, a follower of Wilson's, takes this suggestion further. According to Gershman, not only does the black middle class falsely insist on race being the most important consideration in developing policies for black progress but, perceiving that its advantages depend on the deprivation of the black lower class, it actually *blocks* policies that would help the black lower class. Using Wilson's version of the class theory, Gershman, among other things, argues that black leaders at a national conference in Richmond, Virginia, in 1979 urged policies seriously opposed to the interests of the black lower class. But this charge assumes precisely what Wilson's version of the class theory denies—that racial discrimination is an important impediment to black progress. Gershman concedes this point without realizing it. To illustrate his thesis about the self-serving and destructive nature of the policies urged by the new leadership of the black middle class, he relates how, at a hearing on urban policy conducted by the House Committee on Banking Currency and Housing, Paul R. Porter, an urban specialist, proposed that poor blacks wishing to relocate to areas of industrial growth be assisted by the government. According to Gershman, Representative Parren J. Mitchell (a Democrat from Maryland) opposed this proposal on the grounds that by relocating blacks—moving them out of the central cities—such a policy would "destroy the political base that we blacks have begun to develop in this country." Gershman presents this as evidence of the way in which the black middle class blocks the progress of the black lower class to selfish advantage. But if, as Wilson says, opposition to residential integration has not declined, the exchange is also evidence for the importance of racial discrimination—a view that Gershman, as Wilson's disciple, rejects.

Sowell's argument about the counterproductiveness of color-conscious policies has two phases. First, there is a frontal attack on the effectiveness of those policies. Second, there is a rearguard action in which he concludes that in the long run government intervention creates social and political instabilities.

The frontal attack is simply the accusation that, in Sowell's words, color-conscious policies like affirmative action "have produced little overall pay or employment changes for blacks relative to whites." He backs up this claim with the argument that affirmative action makes it difficult for employers to fire incompetent blacks and so discourages them from hiring blacks in the first place.

But there is a gap in Sowell's argument. He has completely overlooked another effect of affirmative action. Because the policy carries penalties for noncompliance, affirmative action also makes it costly for an employer to hire no blacks at all. Therefore, a fairer assessment of the net effect of affirmative action is that it forces employers to intensify their search for the "right" blacks, that is, as Christopher Jencks notes, "young blacks with educational credentials and mature blacks with steady work histories." Empirical studies suggest that in this respect affirmative action has been productive. Jencks reports that three of the four studies conducted to estimate the effect of affirmative action on employment concluded that it "increased minority employment by 6 to 13 percent," and, while he allows that the effect of affirmative action on income is "less clear cut," he also demonstrates that in this case too the evidence makes it difficult to deny, as Sowell does with assurance, that affirmative action "increased black workers' earnings." The most that Sowell can say, Jencks concludes, is that while affirmative action improved black workers wages, "it also may have made it harder for some blacks to find jobs."

THE ATTACK ON POLITICS AND PROTEST

Sensing, perhaps, the weakness of his frontal attack on the effectiveness of affirmative action, and by extension of all government interference in the free market on behalf of blacks, Sowell invariably falls back on his rearguard argument—that government interference in the market creates instabilities. At this point he admits that this interference is sometimes effective. "At particular historic junctures," he writes, "governmental policy may be beneficial to particular ethnic groups." But he goes on to object that it is unreliable in the long run. "It is the long-run reliance on political action" he warns, "that is questionable in view of the unpredictability of political trends in general." And to drive home his point about the "sheer volatility of governmental policy toward ethnic groups" he reminds us not only of the shifts in U.S. government attitude toward blacks, but of Idi Amin's "brutal mass expulsions of East Indians" from Uganda, "the slaughter of the Ibos in Nigeria," "the severe current official discrimination against the Chinese in Indonesia," and, of course, "Hitler and the Holocaust."

Of Thomas Sowell's many strange arguments, this one is the most bizarre and perverse. The evidence he cites to support his conclusion in fact supports the very opposite. Consider his claim that political activity does not help a minority's progress. His reasons for this are that although political activity may help enact favorable government policy, there are usually economic incentives tempting individuals to "behave at variance with government policy." And Sowell thinks that history proves him right. "The high tide of black political power during Reconstruction," he reminds us, "was not a period of notable economic advance, and in fact included some important retrogressions." And more generally he maintains that

> political success is not only relatively unrelated to economic advance, those minorities that have pinned their greatest hopes on political action—the Irish and the Negroes, for example—have made some of the slowest economic advances. This is in sharp contrast to the Japanese-Americans, whose political powerlessness may have been a blessing in disguise, by preventing the expenditure of much energy in that direction.

Here, of course, he is following Booker T. Washington, whose opposition to engaging in politics to achieve advancement is legendary: "The best course to pursue in regard to the civil rights bills in the South," Washington advised, "is to let it alone."

The most curious property of tunnel vision is not that it blinds. It is that it distorts. Weaknesses appear to be strengths. Washington and Sowell both have a bad case of tunnel vision. Consider again the examples Sowell cites to prove the volatility of government policy in relation to minorities—the Indians in East Africa, the Ibos in Nigeria, the Chinese in Indonesia, and the Jews in Germany. To support Sowell's belief in the ineffectiveness of political power and political action these groups should have been groups with political power and a history of political activity. But the very opposite is true. The Indians in East Africa kept a low political profile, as do the Chinese in Indonesia, and by Sowell's own account the Jews only slowly became involved in politics in this country because they were apolitical in the European countries from which they came originally. Of the groups Sowell mentions, only the Ibos were politically active, and their problems would have been worse had they been less politically involved. Furthermore, these groups were or are doing exactly what Sowell recommends black America do. They kept or keep out of politics, and made or make a lot of money. So if their fate is anything to go by, this is what Sowell plans for us: keep out of politics and make a lot of money, and one day we'll be "brutally expelled," "slaughtered," or suffer a "Holocaust"!

The obvious point to be made here, is, if a person plans to acquire something of value, he had better also plan to acquire a way to keep it, or others will take it away from him. That Washington and Sowell overlook this is amazing. Why else are there locks on doors and guards in banks? And that they overlook it is more amazing still when we recall that their policies are based on the assumption that man is self-interested. For if man is self-interested, what can protect the valuables of the weak from others so motivated? Their oversight literally boggles the mind when we recall that they claim to be examining the experience of black people. I confess that my mind was boggled when I first read Washington's pronouncement that "Harmony will come in proportion that the black man gets something the white man wants." For there was a time when the black man had something the white man wanted. And it did not bring harmony, or even less, justice. It brought the death of one hundred million black people—the number estimated to have died as a result of the slave trade—and two hundred years of slavery. Washington knew this. After noting that the country's immigration laws were framed to keep out people who "might prove a burden upon the tax-payers, because of their poverty and inability to sustain themselves," he boasts that "for two centuries or more it was the policy of the United States to bring in the Negro at almost any cost," concluding rhetorically, "Would any individual or any country have gone to the expense during so many years to import a people that had no economic value?"

Now this boast completely demolishes, of course, the centerpiece of Washington's, and Sowell's, theory—their conviction that all you need to get ahead is to get "something the white man wants" or "something the society values." This really stupid and dangerous idea, which is of a piece with their admonition to eschew politics, does not even state a necessary condition for getting ahead. If you have enough weapons, as kings and conquerors have proved throughout history, you do not need to have something the society values to get ahead. Unless, of course, it is the power to refrain from killing when you can kill.

Every black political thinker worth his salt, with the exception of Washington and his disciples, has acknowledged these elementary truths and has correspondingly concluded that the problem for blacks in America is and has been the problem of the vulnerability of the weak and inarticulate—especially the weak and inarticulate with something the strong want. For example, Martin Delany, the first and wisest of the black nationalists was acutely aware of this. It is the basis of his analysis of black subordination and enslavement. Blacks were subordinated and enslaved, he argued, first because they were weak. They were "least potent in urging their claims." Added to and exacerbating this weakness was the fact that blacks had something whites wanted. Blacks were enslaved, Delany argued, because of their "superior skill and industry." And there was a final factor that determined the enslavement of blacks and made those who practiced it almost immune to moral dissuasion. He observed that those who proscribe others select those who "differ as much as possible . . . from themselves" for this "ensures the greater success" of their proscription as "it engenders the greater prejudice, or in other words, elicits less interest on the part of the oppressing class." And because he supposed that only one of these causes of black subordination could or should be altered—the lack of power—Delany argued that the future of black elevation lay in blacks acquiring power by emigrating to Africa and establishing a great black nation there. A long line of black thinkers, from Marcus Garvey to Stokely Carmichael and Charles V. Hamilton, have endorsed his Black Power solution to the problem of subordination, though they have not always endorsed his idea that emigration was the way to get it.

Assimilationists, for example Delany's great contemporary Frederick Douglass, have, of course, proposed a different solution to the problem of black subordination. But Douglass did not analyze the causes of black subordination any differently than Delany. In particular, he did not deny that part of the cause of their subordination was their powerlessness, and their inability to arouse the whites' sense of justice. He refused to endorse Delany's solution of emigration because he thought it was unrealistic and an evasion of a duty to expose, protest, and combat injustice, and his followers today reject the idea of Black Power for similar reasons. Accordingly, Douglass and his contemporary representatives propose to solve the problem of black subordination by attacking another of its causes, viz., the white majority's belief that blacks differ in some fundamental way from whites. Thus, on the grounds that congregation made blacks more noticeable, and accentuated their difference from whites, Douglass at one time condemned the idea that unity is strength, at least in every circumstance, and urged blacks to disperse themselves among whites. And to back up the effects of this dispersal, since it alone would not solve the problem, Douglass mounted a relentless attack on the idea that prejudice is "natural" and that there is a moral difference between blacks and whites. He employed all his enormous intellectual and oratorical powers to prove and persuade people that "it is all false this talk about the invincibility of prejudice against color," and that despite obvious physical differences, and even differences in origin, "a man's a man for a' that."

It is difficult to say which strategy, that of Black Power, or that of the assimilationists, is superior. Both have advantages and both have disadvantages. The advantages of the Black Power approach include the well-established efficacy of power. Its disadvantages include its tendency to degenerate into cultural chauvinism, to strike poses and to become infected with the racism of black racial superiority. Finally, of course, its goals may simply be impossible to achieve. Many of these disadvantages are precisely the advantages of assimilation. Assimilation utterly rejects racism and concedes nothing to injustice. However, it too has disadvantages. With some advocates, it tends to involve a depreciation of those characteristics which distinguish blacks from whites, and in this way may undermine black self-esteem. Also, it may lead to a preoccupation with protesting injustice and a corresponding disregard for the importance of achievement—there is this much foundation to Washington's fears about political involvement. Finally, of course, like those of Black Power, its aims, too, may be unachievable. Neither strategy is guaranteed to succeed, and each has dangers. Perhaps the best policy would be a judicious combination of the best parts of both. Certainly the worst policy would be to eschew both power and protest. To urge black people to make money, or to acquire skills that will enable them to make money, while at the same time urging them to avoid all means of self-defense, as Washington and Sowell do, is a prescription for disaster.

As I have observed, their recommendations are especially perverse because they are based on a theory which assumes that self-interest is the prime motivation for human beings. Here it should be noted that Washington comes off as less confused than Sowell. For he at least allows that the self-interest of human beings includes an interest in their moral betterment. Thus he could, and did, urge justice by reminding whites of their interest in their souls. But Sowell will have none of this "higher," though still prudential, reasoning. For him, bewildered by his own "causal analysis," it is all "dollars and cents." His saying this, and his urging of policies for blacks of enrichment without self-defense—and this among a people whose history demonstrates the lengths they will go to get dollars and cents—is not mere intellectual blunder. It is reprehensible folly.

Justice as Fairness: For Whom?*

SUSAN MOLLER OKIN

JOHN RAWLS'S *A THEORY OF JUSTICE* has had the most powerful influence of any work of contemporary moral and political theory. The scope of Rawls's influence is indicated by the fact that all the theorists I have discussed [in chapters 3–4 of my work *Justice, Gender, and the Family*] make an issue of their respective disagreements with his method and, in most cases, with his conclusions. Now, I turn to Rawls's theory of justice as fairness, to examine not only what it explicitly says and does not say, but also what it *implies*, on the subjects of gender, women, and the family.

There is strikingly little indication, throughout most of *A Theory of Justice*, that the modern liberal society to which the principles of justice are to be applied is deeply and pervasively gender-structured. Thus an ambiguity runs throughout the work, which is continually noticeable to anyone reading it from a feminist perspective. On the one hand, as I shall argue, a consistent and wholehearted application of Rawls's liberal principles of justice can lead us to challenge fundamentally the gender system of our society. On the other hand, in his own account of his theory, this challenge is barely hinted at, much less developed. After critiquing Rawls's theory for its neglect of gender, I shall ask two related questions: what effects does a feminist reading of Rawls have on some of his fundamental ideas (particularly those most attacked by critics); and what undeveloped potential does the theory have for feminist critique, and in particular for our attempts to answer the question, "Can justice coexist with gender?"

*Excerpt from *Justice, Gender, and the Family* by Susan Moller Okin. Copyright ©1989 by Basic Books, Inc. Reprinted by permission of HarperCollins Publishers, Inc.

Central to Rawls's theory of justice is a construct, or heuristic device, that is both his most important single contribution to moral and political theory and the focus of most of the controversy his theory still attracts, nearly twenty years after its publication. Rawls argues that the principles of justice that should regulate the basic institutions of society are those that would be arrived at by persons reasoning in what is termed "the original position." His specifications for the original position are that "the parties" who deliberate there are rational and mutually disinterested, and that while no limits are placed on the general information available to them, a "veil of ignorance" conceals from them all knowledge of their individual characteristics and their social position. Though the theory is presented as a contract theory, it is so only in an odd and metaphoric sense, since "no one knows his situation in society nor his natural assets, and therefore no one is in a position to tailor principles to his advantage." Thus they have "no basis for bargaining in the usual sense." This is how, Rawls explains, "the arbitrariness of the world . . . [is] corrected for," in order that the principles arrived at will be fair. Indeed, since no one knows who he is, all think identically and the standpoint of any one party represents that of all. Thus the principles of justice are arrived at unanimously. Later in this chapter, I shall address some of the criticisms that have been made of Rawls's original position and of the nature of those who deliberate there. I shall show that his theory can be read in a way that either obviates these objections or answers them satisfactorily. But first, let us see how the theory treats women, gender, and the family.

Justice for All?

Rawls, like almost all political theorists until very recently, employs in A Theory of Justice supposedly generic male terms of reference. Men, mankind, he, and his are interspersed with gender-neutral terms of reference such as individual and moral person. Examples of intergenerational concern are worded in terms of "fathers" and "sons," and the difference principle is said to correspond to "the principle of fraternity." This linguistic usage would perhaps be less significant if it were not for the fact that Rawls self-consciously subscribes to a long tradition of moral and political philosophy that has used in its arguments either such "generic" male terms or more inclusive terms of reference ("human beings," "persons," "all rational beings as such"), only to exclude women from the scope of its conclusions. Kant is a clear example. But when Rawls refers to the generality and universality of Kant's ethics, and when he compares the principles chosen in his own original position to those regulative of Kant's kingdom of ends, "acting from [which] expresses our nature as free and equal rational persons," he does not mention the fact that women were not included among those persons to whom Kant meant his moral theory to apply. Again, in a brief discussion of Freud's account of moral development, Rawls presents Freud's theory of the formation of the male superego in largely gender-neutral terms, without mentioning the fact that Freud considered women's moral development to be sadly deficient, on account of their incomplete resolution of the Oedipus complex. Thus there is a blindness to the sexism of the tradition in which Rawls is a participant, which tends to render his terms of reference more ambiguous than they might otherwise be. A feminist reader finds it difficult not to keep asking, "Does this theory of justice apply to women?"

This question is not answered in the important passages listing the characteristics that persons in the original position are not to know about themselves, in order to formulate impartial principles of justice. In a subsequent article, Rawls has made it clear that sex *is* one of those morally irrelevant contingencies that are hidden by the veil of ignorance. But throughout A *Theory of Justice*, while the list of things unknown by a person in the original position includes "his place in society, his class position or social status, . . . his fortune in the distribution of natural assets and abilities, his intelligence and strength, and the like, . . . his conception of the good, the particulars of his rational plan of life, even the special features of his psychology," "his" sex is not mentioned. Since the parties also "know the general facts about human society," presumably including the fact that it is gender-structured both by custom and still in some respects by law, one might think that whether or not they knew their sex might matter enough to be mentioned. Perhaps Rawls meant to cover it by his phrase "and the like," but it is also possible that he did not consider it significant.

The ambiguity is exacerbated by the statement that those free and equal moral persons in the original position who formulate the principles of justice are to be thought of not as "single individuals" but as "heads of families" or "representatives of families." Rawls says that it is not necessary to think of the parties as heads of families, but that he will generally do so. The reason he does this, he explains, is to ensure that each person in the original position cares about the well-being of some persons in the next generation. These "ties of sentiment" between generations, which Rawls regards as important for the establishment of intergenerational justice—his just savings principle—would otherwise constitute a problem because of the general assumption that the parties in the original position are mutually disinterested. In spite of the ties of sentiment *within* families, then, "as representatives of families their interests are opposed as the circumstances of justice imply."

The head of a family need not necessarily, of course, be a man. Certainly in the United States, at least, there has been a striking growth in the proportion of female-headed households during the last several decades. But the very fact that, in common usage, the term "female-headed household" is used *only* in reference to households without resident adult males implies the assumption that any present male takes precedence over a female as the household or family head. Rawls does nothing to contest this impression when he says of those in the

original position that "imagining themselves to be fathers, say, they are to
ascertain how much they should set aside for their sons by noting what they
would believe themselves entitled to claim of their fathers." He makes the
"heads of families" assumption only in order to address the problem of justice
between generations, and presumably does not intend it to be a sexist assumption. Nevertheless, he is thereby effectively trapped into the public/domestic
dichotomy and, with it, the conventional mode of thinking that life within the
family and relations between the sexes are not properly regarded as part of the
subject matter of a theory of social justice.

Let me here point out that Rawls, for good reason, states at the outset of his
theory that the family *is* part of the subject matter of a theory of social justice.
"For us" he says, "the primary subject of justice is the basic structure of society,
or more exactly, the way in which the major social institutions distribute
fundamental rights and duties and determine the division of advantages from
social cooperation." The political constitution and the principal economic and
social arrangements are basic because "taken together as one scheme, [they]
define men's rights and duties and influence their life prospects, what they can
expect to be and how well they can hope to do. The basic structure is the
primary subject of justice *because its effects are so profound and present from the
start*" (emphasis added). Rawls specifies "the monogamous family" as an example
of such major social institutions, together with the political constitution, the
legal protection of essential freedoms, competitive markets, and private property. Although this initial inclusion of the family as a basic social institution
to which the principles of justice should apply is surprising in the light of the
history of liberal thought, with its dichotomy between domestic and public
spheres, it is necessary, given Rawls's stated criteria for inclusion in the basic
structure. It would scarcely be possible to deny that different family structures,
and different distributions of rights and duties within families, affect men's "life
prospects, what they can expect to be and how well they can hope to do," and
even more difficult to deny their effects on the life prospects of women. There is
no doubt, then, that in Rawls's initial definition of the sphere of social justice,
the family is included and the public/domestic dichotomy momentarily cast in
doubt. However, the family is to a large extent ignored, though assumed, in the
rest of the theory.

THE BARELY VISIBLE FAMILY

In Part 1 of *A Theory of Justice*, Rawls derives and defends the two principles of
justice—the principle of equal basic liberty, and the "difference principle"
combined with the requirement of fair equality of opportunity. These principles
are intended to apply to the basic structure of society. They are "to govern the
assignment of rights and duties and to regulate the distribution of social and

economic advantages." Whenever the basic institutions have within them differences in authority, in responsibility, or in the distribution of resources such as wealth or leisure, the second principle requires that these differences must be to the greatest benefit of the least advantaged and must be attached to positions accessible to all under conditions of fair equality of opportunity.

In Part 2, Rawls discusses at some length the application of his principles of justice to almost all the institutions of the basic social structure that are set out at the beginning of the book. The legal protection of liberty of thought and conscience is defended, as are democratic constitutional institutions and procedures; competitive markets feature prominently in the discussion of the just distribution of income; the issue of the private or public ownership of the means of production is explicitly left open, since Rawls argues that his principles of justice might be compatible with certain versions of either. But throughout all these discussions, the issue of whether the monogamous family, in either its traditional or any other form, is a just social institution, is never raised. When Rawls announces that "the sketch of the system of institutions that satisfy the two principles of justice is now complete," he has paid no attention at all to the internal justice of the family. In fact, apart from passing references, the family appears in *A Theory of Justice* in only three contexts: as the link between generations necessary for the just savings principle; as an obstacle to fair equality of opportunity (on account of the inequalities among families); and as the first school of moral development. It is in the third of these contexts that Rawls first specifically mentions the family as a just institution—not, however, to *consider* whether the family "in some form" is a just institution but to *assume* it.

Clearly, however, by Rawls's own reasoning about the social justice of major social institutions, this assumption is unwarranted. The serious significance of this for the theory as a whole will be addressed shortly. The central tenet of the theory, after all, is that justice as fairness characterizes institutions whose members could hypothetically have agreed to their structure and rules from a position in which they did not know which place in the structure they were to occupy. The argument of the book is designed to show that the two principles of justice are those that individuals in such a hypothetical situation would agree upon. But since those in the original position are the heads or representatives of families, they are not in a position to determine questions of justice within families. As Jane English has pointed out, "By making the parties in the original position heads of families rather than individuals, Rawls makes the family opaque to claims of justice." As far as children are concerned, Rawls makes an argument from paternalism for their temporary inequality and restricted liberty. (This, while it may suffice in basically sound, benevolent families, is of no use or comfort in abusive or neglectful situations where Rawls's principles would seem to require that children be protected through the intervention of outside authorities.) But wives (or whichever adult member[s] of a family are *not* its "head") go completely unrepresented in the original position. If families are just, as Rawls later assumes, then they must become just in some different way (unspecified by him) from other institutions, for it is impossible to see how the viewpoint of their less advantaged members ever gets to be heard.

There are two occasions when Rawls seems either to depart from his assumption that those in the original position are "family heads" or to assume that a "head of a family" is equally likely to be a woman as a man. In the assignment of the basic rights of citizenship, he argues, favoring men over women is "justified by the difference principle . . . only if it is to the advantage of women and acceptable from their standpoint." Later he seems to imply that the injustice and irrationality of racist doctrines are also characteristic of sexist ones. But in spite of these passages, which appear to challenge formal sex discrimination, the discussions of institutions in part 2 implicitly rely, in a number of respects, on the assumption that the parties formulating just institutions are (male) heads of (fairly traditional) families, and are therefore not concerned with issues of just distribution within the family or between the sexes. Thus the "heads of families" assumption, far from being neutral or innocent, has the effect of banishing a large sphere of human life—and a particularly large sphere of most women's lives—from the scope of the theory.

During the discussion of the distribution of wealth, for example, it seems to be assumed that all the parties in the original position expect, once the veil of ignorance is removed, to be participants in the paid labor market. Distributive shares are discussed in terms of household income, but reference to "individuals" is interspersed into this discussion as if there were no difference between the advantage or welfare of a household and that of an individual. This confusion obscures the fact that wages are paid to employed members of the labor force, but that in societies characterized by gender (all current societies) a much larger proportion of women's than men's labor is unpaid and is often not even acknowledged as labor. It also obscures the fact that the resulting disparities in the earnings of men and women, and the economic dependence of women on men, are likely to affect power relations within the household, as well as access to leisure, prestige, political power, and so on, among its adult members. Any discussion of justice *within* the family would have to address these issues. . . .

Later, in Rawls's discussion of the obligations of citizens, his assumption that justice is agreed on by heads of families in the original position seems to prevent him from considering another issue of crucial importance: women's exemption from the draft. He concludes that military conscription is justifiable in the case of defense against an unjust attack on liberty, so long as institutions "try to make sure that the risks of suffering from these imposed misfortunes are more or less evenly shared by all members of society over the course of their life, and that there is no avoidable *class* bias in selecting those who are called for duty" (emphasis added). The complete exemption of women from this major interference with the basic liberties of equal citizenship is not even mentioned.

In spite of two explicit rejections of the justice of formal sex discrimination in part 1, then, Rawls seems in part 2 to be heavily influenced by his "family heads" assumption. He does not consider as part of the basic structure of society the greater economic dependence of women and the sexual division of labor within the typical family, or any of the broader social ramifications of this basic gender structure. Moreover, in part 3, where he takes as a given the justice of the family "in some form," he does not discuss any alternative forms. Rather, he sounds very much as though he is thinking in terms of traditional, gendered family structure and roles. The family, he says, is "a small association, normally characterized by a definite hierarchy, in which each member has certain rights and duties." The family's role as moral teacher is achieved partly through parental expectations of the "virtues of a good son or a good daughter." In the family and in other associations such as schools, neighborhoods, and peer groups, Rawls continues, one learns various moral virtues and ideals, leading to those adopted in the various statuses, occupations, and family positions of later life. "The content of these ideals is given by the various conceptions of a good wife and husband, a good friend and citizen, and so on." Given these unusual departures from the supposedly generic male terms of reference used throughout the book, it seems likely that Rawls means to imply that the goodness of daughters is distinct from the goodness of sons, and that of wives from that of husbands. A fairly traditional gender system seems to be assumed.

Rawls not only assumes that "the basic structure of a well-ordered society includes the family *in some form*" (emphasis added); he adds that "in a broader inquiry the institution of the family might be questioned, and other arrangements might indeed prove to be preferable." But why should it require a broader inquiry than the colossal task in which *A Theory of Justice* is engaged, to raise questions about the institution and the form of the family? Surely Rawls is right in initially naming it as one of those basic social institutions that most affect the life chances of individuals and should therefore be part of the primary subject of justice. The family is not a private association like a church or a university, which vary considerably in the type and degree of commitment each expects from its members, and which one can join and leave voluntarily. For although one has some choice (albeit a highly constrained one) about marrying into a gender-structured family, one has no choice at all about being born into one. Rawls's failure to subject the structure of the family to his principles of justice is particularly serious in the light of his belief that a theory of justice must take account of "how [individuals] get to be what they are" and "cannot take their final aims and interests, their attitudes to themselves and their life, as given." For the gendered family, and female parenting in particular, are clearly critical determinants in the different ways the two sexes are socialized—how men and women "get to be what they are."

If Rawls were to assume throughout the construction of his theory that all human adults are participants in what goes on behind the veil of ignorance, he would have no option but to require that the family, as a major social institution affecting the life chances of individuals, be constructed in accordance with the two principles of justice. I shall begin to develop this positive potential of Rawls's theory in the final section of this chapter. . . . But first I turn to a major problem for the theory that results from its neglect of the issue of justice within the family: its placing in jeopardy Rawls's account of how one develops a sense of justice.

GENDER, THE FAMILY, AND THE DEVELOPMENT OF A SENSE OF JUSTICE

Apart from being briefly mentioned as the link between generations necessary for Rawls's just savings principle, and as an obstacle to fair equality of opportunity, the family appears in Rawls's theory in only one context—albeit one of considerable importance: as the earliest school of moral development. Rawls argues, in a much-neglected section of part 3 of A *Theory of Justice*, that a just, well-ordered society will be stable only if its members continue to develop a sense of justice, "a strong and normally effective desire to act as the principles of justice require." He turns his attention specifically to childhood moral development, aiming to indicate the major steps by which a sense of justice is acquired.

It is in this context that Rawls *assumes* that families are just. Moreover, these supposedly just families play a fundamental role in his account of moral development. First, the love of parents for their children, which comes to be reciprocated, is important in his account of the development of a sense of self-worth. By loving the child and being "worthy objects of his admiration . . . they arouse in him a sense of his own value and the desire to become the sort of person that they are." Rawls argues that healthy moral development in early life depends upon love, trust, affection, example, and guidance.

At a later stage in moral development, which he calls "the morality of association," Rawls perceives the family, though he describes it in gendered and hierarchical terms, as the first of many associations in which, by moving through a sequence of roles and positions, our moral understanding increases. The crucial aspect of the sense of fairness that is learned during this stage is the capacity—which, as I shall argue, is essential for being able to think *as if* in the original position—to take up the different points of view of others and to learn "from their speech, conduct, and countenance" to see things from their perspectives. We learn to perceive, from what they say and do, what other people's ends, plans, and motives are. Without this experience, Rawls says, "we cannot put ourselves into another's place and find out what we would do in his position," which we need to be able to do in order "to regulate our own conduct in the appropriate way by reference to it." Building on attachments formed in the family, participation in different roles in the various associations of society leads to the development of a person's "capacity for fellow feeling" and to "ties of friendship and mutual trust." Just as in the first stage "certain natural attitudes develop toward the parents, so here ties of friendship and confidence grow up among associates. In each case certain natural attitudes underlie the corresponding moral feelings: a lack of these feelings would manifest the absence of these attitudes."

This whole account of moral development is strikingly unlike the arid, rationalist account given by Kant, whose ideas are so influential in many respects on Rawls's thinking about justice. For Kant, who claimed that justice must be grounded in reason alone, any feelings that do not follow from independently established moral principles are morally suspect—"mere inclinations." By contrast, Rawls clearly recognizes the importance of feelings, first nurtured within supposedly just families, in the development of the capacity for moral thinking. In accounting for his third and final stage of moral development, where persons are supposed to become attached to the principles of justice themselves, Rawls says that "the sense of justice is continuous with the love of mankind." At the same time, he acknowledges our particularly strong feelings about those to whom we are closely attached, and says that this is rightly reflected in our moral judgments: even though "our moral sentiments display an independence from the accidental circumstances of our world, . . . our natural attachments to particular persons and groups still have an appropriate place." He indicates clearly that empathy, or imagining oneself in the circumstances of others, plays a major role in moral development. It is not surprising that he turns away from Kant, and toward moral philosophers such as Adam Smith, Elizabeth Anscombe, Philippa Foot, and Bernard Williams in developing his ideas about the moral emotions or sentiments.

Rawls's summary of his three psychological laws of moral development emphasizes the fundamental importance of loving parenting for the development of a sense of justice. The three laws, Rawls says, are

> not merely principles of association or of reinforcement . . . [but] assert that the active sentiments of love and friendship, and even the sense of justice, arise from the manifest intention of other persons to act for our good. Because we recognize that they wish us well, we care for their well-being in return.

Each of the laws of moral development, as set out by Rawls, depends upon the one before it, and the first assumption of the first law is: "given that family institutions are just, ..." Thus Rawls frankly and for good reason acknowledges that the whole of moral development rests at base upon the loving ministrations of those who raise small children from the earliest stages, and on the moral character—in particular, the *justice*—of the environment in which this takes place. At the foundation of the development of the sense of justice, then, are an activity and a sphere of life that, though by no means necessarily so, have throughout history been predominantly the activity and the sphere of women.

Rawls does not explain the basis of his assumption that family institutions are just. If gendered families are *not* just, but are, rather, a relic of caste or feudal societies in which roles, responsibilities, and resources are distributed not in accordance with the two principles of justice but in accordance with innate differences that are imbued with enormous social significance, then Rawls's whole structure of moral development would seem to be built on shaky ground. Unless the households in which children are first nurtured, and see their first examples of human interaction, are based on equality and reciprocity rather than on dependence and domination—and the latter is too often the case— how can whatever love they receive from their parents make up for the injustice they see before them in the relationship between these same parents? How, in hierarchical families in which sex roles are rigidly assigned, are we to learn, as Rawls's theory of moral development requires us, to "put ourselves into another's place and find out what we would do in his position"? Unless they are parented equally by adults of both sexes, how will children of both sexes come to develop a sufficiently similar and well-rounded moral psychology to enable them to engage in the kind of deliberation about justice that is exemplified in the original position? If both parents do not *share* in nurturing activities, are they both likely to maintain in adult life the capacity for empathy that underlies a sense of justice? And finally, unless the household is connected by a continuum of just associations to the larger communities within which people are supposed to develop fellow feelings for each other, how will they grow up with the capacity for enlarged sympathies such as are clearly required for the practice of justice? Rawls's neglect of justice within the family is clearly in tension with the requirements of his own theory of moral development. Family justice must be of central importance for social justice.

I have begun to suggest a feminist reading of Rawls, drawing on his theory of moral development and its emphasis on the moral feelings that originate in the family. This reading can, I think, contribute to the strengthening of Rawls's theory against some of the criticisms that have been made of it. For, in contrast with his account of moral development, much of his argument about how persons in the original position arrive at the principles of justice is expressed in terms of mutual disinterest and rationality—the language of rational choice. This, I contend, leaves what he says unnecessarily open to three criticisms: it involves unacceptably egoistic and individualistic assumptions about human nature; taking an "outside" perspective, it is of little or no relevance to actual people thinking about justice; and its aim to create universalistic and impartial principles leads to the neglect of "otherness" or difference. I think all three criticisms are mistaken, but they result at least in part from Rawls's tendency to use the language of rational choice.

In my view, the original position and what happens there are described far better in other terms. As Rawls himself says, the combination of conditions he imposes on them "forces each person in the original position to take the good of others into account." The parties can be presented as the "rational, mutually disinterested" agents characteristic of rational choice theory only because they do not know *which* self they will turn out to be. The veil of ignorance is such a demanding stipulation that it converts what would, without it, be self-interest into equal concern for others, including others who are very different from ourselves. Those in the original position cannot think from the position of *nobody*, as is suggested by those critics who then conclude that Rawls's theory depends upon a "disembodied" concept of the self. They must, rather, think from the perspective of *everybody*, in the sense of *each in turn*. To do this requires, at the very least, both strong empathy and a preparedness to listen carefully to the very different points of view of others. As I have suggested, these capacities seem more likely to be widely distributed in a society of just families, with no expectations about or reinforcements of gender.

RAWLS'S THEORY OF JUSTICE AS A TOOL
FOR FEMINIST CRITICISM

The significance of Rawls's central, brilliant idea, the original position, is that it forces one to question and consider traditions, customs, and institutions from all points of view, and ensures that the principles of justice will be acceptable to everyone, regardless of what position "he" ends up in. The critical force of the original position becomes evident when one considers that some of the most creative critiques of Rawls's theory have resulted from more radical or broad interpretations of the original position than his own. The theory, in principle, avoids both the problem of domination that is inherent in theories of justice based on traditions or shared understandings, and the partiality of libertarian theory to those who are talented or fortunate. For feminist readers, however, the problem of the theory as stated by Rawls himself is encapsulated in that ambiguous "he." As I have shown, while Rawls briefly rules out formal, legal discrimination on the grounds of sex (as on other grounds that he regards as "morally irrelevant"), he fails entirely to address the justice of the gender system, which, with its roots in the sex roles of the family and its branches extending into virtually every corner of our lives, is one of the fundamental structures of our society. If, however, we read Rawls in such a way as to take seriously both the notion that those behind the veil of ignorance do not know what sex they are and the requirement that the family and the gender system, as basic social institutions, are to be subject to scrutiny, constructive feminist criticism of these contemporary institutions follows. So, also, do hidden difficulties for the application of a Rawlsian theory of justice in a gendered society.

I shall explain each of these points in turn. But first, both the critical perspective and the incipient problems of a feminist reading of Rawls can perhaps be illuminated by a description of a cartoon I saw a few years ago. Three elderly, robed male justices are depicted, looking down with astonishment at their very pregnant bellies. One says to the others, without further elaboration: "Perhaps we'd better reconsider that decision." This illustration graphically demonstrates the importance, in thinking about justice, of a concept like Rawls's original position, which makes us adopt the positions of others— especially positions that we ourselves could never be in. It also suggests that those thinking in such a way might well conclude that more than formal legal equality of the sexes is required if justice is to be done. As we have seen in recent years, it is quite possible to enact and uphold "gender-neutral" laws concerning pregnancy, abortion, childbirth leave, and so on, that in effect discriminate against women. The United States Supreme Court decided in 1976, for example, that "an exclusion of pregnancy from a disability-benefits plan providing general coverage is not a gender-based discrimination at all." One of the virtues of the cartoon is its suggestion that one's thinking on such matters is likely to be affected by the knowledge that one might become "a pregnant person." The illustration also points out the limits of what is possible, in terms of thinking ourselves into the original position, as long as we live in a gender-structured society. While the elderly male justices can, in a sense, imagine themselves as pregnant, what is a much more difficult question is whether, in order to construct principles of justice, they can imagine themselves as women. This raises the question of whether, in fact, sex *is* a morally irrelevant and contingent characteristic in a society structured by gender.

Let us first assume that sex is contingent in this way, though I shall later question this assumption. Let us suppose that it is possible, as Rawls clearly considers it to be, to hypothesize the moral thinking of representative human beings, as ignorant of their sex as of all the other things hidden by the veil of ignorance. It seems clear that, while Rawls does not do this, we must consistently take the relevant positions of both sexes into account in formulating and applying principles of justice. In particular, those in the original position must take special account of the perspective of women, since their knowledge of "the general facts about human society" must include the knowledge that women have been and continue to be the less advantaged sex in a great number of respects. In considering the basic institutions of society, they are more likely to pay special attention to the family than virtually to ignore it. Not only is it potentially the first school of social justice, but its customary unequal assignment of responsibilities and privileges to the two sexes and its socialization of children into sex roles make it, in its current form, an institution of crucial importance for the perpetuation of sex inequality.

In innumerable ways, the principles of justice that Rawls arrives at are inconsistent with a gender-structured society and with traditional family roles. The critical impact of a feminist application of Rawls's theory comes chiefly from his second principle, which requires that inequalities be both "to the greatest benefit of the least advantaged" and "attached to offices and positions open to all." This means that if any roles or positions analogous to our current sex roles—including those of husband and wife, mother and father—were to survive the demands of the first requirement, the second requirement would prohibit any linkage between these roles and sex. Gender, with its ascriptive designation of positions and expectations of behavior in accordance with the inborn characteristic of sex, could no longer form a legitimate part of the social structure, whether inside or outside the family. Three illustrations will help to link this conclusion with specific major requirements that Rawls makes of a just or well-ordered society.

First, after the basic political liberties, one of the most essential liberties is "the important liberty of free choice of occupation." It is not difficult to see that this liberty is compromised by the assumption and customary expectation, central to our gender system, that women take far greater responsibility for housework and child care, whether or not they also work for wages outside the home. In fact, both the assignment of these responsibilities to women— resulting in their asymmetric economic dependence on men—and the related responsibility of husbands to support their wives compromise the liberty of choice of occupation of both sexes. But the customary roles of the two sexes inhibit women's choices over the course of a lifetime far more severely than those of men; it is far easier in practice to switch from being a wage worker to occupying a domestic role than to do the reverse. While Rawls has no objection to some aspects of the division of labor, he asserts that, in a well-ordered society, "no one need be servilely dependent on others and made to choose between monotonous and routine occupations which are deadening to human thought and sensibility" and that work will be "meaningful for all." These conditions are far more likely to be met in a society that does not assign family responsibilities in a way that makes women into a marginal sector of the paid work force and renders likely their economic dependence upon men. Rawls's principles of justice, then, would seem to require a radical rethinking not only of the division of labor within families but also of all the nonfamily institutions that assume it.

Second, the abolition of gender seems essential for the fulfillment of Rawls's criterion for political justice. For he argues that not only would equal formal political liberties be espoused by those in the original position, but that any inequalities in the worth of these liberties (for example, the effects on them of factors like poverty and ignorance) must be justified by the difference principle.

Indeed, "the constitutional process should preserve the equal representation of the original position to the degree that this is practicable." While Rawls discusses this requirement in the context of class differences, stating that those who devote themselves to politics should be "drawn more or less equally from all sectors of society," it is just as clearly and importantly applicable to sex differences. The equal political representation of women and men, especially if they are parents, is clearly inconsistent with our gender system. The paltry number of women in high political office is an obvious indication of this. Since 1789, over 10,000 men have served in the United States House of Representatives, but only 107 women; some 1,140 men have been senators, compared with 15 women. Only one [woman] appointee, Sandra Day O'Connor, has ever served on the Supreme Court. These levels of representation of any other class constituting more than a majority of the population would surely be perceived as a sign that something is grievously wrong with the political system. But as British politician Shirley Williams recently said, until there is "a revolution in shared responsibilities for the family, in child care and in child rearing," there will not be "more than a very small number of women . . . opting for a job as demanding as politics."

Finally, Rawls argues that the rational moral persons in the original position would place a great deal of emphasis on the securing of self-respect or self-esteem. They "would wish to avoid at almost any cost the social conditions that undermine self-respect," which is "perhaps the most important" of all the primary goods. In the interests of this primary value, if those in the original position did not know whether they were to be men or women, they would surely be concerned to establish a thoroughgoing social and economic equality between the sexes that would protect either sex from the need to pander to or servilely provide for the pleasures of the other. They would emphasize the importance of girls' and boys' growing up with an equal sense of respect for themselves and equal expectations of self-definition and development. They would be highly motivated, too, to find a means of regulating pornography that did not seriously compromise freedom of speech. In general, they would be unlikely to tolerate basic social institutions that asymmetrically either forced or gave strong incentives to members of one sex to serve as sex objects for the other.

There is, then, implicit in Rawls's theory of justice a potential critique of gender-structured social institutions, which can be developed by taking seriously the fact that those formulating the principles of justice do not know their sex. At the beginning of my brief account of this feminist critique, however, I made an assumption that I said would later be questioned—that a person's sex is, as Rawls at times indicates, a contingent and morally irrelevant characteristic, such that human beings really can hypothesize ignorance of this fact about them. First, I shall explain why, unless this assumption is a reasonable one, there are likely to be further feminist ramifications for a Rawlsian theory of justice, in addition to those I have just sketched out. I shall then argue that the assumption is very probably not plausible in any society that is structured along the lines of gender. I reach the conclusions not only that our current gender structure is incompatible with the attainment of social justice, but also that the disappearance of gender is a prerequisite for the *complete* development of a nonsexist, fully human theory of justice.

Although Rawls is clearly aware of the effects on individuals of their different places in the social system, he regards it as possible to hypothesize free and rational moral persons in the original position who, temporarily freed from the contingencies of actual characteristics and social circumstances, will adopt the viewpoint of the "representative" human being. He is under no illusions about the difficulty of this task: it requires a "great shift in perspective" from the way we think about fairness in everyday life. But with the help of the veil of ignorance, he believes that we can "take up a point of view that everyone can adopt on an equal footing," so that "we share a common standpoint along with others and do not make our judgments from a personal slant." The result of this rational impartiality or objectivity, Rawls argues, is that, all being convinced by the same arguments, agreement about the basic principles of justice will be unanimous. He does not mean that those in the original position will agree about *all* moral or social issues—"ethical differences are bound to remain"—but that complete agreement will be reached on all basic principles, or "essential understandings." A critical assumption of this argument for unanimity, however, is that all the parties have similar motivations and psychologies (for example, he assumes mutually disinterested rationality and an absence of envy) and have experienced similar patterns of moral development, and are thus presumed capable of a sense of justice. Rawls regards these assumptions as the kind of "weak stipulations" on which a general theory can safely be founded.

The coherence of Rawls's hypothetical original position, with its unanimity of representative human beings, however, is placed in doubt if the kinds of human beings we actually become in society differ not only in respect to interests, superficial opinions, prejudices, and points of view that we can discard for the purpose of formulating principles of justice, but also in their basic psychologies, conceptions of the self in relation to others, and experiences of moral development. A number of feminist theorists have argued in recent years that, in a gender-structured society, the different life experiences of females and males from the start affect their respective psychologies, modes of thinking, and patterns of moral development in significant ways. Special attention has been paid to the effects on the psychological and moral development of both sexes of the fact, fundamental to our gendered society, that children of both sexes are reared primarily by women. It has been argued that the experience of individuation—of separating oneself from the nurturer with whom one is originally psychologically fused—is a very different experience for girls than for boys, leaving the members of each sex with a different perception of themselves and of their relations with others. . . . In addition, it has been argued that the experience of being primary nurturers (and of growing up with this expectation) also affects the psychological and moral perspective of women, as does the experience of growing up in a society in which members of one's sex are in many ways subordinate to the other sex. Feminist theorists have scrutinized and analyzed the different experiences we encounter as we develop, from our actual lived lives to our absorption of their ideological underpinnings, and have filled out in valuable ways Simone de Beauvoir's claim that "one is not born, but rather becomes, a woman."

What seems already to be indicated by the studies, despite their incompleteness so far, is that *in a gender-structured society* there is such a thing as the distinct standpoint of women, and that this standpoint cannot be adequately taken into account by male philosophers doing the theoretical equivalent of the elderly male justices depicted in the cartoon. The formative influence of female parenting on small children, especially, seems to suggest that sex difference is even more likely to affect one's thinking about justice in a gendered society than, for example, racial difference in a society in which race has social significance, or class difference in a class society. The notion of the standpoint of women, while not without its own problems, suggests that a fully human moral or political theory can be developed only with the full participation of both sexes. At the very least, this will require that women take their place with men in the dialogue in approximately equal numbers and in positions of comparable influence. In a society structured along the lines of gender, this cannot happen.

In itself, moreover, it is sufficient for the development of a fully human theory of justice. For if principles of justice are to be adopted unanimously by representative human beings ignorant of their particular characteristics and positions in society, they must be persons whose psychological and moral development is in all essentials identical. This means that the social factors influencing the differences presently found between the sexes—from female parenting to all the manifestations of female subordination and dependence—would have to be replaced by genderless institutions and customs. Only children who are equally mothered and fathered can develop fully the psychological and moral capacities that currently seem to be unevenly distributed between the sexes. Only when men participate equally in what have been principally women's realms of meeting the daily material and psychological needs of those close to them, and when women participate equally in what have been principally men's realms of larger scale production, government, and intellectual and artistic life, will members of both sexes be able to develop a more complete human personality than has hitherto been possible. Whereas Rawls and most other philosophers have assumed that human psychology, rationality, moral development, and other capacities are completely represented by the males of the species, this assumption itself has now been exposed as part of the male-dominated ideology of our gendered society.

What effect might consideration of the standpoint of women in gendered society have on Rawls's theory of justice? It would place in doubt some assumptions and conclusions, while reinforcing others. For example, the discussion of rational plans of life and primary goods might be focused more on relationships and less exclusively on the complex activities that he values most highly, if it were to take account of, rather than to take for granted, the traditionally more female contributions to human life. Rawls says that self-respect or self-esteem is "perhaps the most important primary good," and that "the parties in the original position would wish to avoid at almost any cost the social conditions that undermine [it]." Good early physical and especially psychological nurturance in a favorable setting is essential for a child to develop self-respect or self-esteem. Yet there is no discussion of this in Rawls's consideration of the primary goods. Since the basis of self-respect is formed in very early childhood, just family structures and practices in which it is fostered and in which parenting itself is esteemed, and high-quality, subsidized child care facilities to supplement them, would surely be fundamental requirements of a just society. On the other hand, as I indicated earlier, those aspects of Rawls's theory, such as the difference principle, that require a considerable capacity to identify with others, can be strengthened by reference to conceptions of relations between self and others that seem in gendered society to be more predominantly female, but that would in a gender-free society be more or less evenly shared by members of both sexes.

The arguments of this chapter have led to mixed conclusions about the potential usefulness of Rawls's theory of justice from a feminist viewpoint, and about its adaptability to a genderless society. Rawls himself neglects gender and, despite his initial statement about the place of the family in the basic structure, does not consider whether or in what form the family is a just institution. It seems significant, too, that whereas at the beginning of A *Theory of Justice* he explicitly distinguishes the institutions of the basic structure (*including* the family) from other "private associations" and "various informal conventions and customs of everyday life," in his most recent work he distinctly reinforces the impression that the family belongs with those "private" and therefore nonpolitical associations, for which he suggests the principles of justice are less appropriate or relevant. He does this, moreover, despite the fact that his own theory of moral development rests centrally on the early experience of persons within a family environment that is both loving and just. Thus the theory as it stands contains an internal paradox. Because of his assumptions about gender, he has not applied the principles of justice to the realm of human nurturance, a realm that is essential to the achievement and the maintenance of justice.

On the other hand, I have argued that the feminist *potential* of Rawls's method of thinking and his conclusions is considerable. The original position, with the veil of ignorance hiding from its participants their sex as well as their other particular characteristics, talents, circumstances, and aims, is a powerful concept for challenging the gender structure. Once we dispense with the traditional liberal assumptions about public versus domestic, political versus nonpolitical spheres of life, we can use Rawls's theory as a tool with which to think about how to achieve justice between the sexes both within the family and in society at large.

Social Movements and
the Politics of Difference*

IRIS MARION YOUNG

> The idea that I think we need today in order to make decisions in political matters cannot be the idea of a totality, or of the unity, of a body. It can only be the idea of a multiplicity or a diversity. . . . To state that one must draw a critique of political judgment means today to do a politics of opinions that at the same time is a politics of Ideas . . . in which justice is not placed under a rule of convergence but rather a rule of divergence. I believe that this is the theme that one finds constantly in present day writing under the name "minority."
>
> —Jean-François Lyotard

THERE WAS ONCE A time of caste and class, when tradition decreed that each group had its place, and that some were born to rule and others to serve. In this time of darkness, law and social norms defined rights, privileges, and obligations differently for different groups, distinguished by characteristics of sex, race, religion, class, or occupation. Social inequality was justified by church and state on the grounds that people have different natures, and some natures are better than others.

Then one day Enlightenment dawned, heralding a revolutionary conception of humanity and society. All people are equal, the revolutionaries declared, inasmuch as all have a capacity for reason and moral sense. Law and politics should therefore grant to everyone equal political and civil rights. With these bold ideas the battle lines of modern political struggle were drawn.

For over two hundred years since those voices of reason first rang out, the

---

forces of light have struggled for liberty and political equality against the dark forces of irrational prejudice, arbitrary metaphysics, and the crumbling towers of patriarchal church, state, and family. In the New World we had a head start in this fight, since the American War of Independence was fought on these Enlightenment principles, and our Constitution stood for liberty and equality. So we did not have to throw off the yokes of class and religious privilege, as did our Old World comrades. Yet the United States had its own oligarchic horrors in the form of slavery and the exclusion of women from public life. In protracted and bitter struggles these bastions of privilege based on group difference began to give way, finally to topple in the 1960s.

Today in our society a few vestiges of prejudice and discrimination remain, but we are working on them, and have nearly realized the dream those Enlightenment fathers dared to propound. The state and law should express rights only in universal terms applied equally to all, and differences among persons and groups should be a purely accidental and private matter. We seek a society in which differences of race, sex, religion, and ethnicity no longer make a difference to people's rights and opportunities. People should be treated as individuals, not as members of groups; their life options and rewards should be based solely on their individual achievement. All persons should have the liberty to be and do anything they want, to choose their own lives and not be hampered by traditional expectations and stereotypes.

We tell each other this story and make our children perform it for our sacred holidays—Thanksgiving Day, the Fourth of July, Memorial Day, Lincoln's Birthday. We have constructed Martin Luther King, Jr., Day to fit the narrative so well that we have already forgotten that it took a fight to get it included in the canon year. There is much truth to this story. Enlightenment ideals of liberty and political equality did and do inspire movements against oppression and domination, whose success has created social values and institutions we would not want to lose. A people could do worse than tell this story after big meals and occasionally call upon one another to live up to it.

The very worthiness of the narrative, however, and the achievement of political equality that it recounts, now inspires new heretics. In recent years the ideal of liberation as the elimination of group difference has been challenged by movements of the oppressed. The very success of political movements against differential privilege and for political equality has generated moments of group specificity and cultural pride.

In this chapter I criticize an ideal of justice that defines liberation as the transcendence of group difference, which I refer to as an ideal of assimilation. This ideal usually promotes equal treatment as a primary principle of justice. Recent social movements of oppressed groups challenge this ideal. Many in these movements argue that a positive self-definition of group difference is in fact more liberatory.

I endorse this politics of difference, and argue that at stake is the meaning of social difference itself. Traditional politics that excludes or devalues some persons on account of their group attributes assumes an essentialist meaning of difference; it defines groups as having different natures. An egalitarian politics of difference, on the other hand, defines difference more fluidly and relationally as the product of social processes. An emancipatory politics that affirms group difference involves a reconception of the meaning of equality. The assimilation-ist ideal assumes that equal social status for all persons requires treating everyone according to the same principles, rules, and standards. A politics of difference argues, on the other hand, that equality as the participation and inclusion of all groups sometimes requires different treatment for oppressed or disadvantaged groups. To promote social justice, I argue, social policy should sometimes accord special treatment to groups. I explore pregnancy and birthing rights for workers, bilingual-bicultural rights, and American Indian rights as three cases of such special treatment. Finally, I expand the idea of a heterogeneous public here by arguing for a principle of representation for oppressed groups in democratic decision-making bodies.

COMPETING PARADIGMS OF LIBERATION

In "On Racism and Sexism" [in *Philosophy and Social Issues*, 1980], Richard Wasserstrom develops a classic statement of the ideal of liberation from group-based oppression as involving the elimination of group-based difference itself. A truly nonracist, nonsexist society, he suggests, would be one in which the race or sex of an individual would be the functional equivalent of eye color in our society today. While physiological differences in skin color or genitals would remain, they would have no significance for a person's sense of identity or how others regard him or her. No political rights or obligations would be connected to race or sex, and no important institutional benefits would be associated with either. People would see no reason to consider race or gender in policy or everyday interactions. In such a society, social group differences would have ceased to exist.

Wasserstrom contrasts this ideal of assimilation with an ideal of diversity much like the one I will argue for, which he agrees is compelling. He offers three primary reasons, however, for choosing the assimilationist ideal of liberation over the ideal of diversity. First, the assimilationist ideal exposes the arbitrari-ness of group-based social distinctions which are thought natural and necessary. By imagining a society in which race and sex have no social significance, one sees more clearly how pervasively these group categories unnecessarily limit possibilities for some in existing society. Second, the assimilationist ideal pre-sents a clear and unambiguous standard of equality and justice. According to such a standard, any group-related differentiation or discrimination is suspect.

Whenever laws or rules, the division of labor, or other social practices allocate benefits differently according to group membership, this is a sign of injustice. The principle of justice is simple: treat everyone according to the same principles, rules, and standards. Third, the assimilationist ideal maximizes choice. In a society where differences make no social difference people can develop themselves as individuals, unconstrained by group norms and expectations.

There is no question that the ideal of liberation as the elimination of group difference has been enormously important in the history of emancipatory politics. The ideal of universal humanity that denies natural differences has been a crucial historical development in the struggle against exclusion and status differentiation. It has made possible the assertion of the equal moral worth of all persons, and thus the right of all to participate and be included in all institutions and positions of power and privilege. The assimilationist ideal retains significant rhetorical power in the face of continued beliefs in the essentially different and inferior natures of women, blacks, and other groups.

The power of this assimilationist ideal has inspired the struggle of oppressed groups and the supporters against the exclusion and denigration of these groups, and continues to inspire many. Periodically in American history, however, movements of the oppressed have questioned and rejected this "path to belonging." Instead they have seen self-organization and the assertion of a positive group cultural identity as a better strategy for achieving power and participation in dominant institutions. Recent decades have witnessed a resurgence of this "politics of difference" not only among racial and ethnic groups, but also among women, gay men and lesbians, old people, and the disabled.

Not long after the passage of the Civil Rights Act and the Voting Rights Act, many white and black supporters of the black civil rights movement were surprised, confused, and angered by the emergence of the Black Power movement. Black Power advocates criticized the integrationist goal and reliance on the support of white liberals that characterized the civil rights movement. They encouraged blacks to break their alliance with whites and assert the specificity of their own culture, political organization, and goals. Instead of integration, they encouraged blacks to seek economic and political empowerment in their separate neighborhoods. Since the late 1960s many blacks have claimed that the integration successes of the civil rights movement have had the effect of dismantling the bases of black-organized social and economic institutions at least as much as they have lessened black-white animosity and opened doors of opportunity. While some individual blacks may be better off than they would have been if these changes had not occurred, as a group, blacks are no better off and may be worse off, because the blacks who have succeeded in assimilating into the American middle class no longer associate as closely with lower-class blacks.

While much black politics has questioned the ideal of assimilation in economic and political terms, the past twenty years have also seen the assertion and celebration by blacks of a distinct Afro-American culture, both as a recovery and revaluation of an Afro-American history and in the creation of new cultural forms. The slogan "black is beautiful" pierced American consciousness, deeply unsettling the received body aesthetic which I [have] argued . . . continues to be a powerful reproducer of racism. Afro-American hairstyles pronounced themselves differently stylish, not less stylish. Linguistic theorists asserted that black English is English differently constructed, not bad English, and black poets and novelists exploited and explored its particular nuances.

In the late 1960s Red Power came fast on the heels of Black Power. The American Indian Movement and other radical organizations of American Indians rejected perhaps even more vehemently than blacks the goal of assimilation which has dominated white-Indian relations for most of the twentieth century. They asserted a right to self-government on Indian lands and fought to gain and maintain a dominant Indian voice in the Bureau of Indian Affairs. American Indians have sought to recover and preserve their language, rituals, and crafts, and this renewal of pride in traditional culture has also fostered a separatist political movement. The desire to pursue land rights claims and to fight for control over resources on reservations arises from what has become a fierce commitment to tribal self-determination, the desire to develop and maintain Indian political and economic bases in but not of white society.

These are but two examples of a widespread tendency in the politics of the 1970s and 1980s for oppressed, disadvantaged, or specially marked groups to organize autonomously and assert a positive sense of their cultural and experiential specificity. Many Spanish-speaking Americans have rejected the traditional assumption that full participation in American society requires linguistic and cultural assimilation. In the last twenty years many have developed a renewed interest and pride in their Puerto Rican, Chicano, Mexican, or other Latin American heritage. They have asserted the right to maintain their specific culture and speak their language and still receive the benefits of citizenship, such as voting rights, decent education, and job opportunities. Many Jewish Americans have similarly rejected the ideal of assimilation, instead asserting the specificity and positive meaning of Jewish identity, often insisting publicly that Christian culture cease to be taken as the norm.

Since the late 1960s the blossoming of gay cultural expression, gay organization, and the public presence of gays in marches and other forums have radically altered the environment in which young people come to sexual identity, and changed many people's perceptions of homosexuality. Early gay rights advocacy had a distinctly assimilationist and universalist orientation. The goal was to remove the stigma of being homosexual, to prevent institutional discrimination, and to achieve societal recognition that gay people are "no different" from anyone else. The very process of political organization against discrimination and police harassment and for the achievement of civil rights, however, fostered the development of gay and lesbian communities and cultural expression, which by the mid-1970s flowered in meeting places, organizations, literature, music, and massive street celebrations.

Today most gay and lesbian liberation advocates seek not merely civil rights, but the affirmation of gay men and lesbians as social groups with specific experiences and perspectives. Refusing to accept the dominant culture's definition of healthy sexuality and respectable family life and social practices, gay and lesbian liberation movements have proudly created and displayed a distinctive self-definition and culture. For gay men and lesbians the analogue to racial integration is the typical liberal approach to sexuality, which tolerates any behavior as long as it is kept private. Gay pride asserts that sexual identity is a matter of culture and politics, and not merely "behavior" to be tolerated or forbidden.

The women's movement has also generated its own versions of a politics of difference. Humanist feminism, which predominated in the nineteenth century and in the contemporary women's movement until the late 1970s, finds in any assertion of difference between women and men only a legacy of female oppression and an ideology to legitimate continued exclusion of women from socially valued human activity. Humanist feminism is thus analogous to an ideal of assimilation in identifying sexual equality with gender blindness, with measuring women and men according to the same standards and treating them in the same way. Indeed, for many feminists, androgyny names the ideal of sexual liberation—a society in which gender difference itself would be eliminated. Given the strength and plausibility of this vision of sexual equality, it was confusing when feminists too began taking the turn to difference, asserting the positivity and specificity of female experience and values.

Feminist separatism was the earliest expression of such gynocentric feminism. Feminist separatism rejected wholly or partly the goal of entering the male-dominated world, because it requires playing according to rules that men have made and that have been used against women, and because trying to measure up to male-defined standards inevitably involves accommodating or pleasing the men who continue to dominate socially valued institutions and activities. Separatism promoted the empowerment of women through self-organization, the creation of separate and safe spaces where women could share and analyze their experiences, voice their anger, play with and create bonds with one another, and develop new and better institutions and practices.

Most elements of the contemporary women's movement have been separatist to some degree. Separatists seeking to live as much of their lives as possible in women-only institutions were largely responsible for the creation of the women's culture that burst forth all over the United States by the mid-1970s, and continues to claim the loyalty of millions of women—in the form of music, poetry, spirituality, literature, celebrations, festivals, and dances. Whether drawing on images of Amazonian grandeur, recovering and revaluing traditional women's arts, like quilting and weaving, or inventing new rituals based on medieval witchcraft, the development of such expressions of women's culture gave many feminists images of a female-centered beauty and strength entirely outside capitalist patriarchal definitions of feminine pulchritude. The separatist impulse also fostered the development of the many autonomous women's institutions and services that have concretely improved the lives of many women, whether feminists or not—such as health clinics, battered women's shelters, rape crisis centers, and women's coffeehouses and bookstores.

Beginning in the late 1970s much feminist theory and political analysis also took a turn away from humanist feminism, to question the assumption that traditional female activity expresses primarily the victimization of women and the distortion of their human potential and that the goal of women's liberation is the participation of women as equals in public institutions now dominated by men. Instead of understanding the activities and values associated with traditional femininity as largely distortions and inhibitions of women's truly human potentialities, this gynocentric analysis sought to revalue the caring, nurturing, and cooperative approach to social relations they found associated with feminine socialization, and sought in women's specific experiences the bases for an attitude toward the body and nature healthier than that predominant in male-dominated Western capitalist culture.

None of the social movements asserting positive group specificity is in fact a unity. All have group differences within them. The black movement, for example, includes middle-class blacks and working-class blacks, gays and straight people, men and women, and so it is with any other group. The implications of group differences within a social group have been most systematically discussed in the women's movement. Feminist conferences and publications have generated particularly fruitful, though often emotionally wrenching, discussions of the oppression of racial and ethnic blindness and the importance of attending to group differences among women. From such discussions emerged principled efforts to provide autonomously organized forums for black women, Latinas, Jewish women, lesbians, differently abled women, old women, and any other women who see reason for claiming that they have as a group a distinctive voice that might be silenced in a general feminist discourse. Those discussions, along with the practices feminists instituted to structure discussion and interaction among differently identifying groups of women, offer some beginning models for the development of a heterogeneous public. Each of the other social movements has also generated discussion of group differences that cut across their identities, leading to other possibilities of coalition and alliance.

EMANCIPATION THROUGH THE POLITICS OF DIFFERENCE

Implicit in emancipatory movements asserting a positive sense of group difference is a different ideal of liberation, which might be called democratic cultural
pluralism. In this vision the good society does not eliminate or transcend group
difference. Rather, there is equality among socially and culturally differentiated
groups, who mutually respect one another and affirm one another in their
differences. What are the reasons for rejecting the assimilationist ideal and
promoting a politics of difference?

Some deny the reality of social groups. For them, group difference is an
invidious fiction produced and perpetuated in order to preserve the privilege of
the few. Others, such as Wasserstrom, may agree that social groups do now exist
and have real social consequences for the way people identify themselves and
one another, but assert that such social group differences are undesirable. The
assimilationist ideal involves denying either the reality or the desirability of
social groups.

Those promoting a politics of difference doubt that a society without group
differences is either possible or desirable. Contrary to the assumption of modernization theory, increased urbanization and the extension of equal formal
rights to all groups has not led to a decline in particularist affiliations. If
anything, the urban concentration and interactions among groups that mod-
ernizing social processes introduce tend to reinforce group solidarity and differentiation. Attachment to specific traditions, practices, language, and other
culturally specific forms is a crucial aspect of social existence. People do not
usually give up their social group identifications, even when they are oppressed.

Whether eliminating social group difference is possible or desirable in the long
run, however, is an academic issue. Today and for the foreseeable future
societies are certainly structured by groups, and some are privileged while others
are oppressed. New social movements of group specificity do not deny the official
story's claim that the ideal of liberation as eliminating difference and treating
everyone the same has brought significant improvement in the status of excluded
groups. Its main quarrel is with the story's conclusion, namely, that since we
have achieved formal equality, only vestiges and holdovers of differential privilege remain, which will die out with the continued persistent assertion of an ideal of
social relations that make differences irrelevant to a person's life prospects. The
achievement of formal equality does not eliminate social differences, and rhetorical
commitment to the sameness of persons makes it impossible even to name how
those differences presently structure privilege and oppression.

Though in many respects the law is now blind to group differences, some
groups continue to be marked as deviant, as the Other. In everyday interactions,
images, and decisions, assumptions about women, blacks, Hispanics, gay men
and lesbians, old people, and other marked groups continue to justify exclusion,

avoidance, paternalism, and authoritarian treatment. Continued racist, sexist, homophobic, ageist, and ableist institutions and behavior create particular circumstances for these groups, usually disadvantaging them in their opportunity to develop their capacities. Finally, in part because they have been segregated from one another, and in part because they have particular histories and traditions, there are cultural differences among social groups—differences in language, style of living, body comportment and gestures, values, and perspectives on society.

Today in American society, as in many other societies, there is widespread agreement that no person should be excluded from political and economic activities because of ascribed characteristics. Group differences nevertheless continue to exist, and certain groups continue to be privileged. Under these circumstances, insisting that equality and liberation entail ignoring difference has oppressive consequences in three respects.

First, blindness to difference disadvantages groups whose experience, culture, and socialized capacities differ from those of privileged groups. The strategy of assimilation aims to bring formerly excluded groups into the mainstream. So assimilation always implies coming into the game after it is already begun, after the rules and standards have already been set, and having to prove oneself according to those rules and standards. In the assimilationist strategy, the privileged groups implicitly define the standards according to which all will be measured. Because their privilege involves not recognizing these standards as culturally and experientially specific, the ideal of a common humanity in which all can participate without regard to race, gender, religion, or sexuality poses as neutral and universal. The real differences between oppressed groups and the dominant norm, however, tend to put them at a disadvantage in measuring up to these standards, and for that reason assimilationist policies perpetuate their disadvantage. Later in this chapter, I shall give examples of facially neutral standards that operate to disadvantage or exclude those already disadvantaged.

Second, the ideal of a universal humanity without social group differences allows privileged groups to ignore their own group specificity. Blindness to difference perpetuates cultural imperialism by allowing norms expressing the point of view and experience of privileged groups to appear neutral and universal. The assimilationist ideal presumes that there is a humanity in general, an unsituated group-neutral human capacity for self-making that left to itself would make individuality flower, thus guaranteeing that each individual will be different. Because there is no such unsituated group-neutral point of view, the situation and experience of dominant groups tend to define the norms of such a humanity in general. Against such a supposedly neutral humanist ideal, only the oppressed groups come to be marked with particularity; they, and not the privileged groups, are marked, objectified as the Others.

Thus, third, this denigration of groups that deviate from an allegedly neutral standard often produces an internalized devaluation by members of those groups themselves. When there is an ideal of general human standards according to which everyone should be evaluated equally, then Puerto Ricans or Chinese Americans are ashamed of their accents or their parents, black children despise the female-dominated kith and kin networks of their neighborhoods, and feminists seek to root out their tendency to cry, or to feel compassion for a frustrated stranger. The aspiration to assimilate helps produce the self-loathing and double consciousness characteristic of oppression. The goal of assimilation holds up to people a demand that they "fit," be like the mainstream, in behavior, values, and goals. At the same time, as long as group differences exist, group members will be marked as different—as black, Jewish, gay—and thus as unable simply to fit. When participation is taken to imply assimilation the oppressed person is caught in an irresolvable dilemma: to participate means to accept and adopt an identity one is not, and to try to participate means to be reminded by oneself and others of the identity one is.

A more subtle analysis of the assimilationist ideal might distinguish between a conformist and a transformational ideal of assimilation. In the conformist ideal, status quo institutions and norms are assumed as given, and disadvantaged groups who differ from those norms are expected to conform to them. A transformational ideal of assimilation, on the other hand, recognizes that institutions as given express the interests and perspective of the dominant groups. Achieving assimilation therefore requires altering many institutions and practices in accordance with neutral rules that truly do not disadvantage or stigmatize any person, so that group membership really is irrelevant to how persons are treated. Wasserstrom's ideal fits a transformational assimilation, as does the group-neutral ideal advocated by some feminists. Unlike the conformist assimilationist, the transformational assimilationist may allow that group-specific policies, such as affirmative action, are necessary and appropriate means for transforming institutions to fit the assimilationist ideal. Whether conformist or transformational, however, the assimilationist ideal still denies that group difference can be positive and desirable; thus any form of the ideal of assimilation constructs group difference as a liability or disadvantage.

Under these circumstances, a politics that asserts the positivity of group difference is liberating and empowering. In the act of reclaiming the identity the dominant culture has taught them to despise, and affirming it as an identity to celebrate, the oppressed remove double consciousness. I am just what they say I am—a Jewboy, a colored girl, a fag, a dyke, or a hag—and proud of it. No longer does one have the impossible project of trying to become something one is not under circumstances where the very trying reminds one of who one is. This politics asserts that oppressed groups have distinct cultures, experiences, and perspectives on social life with humanly positive meaning, some of which may even be superior to the culture and perspectives of mainstream society. The rejection and devaluation of one's culture and perspective should not be a condition of full participation in social life.

Asserting the value and specificity of the culture and attributes of oppressed groups, moreover, results in a relativizing of the dominant culture. When feminists assert the validity of feminine sensitivity and the positive value of nurturing behavior, when gays describe the prejudice of heterosexuals as homophobic and their own sexuality as positive and self-developing, when blacks affirm a distinct Afro-American tradition, then the dominant culture is forced to discover itself for the first time as specific: as Anglo, European, Christian, masculine, straight. In a political struggle where oppressed groups insist on the positive value of their specific culture and experience, it becomes increasingly difficult for dominant groups to parade their norms as neutral and universal, and to construct the values and behavior of the oppressed as deviant, perverted, or inferior. By puncturing the universalist claim to unity that expels some groups and turns them into the Other, the assertion of positive group specificity introduces the possibility of understanding the relation between groups as merely difference, instead of exclusion, opposition, or dominance.

The politics of difference also promotes a notion of group solidarity against the individualism of liberal humanism. Liberal humanism treats each person as an individual, ignoring differences of race, sex, religion, and ethnicity. Each person should be evaluated only according to her or his individual efforts and achievements. With the institutionalization of formal equality some members of formerly excluded groups have indeed succeeded by mainstream standards. Structural patterns of group privilege and oppression nevertheless remain. When political leaders of oppressed groups reject assimilation they are often affirming group solidarity. Where the dominant culture refuses to see anything but the achievement of autonomous individuals, the oppressed assert that we shall not separate from the people with whom we identify in order to "make it" in a white Anglo male world. The politics of difference insists on liberation of the whole group of blacks, women, American Indians, and that this can be accomplished only through basic institutional changes. These changes must include group representation in policy-making and an elimination of the hierarchy of rewards that forces everyone to compete for scarce positions at the top.

Thus the assertion of a positive sense of group difference provides a standpoint from which to criticize prevailing institutions and norms. Black Americans find in their traditional communities, which refer to their members as "brother" and "sister," a sense of solidarity absent from the calculating individualism of white professional capitalist society. Feminists find in the traditional female values of nurturing a challenge to a militarist worldview, and lesbians find in their relationships a confrontation with the assumption of complementary gender roles in sexual relationships. From their experience of a culture tied to the land American Indians formulate a critique of the instrumental rationality of

European culture that results in pollution and ecological destruction. Having revealed the specificity of the dominant norms which claim universality and neutrality, social movements of the oppressed are in a position to inquire how the dominant institutions must be changed so that they will no longer reproduce the patterns of privilege and oppression.

From the assertion of positive difference the self-organization of oppressed groups follows. Both liberal humanist and leftist political organizations and movements have found it difficult to accept this principle of group autonomy. In a humanist emancipatory politics, if a group is subject to injustice, then all those interested in a just society should unite to combat the powers that perpetuate that injustice. If many groups are subject to injustice, moreover, then they should unite to work for a just society. The politics of difference is certainly not against coalition, nor does it hold that, for example, whites should not work against racial injustice or men against sexist injustice. This politics of group assertion, however, takes as a basic principle that members of oppressed groups need separate organizations that exclude others, especially those from more privileged groups. Separate organization is probably necessary in order for these groups to discover and reinforce the positivity of their specific experience, to collapse and eliminate double consciousness. In discussions within autonomous organizations, group members can determine their specific needs and interests. Separation and self-organization risk creating pressures toward homogenization of the groups themselves, creating new privileges and exclusions. But contemporary emancipatory social movements have found group autonomy an important vehicle for empowerment and the development of a group-specific voice and perspective.

Integration into the full life of the society should not have to imply assimilation to dominant norms and abandonment of group affiliation and culture. If the only alternative to the oppressive exclusion of some groups defined as Other by dominant ideologies is the assertion that they are the same as everybody else, then they will continue to be excluded because they are not the same.

Some might object to the way I have drawn the distinction between an assimilationist ideal of liberation and a radical democratic pluralism. They might claim that I have not painted the ideal of a society that transcends group differences fairly, representing it as homogeneous and conformist. The free society envisaged by liberalism, they might say, is certainly pluralistic. In it persons can affiliate with whomever they choose; liberty encourages a proliferation of life-styles, activities, and associations. While I have no quarrel with social diversity in this sense, this vision of liberal pluralism does not touch on the primary issues that give rise to the politics of difference. The vision of liberation as the transcendence of group difference seeks to abolish the public and political significance of group difference while retaining and promoting both individual and group diversity in private, or nonpolitical, social contexts. This way of distinguishing public and private spheres, where the public represents universal citizenship and the private individual differences, tends to result in group exclusion from the public. Radical democratic pluralism acknowledges and affirms the public and political significance of social group differences as a means of ensuring the participation and inclusion of everyone in social and political institutions.

RECLAIMING THE MEANING OF DIFFERENCE

Many people inside and outside the movements I have discussed find the rejection of the liberal humanist ideal and the assertion of a positive sense of group difference both confusing and controversial. They fear that any admission by oppressed groups that they are different from the dominant groups risks justifying anew the subordination, special marking, and exclusion of those groups. Since calls for a return of women to the kitchen, blacks to servant roles and separate schools, and disabled people to nursing homes are not absent from contemporary politics, the danger is real. It may be true that the assimilationist ideal that treats everyone the same and applies the same standards to all perpetuates disadvantage because real group differences remain that make it unfair to compare the unequals. But this is far preferable to a reestablishment of separate and unequal spheres for different groups justified on the basis of group difference.

Since those asserting group specificity certainly wish to affirm the liberal humanist principle that all persons are of equal moral worth, they appear to be faced with a dilemma. Analyzing W. E. B. Du Bois's arguments for cultural pluralism, Bernard Boxill poses the dilemma this way: "On the one hand, we must overcome segregation because it denies the idea of human brotherhood; on the other hand, to overcome segregation we must self-segregate and therefore also deny the idea of human brotherhood." Martha Minow finds a dilemma of difference facing any who seek to promote justice for currently oppressed or disadvantaged groups. Formally neutral rules and policies that ignore group differences often perpetuate the disadvantage of those whose difference is defined as deviant; but focusing on difference risks recreating the stigma that difference has carried in the past.

The dilemmas are genuine, and exhibit the risks of collective life, where the consequences of one's claims, actions, and policies may not turn out as one intended because others have understood them differently or turned them to different ends. Since ignoring group differences in public policy does not mean that people ignore them in everyday life and interaction, however, oppression continues even when law and policy declare that all are equal. Thus, I think for many groups and in many circumstances it is more empowering to affirm and acknowledge in political life the group differences that already exist in social life.

One is more likely to avoid the dilemma of difference in doing this if the meaning of difference itself becomes a terrain of political struggle. Social movements asserting the positivity of group difference have established this terrain, offering an emancipatory meaning of difference to replace the old exclusionary meaning.

The oppressive meaning of group difference defines it as absolute otherness, mutual exclusion, categorical opposition. This essentialist meaning of difference submits to the logic of identity. One group occupies the position of a norm, against which all others are measured. The attempt to reduce all persons to the unity of a common measure constructs as deviant those whose attributes differ from the group-specific attributes implicitly presumed in the norm. The drive to unify the particularity and multiplicity of practices, cultural symbols, and ways of relating in clear and distinct categories turns difference into exclusion. Thus the appropriation of a universal subject position by socially privileged groups forces those they define as different outside the definition of full humanity and citizenship. The attempt to measure all against some universal standard generates a logic of difference as hierarchical dichotomy—masculine/feminine, civilized/savage, and so on. The second term is defined negatively as a lack of the truly human qualities; at the same time it is defined as the complement to the valued term, the object correlating with its subject, that which brings it to completion, wholeness, and identity. By loving and affirming him, a woman serves as a mirror to a man, holding up his virtues for him to see. By carrying the white man's burden to tame and educate the savage peoples, the civilized will realize universal humanity. The exotic orientals are there to know and master, to be the completion of reason's progress in history, which seeks the unity of the world. In every case the valued term achieves its value by its determinately negative relation to the Other.

In the objectifying ideologies of racism, sexism, anti-Semitism, and homophobia, only the oppressed and excluded groups are defined as different. Whereas the privileged groups are neutral and exhibit free and malleable subjectivity, the excluded groups are marked with an essence, imprisoned in a given set of possibilities. By virtue of the characteristics the group is alleged to have by nature, the ideologies allege that group members have specific dispositions that suit them for some activities and not others. Difference in these ideologies always means exclusionary opposition to a norm. There are rational men, and then there are women; there are civilized men, and then there are wild and savage peoples. The marking of difference always implies a good/bad opposition; it is always a devaluation, the naming of an inferiority in relation to a superior standard of humanity.

Difference here always means absolute otherness; the group marked as different has no common nature with the normal or neutral ones. The categorical opposition of groups essentializes them, repressing the differences within groups. In this way the definition of difference as exclusion and opposition actually denies difference. This essentializing categorization also denies difference in that its universalizing norms preclude recognizing and affirming a group's specificity in its own terms.

Essentializing difference expresses a fear of specificity, and a fear of making permeable the categorical border between oneself and the others. This fear is not merely intellectual and does not derive only from the instrumental desire to defend privilege, though that may be a large element. It wells from the depths of the Western subject's sense of identity, especially, but not only in the subjectivity of privileged groups. The fear may increase, moreover, as a clear essentialism of difference wanes, as belief in a specifically female, black, or homosexual nature becomes less tenable.

The politics of difference confronts this fear, and aims for an understanding of group difference as indeed ambiguous, relational, shifting, without clear borders that keep people straight—as entailing neither amorphous unity nor pure individuality. By asserting a positive meaning for their own identity, oppressed groups seek to seize the power of naming difference itself, and explode the implicit definition of difference as deviance in relation to a norm, which freezes some groups into a self-enclosed nature. Difference now comes to mean not otherness, exclusive opposition, but specifically, variation, heterogeneity. Difference names relations of similarity and dissimilarity that can be reduced to neither coextensive identity nor overlapping otherness.

The alternative to an essentializing, stigmatizing meaning of difference as opposition is an understanding of difference as specificity, variation. In this logic, as Martha Minow suggests, group differences should be conceived as relational rather than defined by substantive categories and attributes. A relational understanding of difference relativizes the previously universal position of privileged groups, which allows only the oppressed to be marked as different. When group difference appears as a function of comparison between groups, whites are just as specific as black or Latinos, men just as specific as women, able-bodied people just as specific as disabled people. Difference thus emerges not as a description of the attributes of a group, but as a function of the relations between groups and the interaction of groups with institutions.

In this relational understanding, the meaning of difference also becomes contextualized. Group differences will be more or less salient depending on the groups compared, the purposes of the comparison, and the point of view of the comparers. Such contextualized understandings of difference undermine essentialist assumptions. For example, in the context of athletics, health care, social service support, and so on, wheelchair-bound people are different from others, but they are not different in many other respects. Traditional treatment of the disabled entailed exclusion and segregation because the differences between the disabled and the able-bodied were conceptualized as extending to all or most capacities.

In general, then, a relational understanding of group difference rejects exclusion. Difference no longer implies that groups lie outside one another. To say that there are differences among groups does not imply that there are not overlapping experiences, or that two groups have nothing in common. The assumption that real differences in affinity, culture, or privilege imply oppositional categorization must be challenged. Different groups are always similar in some respects, and always potentially share some attributes, experiences, and goals.

Such a relational understanding of difference entails revising the meaning of group identity as well. In asserting the positive difference of their experience, culture, and social perspective, social movements of groups that have experienced cultural imperialism deny that they have a common identity, a set of fixed attributes that clearly mark who belongs and who doesn't. Rather, what makes a group a group is a social process of interaction and differentiation in which some people come to have a particular affinity for others. My "affinity group" in a given social situation comprises those people with whom I feel the most comfortable, who are more familiar. Affinity names the manner of sharing assumptions, affective bonding, and networking that recognizably differentiates groups from one another, but not according to some common nature. The salience of a particular person's group affinities may shift according to the social situation or according to changes in her or his life. Membership in a social group is a function not of satisfying some objective criteria, but of a subjective affirmation of affinity with that group, the affirmation of that affinity by other members of the group, and the attribution of membership in that group by persons identifying with other groups. Group identity is constructed from a flowing process in which individuals identify themselves and others in terms of groups, and thus group identity itself flows and shifts with changes in social process.

Groups experiencing cultural imperialism have found themselves objectified and marked with a devalued essence from the outside, by a dominant culture they are excluded from making. The assertion of a positive sense of group difference by these groups is emancipatory because it reclaims the definition of the group by the group, as a creation and construction, rather than a given essence. To be sure, it is difficult to articulate positive elements of group affinity without essentializing them, and these movements do not always succeed in doing so. But they are developing a language to describe their similar social situation and relations to one another, and their similar perceptions and perspectives on social life. These movements engage in the project of cultural revolution I recommended in chapter [5 of *Justice and the Politics of Difference*], insofar as they take culture as in part a matter of collective choice. While their ideas of women's culture, Afro-American culture, and American Indian culture rely on past cultural expressions, to a significant degree these movements have self-consciously constructed the culture that they claim defines the distinctiveness of their groups.

Contextualizing both the meaning of difference and identity thus allows the acknowledgment of difference within affinity groups. In our complex, plural society, every social group has group differences cutting across it, which are potential sources of wisdom, excitement, conflict, and oppression. Gay men, for example, may be black, rich, homeless, or old, and these differences produce different identifications and potential conflicts among gay men as well as affinities with some straight men. . . .

BIBLIOGRAPHY

Ackerman, Bruce A. *Social Justice and the Liberal State*. New Haven, CT: Yale University Press, 1980.

Atkinson, A. B. *Social Justice and Public Policy*. Cambridge, MA: MIT Press, 1983.

Barker, Ernest. *Principles of Social and Political Philosophy*. 1951. Westport, CT: Greenwood Press, 1980.

Barry, Brian. *Democracy, Power, and Justice*. New York: Oxford University Press, 1990.

Barry, Brian, and R. I. Sikora. *Obligation to Future Generations*. Philadelphia: Temple University Press, 1978.

Bookchin, Murray. *Remaking Society*. Montreal: Black Rose Books, 1989.

Boxill, Bernard R. *Blacks and Social Justice*. 2d ed. Totowa, NJ: Rowman and Littlefield, 1991.

Buchanan, Allen. *Ethics, Efficiency, and the Market*. Totowa, NJ: Rowman and Littlefield, 1988.

Cohen, G. A. *History, Labour, and Freedom*. Oxford: Clarendon Press, 1988.

Commoner, Barry. *Making Peace with the Planet*. New York: Pantheon Books, 1990.

Elster, Jon. *Making Sense of Marx*. New York: Cambridge University Press, 1985.

Ezorsky, Gertrude. *Racism and Justice*. Ithaca, NY: Cornell University Press, 1991.

Fisk, Milton. *Ethics and Society*. New York: New York University Press, 1980.

———. *The State and Justice*. New York: Cambridge University Press, 1989.

Gibson, Mary. *Workers' Rights*. Totowa, NJ: Rowman and Allanheld, 1983.

Gramsci, Antonio. *Prison Notebooks*. Vol. 1–5. Edited by J. A. Buttigieg. New York: Columbia University Press, 1992.

Habermas, Jürgen. *Moral Consciousness and Communicative Action*. Translated by C. Lenhardt and S. Weber Nicholsen. Cambridge, MA: MIT Press, 1990.

Heller, Agnes. *Beyond Justice*. Oxford: Basil Blackwell, 1987.

Husak, Douglas N. *Philosophy of Criminal Law*. Totowa, NJ: Rowman and Littlefield, 1987.

Hutchinson, Allan C., ed. *Critical Legal Studies*. Totowa, NJ: Rowman and Littlefield, 1989.

Kirzner, Israel M. *Discovery, Capitalism, and Distributive Justice*. New York: Basil Blackwell, 1989.

Kymlicka, Will. *Liberalism, Community, and Culture*. New York: Oxford University Press, 1989.

Lucas, J. R. *On Justice*. New York: Oxford University Press, 1980.

Luper-Foy, Steven, ed. *Problems of International Justice*. Boulder, CO: Westview Press, 1988.

Machan, Tibor. *Individuals and Their Rights*. La Salle, IL: Open Court, 1989.

MacIntyre, Alasdair. *After Virtue*. Notre Dame, IN: University of Notre Dame Press, 1981.

———. *Whose Justice? Which Rationality?* Notre Dame, IN: University of Notre Dame Press, 1988.

MacKinnon, Catherine. *Toward a Feminist Theory of the State*. Cambridge, MA: Harvard University Press, 1989.

Macpherson, C. B. *The Rise and Fall of Economic Justice and Other Essays.* New York: Oxford University Press, 1985.

Marable, Manning. *Race, Reform, and Rebellion: The Second Reconstruction in Black America, 1945–1990.* 2d ed. Jackson, MS: University of Mississippi Press, 1991.

Mohr, Richard D. *Gays/Justice.* New York: Columbia University Press, 1988.

Moore, Barrington, Jr. *Injustice: The Social Bases of Obedience and Revolt.* Armonk, NY: M. E. Sharpe, Inc., 1978.

Nielsen, Kai. *Equality and Liberty.* Totowa, NJ: Rowman and Allanheld, 1984.

Nielsen, Kai, and Steven C. Patten, eds. *Marx and Morality. Canadian Journal of Philosophy,* supplementary volume 7 (1981).

Nozick, Robert. *Anarchy, State, and Utopia.* New York: Basic Books, 1974.

Okin, Susan Moller. *Justice, Gender, and the Family.* New York: Basic Books, 1989.

Posner, Richard A. *The Economics of Justice.* Cambridge, MA: Harvard University Press, 1981.

Rakowski, Eric. *Equal Justice.* New York: Oxford University Press, 1991.

Rawls, John. *A Theory of Justice.* Cambridge, MA: Belknap Press of Harvard University Press, 1971.

———. "The Idea of Overlapping Consensus." *Oxford Journal of Legal Studies* 7, no. 1 (1987).

Reiman, Jeffrey. *Justice and Modern Moral Philosophy.* New Haven, CT: Yale University Press, 1990.

Roemer, John. *Free to Lose.* Cambridge, MA: Harvard University Press, 1988.

Sandel, Michael. *Liberalism and the Limits of Justice.* New York: Cambridge University Press, 1982.

Sen, Amartya K. *Poverty and Famines.* New York: Oxford University Press, 1981.

Shklar, Judith N. *The Faces of Injustice.* New Haven, CT: Yale University Press, 1990.

Sterba, James P. *How to Make People Just.* Totowa, NJ: Rowman and Littlefield, 1988.

Walzer, Michael. *Spheres of Justice.* New York: Basic Books, 1983.

Wenz, Peter S. *Environmental Justice.* Albany, NY: State University of New York Press, 1987.

Wilson, William Julius. *The Truly Disadvantaged.* Chicago: University of Chicago Press, 1987.

Winfield, Richard Dien. *The Just Economy.* New York: Routledge, Chapman, and Hall, 1988.

Wood, Allen. *Karl Marx.* London: Routledge and Kegan Paul, 1981.

Young, Iris Marion. *Justice and the Politics of Difference.* Princeton, NJ: Princeton University Press, 1990.

Zinn, Howard. *Declarations of Independence.* New York: HarperCollins, 1990.

INDEX

Abortion, 142–43
Absolutism, 2, 5; Hume against, 3; and group difference, 308

Birth rate: and the living standard, 215; and the infant mortality rate, 217
Blacks: economic status of, 241; discrimination as cause of subordination of, 263; and color-conscious policies for, 271; and group difference, 299

Capitalism, 30–31, 135; Marx's denial that it is unjust, 167; instability of, 171; conflict between forces and relations within, 176; and morality, 177; exploitation inevitable under, 186, 203; for Roemer not unjust due to exploitation, 197
Class, 181; and minorities, 248; and discrimination, 265
Communism, 126–27; distribution in, 31; and unforced labor, 181
Community: MacIntyre on, 3–4; Dewey on, 4; Green on, 44; Walzer on, 70; cohesion of and expulsion from, 72–75; and mutual aid, 77; divided, 79; and provision for needs, 81–83; and integrity, 145; and responsibility, 153; true versus bare in Dworkin, 153–54; and the view of law as compromise, 160; based on principle, 161
Compensation: to poor countries, 221, 234; for depletion of resources, 232; and the disadvantaged, 248
Compromise: Solomonic, 139; and inconsistency, 146
Conflict: Plato on, 1; and political justice, 52; among principles, 139; generates new society, 175
Consciousness: collective, 125–26; and culture of acceptance, 131; and separatist organization, 306
Consensus: overlapping in Rawls, 64

Constructivism: Kantian, 53
Control: of product, 187; of labor, 188; and exploitation, 191, 203
Cooperation: social, 54

Democracy: conception of justice for, 50; public culture of, 54; promoted by distribution of goods in Athens, 85
Dialogue: and ethical validity in Habermas, 93–94
Difference: between groups, 296; politics of, 297; celebration of, 300; and democratic cultural pluralism, 302
Discourse: poststructuralism on, 6; as means of reaching ethical agreement, 94; role-taking model of, 93; as breaking limits of lifeworld, 99; feminist, 301
Discrimination: as obstacle to black progress, 265
Distribution: to labor of product, 26; equitable, 29; according to need in Marx, 31; depends on production, 32; of membership, 68–71; just when it reflects mode of production, 172; of food between nations, 213; between generations, 228; intra- and inter-generational, 233; of income within family, 282; and unpaid labor, 282
Duty, 16; to support institutions, 149

Economic growth: and ecology, 208; limits to, 209; to help poor minority members, 251
Economy: and right, 29; context for social change, 122–23
Emancipation: of working class, 32–34, 126; of women, 301
Environment: crisis of the, 206; and population, 206–7; Bruntland report on, 212; and poverty, 221; greenhouse effect, 224
Equality, 13; competing views of, 51; in community, 154; of opportunity for